W9-CBW-887

THE KAISER

Books by Virginia Cowles

LOOKING FOR TROUBLE

NO CAUSE FOR ALARM

WINSTON CHURCHILL
The Era and the Man

GAY MONARCH
The Life and Pleasures of Edward VII

THE PHANTOM MAJOR
The Story of David Stirling and His Desert Command

THE GREAT SWINDLE
The Story of the South Sea Bubble

THE KAISER

Virginia Cowles

THE KAISER

HARPER & ROW, PUBLISHERS
NEW YORK AND EVANSTON

FIRST EDITION

LIBRARY OF CONGRESS CATALOG CARD NUMBER: 63-20288

Contents

Illustrations

These illustrations, grouped in a separate section, will be found following page 192

Selected genealogy showing the relationship between the Kaiser, George V, Czar Nicholas and the Czarina

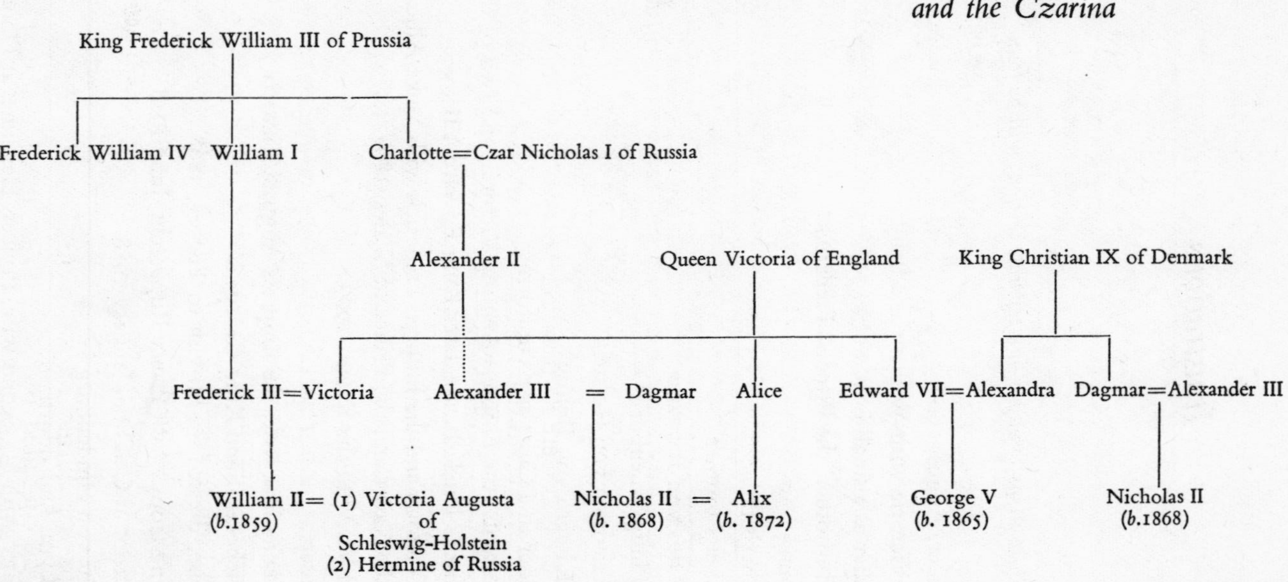

1. *His Mother*

A salute of 101 guns told the people of Berlin, on the winter afternoon of January 27th, 1859, that a future king of Prussia had been born. The eighteen-year-old mother, the English-born Princess Frederick, lay dangerously ill. The labour had been long and difficult, no anaesthetics had been given, and in the end forceps had been used. Only German doctors were in attendance, for the messenger sent to summon the Princess's English doctor had misunderstood his instructions and posted the letter instead of delivering it. During the hours of agony the Prince had sat by his wife's bed, sometimes holding her in his arms. At one point the German doctors said aloud that they did not think either mother or child would survive; the newspapers were informed and set up obituary notices. When, at last, the delivery was accomplished, the relief and confusion were so great, no one noticed that the baby's left arm had been wrenched from the shoulder socket. A day later the nurse reported that it was hanging in a peculiarly limp way. The doctors were confounded; after long consultation they announced that nothing could be done.

The Princess was not allowed to sit up for nearly a month. At the end of February she wrote to her mother, Queen Victoria: "Your grandson is exceedingly lively and when awake will not be satisfied unless kept dancing about continually. He scratches his face and tears his caps and makes every sort of extraordinary little noise. I am so thankful, so happy, he is a boy. I longed for one more than I can describe, my whole heart was set upon a boy, therefore I did not expect one . . . I feel very proud of him and very proud of being a Mama . . ."[1] It was a brave letter for she did not mention her distress over her child's arm. During the next few years she consulted many doctors, but they always gave her the same negative answer.

[1] *Letters of the Empress Frederick.*

The Princess's letters were read by Queen Victoria and Prince Albert with avid interest. " Vicky "—as she was called in the family circle—was the Queen's eldest child and Princess Royal of England; she also was the favourite of both parents. She not only was attractive but brilliantly clever. Her precociousness had become apparent at the age of three when she began to produce a remarkable vocabulary in three languages. When she was eight, her governess, Lady Lyttelton, was writing: " The Princess Royal might pass, if not seen, but only overheard, for a young lady of seventeen in whichever of her three languages she chose to entertain the company." Even the crabbed German pedant, the Baron Stockmar, who was Prince Albert's closest adviser, wrote: " I think her to be exceptionally gifted in some things, even to the point of genius."

The Princess's talents threw an unkind light on her brother and sister, " Bertie " and Alice. By comparison Alice, who was two years younger, seemed dull, while Bertie, one year younger, appeared positively backward. However, they were good-tempered, jolly children and the praise showered on Vicky did not create a breach of any kind. Indeed, all three remained devoted to one another for the rest of their lives—even though these lives were fated to cross each other in a tragic pattern. Vicky was destined to become the mother of Kaiser William II and Alice the mother of the last Czarina of Russia; while Bertie would ascend the throne as Edward VII and play no small part in the events leading to the First World War.

Vicky's childhood did not last long. At the age of fourteen she became engaged to Prince Frederick William of Prussia. This tall, good-looking, twenty-four-year-old prince, who one day would become King of Prussia, arrived at Balmoral for a visit in the summer of 1855 and informed the Queen and Prince Albert that he had fallen in love with the ten-year-old Vicky when he had met her at the Great Exhibition in Paris four years earlier. The royal parents welcomed the match, but hesitated before allowing " Fritz " to propose. "... we were uncertain on account of her extreme youth," the Queen noted in her diary, " whether he should speak to her himself, or wait until he came back again. However, we felt it was better he should do so, and during our ride up Craig-na-Bain this afternoon, he picked a piece of white heather (the emblem of

' good luck,') which he gave to her; and this enabled him to make an allusion to his hopes and wishes as they rode down Glen Girnoch. . . ."[1] The Princess was not in the least disconcerted by the Prince's declaration, and accepted him with enthusiasm. " She manifested toward Fritz and ourselves the most childlike simplicity and candour," wrote her father. " The young people are ardently in love with one another. . . ."

Prince Albert adored his daughter. His love was almost Narcissus-like, for she seemed to be a reflection of himself—a twin soul who mirrored his innermost thoughts. He had played an active part in her education, and nothing delighted him more than to plant ideas in her fertile brain and watch them flower into his own beliefs. He felt that her marriage with Prince Frederick would result not only in happiness, but give her the opportunity to play an historic role upon the world stage. Prince Albert and Baron Stockmar came from the small principality of Saxe-Coburg which in recent years had become a centre of progressive thought. They dreamed of the day when Prussia would model itself upon the English constitutional monarchy—that miracle of the nineteenth century—and under the banner of liberalism would unite the independent German states and kingdoms into one powerful nation; and with Vicky on the throne the new Germany would ally itself with Great Britain to preserve peace and order throughout the world.

Albert's dreams were not altogether fanciful, for ever since the Congress of Vienna, in 1815, the German states had been linked together in a loose confederation. They each sent delegates to a Diet at Frankfurt, which, although it had no specific powers, was a sounding board for opinion and promoted a spirit of cohesion. Then came the great liberal wave of 1848, inspired by the ideals of the French revolution and the practical example of the English parliamentary system, which rolled across Europe inciting " revolutionary mobs " to clamour for the vote. In Berlin the crowds clashed with the army, and the King, fearful of civil war, gave way. For the first time in history Prussia was permitted a parliament based on popular representation; and at Frankfurt a German national Assembly sprang into being elected by universal suffrage.

[1] *Leaves from the Journal of our Life in the Highlands:* Queen Victoria.

Unfortunately the period of freedom was short-lived. A year later the national assembly invited the King of Prussia, Frederick William IV, to accept the crown of a united Germany under a liberal constitution. But the King was a hide-bound reactionary, and was more impressed (and a little frightened) by the fiery speeches of a political new-comer, Otto von Bismarck, who declared that Frankfurt's " middle-class " liberalism would destroy the supremacy of Prussia and the glories of Junker rule. So Frederick William plucked up his courage and declined the throne of Germany on the grounds that it had not been offered to him by the German princes, adding petulantly that he did not wish to pick up a crown " from the gutter." Then, with the backing of Russia and Austria, he reorganised his army and refused to recognise the national assembly as an over-riding authority. As this body lacked both financial and military support the Prussian king's defiance finally brought about its collapse; and all that was left in the ruin was the old impotent Frankfurt Diet.

Although Albert was bitterly disappointed by the climax of these stirring events, he remained optimistic. After all, Prussia had benefited from the upheaval, for the King would scarcely dare to withdraw the constitution he had been forced to bestow upon his country, and the people now had an assembly, no matter how feeble its authority, based on a limited franchise. Albert regarded the new chamber as " a framework " for democracy. With a progressive monarch on the Prussian throne the constitution could be developed and expanded; and his future son-in-law, Prince Frederick, was the right man for the task. The Prince was not clever, but he was high-minded and brave and a firm adherent of parliamentary government. Furthermore, he was almost as impressed by the Princess Royal as her parents were. Vicky would supply the intellect and together they would move forward on the path that the Prince Consort had chosen for them.

So Albert flung himself eagerly into the task of preparing his daughter for the work that lay before her. If he adored Vicky she, in turn, idolised her father. No one, not even her husband, ever acquired the same influence over her. He grounded her thoroughly in politics and was the final arbiter of her opinions. She was a natural blue-stocking and delighted in producing learned papers for his perusal, ranging from historical précis to treatises on British cabinet responsibility and parliamentary procedure. "She comes to me every evening from six to seven," Prince Albert wrote to his future son-in-law, "when I put her through a kind of general catechising. In order to make her idea clear, I let her work out subjects for herself, which she brings to me for correction. She is at present writing a short compendium of Roman history."[1] So that he could implant his vision of how German political institutions might develop, he instructed her to translate an almost unreadable thesis by a German scholar entitled *Karl August und die Deutsche Politik.* He was so proud of her work that he sent a copy to Lord Clarendon, the Foreign Secretary. The latter congratulated the translator, saying: "The Princess's manner is . . . the reflection of a highly cultivated intellect."

The Princess's engagement was kept secret until she was sixteen, when it was announced that the wedding would take place in nine months' time on January 25th, 1858. From this moment on Queen Victoria's sentimentality threatened to engulf all those around her. Everything took on the tragedy of "a last time." The Princess was forever saying farewell to places, things, and people. The wedding ceremony was scheduled to take place at St. James's Chapel in London, after which Vicky would return to Windsor for her honeymoon. Just before the royal family left Windsor for Buckingham Palace, the Queen wrote in her diary: "Went to look at the rooms prepared for Vicky's 'Honeymoon.' It quite agitated me to look at them. Poor, poor child! We took a short walk with Vicky who was dreadfully upset with this real break in her life; the real separation from her childhood! She slept for the last time in the same room with Alice. Now all this is cut off."[2]

However, the Queen managed to check her emotions when British prestige required it. When, for instance, there were murmurs from German quarters that, since Prince Frederick one day would become King of Prussia, the wedding ought to take place in Berlin, she reacted strongly. Prussia might be destined for great things, but as yet she was a second-class power, and ought not to forget it. "The Queen *never* could consent to it," she wrote indignantly to her Foreign Secretary, "and the assumption of its being *too much* for a

[1] *The Life of the Prince Consort:* Sir Theodore Martin.

[2] *The Empress Frederick: A Memoir.*

Prince Royal of Prussia to *come* over to marry the *Princess Royal of Great Britain* IN England is too *absurd*, to say the least. . . . Whatever may be the usual practice of Prussian Princes, it is not *every* day that one marries the eldest daughter of the Queen of England. The question therefore must be considered as settled and closed."[1]

Closed it was, and the Queen promptly returned to her tearful sentiments. She described the wedding in her diary as " the second most eventful day in my life as regards feelings." The ceremony itself went off without a hitch. Royalties from all over Europe were present and the bride looked enchanting. " She is not at all short," wrote one of the Maids of Honour, " and has a beautiful countenance, so gentle and childlike, and has quite a nice figure, fine hair and beautiful eyes."[2] Although the Princess was very much in love with her husband she was deeply affected by her mother's emotions. She gave the Queen lockets filled with her hair and clung to her, sobbing: " I think it will kill me to take leave of dear Papa."

At last the day of departure came. The couple had returned from their Windsor honeymoon and Princess Mary of Cambridge wrote in her diary that she drove to Buckingham Palace to see " poor, dear Vicky off" and found the Queen in her closet " surrounded by a number of crying relations." The Queen herself wrote: " A dreadful moment and a dreadful day. Such sickness came over me, real heartache, when I thought of our dearest child being gone, and for so long—all, all being over! It began to snow before Vicky went, and continued to do so without intermission all day. At times I could be quite cheerful, but my tears began to flow afresh frequently, and I could not go near Vicky's corridor."[3]

Despite the snow the newly-weds rode to the station in an open carriage to wave to the populace. The Prince Consort and the bride's sixteen-year-old brother Bertie accompanied them to Gravesend where the royal yacht, the *Victoria and Albert*, was waiting to take them across the Channel. The Prince Consort managed to keep back the tears, but Bertie wept unashamedly. *The Times* added the final touch of gloom by writing prophetically: " We only trust and pray that the policy of England and Prussia may

[1] *Letters of Queen Victoria.*

[2] *Embassies of Other Days:* Walpurga Paget.

[3] *The Empress Frederick: A Memoir.*

never present any painful alternatives to the Princess now about to leave our shores. . . ."

With such a leave-taking it is not surprising that the long trip to Berlin did not begin with much gaiety. However, the Princess was fortunate in one of her German ladies-in-waiting—the beautiful, high-spirited Countess Walpurga von Hohenthal. When this charming young lady was introduced to Queen Victoria, the latter remarked laughingly: "The Princess is seventeen, the Maid of Honour eighteen. What a respectable court that will make!" The Countess's sparkle and gaiety, and her love of all things English, quickly won the bride's heart and before the journey was over "Walpurga" had become "Wally" and the two young ladies were finding much to amuse them. The train made many stops before Berlin. At Wittenberg, a town noted for its pastry, the Princess was presented by the Mayor with a huge apple tart. Shortly afterwards, Field Marshal von Wrangel boarded the train, complimented the Princess, and sat down on the tart. The bride and her lady-in-waiting went into peals of laughter, and the Field Marshal asserted gallantly that he was delighted to have provoked so much merriment.

The state entry into Berlin, however, offered no such lighter moments. The weather was icy, yet the Princess and her ladies-in-waiting were obliged to change into evening dress at Potsdam, and ride through the streets of Berlin in open carriages, with no wraps, and windows down. When they arrived at the Old Schloss, which was to be the couple's Berlin residence, the King and Queen of Prussia were waiting to greet them. The Queen, who hated England, asked haughtily: "Are you not frozen?" "All except my heart, which is warm," replied the Princess with perfect control.

The Queen of Prussia, Prince Frederick's aunt, was by no means the only person in Berlin who was anti-English. The hostility sprang mainly from the fact that Prussia had sympathised strongly with Russia against England in the Crimean War which had ended barely two years earlier. It also came from a dislike of English "liberalism," which, it was feared, might infect the rigid Prussian system and prove the undoing of the ruling class. The antagonism was fanned constantly by *The Times* newspaper which, under the editorship of the passionately liberal Mr. Delane, delighted in jibing at Prussian autocracy. When the Princess Royal's engagement was announced, he referred to the Hohenzollerns as a "paltry German dynasty." This was needlessly insulting and caused a storm of anger in Berlin. But it was the Junkers—and not the royal family—who found the smug superiority of *The Times* most unbearable. Compared to the great British land-owning aristocracy the Junkers were dowdy and provincial and, like poor relations, immensely touchy. Furthermore they resented the fact that English noblemen could preach democracy and still retain their vast properties, whereas in semi-feudal Prussia democracy would spell the end of Junkerdom. The fact that the English seemed to have devised a magic formula which gave them the best of all worlds only served to increase the resentment.

Vicky could not fail to sense the atmosphere and picked her way warily. Although many Berliners secretly were proud of the fact that their Prince had married Queen Victoria's daughter, they watched her critically, ready to take offence at any slight. But she was clever enough to emphasise repeatedly how proud she was to be "a Prussian" and soon old Field Marshal von Wrangel, who had sat on the apple tart, was calling her an angel, and the German-born Duchess of Manchester was writing to Queen Victoria that "the English could not help feeling proud of the way the Princess Royal is spoken of, and the high esteem she is held in."[1]

Life was not easy for the Princess. In the first place the old King—the same gentleman who had refused the Frankfurt crown—was senile; yet his permission was necessary before the smallest alteration could be made in any of the royal palaces. Her Berlin home, the Old Schloss, offered a bleak contrast to English royal houses with their carpets and books and blazing fires. It was cold, dark, and filled with black antique furniture. Indeed, it was mediaeval in everything including the plumbing, and even worse, it was said to be haunted. "I do not believe that anyone washed in former days," wrote the Countess von Hohenthal, "for if you were lucky you found a basin, the size of an entrée dish of some precious porcelain, Dresden or Carl Theodore, and a bottle of water of priceless ruby glass. . . . The rooms were immense, the walls covered with full-length pictures, the great furniture creaked and the wind, on a winter's night, shrilled through the ill-fitting doors

[1] *The Empress Frederick : A Memoir.*

and windows. I lived in constant dread of meeting the White Lady, especially as there was a report that a sentry had seen her not so very far from the part occupied by us, outside her usual 'beat.' "[1]

However, worse was to come. The Old Schloss seemed luxurious compared to the New Palace at Potsdam and the country house at Bornstedt into which the Prince and Princess soon moved. The appalling discomfort remained a vivid memory to Vicky all her life; even forty years later when she described conditions to her daughter, Sophie, she wrote with emotion. "I must tell you, when I was a young thing, Berlin was an awful hole. No drainage, fearful pavements, awful smells. I spent the first year without W.C., baths or water to be got at, no cupboards for my clothes, my things had to all remain in boxes. The servants horrified me by their dishonesty and impertinence, their rough, untidy, dirty ways, their disobedience. A lady was nothing, not to be listened to . . . 1000's of dead bats I found in one big empty room, and bugs by the 100's. The beds I begged all to have burnt, but they were not. . . . Every drop of water was fetched for every bath and for the kitchen etc. by soldiers, a battalion of men. At Bornstedt (a house near Potsdam) when we first took it, no farm servant had *ever* had a mattress or sheets or blankets! They never undressed to go to bed, but kept on their clothes and enormous leather boots!—never washed and had no place to have meals, but sat and ate anywhere in the yard, stable or on the staircase. . . ."[2]

Luckily for the Princess the old King became so mad that Frederick's father was appointed Regent at the end of 1858, and during the following year she was able to unpack and introduce some method and hygiene. However, the dirt and the lack of plumbing were not her only worries. No matter how hard she tried, she could not get used to the stiffness of Prussian etiquette and the interminably long ceremonies. By comparison Queen Victoria's court seemed positively abandoned. To Vicky, the rigid emphasis on trivial details appeared ridiculous and provincial. Once the Queen rebuked her for sneezing during a ceremony and she replied tartly: "But I have a cold, Ma'am." The Queen snapped back that it made no difference; no one was permitted to sneeze in front

[1] *Embassies of Other Days:* Walpurga Paget.

[2] *The Empress Frederick Writes to Sophie:* edited by Arthur Gould Lee.

of the Sovereign. And Vicky could not resist saying acidly: "We do not have customs like that in our Court at home."

Another ordeal was the strange hours of the meals. There was no such thing as the English dinner party. In Prussia dinner took place in mid-afternoon, and the evening meal at eight was merely tea. Even the German-born Countess von Hohenthal refers to "these ghastly hours and modes of feeding." "I could never achieve satisfactorily," she wrote, "the early dinner by daylight in full evening dress. The crude white lights streaming in at the windows used to blind and tire me and many a time I have had to leave the table in a half-fainting state. The afternoons were passed by the victims of these barbarous customs in a state of coma, almost unable to move, and certainly to occupy themselves. . . ."[1] Vicky found a sympathetic ear when she complained to Wally of the Prussian habit of dinner guests gargling into their finger-bowls; and she developed an almost psychopathic loathing for Prussian boots. Why could none of the gentlemen ever appear in civilian attire?

On the whole these were minor irritants. What the Princess missed most of all was intellectual freedom and its natural companion, good conversation. English society had a vitality which was lacking on the continent. This was due to the fact that the British aristocracy was constantly revitalized by the creation of new peers drawn from the middle classes—the best brains in politics, industry, and the arts. The Prussian aristocracy on the other hand was static. Since Prussia had not yet begun to industrialise it was composed entirely of Junkers, who not only owned the land but dominated the civil service and the army, the only two dignified occupations open to them. Society drawn exclusively from these limited spheres was not apt to be lively; of course there was a group of middle-class intellectuals who might have added some spice, but as most of them were radicals they were regarded as beyond the pale.

Since the Princess herself was a radical and a free-thinker she found the company of the Junkers stultifying. They were narrow-minded and censorious and she wrote her mother that "the very approach of a Tory reactionary seems to freeze me up." One of these reactionaries was the towering, shaggy-haired diplomatist,

[1] *Embassies of Other Days*: Walpurga Paget.

Otto von Bismarck. Bismarck had remained in prominence ever since the revolutionary days of 1848 when he had stemmed the liberal tide by his passionate defence of autocracy and feudalism, and above all of Prussian supremacy. " We all desire the Prussian eagle to spread its guardian and governing wings from the Memel to the Donnersberg," he had cried, " but free we will see him . . . not sheltering under the levelling vultures from Frankfurt . . . Prussians we are and Prussians we will remain." He had written the King such hysterical letters of support at the time that the old man—a die-hard himself—was slightly embarrassed and catalogued him as a " red revolutionary, smacking of blood, only to be employed when the bayonet reigns without reservation." However, when the old, reactionary Frankfurt Diet was restored in 1850 the King thought better of Bismarck and sent him to Frankfurt as Prussia's representative. Thus he was launched on a diplomatic career. A few years later he was transferred to St. Petersburg, then to Paris.

It was during this phase, when he was in his middle forties, that he first met the Princess Royal. He had received the news of her engagement to Frederick with reservation as he did not want British democratic ideas infecting Prussia. " If the Princess can leave the English women at home and become a Prussian, then she may be a blessing to the country," he remarked guardedly to a friend. But when he met her he sensed that she was an opponent. At first he did not realise how deep her political convictions lay, and that her hostility sprang from the role he had played in 1848. He wrote in his reminiscences that he was startled to find that she did not approve of his character. " Even soon after her arrival in Germany, in February 1858, I became convinced, through members of the Royal House and my own observations, that the Princess was prejudiced against me personally. The fact did not surprise me so much as the form in which her prejudice against me had been expressed in the narrow family circle—' she did not trust me.' "

The Princess did not worry about Bismarck. To her he was just another Junker reactionary. She made contacts of her own with the intellectuals in Berlin and even took private lessons in science and mathematics. She had unlimited energy; she painted and sculptured, wrote poetry and organised musical glee clubs. The Prussians looked askance, for they believed that women should occupy themselves with husband and children and not meddle in the great world. She sensed the disapproval and at times was overcome with longing for her father. "You don't know," she wrote to her brother, the Prince of Wales, "how one longs for a word from him when one is distant." Instead, she had to content herself with letters. Every week she sent Prince Albert a long dissertation on politics or philosophy—and sometimes on her own emotions. He gave her constant reassurance. "That you should sometimes be oppressed by home-sickness is most natural. This feeling, which I know right well, will be sure to increase with the sadness which the reviving spring and the quickness of all nature that comes with it, always develops in the heart."[1] The weekly letters were not enough. Albert was dissatisfied unless he could exchange visits with his daughter every few months. The June after her marriage he spent six days with her in Berlin; and later in the summer returned to pay a second visit with Queen Victoria. The following year the Princess made two trips to England and the third year Queen Victoria and Prince Albert made a long visit to Coburg where all their relations gathered.

The Queen's relationship with her daughter was of a different nature, less exalted and more exacting. She wanted to know every detail of the Princess's life. She instructed the Maids of Honour to write her regularly and the Countess Walpurga remembers warnings from the Princess: "Don't tell Mama that." The Princess herself wrote to her mother once and sometimes twice a day. Baron Stockmar thought the Queen's demands insatiable and even harmful. After a visit to Berlin, he complained to Lord Clarendon that "the Queen wishes to exercise the same authority and control over her that she did before her marriage. . . ."[2] This was unfair. Victoria's chief concern was to help her daughter through a difficult period, but Baron Stockmar was not the only person to complain. Soon Prussian critics were whispering of the dangers of "petticoat rule."

The Princess's first child was named Frederick William Victor Albert, and known as Prince William. Queen Victoria was hurt and irritated at not being able to attend the christening. A cabinet

[1] *The Life of the Prince Consort:* Sir Theodore Martin.

[2] *Greville Diaries*: edited by Philip Whitwell Wilson.

crisis prevented her from leaving England, and her daughter wrote that it was impossible to postpone the date of the ceremony, which took place a week after William was born. " Never," wrote the Queen to her Uncle Leopold, " have I been so bitterly disappointed *about anything* as this. . . . It is a stupid law in Prussia, I must say, to be so particular about having the christening so soon."[1] The Princess wrote to her mother that she had promoted her trusted English maid, Mrs. Georgina Hobbs, to the post of nanny, and was organising her nursery on strictly English lines. The Queen and the Prince did not see their first grandchild until they made a trip to Coburg when he was twenty months old. Anything that belonged to Vicky was perfect in Albert's eyes and the Queen eagerly reflected her husband's sentiments. The poor, maimed little arm was not mentioned, even in her diary. She could not bear to refer to it for she knew how distressed Vicky was by the child's infirmity and how she still consulted new doctors, although they always said that nothing could be done. " Our darling grandchild was brought," she wrote, " such a little love! He came walking in at Mrs. Hobbs' hand, in a little white dress with black bows and so good. He is a fine, fat child, with a beautiful white soft skin, very fine shoulders and limbs, and a very dear face, like Vicky and Fritz, and also Louise of Baden. He has Fritz' eyes and Vicky's mouth, and very fair curly hair. We felt so happy to see him at last."[2]

By this time William was not the only child in the nursery. Despite the fact that Vicky had almost died in giving birth to him, and despite her father's warnings about having children in too quick succession, she produced babies with clock-work regularity. In 1860 a daughter, Charlotte, was born, and in 1862 a second son, Henry. Altogether she gave birth to four sons and four daughters. She created her large family less from a strong maternal instinct than a sense of royal duty. Although she was proud of her children and conscientious about their welfare, in the first years of her married life her interest was centred almost exclusively on her husband.

Like all Prussian princes, Fritz was in the army, but a less typical Prussian officer could scarcely be found. He was gentle and diffident and disliked the routine and heartiness of military life; furthermore

[1] *Letters of Queen Victoria.*

[2] *The Empress Frederick: A Memoir.*

he treated his wife as an equal which was almost unheard of in Berlin. He not only loved her but was enchanted by her flashing intellect and liked to spend long hours discussing complex subjects with her. She, in turn, felt herself indispensable to him. She returned his adoration with a deep devotion tinged by an almost prophetic desire to protect him. She followed him about on tours of inspection, and moved house to be with him on manœuvres. Sometimes Walpurga Hohenthal felt that she was seeing too few people. "The Princess had at that time a passionate but simple nature. . . . During the whole of those weeks at Berlin she never once went out in the daytime, but used to wait until the Prince came home and then take a drive with him."[1] But Vicky was blissful in her married life. On her third wedding anniversary she wrote to her father: "Every time our dear wedding day returns I feel so happy and thankful . . . not a hope has been disappointed, not an expectation that has not been realised. . . ."

The only demands that could draw the Princess away from Fritz were trips to England to visit her parents and, on one occasion, a special commission for her father. It was a strange request. In 1859 the Prince Consort confided to Vicky that he was worried about the eighteen-year-old Prince of Wales's development. The boy seemed to have no intellectual interests, and, even more alarming, was definitely pleasure-loving. Albert thought that he might get into mischief unless a stable influence could be brought into his life, and had decided that he must marry young. The difficulty lay in finding a suitable bride. Could not Vicky survey the field and produce the right person?

The Princess accepted the assignment and when she returned to Germany enlisted Walpurga Hohenthal's help. The first move on the part of the two young ladies was to attend a large supper party in Düsseldorf, given by the Prince of Hohenzollern, at which every eligible young German princess would be present. The Countess disapproved of the scheme, arguing that the Prince of Wales was much too young for an engagement. Nevertheless, they attended the party, but luckily all the princesses were "too plain to be considered." "We therefore returned to Berlin having done nothing," wrote the Countess with relief.

However, the incident had a sequel. A year later, Walpurga

[1] *Embassies of Other Days:* Walpurga Paget.

married a British diplomat, Mr. Arthur Paget, who was sent *en poste* to Copenhagen. The Princess was desolate at losing her beloved " Wally " but the two corresponded regularly. One day a letter arrived saying that the Countess had met an enchanting Danish Princess by the name of Alexandra who might make an excellent wife for the Prince of Wales. The Princess replied immediately, asked Wally to arrange a meeting (with as much discretion as possible) between herself and the young lady at Stretlitz. It took nearly a year before an occasion could be found, and the Countess waited nervously for the Princess's verdict. At last the letter arrived. " Quite enchanted I returned from Stretlitz and you are the first to whom I hasten to impart my impression. Princess Alix is the most enchanting creature in the world, you did not say nearly enough. For a long time I have seen nobody who pleased me so much as this lovely and charming girl, not to speak of a Princess. I am so grateful to you, dear Wally, that you have arranged all so well. . . . I have never seen Fritz so taken with anyone as he was with her. I have to think of you so continually here in the dear *Neue Palais*, I feel so sad when I pass your windows where, for two summers, your dear face always looked out with eyes brimful of mischief. . . . The children have grown much, the little boy [Prince William] had a nasty inflammation of the eyes which however, God be praised, is over now, but he still looks pale—not at all well—because, after the much-beloved German system, he has been kept locked up indoors for ages. . . ."[1] On the same day the Princess sent an equally enthusiastic report about " Alix " to her father.

Vicky was now Crown Princess of Prussia. In January 1861 the mad old King had died and Prince Frederick's father had ascended the throne as William I. Vicky was approaching her twenty-first birthday and in the full bloom of vitality and good looks. The American historian, Mr. Motley, who met her in Vienna, wrote to his mother: " She is rather *petite*, has a fresh young face with pretty features, fine teeth, and a frank and agreeable smile. . . . Nothing could be simpler or more natural than her style, which I should say was the perfection of good breeding."[2] Prince Albert's heart was filled with pride. " As for Vicky," he wrote the faithful Stockmar,

[1] *Scenes and Memories:* Walpurga Paget.
[2] *The Empress Frederick: A Memoir.*

"unquestionably she will turn out a very distinguished character whom Prussia will have cause to bless." To Vicky herself he sent congratulations on her twenty-first birthday in November 1861. "May your life which has begun so beautifully expand still further to the good of others and the contentment of your own mind. . . ."[1]

A month later Prince Albert was dead of typhoid fever. The blow fell with stunning impact on both his widow and daughter. The Princess was so distraught that she declared hysterically that her life was "over"—much to her husband's bewilderment. "She is very miserable and has bursts of grief which are painful to witness," wrote one of her German ladies-in-waiting to Walpurga Paget's husband. "Her health at present is very good, but I am always in fear that the continual emotions may be detrimental to her . . . she certainly has the kindest and most devoted of nurses (I may almost say) in the excellent Crown Prince, who seems to think of nothing else but how to try and alleviate her sorrow."[2]

The death of Prince Albert was more than a personal loss; it coincided with political events which marked a turning point in the life of Prussia, in the life of Europe, and in the life of the Princess. First of all, the Princess's determination to express her father's liberal ideas became almost an obsession. She was highly strung and impulsive, and now she seemed to lose all poise and discretion. "She was like a ship in full sail," wrote Walpurga Paget, "when the ballast is suddenly thrown overboard." And at the exact moment that the Princess moved in one direction, the Prussian ship of state veered and turned the opposite way.

It is surprising that Vicky did not foresee the likely change of course when her father-in-law, William I, succeeded as King of Prussia. William was even more of a reactionary than his predecessor. Indeed, during the revolutionary days of 1848 he had been bundled out of the country for safety. He believed in the Divine Right of Kings; and in Junker supremacy which meant an army dominated by the Junker class. He loathed all liberals and his first move was to expand the country's military forces and reorganise them in such a way as to rid them of liberal elements which had crept in over the past ten years. But here he hit a snag. The lower house of the Prussian assembly had a liberal majority,

[1] *The Life of the Prince Consort:* Sir Theodore Martin.
[2] *Embassies of Other Days:* Walpurga Paget.

and, although the assembly had very few powers, its one indisputable function was to approve the King's bills. But what if it did not approve? What happened then? No one knew. The Constitution of 1850 had left this point delightfully vague.

This was the problem with which William was faced. The upper house, composed of aristocrats, passed his huge financial budget, but the lower assembly, unwilling to see its political supporters expunged from the army during the period of expansion, refused to give its sanction. William I was advised to send for the shrewd, fiercely conservative Otto von Bismarck. If anyone could find a way to thwart the assembly it was he. The King offered him the job of Minister-President of Prussia, but Bismarck saw the chance for real power; he could not accept the position, he said, unless he was given control of Prussia's foreign policy. After much hesitation, the King agreed and the direction of the nation passed into the hands of a man destined to stand as a breakwater against the democratic tide moving across Europe. Even the King was taken aback by the bluntness of Bismark's speeches. In his first address to the budget Commission of the assembly, he jeered at liberal ideas and declared: "The great questions of the day will not be settled by resolutions and majority votes—that was the mistake of the men of 1848—but by blood and iron."

This sentence reverberated through Europe and alarmed Prussia's neighbours. The King was so annoyed at what he regarded as unnecessary provocation that he decided to dismiss Bismarck—but in the end the forty-seven-year-old statesman got round him. He announced that he had found a way out of the impasse with the assembly. His solution was simple enough—merely to rule without Parliament—yet it had a clever angle. The King must insist that his action was legal on the grounds that the constitution had a "hole" in it. Although money could only be spent with the assent of the two houses of Parliament, Prussia could not remain in a state of paralysis simply because the two houses refused to agree. Therefore the King must spend the money until they resolved their dispute. This was not all. In order to prevent trouble, Bismarck inveigled the King into muzzling the press. William I was dubious about these methods and although he agreed he remarked gloomily: "I see how it will end—on the gallows. You will suffer the fate of Strafford and I of Charles I."

The Crown Princess was shocked and angry. She had never liked Bismarck—he was the antithesis of all she had been taught to admire—and here he was with one stroke abrogating the Constitution and destroying the liberal frame-work on which her beloved father had pinned his hopes. Furthermore, she was enraged that the assembly and the press should accept their defeat so tamely. "Thank God I was born in England," she wrote heatedly to her mother, "where people are not slaves and too good to allow themselves to be treated as such."[1]

At least she and her husband would not acquiesce in Bismarck's unconstitutional acts. Prince Frederick would make his position clear. He was not in Berlin but the Princess followed him to Graudenz. She found him reluctant to comply. After all, his father, the King, stood behind Bismarck. "Think if it was your father," he protested. "Would you like to disobey him and make him unhappy?"[1] In the end she got round him and he promised to reveal his opposition in a speech at Danzig. His words sound mild enough but they nearly landed him in a fortress. "Of the proceedings which brought it [the constitutional change] about I know nothing," he said, "I was absent. I have had no part in the deliberations which produced the result."[1]

The fact that the Crown Prince dissociated himself from the King's actions was enough to cause a sensation, not only in Prussia but throughout Europe. *The Times* newspaper made matters worse by congratulating the young couple on their courageous stand. Now it was the King's turn to be furious. He wrote to the Prince demanding an apology; the Prince refused and offered to resign his office. The King considered all sorts of punishments—including the fortress—then finally decided to end the matter by forbidding the Crown Prince to make any further public utterances. The Princess was unrepentant. She wrote to her mother proudly that she had exercised a decisive influence on Fritz, "knowing how necessary it was that he should once express his sentiments openly and disclaim having any part in the last measures of the Government." This was not all. She then encouraged Frederick to write to Bismarck (and to send a copy of the letter to the King), which was nothing less than a declaration of war. It ended with the words: "I will tell you what results I anticipate from your policy . . . whether you intend it

[1] *Letters of the Empress Frederick.*

or not, you will pass from one venturesome interpretation to another until you are finally driven into an open breach of the Constitution. I regard those who lead his Majesty the King, my most gracious father, into such courses as the most dangerous advisers for Crown and country."[1] Bismarck spotted the hand of the Crown Princess. " She has decided upon a course of opposition to the present government," he dictated in a memorandum, ". . . in order to bring her husband more and more into prominence. . . ."

Meanwhile the Crown Princess had written to her mother gaily that both she and Fritz would do the same again " in the face of all the Kings and Emperors in the whole world." " I enjoy a pitched battle when it comes to it exceedingly," she commented happily. Yet the truth was that she had committed an irrevocable blunder. Not only had she caused a severe breach between father and son and made an enemy of Bismarck, but she had encouraged her husband to take a stand which, as a royal prince, he was not in a position to defend or exploit. Bismarck had won the battle for now he was the King's sole adviser, while Frederick, by nailing his opposition colours to the mast, had destroyed the only weapon he possessed: indirect influence.

The Crown Princess seemed to have no idea of the impossible situation she had put herself in. She was only twenty-two and did not understand that in politics courage requires the companionship of sagacity. She was to learn by sad experience that the rift between King and Prince would never completely close; that she had made enemies with a man who would rule Germany for twenty-seven years; and that she had sown the seeds of discord which one day would separate her from her eldest son.

[1] *Letters of the Empress Frederick.*

2. *His Youth*

Prince William made his first visit to England when he was two and a half, just six months before the Prince Consort died. His mother took him to Osborne and in later life William claimed to have a vivid recollection of Grandpapa Albert, who, he said, swung him about in a huge white damask table-napkin. Not only did the boy hold a special position as the first grandchild, but Prince Albert had pronounced that he was "a pretty, clever child—a compound of both parents, just as it should be"; and this was enough for the Queen to stud her diary with praise. "The dear little boy is so intelligent and pretty, so good and affectionate." "The darling little boy was with us for nearly an hour, running about so dearly and merrily."

William's second trip to England was eighteen months later, when he was just four. He was taken to Windsor for the marriage of his twenty-one-year-old Uncle "Bertie" to the Princess Alexandra of Denmark. For months beforehand a buzz of excitement had enlivened his mother's house, for the Crown Princess considered herself personally responsible for the match. She had written her father glowing accounts of the Danish Princess, and Albert had told Victoria that he regarded the affair as good as settled. He had been struck down before any formal steps could be taken, but six months after his death the Queen wrote to Prince Christian, nephew and heir to the King of Denmark, formally requesting his daughter's hand for the Prince of Wales.

Bertie had never seen Alexandra but he admired her picture; he was eager to marry in order to have his own establishment and escape from his mother's surveillance. The Queen would not let him propose, however, until she had met the young lady, and a family gathering at Laecken was duly arranged by Uncle Leopold, King of the Belgians. Princess Alexandra was warned to dress simply and not to smile, for the Queen could not bear to see anyone looking happy. She made a good impression on Victoria, and, even more important, on Bertie, who was delighted by her charm and beauty. He was so attentive that a few weeks later Uncle Leopold wrote to Victoria: " The match is quite a love-match. Bertie is extremely happy and in admiration of his very lovely bride. All the arguments that one forced him to marry a young lady that he had never seen fall most completely to the ground. All this is important, particularly for England, where it will please people very much that the Prince of Wales, like his parents, should marry from affection."[1]

The Queen would not allow her son to have a large wedding, saying that the ordeal would be too much for her. The ceremony took place at St. George's Chapel, Windsor, and since space was limited, most of the guests were royal relations. Little Prince William attended his uncle's wedding dressed in a Highland costume presented to him by his grandmother. He was immensely proud of his sporran and the tiny dirk in his stocking, but he found the ceremony interminably long. His eighteen-year-old Uncle Alfred —the Duke of Edinburgh—was put in charge of him. When he bade the small Prince be quiet William drew his dirk in a threatening manner; and when he remonstrated with him for throwing his sporran into the choir William bit him in the leg. Queen Victoria sat weeping in the gallery above the chancel, and remained ignorant of her grandson's aggressive tendencies. She wrote to Uncle Leopold that he was " a clever, dear good little child, the great favourite of my beloved Angel."

The fact that William was the only grandchild who could recall Grandfather Albert gave him first place in Victoria's heart. The boy —and his brothers and sisters—visited her regularly throughout their childhood years, and William was always touched by his grandmother's indulgences. " The Queen," he wrote, " was always particularly kind to me from the very first, she was a real grandmother, and our relations to one another were never changed or dimmed to the end of her life. I was allowed to play with the same toys and in the same places as did formerly my English uncles and aunts when they were my age. And by the same token we could go and drink tea and make butter and cream cheese in the little kitchen fitted out for them in the dairy at Frogmore, which was in Windsor Park.

[1] *Letters of Queen Victoria.*

At Osborne I could play with the same old iron cannon on a model redoubt where my uncles had played when they were boys. And I remember a lottery organised for us children at Windsor of which the winning prize was arranged by my grandmother to be a huge English cake. . . . I was supposed to have been ' very brave ' when having a tooth extracted by the celebrated Dr. Evans, so my grandmother gave me a brand new gold pound that I kept for the whole of my life. . . ."[1]

The Queen intimidated many people, including her own relations, but William was one of the few who was always at ease with her. He found her cosy and sympathetic and remembered how hard she had laughed at a *gaffe* made by Admiral Foley. The incident took place at a family lunch party at Osborne when William was twelve. The British sailing-frigate *Eurydice* had been sunk near Portsmouth, salvaged, and towed into harbour. " The Queen," recounted William, " had commanded Admiral Foley to luncheon at Osborne to receive his report of it. After she had exhausted this melancholy subject, my grandmother, in order to give the conversation a more cheerful turn, inquired after his sister, whom she knew well, whereon the Admiral, who was hard of hearing and still pursuing his train of thought about the *Eurydice*, replied in his stentorian voice : ' Well, Ma'am, I am going to have her turned over and take a good look at her bottom and have it well scraped.' The effect of this answer was stupendous. My grandmother put down her knife and fork, hid her face in her handkerchief and shook and heaved with laughter until the tears rolled down her face."[1]

No doubt Queen Victoria's kindness to William assumed exaggerated proportions in contrast to the harsh life the Prince was obliged to live in Berlin. At four, he had two companions in the nursery, a three-year-old sister, Charlotte, and a one-year-old brother, Henry. They were happy with their jolly English nurse " Hobbsy," but when more babies continued to arrive Mrs. Hobbs was delegated to the younger ones, and the three eldest were put in charge of Fräulein von Dobeneck. Life became a torment of restrictions and punishments ; but even more gruelling experiences were in store for them.

When William was seven his mother decided that the time had

[1] *My Early Life :* William II.

come to hand him over to a tutor. Although she described herself as a "free-thinker," there was no trace of originality in the upbringing of her children. She faithfully copied the grim German regime that her father had laid down for her unfortunate brother Bertie, and, if anything, made it even more severe. As William's tutor, she selected a stern unbending Calvinist school-master by the name of George Hintzpeter. This gaunt, joyless creature emphasized the Spartan ideas of duty and renunciation; anything in the name of pleasure was harmful to the character. William's brother Henry was soon forced to share the routine and the two boys regarded themselves as little better than prisoners. Their existence became a nightmare of austerity, and, as far as William was concerned, even of fear and pain. Lessons began at six in the morning and continued all day—with only a few brief breaks for meals and physical exercise—until six or seven at night. The children were given dry rusks for breakfast to emphasise "renunciation;" and when their cousins came to visit them were made to offer them cakes, but to take none for themselves. All praise was rigidly excluded from their lives. The impossible was expected of them, Hintzpeter explained, in order to force them "to the nearest degree of perfection;" and since this could never be achieved there was no occasion for praise. Apart from the relentless scholastic regime, Prince William was made to undergo electric treatments on his powerless left arm. The experiments proved abortive and caused him excruciating pain.

He was also made to ride. Prussia was a military nation and a future king must be able to cut a fine ceremonial figure at the head of his cavalry. But how could he be taught? The child's infirmity presented a serious problem. Hintzpeter finally found the answer. "Riding," he wrote, "at first actually dangerous and forced upon him with stern discipline, despite his tearful resistance, was finally mastered with delight and skill . . . When the Prince was eight and a half years old a lackey still had to lead his pony by the rein, because his balance was so bad that his unsteadiness caused intolerable anxiety to himself and others. So long as this lasted he could not learn to ride: it had to be overcome no matter at what cost. Neither groom nor riding master could do it. Therefore the tutor [Hintzpeter], using a moral authority over his pupil that by now was absolute, set the weeping Prince on his horse without stirrups and compelled him to go through the various paces. He fell off continually: every time, despite his prayers and tears, he was lifted up and set upon its back again. After weeks of torture, the difficult task was accomplished: he had got his balance."[1] William's brother Henry howled with anguish when he was forced to witness these ordeals but the Crown Princess showed iron control, for she was convinced that Hintzpeter's tactics were both right and necessary. On one occasion, when William came riding across the park at Potsdam his hat fell off, the pony reared, and he was thrown on his back. The Court Chamberlain, Herr Pulitz, could see the agitation in the Princess's eyes but he wrote his wife admiringly that she did not allow a single exclamation to escape her lips.

To William his mother seemed a remote and even frightening figure. In later years he wrote that she did not show the same tenderness towards her three elder children as with her younger. Although she supervised her nurseries conscientiously she seldom laughed or played and only seemed to intervene to uphold the strictures of his tormentors, so that William always associated her with his misery. He could not know that during the years of his early boyhood—years that stretched from his mother's twenty-fourth to thirtieth birthday—she was caught up in events that were changing the face of Europe, causing her an agonising inner conflict which led to many bitter tears.

Bismarck was at the root of all her trouble. He was a formidable enemy, for he was wily, ruthless, and cruelly vindictive. He believed that the end justified any means and did not hesitate to slander, distort, intimidate, or even blackmail, when it served his purpose. The Crown Princess was an easy target for she was English. He simply spread the story that she was an agent of Queen Victoria and a traitor to Prussia. Her advisers, Sir Robert Morier, the British diplomat, and Ernest Stockmar, her secretary, were also part of the " Anglo-Coburg " conspiracy to make Prussia a British satellite. Note how often the Princess journeyed to Windsor and Balmoral; note how persistently she referred to England as " home; " note how determinedly she employed English nurses for her children. She was always making disparaging remarks about Prussia; Bismarck himself had heard her

[1] *My Early Life:* William II.

say that there was more silver-plate in Liverpool than the whole of Prussia. Could anyone regard her as a Prussian patriot? Bismarck even convinced the King that she was not to be trusted; and since Frederick told his wife everything, persuaded the old man that it was not wise to allow the Crown Prince to see or hear any state secrets.

The Princess was sickened and outraged by these tales, but they did not produce the deep emotional stress that later darkened her existence. It was not until Bismarck launched out on his wars of aggression that her torment began. During the years between 1864 and 1871 he plunged the nation into three conflicts, first with Denmark, then Austria, then France; and Prussia emerged not only the victor but as the leader of a united Germany and the strongest power on the continent. The Princess hated war, hated autocracy, and hated Bismarck. But how could she decry events that were transforming Fritz's small country into a mighty empire which one day would be his heritage? Even worse, Fritz was a general in the Prussian Army and was obliged to take part in the campaigns. It was unbearable for her to feel that he was risking his life in an unjust war.

Prince Albert had boasted that his daughter had a "man's mind," but now the woman's temperament took over. Torn between reason and impulse she moved first in one direction, then another, pouring out passionate and illogical sentiments to her mother. For instance, when Bismarck first challenged Denmark over the ownership of the Schleswig-Holstein Duchies, she scoffed at his claim, but as soon as war broke out she not only reversed her views but became incensed at England's pro-Danish sympathies. Most countries in Europe deplored the attack on a small defenceless nation, and England was particularly concerned because the father of the Princess of Wales was King of Denmark. The beautiful Alexandra went about with tears in her eyes, saying, "The Duchies belong to Papa," and feeling in Parliament rose to such a pitch it looked for a time as though England might intervene. Queen Victoria's uncle, the King of the Belgians, could not refrain from writing mischievously: "Vicky little dreamt in selecting a charming princess [for her brother] that she would become a source of difficulties for England, and perhaps the cause of a popular war against Prussia."

Queen Victoria stood firmly for neutrality and in the end British interference went no further than speeches in the House and articles in *The Times*. But even this annoyed the Crown Princess. " The continual meddling and interfering in other people's affairs has become so ridiculous abroad that it almost ceases to annoy," she wrote angrily to her mother. Although the conflict was soon over it had opened a breach between the Crown Princess and the Prince and Princess of Wales that did not heal quickly. Queen Victoria begged Bertie and Alix to stop off in Germany on their way home from Denmark and patch things up, but the brief visit was not a success. The Prince of Wales wrote Lord Spencer that it was not pleasant to see his brother-in-law in a Prussian uniform " flaunting before our eyes a most objectionable ribbon which he received for his *deeds of valour*??? against the unhappy Danes."

Once peace was established Vicky resumed her hostile attitude towards Bismarck. Two years later, in the spring of 1866, she saw that he was bent on a clash with Austria in order to settle the leadership of the German states. She complained to Queen Victoria: " Not a day passes when the wicked man does not with the greatest ability counteract and thwart what is good, and drive on towards war." The conflict broke out a month later and ended seven weeks later with a smashing Prussian victory at Sadowa. This time Fritz led his troops into action and emerged as a hero so once again Vicky changed her views. " I assure you that if the rest of Europe did but know the details of this war—the light in which our officers and men and our public at large have shown themselves—the Prussian people would stand high in the eyes of everyone, and I feel that I am *now* every bit as proud of being a Prussian as I am of being an Englishwoman and that is saying a very great deal, as you know what a 'John Bull' I am and how enthusiastic about my home. I must say the Prussians are a superior race, as regards intelligence and humanity, education and kind-heartedness. . . ."[1] Queen Victoria was upset to hear that Prussia was annexing the Kingdom of Hanover and part of Hesse-Darmstadt, both of which were ruled by her near relations, but Vicky was unsympathetic. " Those who are now in such precarious positions might have *quite well* foreseen what danger they were running into . . . they *chose* to go with Austria and they now share the sad fate she confers

[1] *Letters of the Empress Frederick.*

upon her Allies . . . I know it is difficult to make you or any other non-German see how our case lies. We have made enormous sacrifices, and the nation expects them not to be in vain."[1]

They were not in vain. Only one more obstacle blocked Bismarck's way to real power: France. When he launched his third and last war, Vicky for once did not have to argue with her mother. Queen Victoria remembered that dear Albert had always considered France "vainglorious and immoral;" and since Bismarck had managed to trap Napoleon III into the role of aggressor, she became highly partisan and told Sir Theodore Martin: "It was merciful that the beloved Prince was taken, for had he lived I could never have prevented him from joining the German armies." Only the Prince and Princess of Wales remained steadfastly anti-Prussian. Vicky was so annoyed by her brother's sentiments that she tried to make trouble for him by telling her mother that he was reported to have "loudly expressed at a dinner at the French ambassador's . . . his hope that we should fare ill."

In the beginning everyone trembled for poor Prussia. How could this little nation hope to vanquish mighty France? But after a few weeks it became apparent that France was no longer mighty —only disorganised and demoralised. On September 1, 1870, less than two months after the opening of hostilities, the Prussians scored a decisive victory at Sedan. "What will Bertie and Alix say to all these marvellous things!" crowed Vicky. "May we all learn what frivolity, conceit and immorality lead to! The French people have trusted in their own excellence, have completely deceived themselves. . . . They despised and hated the Germans whom they considered it quite lawful to insult. How they have been punished!" She could not resist taking a cut at her brother. "I am sure dear Bertie must envy Fritz who has such a trying, but useful life."[2]

The war lasted another five months. The Parisians refused to surrender their city and held on doggedly despite famine and bombardment. A few weeks before the capitulation of the invested capital, the Prussians held an imposing ceremony in the Palace of Versailles where King William was proclaimed German Emperor. When peace was finally signed, the terms were so hard that the Crown Princess refused to believe them: France was to pay a huge

[1] *Letters of Queen Victoria.*

[2] *Letters of the Empress Frederick.*

indemnity and surrender the province of Alsace and a large part of Lorraine. The report, she informed her mother, "was invented by a German newspaper correspondent, I never believed it for a moment." But it was true; she wrote again, this time explaining that it was necessary to have Alsace and Lorraine for defensive purposes—in case France ever launched another attack.

Now that Germany was a great power the Crown Princess hated Bismarck more than ever. She saw nothing illogical in the fact that she had supported him at each crucial step, for her hatred was swollen by personal grievances and jealousy. He had usurped the position that the Prince Consort had intended for Fritz and herself, for his views and his views alone prevailed. The Emperor had rewarded him with vast estates in Prussia and the rank and style of Prince and, even more galling, he was recognised universally as the greatest statesman in Europe. He certainly was the most devious and the most difficult to fathom, for everything about him was contradictory. A physical giant with the intuition of a woman; a passionate Prussian with the subtlety of a Latin; a man who made no pretensions to being an intellectual and never read a book, but expressed himself in such provocative, piquant, and droll language that he created a new literature often compared to Goethe. He had no knowledge of the arts, furnished his house in abominable style, ate Gargantuan meals, and shocked the connoisseurs by pouring beer and champagne together and calling it a "Black Velvet." He took long walks and spent hours in solitary reflection. He believed that he was serving God when he was serving his King; and that he was serving his King when he followed his own inclinations. Thus he was free of all scruples and restraints.

Bismarck now adopted as his daily garb the Prussian military uniform (explaining to friends that it was cheaper than civilian dress), while his curious, rough, almost benign countenance hid a spirit more cunning, more vindictive, more tyrannical than ever. He not only continued to persecute the Crown Prince and Princess but manifested an attitude of scorn which made Vicky boil with indignation. Her gentle, high-minded husband, however, refused to be agitated by personal resentment and clung to principles. He loathed Bismarck's use of force. During the Franco-Prussian war he had shocked a well-known German writer, Herr Freytag, by declaring: "I hate this slaughter. I never desired the honours of war, and would gladly have left such glory to others. Nevertheless, it is my hard fate to go from battlefield to battlefield, from one war to another, before ascending the throne of my ancestors."[1] He had tried to dissuade Bismarck from subjecting Paris to bombardment, warning him that European opinion would veer away from Prussia and range itself with France. His advice was not heeded and he was proved right. "Bismarck has made us great and powerful," he wrote in his diary, "but he has robbed us of our friends, the sympathies of the world and—our conscience."

When the Crown Prince and Princess visited England shortly after the end of the war, they made no secret of their detestation of the "Iron Chancellor." Needless to say, their sentiments found favour with the Prince and Princess of Wales, and the long-standing breach between the two couples was closed. "Fritz is so fair, kind and good," wrote Queen Victoria, "and has the intensest horror of Bismarck, says he is no doubt energetic and clever, but bad, unprincipled and *all*-powerful; he is, in fact, Emperor which Fritz' father does not like, but still cannot help."[2]

Prussia's three victories and the emergence of united Germany took place in the seven years which fell between Prince William's fifth and twelfth birthdays; and what a glorious contrast these stirring events offered to the child's own dull, unhappy existence! It provided him with his only channel of escape, and he lived in a vicarious haze of great deeds and imperial pomp.

Of course the Prussians had always been a martial race. "The memory of any child born in Berlin must be tinged with military colour," wrote William. "It was impossible to think of the capital of Prussia without soldiers and regimental bands." With the advent of Bismarck, however, the soldiers had taken on a more menacing character, and no one rejoiced more than the young Prince. He put up maps in the schoolroom; pored over books and magazines, and was thrilled to see pictures of his father on a prancing steed, leading his army at the front. How he revelled in the victory parades that passed with such precision through the Brandenburger Tor! How he exulted in the news that an Emperor's laurels had been accorded to his grandfather in the Palace of Versailles! And

[1] *The Empress Frederick: A Memoir.*
[2] *Letters of Queen Victoria.*

what a day it was when grandfather and father returned from France! The Prince was twelve years old and he drove with his family to Wildpark Station in Potsdam " to meet the conquerors." " With what an ecstasy I flung myself into my father's arms and saw my much respected grandfather for the first time as German Emperor! "

Yet there were things that troubled William. Why were the relations between his parents and his grandfather so cool? They never met in cosy family gatherings, only on formal state occasions. It could not be his grandfather's fault for the Emperor seemed to William a benign kindly old man. He often invited the boy to dine alone with him. " On such occasions," wrote William, " the meal was served in the drawing-room, which led into his study, at a small, green card-table, that was very shaky and needed extremely careful handling. With the joint, a bottle of champagne was put on the table, which the Emperor himself uncorked and with his own hands filled two glasses for himself and for me. After the second glass he would hold the bottle up to the light, and make a pencil mark on the label at the height of the contents; in this way, for he was very economical, he could prove whether the servants kept the bottle for further use or, somewhat against his order, set a fresh one before him the next day."[1]

But even more disturbing than the coolness of his parents towards the Emperor was their attitude towards the Imperial Chancellor. While all Germany bowed to Bismarck, William's father and mother could not bear to hear a word in his favour. They even criticised his new constitution. The boy studied it with Hintzpeter and could find nothing wrong with it; indeed, he marvelled at its ingenuity. Federal Germany had been given an assembly consisting of two houses. The upper house was composed of princes and controlled by the Emperor, while the lower house was elected by universal male suffrage, a " democratic " innovation created to silence the liberals. But the truth was that its members had very little say. The Chancellor governed the nation in the Sovereign's name and was not responsible to the assembly, only to the Emperor. He controlled all the civil departments of state including the Foreign Office. The lower house was not allowed to introduce legislation but its assent was necessary before bills became law. However, if

[1] *My Early Life:* William II.

it proved obstinate in providing a rubber stamp the Emperor could always dissolve the chamber and hold new elections. Prince William saw that Bismarck had designed the edifice to give himself the mastery of Germany; he also saw that he wielded his authority by permission of the Emperor. The Sovereign could appoint and dismiss his chancellors as he liked. Although his grandfather relied on Bismarck, the day might come when another emperor would choose to rule himself.

William could not help thinking his mother rather foolish to object to the splendid gift of unchallenged autocracy that Bismarck had bestowed upon the House of Hohenzollern. He did not understand his mother. Although he saw far more of her than most royal children he always felt uneasy with her. He and his brother Henry had breakfast with their parents every morning and during the holidays they were taken on many " worth-while " sight-seeing expeditions; frequently William accompanied his mother on visits to England—and once on a long trip to the South of France. Yet she often was so stern and critical that he felt she was disappointed in him, and at times had a despairing sense of inadequacy. He vividly remembered her grief at the death of his two-year-old brother, Sigismund. He was only seven at the time and his father was away, fighting in the Austrian war, but all his life he remembered how wildly distraught she had been; and although he could not analyse his feelings then, realised later with a bitter pang that she was capable of the deepest love—but not for him. He was not wrong in his intuition, for she lamented to Queen Victoria that she had lost her favourite child. " Oh how I loved that little thing, from the first moments of its birth, it was more to me than its brothers and sisters . . . so wonderfully forward and intelligent, so clever, much more than either of the others, and I thought he was going to be like Papa."[1] She wrote a poem about Sigismund which William was obliged to memorise and recite to his father when the Prince returned from the war. Meanwhile she had erected a shrine in the dead child's room, and nailed a cross upon the wall. No one was allowed to enter. Years later Lady Macdonald, the wife of a British diplomat, was taken by the Crown Princess along a corridor in the New Palace, and a locked door was

[1] *Letters of Empress Frederick.*

opened. "I saw a cradle, and in it a baby boy, beautiful to look upon, but it was only the waxen image of the former occupant, Prince Sigismund, who had died when the Crown Prince went to the war in 1866. How pathetic it was to note the silver rattle and ball lying as though flung aside by the little hand, the toys which had amused his baby mind arranged all about the cradle, his little shoes waiting, always waiting—at the side."[1]

It was not until William was eleven that his mother turned her full gaze upon him. The time had arrived, she decided, to supervise his development herself. What a pity that he had a crippled arm! Why had it had to happen to her eldest son! Sometimes she felt that Providence singled her out for misfortune. She often had moments of depression, and the only antidote was to pour out her feelings on paper. In such a mood she wrote to her mother: "The poor arm is no better, and William begins to feel being behind much smaller boys in every exercise of the body—he cannot run fast, because he has no balance, nor ride, nor climb, nor cut his food etc. . . . I wonder he is so good-tempered about it. His tutor thinks he will feel it much more, and be much unhappier about it as he grows older, and feels himself debarred from everything which others enjoy, and particularly since he is so strong and lively and healthy. It is a hard trial for him and for us. Nothing is neglected that can be done for it, but there is so little to be done. . . ."[2] It was a curiously distorted letter for, in fact, William's tutor testifies that this pupil could ride "with skill and delight." He could also swim, fence, skate, and even handle a gun. "I shot my first game in the year 1872; it was a pheasant," wrote the Prince. "Soon after I brought down my first hare. I shot my first stag in Wildpark in the autumn of 1876."

William was not enthusiastic about his mother's supervision for she possessed her father's thoroughness. Even Queen Victoria was apprehensive, for she knew how seriously Vicky regarded the task of moulding the character of a future emperor and was afraid of her intensity. When Vicky wrote her proudly in 1871, "I watch over him myself, over every detail, even the minutest, of his education . . . ," the Queen replied warningly: "I am sure you watch over your dear boy with the greatest care, but I often think

[1] *The Empress Frederick: A Memoir.*
[2] *Letters of the Empress Frederick.*

too great care, too much constant watching, leads to the very dangers hereafter which one wishes to avoid." However, the Princess did not heed her mother's advice for she believed that there was much to teach William that only she could give him. She prided herself on a knowledge of music, literature, painting, architecture, and even archaeology, and was determined that William should also acquaint himself with these subjects. He was well versed in Greek, Latin, French, and English, and had read widely in his own language. Now more tutors were engaged and more professors bidden to enlighten him. His school hours were lengthened and his relaxations curtailed. Every moment had to be utilised. On Sundays, after church, his mother took him to visit artists in their studios, and in the afternoons his father accompanied him to museums. His treats were Shakespearean plays or the opera. Even when he went riding with Hintzpeter the time was not allowed to be wasted. As he cantered along, he was compelled to recount the Greek epics in order to acquire fluency of expression. His instructors were told to report personally to the Crown Princess and in the spring of 1870 his English tutor, Mr. Dealtry, wrote that he had read most of the works of Sir Walter Scott and a great deal of Tennyson and Macaulay. "His Royal Highness has, I think, advanced satisfactorily in his knowledge of the English language, and has evinced a real love for English literature. His interest in his studies has added much to the enjoyment of the hours I have passed with him. His pronunciation and accent still need cultivation. I have been greatly struck by his generous and manly instincts. Indeed both the princes are remarkable for their gentlemanly tone of thought and feeling. . . ."

The Crown Princess was not so lenient in her judgement of William's capacities. It was too bad that he did not have more of his grandfather in him. Thought and learning had been Albert's delight whereas William seemed to regard them as a laborious duty. On the other hand he was often a pleasing companion, and she particularly enjoyed the hours he spent reading to her while she painted in her studio. In the spring of 1871 she wrote a letter to the Queen containing the warmest allusions to the boy she was ever to make. "I am sure you would be pleased with William if you were to see him—he has Bertie's pleasant amiable ways—and can be very winning. He is not possessed of brilliant abilities, nor of any strength of character or talents, but he is a dear boy, and I hope and trust will grow up a useful man. He has an excellent tutor, I never saw or knew a better, and all the care that can be bestowed on mind and body is taken of him. I am happy to say that between him and me there is a bond of love and confidence, which I feel sure nothing can destroy. He has very strong health and would be a very pretty boy were it not for that wretched unhappy arm which shows more and more, spoils his face (for it is on one side), his carriage, walk and figure, makes him awkward in all his movements, and gives him a feeling of shyness, as he feels his complete dependence, not being able to do a single thing for himself. It is a great additional difficulty in his education, and is not without its effect on his character. To me it remains an inexpressible source of sorrow! I think he will be very good-looking when he grows up, and he is already a universal favourite, as he is so lively and generally intelligent. He is a mixture of all our brothers—there is very little of his Papa, or the family of Prussia, about him."[1]

Was there really a bond of love and confidence between them? There is no hint of this from William's pen, either as a schoolboy or in retrospect. Was he really shy and awkward? Hintzpeter suggests that he was becoming alarmingly autocratic. His head was filled with romantic notions and he was still in a haze of ecstasy over the newly created German Empire. About this time, he accompanied his father and mother to England to stay with his grandmother. Shortly after his return, the Queen cautioned her daughter not to keep William's circle too narrow. Perhaps she, too, had thought him a bit imperious, for she regretted that he did not come into contact more often with ordinary people—military training would not suffice. Apparently the Crown Princess misunderstood her mother's meaning, for the Queen wrote again. "I . . . wish just to touch on your answer to my observations and hopes respecting Willy. The vehemence with which you speak of 'the horror of low company' would make it appear as though I had advocated it! What I meant (but what I fear your position in Prussia, living always in a Palace with the ideas of immense position of Kings and Princes, etc.) is: that the Princes and Princesses should be thoroughly kind, *menschlich*, should not feel that they were of a different flesh and blood to the poor, the peasants and working

[1] *Letters of the Empress Frederick.*

classes and servants, and that going amongst them, as we always did and do, and as every respectable lady and gentleman does here—was of such immense benefit to the character of those who have to reign hereafter. The mere contact with soldiers *never* can do that, or rather the reverse, for they are bound to obey and no independence of character can be expected in the ranks. . . ."[1]

Queen Victoria's words did not have much effect at the time but three years later they bore unexpected fruit. When William was fifteen an announcement was made which astonished the Prussian aristocracy. William and his brother Henry would move to Cassel and attend the state-run grammar school. They would do their lessons with ordinary boys. Even today royal princes are seldom sent to state schools, so it is not difficult to imagine the indignation the plan drew from the privileged world of 1874. The aging Emperor protested angrily and Bismarck raised his hands in sharp disdain. The Crown Princess was to blame. This obviously was an English notion. As usual she was trying to force the practices of her native land upon the Prussian way of life. Nothing could have been farther from the truth, for the English aristocracy—much less its royalty—would have been just as shocked as the Prussians at the thought of a prince attending a state school. The idea had originated with George Hintzpeter, and it had taken him months to persuade the Crown Princess to accept it.

Hintzpeter was convinced that the only cure for William's growing arrogance was to mix with middle-class boys. He must learn that although he occupied an exalted position many of the sons of professional people were more gifted intellectually than himself. Competition on a serious scale was essential, and might induce a more humble approach to life. William himself was appalled by the plan. "I was not exactly pleasantly surprised. For now I . . . was to be given into the hands of new teachers, and now, all at once, was to learn with strange boys in a public school, was to compete with them—and to come out lower on the lists!"[2]

William and his brother soon found themselves plunged into an odd mixture of pomp and simplicity. Hintzpeter got it into his head that they must hike to Cassel like "travelling students." He

[1] *Letters of the Empress Frederick.*
[2] *My Early Life:* William II.

accompanied them and for hours they climbed over mountains and marched through valleys, arriving in the town looking like tramps. The Emperor was expected the same day, which was all part of Hintzpeter's plan. "We entered Cassel in a peculiar fashion, in deliberate antithesis to the public imagination," he recorded pompously in his diary. "We cheerfully sat in the enclosure for yeomen on the bowling green of a coachman's beer-house, partaking of sour beer and hard bread. It was raining, and I held my umbrella over the lunch to prevent the beer becoming still more watery, for we needed strengthening after a hard march. Then we heard the whistle of an engine, and by this knew that at that moment the Emperior was arriving in Cassel in triumph, in a comfortable saloon car, honoured, extolled, well-dined, in complete enjoyment of a hard-earned position after a lifetime's work; while Prince William, having quite insufficiently breakfasted, with tired legs and empty stomach, walked to Cassel and entered Cassel in the true manner of a travelling student. And this moral sermon was fully exemplified in word and deed. So as not to be with the Emperor in Cassel we wander about in the surrounding country, obtain, with difficulty, a cup of coffee in some pleasure grounds, wherein we blissfully soak a pocketed crust of bread. . . ."[1] After this, the tutor and the two princes walked to the large palace on the main street which was to be their home. The porter, dressed in a splendid uniform, refused to believe they were who they said, and only let them in after protracted argument.

Hintzpeter's attempts to democratise Prince William were not altogether successful. Although he quickly adjusted himself to his new life and soon enjoyed the games and rivalry, he refused to shed his condescension. Apparently it did not matter, for his tutor wrote that "his school-fellows soon found out, in spite of an ever-tactful reserve which forbade all familiarity, he could be, and actually was, a very good fellow. . . ."

Hintzpeter was not the right person to deal with William's pompousness. Heavy and unimaginative, he lacked the humour necessary to jostle him out of his pretentiousness. Indeed, he himself had a tendency to treat trivial matters with ridiculous solemnity. Once Bismarck, who was curious to know what sort of a man was instructing Prince William, honoured him with a talk.

[1] *My Early Life*: William II.

Afterwards the Crown Princess asked him casually what the Chancellor had said. Before he felt able to reply, he drew up a draft of the conversation and sent it to Bismarck asking if he had quoted him correctly. Needless to say, he received no acknowledgement.

During the three years William and his brother spent at Cassel, Hintzpeter arranged a weekly dinner party to which he summoned distinguished men from different walks of life. His object, he explained, was to mix the " classes," and he dubbed his parties " conciliation dinners." These occasions were not gay ; the guests stood about stiffly, conscious that they were in the presence of their future ruler. And William, far from inhaling a spirit of equality, was so pleased by the awe his presence inspired that he became more arrogant than ever.

Hintzpeter wrote the Crown Princess regularly and often complained of William's laziness. Considering, however, that the boys had to do two hours of homework before breakfast, and lessons went on until eight at night, this weakness had little opportunity to develop. The final examinations came in January 1877, a few weeks before the Prince's eighteenth birthday. He passed tenth in a class of sixteen. Now the moment had arrived for his brother to enter the navy, and for him to do six months' military service before proceeding to Bonn University. He returned to Berlin for his birthday celebrations. He learned that his Prussian grandfather was planning to bestow upon him the Order of the Black Eagle. He also learned that his English grandmother was making arrangements to send him the Grand Companionship of the Bath. He told his mother flatly that this would not do. He made such a fuss that she finally wrote to Queen Victoria pointing out that the Emperors of Russia and Austria, and the King of Italy, had already sent the Prince the highest orders at their disposal. The Order of the Garter, she urged, was the only one that would suffice. " Willie," she added, " would be satisfied with the Bath, but the nation would not."[1] Queen Victoria gave way and sent her grandson the Garter.

" It is impossible to find two nicer boys than William and Henry," commented the Prince of Wales in 1878. The Crown Princess, however, was having trouble with William. He was studying Jurisprudence and Political Science at Bonn University, and when

[1] *Letters of the Empress Frederick.*

he came home for the holidays she was startled to find how dogmatic and aggressive he had become. He knew best about everything, and even began to quarrel with his parents over politics, sometimes making wounding and offensive remarks. The fact that he was deeply religious only seemed to make matters worse, for his religion was based on a conviction that God had personally selected him as heir to the German throne; and since he was deeply favoured, he also must be deeply endowed. Vicky wrote to her younger sister Alice, who was married to the Grand Duke of Hesse-Darmstadt, and lived only a few miles from Bonn, and asked her to keep an eye on him. Perhaps she could make him less intractable.

Prince William enjoyed the university but formed no close friendships, for, just as at Cassel, he was always mindful of his high position. He lived in a palace with a governor and a retinue of aides and entered into student life with a mixture of pleasure and condescension. Moral questions caused him no difficulties, as Hintzpeter's Calvinism, with its neat simple answers, had stamped his mind. He was a tremendous prig. He objected to gambling and tried to make his fellow students curtail their drinking habits. When he learned that his close friend, Prince Rudolf, son of the Austrian Emperor, was leading a promiscuous life, he turned his back on him. "I was forced to notice in the course of years that he did not take religion seriously. . . . Nor could I help becoming aware of other faults of character so much as to destroy my original confidence, and we drifted further and further apart."[1] Even Paris incurred his disapproval. He visited the city for the first time in the autumn of 1878; and although he was impressed by the museums and churches, and went up in a balloon from the Tuileries, delighting in an "indescribable view," he found the levity of the French uncongenial. "The feverish haste and restlessness of Parisian life repelled me," he wrote in his memoirs. "I never wanted to see the French capital again."[1]

Princess Alice welcomed William as one of her own family. She was a dumpy, homely little woman of thirty-five, almost the complete opposite of Vicky. Not particularly interested in politics, she was unambitious and placid, and inclined to regard royalty as a bit of a joke. Her family consisted of five daughters and one

[1] *My Early Life*: William II.

surviving son. She brought them up not by theory but according to the dictates of her heart. They were jolly uninhibited children and adored their mother. The two eldest, Elisabeth (known as Ella) and Victoria,[1] were only fourteen and fifteen years old when William came to Bonn, and did not find him sympathetic. " They disliked his restlessness and complained that his rapid changes of mood made him an impossible companion. At one moment he would want to go rowing, then it would be riding, or a game of tennis, always eager to show how proficient he was in spite of his crippled arm. He would rein in his horse, or throw down his racket in the middle of a game, and order them all to come and listen to him reading the Bible. Whether he was riding, playing games, or reading, he wanted his cousin Ella to be near him, always his brilliant eyes followed her movements, and when she spoke he was silent, listening to every inflection of her voice."[2]

When William was in his last term at Bonn a tragedy overtook his aunt's household. Her six-year-old daughter Alix, nicknamed Sunny, and one day to be known as the grim unsmiling Czarina of Russia, caught diphtheria. The child recovered but the disease raged through the family. Four-year-old Marie died, and finally, when all the others were mending, Princess Alice, worn out from nursing her children, came down with the illness herself, and succumbed. Vicky was shattered by the news and Queen Victoria found it " almost incredible and most mysterious " that beloved Alice had been called to Albert's side on the very anniversary of his death.

Had William fallen in love with his cousin Elisabeth? Meriel Buchanan, the daughter of the British minister to Darmstadt, claims that " there can be little doubt that he was greatly attracted to Princess Elisabeth of Hesse, but it is not certain whether she herself refused his proposal, or whether he ever actually asked for permission to marry her, but, judging from a letter the Crown Princess wrote to her mother, some years later, in which she said that it " had not been considered advisable for him to marry a cousin,' there must at some time have been a question of their engagement. . . . It is known that for several years, even after he had succeeded his father as German Emperor, and after Elisabeth of Hesse had

[1] Victoria married Prince Louis of Battenberg.

[2] *Queen Victoria's Relations*: Meriel Buchanan.

become the Grand Duchess Serge of Russia, he refused obstinately to meet her, never going to see her if she was passing through Berlin, and deliberately keeping at a distance if circumstances forced them to be together on some State occasion. Questioned as to this marked avoidance of his cousin, he sometimes refused to reply, or if he did, said harshly that he could never forget how much she had meant to him in the past and how much he had loved her."[1]

Not until William was an old man, living in exile in Holland, did he refer to his love for Elisabeth. He then admitted to an American journalist, George Viereck, that when he was a young man at Bonn University he had spent much of his time writing love poems to his beautiful cousin. This unrequited passion helps to explain his sudden engagement, only four months after leaving Bonn and beginning his military career at Potsdam, to "Dona," the Princess Augusta Victoria of Schleswig-Holstein. "Willy has written most touching letters (in his own funny style) about his great happiness," the Princess confided to her mother in February 1880. Yet William made no pretence of being in love with Dona; nor was Dona beautiful or clever or rich or even thought to be a particularly good match. All that could be said was that William had known her a long time and wished to settle down.

The Crown Princess welcomed the idea. Although Willy was only twenty-one she remembered that her father had approved of early marriage for princes, and particularly for future kings. Apart from this, she hoped that Dona might make her son less intractable. She was worried about William for he seemed to be growing farther away from his parents all the time. He not only showed a marked lack of sympathy for their liberal views but was often boastful and rude. At first she had put his rebelliousness down to youth but now she was beginning to be frightened by the cold, almost cruel streak that she noticed in him. At times he adopted such a patronizing air with his father and was so dogmatic with his mother that they were deeply offended. If only they could make Dona fond of them William might become more amenable. Although she was a dull girl—a rosy-cheeked *Hausfrau* without a trace of intellect—she was kind and gentle and surely would remind him of the respect he owed his parents.

The wedding did not take place until February 1881, a year after

[1] *Queen Victoria's Relations:* Meriel Buchanan.

the engagement. In January William came home to prepare for the event and Vicky, like her mother before her, made a great fuss over " last times." Never again would he sleep in the same house with them, never again in the same rooms! " He thinks me absurdly sentimental to observe this," she wrote to the Queen, " and says it is all the same to him in what place, or house, or room he lives."

3. *The Ninety-nine Days*

"I wonder why he [Prince Bismarck] does not say straight out, 'As long as I live both the constitution and the Crown are suspended;' because that is the exact state of the matter," wrote the Crown Princess to Queen Victoria in the autumn of 1881. "He thinks a great central power is necessary and that one will must decide and that the state be everything and do everything like one vast set of machinery. . . ."[1]

Germany was a dictatorship although not nearly so efficient as the dictatorships of the present century. It had some of the paraphernalia of the modern totalitarian state but it also had many loopholes. Bismarck controlled a large section of the press and set it snapping and snarling at whomever he liked, yet some papers served other masters and thus provided an opposition; there were severe anti-socialist laws which enabled the State to confiscate property and even imprison without warrant, yet the Social Democrat party, which promulgated socialism, was legal and increased its vote at each election. There was a rather inefficient secret police system, which sent voluminous intelligence reports to the Chancellor who did not bother to read them.

English people, however, found such practices distasteful, and when Lady Ponsonby, the wife of Queen Victoria's secretary, visited Berlin in 1882 she was shocked to learn that Bismarck even had spies in the Crown Princess's household. "I don't think the Queen realises what an extraordinary state of things exists in Germany in the way of espionage and intrigue," she wrote her husband.

Scarcely a day passed without the Crown Princess inveighing against the corrupting influence of Bismarck and the harm he was doing to the national character. She longed for the power to intervene, but found it difficult to exert the smallest influence as

[1] *Letters of the Empress Frederick.*

people avoided seeing her for fear of incurring the Chancellor's displeasure. At times the frustration of her position seemed almost unbearable. When she had come to Germany as a bride, the throne had seemed close. In 1861 the King had celebrated his sixty-fourth birthday and the Queen had remarked resignedly: "We are old people; all we can do is work for the future." That was over twenty years ago, and the Crown Princess was still waiting for the cue that never came.

Her lot was made even harder by the fact that Bismarck's campaign against her had never abated, and she was always depicted as an English princess working for English aims. Frederick did his best to smooth his wife's path, but his solicitude, so alien to the Prussian character, was twisted into pusillanimity and people declared that he grew "weaker every year." Even his private secretary, Colonel Sommerfeld, turned against him. "You only have to look what she's made of him," he expostulated. "But for her he'd be the average man, very arrogant, good-tempered, of mediocre gifts and with a good deal of common sense. But *now* he's not a man at all, he has no ideas of his own, unless she allows him. He's a mere cipher. 'Ask my wife' or 'Have you discussed the matter with the Crown Princess?' and there's no more to be said."[1]

With this atmosphere, it is not surprising that the Princess often loathed her husband's country. At times she felt that she could not bear the ugly streets of Berlin a day longer, the lack of elegance, the clicking army boots, the censoriousness, the sycophantic acceptance of despotism. Occasionally she poured out her heart to English friends. In the winter of 1879 Sir Howard Elphinstone, the Comptroller of Prince Arthur's household, visited Berlin and called upon the Princess. "She spoke in a most disparaging tone of the German people," he wrote to his wife. "There is no one of whom she could make a friend and she feared she was generally unpopular in consequence of the free-thinking tone she took up. There is no doubt the society here is made up of very small 'sets.' Each set is quite exclusive and will not even look at the other. The aristocracy as such is not to my liking, being very vain, small minded and decidedly dull. Of politics they are afraid to talk, of art and literature they know little. Consequently bitter tittle-tattle is their element, in which they excel."

[1] *The Holstein Papers*: edited by N. Rich and M. H. Fisher.

Sir Howard found the atmosphere almost as depressing as the Princess did, and each letter grew more depressed. " My stay here is a wretched one. I hate the place. . . . There is not a chance of my staying willingly a day longer than I can help." A party at the old Emperor's dampened his spirits even further. " We first sat down at little round tables, and cups of tea were handed to us, and when these were cleared away Professor Homan gave us a chemical lecture. It was rather good, but too long I thought unfortunately. We then again sat down to the small tables and continued our supper, consisting of pâté de foie gras on bread, oranges and ices. I need not tell you that I did not partake of this mixture. . . ." Even the window displays distressed him. " Not a shop that contains a thing of state or that one could care about. The ornaments are simply hideous or vulgar. I have not seen a single thing that I should like to bring back as a present to you. . . ."[1]

Despite her dislike of Germany, Vicky wrote her mother repeatedly how blessed she was in her marriage. Unfortunately her relations with William continued to deteriorate and even her second son, Henry, was becoming difficult under the influence of his brother. Once she lamented to her mother : " The dream of my life was to have a son who should be something of what our beloved Papa was, a real grandson of his, in soul and intellect, a grandson of yours. . . . One must learn to abandon dreams and take things as they come and characters as they are—one cannot quarrel with nature, and I suppose it knows best, though to us it seems cruel, perverse and contrary in the extreme. . . ."[2]

Cruel and perverse ; the Crown Princess could never rid herself of the feeling that Providence was using her unfairly. She had expected to instruct and guide her son as her father had guided her, but now he praised Bismarck's policies openly and seemed to care nothing for the mortification he caused her ; while Dona, far from trying to heal the breach, played the role of an adoring slave approving whatever he did.

The truth was that William did not like his mother. He had never found her sympathetic and as he grew older he became increasingly critical. In many ways they were too much alike to be drawn to

[1] *The Queen Thanks Sir Howard :* Mary McClintock.

[2] *Letters of the Empress Frederick.*

one another. Both were dogmatic, impulsive, and self-willed, but whereas the Princess had deep loyalties and a heart capable of pity, William was hard and unyielding. He resented his mother's efforts to dominate him and suspected that her sentiment was only a trap to ensnare him. What he disliked most, however, was the same failing that she so often criticised in him: the fact that she always knew best about everything. When he differed with her, she told him that he was "green" and lectured him as severely as a child. One of the reasons he had been glad to marry was to escape from her vigilant concern.

What relief his freedom gave him! He loved the life of a Prussian officer, and now that he had his own household he was happy for the first time. Everything about the army delighted him; the conviviality of the mess, the study of tactics and strategy, the complicated exercises, the *esprit de corps*. He had begun as a lieutenant in the foot-guards and was promoted rapidly through the grades to the rank of colonel; then, a year after his marriage, transferred to the cavalry. The riding instructor was doubtful whether, with his crippled arm, he could reach the high and exacting standard of horsemanship required, but the Prince showed remarkable prowess. His grandfather the Emperor and his uncle "The Red Prince," one of the finest horseman in Europe, came to watch the manœuvres. William led his cavalry unit through a series of dashing and complicated exercises without a mistake. "Well done!" cried the Red Prince. "I never thought you could do it!" The Old Emperor's eyes filled with tears of pride, for this was a triumph worthy of any Hohenzollern prince. "Never," wrote Hintzpeter, "was a young man enrolled in the Prussian army who seemed so physically unfitted to become a keen and brilliant cavalry-officer. The few who could estimate the significance of this victory of moral force over bodily infirmity felt justified in their proudest hopes for this royal personage."[1]

Success strengthened William's attachment for the army, but apart from this he found the atmosphere of the Junker mess, with its feudal outlook and talk of war, far more congenial than his parents' home. For the first time he had companions who shared his own feelings and who believed passionately in Germany. For years he had been forced to listen to his mother's insistence that everything

[1] *Kaiser Wilhelm II*: George Hintzpeter.

in England was better, and to hear her bitter remarks about German provincialism, German intolerance, German absolutism. Now, at last, he had friends who, far from being ashamed of German autocracy, revelled in it; friends who revered Bismarck instead of calling him " a wicked man."

Prince William was particularly taken with the sophisticated Quartermaster General, Count von Waldersee, who talked a great deal about war and hoped to become Chief of the Imperial General Staff. Waldersee was in close touch with the Chancellor's son, the clever, ill-mannered Count Herbert Bismarck, who was too busy carrying out his father's orders in the Foreign Office to think of marriage, and who reaped his reward in 1886 when he became State Secretary; and before long William found himself a member of the Chancellor's family circle. The old man often invited the Prince to take meals with him—usually breakfast—and after these enormous repasts would recline on a sofa and allow William to light his pipe for him. He enchanted the Prince with his pungent, provocative observations and captivated him with his subtle flatteries. Once he remarked to a friend that William had such talents that one day he probably would be his own chancellor—and made sure that the friend repeated it back to William. All this increased the young Prince's hero-worship and heightened his contempt for liberalism—even for the feeble powers of the Reichstag. " If his parents have trained him to be a constitutional monarch ready to bow to the rule of a parliamentary majority," observed Waldersee in 1883, " they have failed. The very opposite would seem to be the result."[1]

Now every time William went to his family home there was a row. His mother was horrified to learn that he was consorting with the Bismarcks and told him that he was betraying and insulting his father by making friends with a man who had done so much to harm him. At each meeting tempers flew and ugly exchanges took place, with the result that William avoided his parents as much as possible. Bismarck was delighted when he heard of the rift, and did all that he could to further it. Until now William had only thought of his mother as a censorious and stubborn English die-hard, an inevitable product of her upbringing, but gradually the Bismarcks and Count von Waldersee planted a different picture in

[1] *A Field Marshal's Memoirs:* Count von Waldersee.

his mind. They made him see his parents as the Iron Chancellor had depicted them over the years: the weak father dominated by the clever, strong-willed Princess who was working deliberately to further British aims to the detriment of Germany. William's imagination flared up and his mother began to appear in the guise of a traitor. "To his grief," wrote Waldersee, "he is able to see quite clearly that his mother has not become a Prussian Princess but has remained an Englishwoman—not merely as regards habits of life but in her heart, especially in relation to political matters. He knows that she is consciously in favour of English interests as against Prussian and German. With his own out and out Prussian feeling this hurts him deeply, and he often finds it difficult to curb his fiery temperament."[1]

Waldersee played on the "fiery temperament" and excited the Prince still further by his talk of war. Germany would have to conquer France and Russia in turn, he said; but even more important—if she wished to be a great world power—she would have to break the might of England. William was so taken with this thought that when the Prince of Wales arrived in Berlin in 1883 for his sister's Silver Wedding celebrations he greeted him coolly. He thanked him politely for his gift of a Highland costume; then he had his picture taken in it and sent copies to his friends with the words written underneath "I bide my time." The British military attaché, Colonel Swaine, found the incident so curious that he reported it to London.

Prince Bismarck did not want war and was irritated by Count von Waldersee's wild talk. Germany was industrialising rapidly and developing markets all over the globe. Her population was increasing, her standard of living rising, and soon she might outstrip Britain as the world's leading manufacturer. What Germany needed was a period of peace and security; Bismarck's problem was how to achieve it. Two of her neighbours, Russia and Austria, were always at loggerheads over the Balkans, and if they went to war with each other Germany would find herself in an impossible dilemma; if she remained neutral Russia might stretch out to France for an alliance, and Germany would be in a trap; on the other hand if Germany took sides she would make an enemy of the

[1] *A Field Marshal's Memoirs:* Count von Waldersee.

defeated nation and a rival of the victor. The only solution was not to allow these contingencies to arise.

Bismarck's policy, therefore, was to remain on friendly terms with Russia and Austria and, above all, to keep them on friendly terms with each other. In 1873 he managed to establish the League of the Three Emperors by which Russia, Austria, and Germany promised to consult each other in case of divergencies and to help each other if attacked. But these bonds were tenuous for Austria and Russia believed that the Ottoman Empire was on the verge of a break-up, and each was determined to get the largest share of the spoils. Bismarck nevertheless succeeded in persuading the two countries to come to a private arrangement before Russia attacked Turkey in 1877. However, when the war ended with Russian troops on the outskirts of Constantinople, and the Czar announced that Turkey had agreed to cede her Bulgarian provinces to him, and that he, in turn, proposed to expand the present Bulgaria into a large vassal state with ports along the Aegean, Europe rose in alarm. Austria was outraged and Britain said she could not permit it, as it would constitute a danger to the Suez Canal. The Russians finally were forced to submit the problem to a Congress, held in Berlin, with Bismarck acting as " the honest broker."

Austria won the right to occupy and administer the Turkish provinces of Bosnia and Herzegovina, and Russia emerged with large territories between the Black and the Caspian Seas, and the recovery of Bessarabia which she had lost in 1856. But not Turkish Bulgaria. St. Petersburg was enraged and accused Bismarck of ingratitude in view of Russia's neutrality at the time of the Franco-Prussian war. She increased her armaments and moved troops near the German frontier; and the Czar wrote to Bismarck warning him of " the disastrous consequences which might follow." Consequently, in October 1879, Bismarck signed a secret alliance with Austria, by which both countries promised to defend each other in the event of a Russian attack. The object of this treaty was not only defensive but to prevent Russian expansion in the Balkans, and it remained the corner-stone of German foreign policy until the first world war.

Bismarck, however, had no intention of allowing Austria to expand in the Balkans any more than Russia, and worked hard to revive the League of the Three Emperors. He succeeded in 1881, and the clauses of the new treaty, which provided for a demarcation line in the Balkans, with Serbia in the Austrian sphere of influence and Bulgaria in the Russian, were so secret that he wrote them out in his own hand and kept them under lock and key. But the harmony soon began to disintegrate. Russia accused Austria of setting the Serbs against the Bulgarians, and although the treaty did not expire until 1887 the Czar became acutely hostile to Vienna. Bismarck concentrated all his attention on trying to patch up the crumbling bridge.

This was the situation in May 1884 when Prince Bismarck decided to send William to Russia to celebrate the coming-of-age festivities of the Czarevitch, the future Nicholas II. It amused him to mortify the Crown Prince by persuading the Kaiser to overlook the son he did not find congenial for the grandson he admired. Furthermore William seemed ideally suited by temperament to placate the despotic Alexander. In January 1884 Baron Holstein, a clever and sinister Foreign Office official, generally regarded as Bismarck's "tool," succinctly summed up the Prince's character. "He is self-willed, devoid of all tenderness, an ardent soldier, anti-democratic, anti-English. He shares the Kaiser's view on everything and has the greatest admiration for the Chancellor."[1]

Prince William, of course, knew nothing of the secret clauses of the Emperors League but he was told that he must do everything to promote better relations between Germany, Austria, and Russia. His mission was a brilliant success. He arrived in St. Petersburg in February 1884 accompanied by Count von Waldersee, attended ceremonies and balls, watched military displays, invested the Czarevitch with the Order of the Black Eagle, and went bear hunting with Prince Radzivill. Most important of all, he charmed the Czar. Since Alexander's father had been blown to pieces by an assassin's bomb three years earlier, he had ruled with iron severity. It was not difficult for William, with his own imperious notions, to play convincingly on these sentiments. He argued that despite the dissensions between Austria and Russia the three emperors must work in the closest harmony to hold back the flood-tide of liberal democracy. The next day M. Giers, the Russian Foreign Secretary, called on Count Herbert Bismarck, who had travelled to St.

[1] *The Holstein Papers:* edited by N. Rich and M. H. Fisher.

Petersburg for the occasion, and said ecstatically: "I wish good luck to whoever it was who had the idea of sending Prince William. . . . The Emperor is entirely taken up with him. . . . He said to me yesterday: 'Prince William expressed himself very well. We need a bond of friendship and a triple *entente* to combat the waves of anarchy.' That is the first time the Emperor has said 'triple.' He has always and habitually said 'dual,' and even accentuated the dual alliance. This is a great triumph for Prince William. In two days he has reached a point to which all our diplomacy has failed to bring the Emperor in six months." M. Giers was not over-optimistic for in September the Czar agreed to meet the Austrian Emperor and the German Kaiser at Skerniewski in Poland to discuss their problems. At the bottom of a letter to his father Count Herbert wrote: "Prince William is really excellent."[1]

The Prince arrived home flushed with triumph, to find that the Prince of Wales was again in Berlin visiting his mother. Why had he come? No doubt to try and sabotage William's good work. Britain was having trouble with Russia on the Afghanistan frontier and would like Germany's support; German friendship with Russia was the last thing she wanted. Uncle Bertie probably would persuade the Crown Princess to try and undermine the cordial relations between Berlin and St. Petersburg by instigating an anti-Russian campaign in Berlin. William would show them. Impulsively he sat down and dashed off a letter to Alexander telling him that the Prince of Wales had arrived in Germany to organise a conspiracy against Russia. "The visit of the Prince of Wales has yielded and is still bringing extraordinary fruit, which will continue to multiply under the hands of my mother and the Queen of England. But these English have accidentally forgotten that I exist! I swear to You, my dear cousin, that anything I can do for You or Your country I will do, and I swear that I will keep my word! But only it will take a long time and have to be done slowly."

William's letter was a mistake, for the one constant factor in Alexander's character was deep family loyalty, and he was rather shocked by the young Prince's allusions to his mother. Furthermore, his wife, the former Princess Marie of Denmark, was a sister of the Princess of Wales and the two families often met at Copenhagen. He doubted whether the pleasure-loving Bertie would trouble

[1] *My Early Life*: William II.

himself with a conspiracy. He regarded the Prince's letter as both naive and unfilial, and gradually began to revise his opinion of him.

The Czar was not the only person who noted William's disrespect for his parents. In 1885, a year after his Moscow trip, the Prince became embroiled in a fresh family row and talked so freely against his mother that even Count von Waldersee was critical. His sister, the Princess Victoria, became engaged to Prince Alexander of Battenberg, whom the Russians had created puppet ruler of Bulgaria. But Alexander had aroused the enmity of the Czar by refusing to do what he was told; and Bismarck, unwilling to jeopardise friendly Russo-German relations, had advised the old Kaiser to forbid the marriage. The Crown Princess, of course, did not know of the secret alliance behind the three emperors, which recognised Bulgaria as a Russian preserve, and regarded this act as pure spite. William sided with Bismarck and scenes took place which left him enraged with his mother. Waldersee told Holstein that the Prince was declaring wildly that when his father came to the throne it might be necessary to arrest his mother. " By what means this weak man [the Crown Prince] now completely under his wife's thumb is to be brought to such a monstrous decision is not clear,' mused Holstein in his diary.[1] And Waldersee wrote uneasily: " the Prince has been very inconsiderate and above all very indiscreet regarding his mother . . . were the Crown Prince now suddenly to become Kaiser there would be nothing for it but to station him in some remote garrison."[2]

Bismarck was not troubled; the family quarrels amused him and he continued to employ William as an envoy, if only for the fun of keeping the Crown Prince permanently annoyed. In June 1886 he sent him to Gastein to a meeting of the three emperors. " We are rather horrified at hearing that William was at the interview of the Emperors at Gastein," Vicky wrote wearily to Queen Victoria, " and that he is going to Skerniewski to see the Emperor of Russia! It is perhaps not true, but as such things are always arranged between the Emperor and William without consulting or informing us, it may be, and I need hardly say that it would make endless mischief and do endless harm. William is as blind and green, wrong-headed

[1] *The Holstein Papers:* edited by N. Rich and M. H. Fisher.

[2] *A Field Marshal's Memoirs:* Count von Waldersee.

and violent on politics as can be. . . . It is really rather hard upon us, and our position a very painful one. I still hope it may not be." Frederick found it difficult to forgive his father for these slights and Baron von Holstein commented acidly: "The relations between the three generations of our royal family are remarkable, not to say comic. The Kaiser ignores the Crown Prince completely and so far as possible never informs him of anything. The Crown Prince, in turn, ignores Prince Wilhelm in the same way. At this year's Rhine manœuvres the father . . . treated the son as though he didn't exist."[1]

Where would it all end? In 1886 the old Emperor, who was in his ninetieth year, fell ill and a wave of panic swept through the Bismarck entourage. He had lived so long no one had faced up to the day of reckoning. What would happen to them when the Crown Prince came to the throne? Count Herbert Bismarck threw his hands in the air and declared it would be "all up with Germany anyway." Count von Waldersee wrote to Baron von Holstein, at the Foreign Office, and suggested a *coup d'état* against the Prince; and Holstein himself was said to recommend poisoning the Crown Prince![2] Only the Iron Chancellor kept his nerve. He had baited the Crown Princess too long to hope for any real reconciliation so he would continue as before. In the autumn of 1886 he announced that Prince William would be given access to the Foreign Office, a privilege always denied to Frederick. The Crown Prince begged Bismarck to reconsider his plan, insisting bluntly in a letter that his son's lack of judgement "together with his leaning toward vanity and presumption and his overweening estimate of himself" made him totally unfit for the job.[3] But the Chancellor refused to change his mind.

The quarrel between Prince William and his parents reached its climax in a bitter tragedy. The drama began in January 1887 when the Crown Prince complained of hoarseness. At first his physician, Dr. Wagner, thought it was merely the aftermath of an attack of measles, but when March came and the hoarseness persisted he summoned a consultant, Dr. Gerhardt, a Professor of Medicine at

[1] *The Holstein Papers:* edited by N. Rich and M. H. Fisher.
[2] *Philip Eulenburg, the Kaiser's Friend:* Johannes Haller.
[3] *Reflections and Memories:* Otto von Bismarck.

Berlin University. Gerhardt diagnosed a small growth on the left vocal chord, which he treated locally, burning it off with a hot wire. He then suggested that the Crown Prince should take a rest cure at Elms. The Princess wrote to her mother cheerfully: "Fritz now eats and sleeps and looks well. Of course he takes no long walks and does not go uphill so as to fatigue or heat himself, and is asked to talk as little as possible. . . ."

When the Crown Prince returned to Berlin in May, however, Gerhardt could find no sign of improvement; the growth had reappeared, the hoarseness remained and the wound caused by the treatment had not healed. He called Professor Ernst von Bergmann, an eminent surgeon, for consultation. This doctor gave an alarming verdict. He could not say whether or not the growth was malignant, but he believed that it should be removed by a surgical operation. "It cannot be got at from inside the throat," the Crown Princess wrote to Queen Victoria, "as it may also exist under the larynx in a fold, where it cannot be reached. The celebrated surgeon, Professor Bergmann, is for operating from the outside, and you can imagine that this is not an easy operation or a small one. I own I was more dead than alive with horror when I heard this. The idea of a knife touching his dear throat is terrible to me. Of course Fritz is not to know a word about this. He is at times so very depressed . . . that he now often thinks his father will survive him, and I have fine work to make these passing sad thoughts clear away, which I am happy to say they do after a short while. . . . My fear and dread is that a swelling of that kind, if not removed by some means or other, might in time develop into a growth of a malignant and dangerous character. I hope and trust and believe that there is no such danger present. . . ."[1]

Now we come to the crux of the matter. The operation proposed by Gerhardt and Bergmann was known as "thyrotomy" and involved splitting the larynx. How serious was it? Months later the German doctors, loudly supported by Prince William, declared that it was not serious at all; that it could be performed successfully seven times out of ten, that it would not have rendered the Crown Prince speechless, but merely left him hoarse. This, however, was not the impression that the doctors gave at the time—either to the Crown Princess or to Prince Bismarck. On May 19th the Princess

[1] *Letters of the Empress Frederick.*

wrote to Queen Victoria: "I spent a terrible day yesterday; it is so difficult to appear unconcerned when one's heart is torn. . . . I am so distressed to think that his dear voice, which is so necessary to him in his position in the country and army etc., will be gone, and I know what an awful trial it will be to him. . . ."[1]

Prince Bismarck took such a grave view of the operation that he intervened. "The doctors," he wrote, "determined to make the Crown Prince unconscious and to carry out the removal of the larynx without having informed him of their intention. I raised objections, and required that they should not proceed without the consent of the Crown Prince. . . . The Emperor, after being informed by me, forbade them to carry out the operation without the consent of his son."[2] Bismarck arranged for further consultation and three more doctors were called in. They gave the opinion that cancer was present. Before recommending the operation, however, they decided to send for the eminent English laryngologist, Dr. Morell Mackenzie, whose text books had been translated into German and whose work was familiar to all of them.

Mackenzie arrived on the evening of May 20th. He examined the Prince's throat and said that the operation should not take place unless the growth was proved scientifically to be malignant. He asked that a fragment of the larynx should be examined by the celebrated anthropologist and pathologist, Rudolph Virchow. This was done and Virchow reported that he could find no evidence of cancer. Gerhardt and Bergmann protested hotly, declaring that the reason they had not sought the advice of a pathologist was because this science was in so elementary a state that it was not possible to exact proof one way or the other. They remained obdurate that their original diagnosis was correct. "I regard the matter with increasing anxiety," Gerhardt told the Crown Princess. "Where M. Mackenzie removed a small portion it has grown again—the tumour is suppurating etc., on the other side of the throat, the other vocal chord, which hitherto has remained healthy, is attacked—there is already a considerable amount of damage done. If Dr. M. Mackenzie cannot assist and cure it there is no chance of recovery save in the operation known as 'laryngotomy.' It would have to be performed under far less favourable conditions than would have been

[1] *Letters of the Empress Frederick.*

[2] *Reflections and Memories:* Otto von Bismarck.

the case fourteen days ago. Therefore my only hope is that Dr. Mackenzie may be right in his opinion, and that his treatment may be successful, for we have nothing else to offer."[1]

Mackenzie on the other hand was equally emphatic that it was not cancer. He declared brightly that it was simply a fibromatosis swelling; and if the Crown Prince would attend his clinic in London like "any ordinary mortal" he would cure him in two months. In view of Mackenzie's reputation and his confidence, it is not surprising that the Crown Princess decided to follow his advice rather than Gerhardt's. Would any wife have done differently? What hope and relief, she wrote her mother, the blessed Mackenzie had given her. However, she could not completely quell her forebodings, for she wrote the Queen that she would accompany Fritz to England the middle of June for his treatments; and would her mother mind if they brought their private papers, and stored them at Windsor for safe-keeping?

The royal couple arrived in England a week before Queen Victoria's Jubilee, commemorating her fifty years' reign. When the day came, Prince Frederick felt well enough to take part in the procession. All eyes were upon him as he rode through the streets on a magnificent horse, dressed in white from head to toe, his silver breastplate and eagle-crested helmet gleaming in the sun, like a figure from *Lohengrin*. After the celebrations the couple spent two months in England then departed for Toblach in the Alps; and after that to Venice.

Soon letters were arriving from Berlin, pressing the Crown Prince to return. The old Emperor had fallen ill again, was failing rapidly and could not survive much longer. Prince William, alone and unchecked, was behaving as though he already wore the crown. It was not wise, friends said, for Prince Frederick to remain away from the capital. The Princess refused to listen. The only thing that mattered was beloved Fritz's health, and she would not risk the damp Berlin atmosphere until he had thoroughly recovered. Every day she wrote to her mother, confiding her problems but trying to conceal the gnawing anxiety that never left her.

She might have expected loyalty from her household at such a period, but the Crown Prince's Court Chamberlain, Count Lynkar, seized the opportunity to ingratiate himself with the Bismarck

[1] *Letters of the Empress Frederick.*

clique, by writing singularly unpleasant letters to the Foreign Office. " Oh, this Crown Princess. I am glad for the Crown Prince's sake that he will be alone for a few days. But it is a real rest-cure for me too. I cannot tell you how that woman gets on my nerves. Now, when it is so bitterly cold that all our teeth are chattering with the frost and the Princesses are going around with blue noses and their hands in mittens, she declared the weather is unbearably hot and has the windows opened; then, mark you, she puts on a great thick shawl. . . . During our walks she runs ahead like a mad thing until the Crown Prince comes to a standstill, exhausted, and says: 'I can't go any further. My wife is racing ahead again.' I stay with him then, but the Princess just walks on, saying with a soft upward glance: 'You will walk really slowly, won't you, dear Fritz, so that you don't get too hot?' and so on. I cannot bear to see that everlasting smile on her face—the woman has driven every good genius out of her house with that smile."

No man had a more devoted wife than the Crown Prince, yet Baron von Holstein, reputed to possess the shrewdest brain in Berlin and destined to direct his country's foreign policy during the fateful years from 1890 to 1906, apparently believed all the foolish, malicious gossip he heard, for here are some excerpts from his diary. "Sept. 24, 1887. The Crown Princess's behaviour is typical. Gay and carefree with but one idea—never to return to Prussia. I persist in my view, which is now shared by others, namely that from the very beginning she accepted the idea that the worst would happen. Judging by all I have heard of her in recent months, I am tempted to call her a degenerate or corrupt character. . . . She has always despised her husband. She will greet his death as the moment of deliverance."

" Nov. 9, 1887. The Crown Princess's behaviour has been incredible. In Toblach Mackenzie said the Crown Prince was dangerously ill and must go at once to Cairo or Madeira. When the Crown Princess heard this she exclaimed: 'That will never do. Where am I to stay? It would be all right if I could spend the winter in Rome, but not otherwise.' Despite the doctors' request she refused in Toblach to alter the time for lunch. As a result, just when the midday sun was at its height, the Crown Prince was sitting at table instead of being out of doors. . . . In Munich she received a telegram from the hotel proprietor in Toblach advising them not to come because the climate was too harsh for the Crown Prince. She took no notice; she had there, as the Crown Prince himself put it, good subjects to paint, she wanted to go for walks and grow slimmer."[1]

Early in November, while Holstein was recording these silly untruths, the couple moved from Venice to San Remo, on the Mediterranean, where the Crown Princess had rented a villa for the winter. They had been there less than twenty-four hours before the Crown Prince's condition drastically changed for the worse. Mackenzie was summoned from England, and two more specialists called from Vienna and Berlin. After the patient's throat had been examined the Crown Prince asked Mackenzie bluntly if he now thought it was cancer. "I am sorry to say, sir, it looks very much like it, but it is impossible to be certain." When the doctor left the room and the stricken man was alone with his wife, he broke down for the first time. His anguish was not for himself but for her. "To think that I should have such a horrid, disgusting illness! that I shall be an object of disgust to everyone, and a burden to you all! I had so hoped to be of use to my country. Why is Heaven so cruel to me? What have I done to be stricken and condemned? What will become of you? I have nothing to leave you!" The Crown Princess tried to comfort her husband, but to her mother she wrote: "My darling has got a fate before him which I hardly dare to think of! How I shall ever have the strength to bear it I do not know!!"[2]

Two days later Prince William suddenly arrived, unbidden and unannounced, at San Remo. The moment he learned that doctors had been summoned hurriedly, he surmised that Mackenzie's diagnosis was proving incorrect and that his father had cancer. From the beginning he had been indignant that his mother had chosen to follow the advice of an English specialist rather than heed the German consultants, but now dark suspicions, suggested to him by the Bismarck circle, began to gain control of his mind. Prince Bismarck believed that Mackenzie had known all along that the Crown Prince had cancer, but that the Crown Princess had implored him not to divulge it for fear that Frederick would give up the throne if he knew the truth. The implications of this theory

[1] *The Holstein Papers:* edited by N. Rich and M. H. Fisher.
[2] *Letters of the Empress Frederick.*

were obvious and William accepted them fully; his mother had kept his father in ignorance of his fatal disease in order to acquire the title of Empress and to taste the delights of power if only for a moment: for this reason she had refused to allow the operation to be performed which, although it would have left him speechless and undoubtedly forced him to abdicate, might have prolonged his life for several years.[1]

In a passion of self-righteousness William went to his dying grandfather and told him that he had reason to doubt the integrity of the English physician looking after his father. He asked the old Emperor to authorise him to visit San Remo with a German doctor and to bring back a true report of the Crown Prince's condition. Even the unscrupulous Count von Waldersee was shocked by this news. " Prince William came to me to-day at 11 a.m.; he told me that the news of the Crown Prince was really bad and that by the Kaiser's command he was off to San Remo to-day in order to find out the truth of his father's condition. . . . It does not seem to me right that Prince William should go to San Remo. He can't help and should he try to get rid of the English physician against his mother's will he must fail in the effort; he will only give occasion for excited scenes and cause more distress to his father, already the object of much pity. . . ."[2]

Nevertheless William went. " When I entered the Villa Zirio, situated on the Mediterranean, amid a grove of olives," he wrote in his memoirs, " my arrival gave little pleasure to my mother. She was doubtless afraid that the house of cards on which she had set her life's hope would now come tumbling down. Standing at the foot of the stairs, I had to allow the flood of her reproaches to pass over me, and to hear her decided refusal to allow me to see my father. . . . My father's condition, in my mother's opinion, gave no cause whatever for alarm, but the stony expression on her face, utterly different from what it had been at Baveno—proof enough of the hard struggle between her iron will and her growing anxiety—gave the lie to what her lips uttered, and fell like a crushing weight upon my heart. Then I heard a rustling at the top of the stairs, looked up, and saw my father smiling a welcome to me. I rushed

[1] Prince Bismarck expressed this opinion in an anonymous article in the *Norddeutsche Allgemeine Zeitung*. See Emil Ludwig's *Kaiser Wilhelm II.*

[2] *A Field Marshal's Memoirs:* Count von Waldersee.

up the stairs, and with infinite emotion we held each other embraced, while in low whispers he expressed his joy at my visit. During the heavy days that followed we came in spirit very close to one another."

The Crown Princess described the same scene, but gave a somewhat different picture. "You ask," she wrote Queen Victoria, "how Willy was when he was here! He was as rude, as disagreeable and as impertinent to me as possible when he arrived, but I pitched into him with, I am afraid, considerable violence, and he became quite nice and amiable and gentle (for him)—at least quite natural, and we got on very well! He began with saying that he would not go out walking with me 'because he was too busy—he had to speak to the doctors.' I said the doctors had to report to me and not to him, upon which he said he had the Emperor's orders 'to insist upon the right thing, to see that the doctors were not interfered with, and to report to the Emperor about his Papa!' I said it was not necessary, as we always reported to the Emperor ourselves. He spoke before others and half turning his back to me, so I said I would go and tell his father how he behaved and ask that he should be forbidden the house—and walked away. Upon which he sent Count Radolinsky flying after me to say he had not meant to be rude and begged me to say nothing to Fritz 'but that it was his duty to see that the Emperor's commands were carried out.' I instantly said that I had no malice, but I would suffer no interference. So it all went on quite smoothly and we had many a pleasant little walk and chat together."[1]

On November 12th a bulletin was issued in Berlin announcing that the Crown Prince was suffering from cancer. The old Emperor was sinking, and all Europe now began to watch the macabre race with death between father and son. Neither Prince Bismarck nor Prince William, however, were content to play the role of spectator. They seized the moment to inspire a press campaign against Mackenzie and the Crown Princess. Her Anglo-mania, declared the newspapers, had prompted her to call in a second-rate English doctor rather than follow the advice of the German physicians. The operation recommended in May was of a minor character and probably would have effected a complete cure; now

[1] *Letters of the Empress Frederick.*

it was too late. Even William's brother, Henry, echoed these accusations. "Henry maintains that his Papa is lost through the English doctors and me . . ." the Princess wrote her mother. She spared herself nothing for every morning she insisted on seeing the press cuttings and many of them insinuated that she was responsible for the tragedy by preventing the operation in May, forcing Sir M. Mackenzie on her husband and keeping everyone else away. "They say I try to hide the gravity of the situation from him," she wrote to her mother, "that he ought to feel more what danger he is in. . . . Even good and well-meaning people have not *le tact du cœur* and would not try to save a person one moment's agony or distress of mind. You know how sensitive and apprehensive, how suspicious and despondent Fritz is by nature! All the more wrong and positively dangerous (let alone the cruelty of it) to wish him to think the worst! We should not keep him going at all, if this were the case. . . ."[1]

At this point the British Ambassador in Berlin, Sir Edward Malet, was forced to intervene, for even Queen Victoria was being dragged into the controversey. "Dear Count Bismarck," he wrote on November 14th, "Will you kindly glance your eye at the passage which I have marked in this evening's *Nordeutsche Allgemeine Zeitung*? You will see that to the Queen of England *also* is to be attributed that the Crown Prince was committed to the care of an English specialist. The context indicates that the word 'also' means that the other person was the Crown Princess. Now as a matter of fact, of which I am sure you are aware, the Crown Princess had nothing to do with calling in Sir Morell Mackenzie, still less the Queen. The report that the Crown Princess sent for him originally is doing her great injury, and is devoid of truth.

"Would it be possible, with reference to this paragraph, which gains credence through appearing in the semi-official paper, to state authoritatively in the same paper, or in the *Reichs Anzeiger*, that Mackenzie was called in by decision of the physicians attending the Crown Prince, and that the Crown Princess was not even consulted and that certainly the Queen of England had nothing to do with it?" Sir Edward ended his letter: "I am sure your chivalry will make you feel as I do about these statements."[2] But he was wrong,

[1] *Letters of the Empress Frederick.*
[2] *British Documents on the Origins of the War.*

there was no chivalry. Count Bismarck promised to take up the matter with his father, and the attacks continued.

Meanwhile the Crown Prince rapidly grew worse. He had spasms of suffocation and in February 1888 it was necessary to perform an operation which deprived him of his voice but enabled him to breathe through a tube inserted in his throat. A month later the old monarch died with his grandson at his bedside, and the news was telegraphed to Italy. The voiceless Frederick was German Emperor. The scene at San Remo was pitiful. The moment the news was received the household gathered in the drawing-room. The new Emperor wrote out the announcement of his succession as Frederick III. Next he invested his beloved consort with the highest order in his power to give—the ribbon of the Black Eagle. Then he greeted Sir Morell Mackenzie and wrote on a piece of paper: "I thank you for having made me live long enough to reward the valiant courage of my wife." Finally he sent a telegram to Queen Victoria. "At this moment of deep emotion and sorrow at the news of my father's death, my feelings of devoted affection to you prompt me, on succeeding to the throne, to repeat to you my sincere and earnest desire for a close and lasting friendship between our two nations. Frederick."[1] That night the new Empress wrote to her mother: "To think of my poor Fritz succeeding his father as a sick and stricken man is so hard! How much good he might have done! I pray that it may be and that he may be spared to be a blessing to his people and to Europe."[2]

The Emperor was not fit to travel, yet he had no recourse but to return to Germany. Instead of moving into the Berlin Schloss he took up residence in the Palace of Charlottenburg, a few miles outside the capital, as the doctors felt that the air would be more beneficial. People who saw him were appalled. He could barely stand. He made a painful effort to hold himself erect, but his emaciated frame and the look of agony in his deep, tragic eyes revealed only too clearly that the hand of death was on him. News spread through the Bismarck entourage that his reign was a matter of weeks. This was the signal not merely for indifference but for

[1] *Letters of Queen Victoria.*

[2] *Letters of the Empress Frederick.*

cruel defiance. Not that the Emperor contemplated any far-reaching changes. There was no longer any question of implementing the plans that he and Vicky had discussed so often. Bismarck would have to reign, and the autocratic regime would continue undisturbed. All he could do was to reward his liberal friends with decorations and promote a few of them to government positions. Nevertheless, even the smallest decisions made by his wife and himself were mocked. When the Empress dismissed the German physician, Professor Bergmann, because she felt he had handled Frederick's throat too roughly, causing unnecessary pain, William received the doctor to show his respect. When the Emperor demanded the resignation of Herr von Puttkamer, the Minister of the Interior, because of corrupt practices in conducting the recent Reichstag elections, Bismarck ostentatiously gave a dinner in his honour. Colonel Swaine, the British military attaché in Berlin, was so shocked by the behaviour of Prussian officialdom that he wrote to the Prince of Wales: " We are living in sad times here in Berlin. Not sad alone because we have an Emperor at death's door, nor sad only because there are family disagreements, but sad, doubly sad, because almost all officials—perhaps with exceptions, but I know them not—are behaving in a way as if the last spark of honour and faithful duty had gone—they are all trimming their sails. It seems as if a curse had come over this country, leaving but one bright spot and that is where stands a solitary woman doing her duty faithfully and tenderly by her sick husband against all odds. It is one of the most, if not *the* most tragic episode in a country and life ever recorded in history."[1]

The unpleasant atmosphere grew venal when rumour swept the capital that the Empress was planning to exploit her brief moment of power by insisting upon the marriage of her daughter to Prince Alexander of Battenberg. The Prince was no longer ruler of Bulgaria. He had been kidnapped by the Russians and forced to sign a paper of abdication at the point of a gun. As he was now a private citizen, there was no real reason why the wedding should not take place. But both Prince Bismarck and Prince William still insisted that Russia would take umbrage, and instructed the press to open a campaign against the proposal.

In the midst of this uproar, Queen Victoria arrived in Berlin to

[1] *Letters of the Empress Frederick.*

visit her stricken son-in-law. Lord Salisbury had been apprehensive about the trip. He was afraid Bismarck might not show her proper respect, or that William might be rude to her. He need not have worried. Her dumpy figure, swathed in black, was the symbol of majesty. Her immense prestige, coupled with tact and firmness, enabled her to carry off her difficult role perfectly. She charmed Bismarck who had never met her before; she cheered the Emperor; she warned her daughter not to press the marriage with Alexander unless William consented; and she implored William to be more considerate of his mother. While she was present the meanness and maliciousness faded away; but as soon as she departed it rolled back again like a sultry storm.

On May 24th the Emperor attended the wedding of his son Prince Henry to Princess Irene, daughter of Princess Alice. All eyes were upon him. The collar of his uniform was cut high in order to hide the tube in his throat, but those near him could see his breast heaving as he fought for breath. He was a pitiful object, so white, so wasted, so sad; but Count von Waldersee, who sat not far from him, could only exult. "How wonderfully everything is turning out!" he wrote in his diary on May 30th. "What a terrible misfortune it would have been if we now had a healthy Kaiser Frederick over us! Under his wife's leading he would have put the whole German Empire out of joint. . . . All are looking with high hope to the Crown Prince. Who would have believed it a year ago?"[1]

A week after the wedding the Emperor asked to be taken to the New Palace at Potsdam. This was where he had been born and where he had spent the first year of his marriage. He was carried down the river by barge, as it was the least painful way to move him. As soon as he arrived, he wrote on a slip of paper that he rechristened the palace "Friedrichskron." It was the only immortality he sought.

Ten days later the Empress telegraphed her mother that her husband's condition had taken a turn for the worse, and on the 14th June the doctors cabled that he was sinking. The Queen immediately wired William: "Am in great distress at these terrible news and so troubled about poor dear Mama. Do all you can, as I asked you, to help her at this terrible time of dreadful trial

[1] *A Field Marshal's Memoirs:* Count von Waldersee.

and grief. God help us!"[1] On that same day Prince Bismarck was received by the dying man. The Emperor took his wife's hand and placed it inside the Chancellor's, imploring the old man, with his eyes, to look after her. His sons and daughters filed in to see him; the Empress kept vigil at the bedside.

That night there were mysterious movements in the palace. Army officers with permits signed by Prince William moved into one of the wings; and the Master of the Household was told that he was already superseded by a new man—a nominee of the Prince. The next morning the Emperor died. But there was little time to think of this, for the palace was suddenly in a state of siege, surrounded by soldiers. No one could move in or out without permission from the officer in charge. Prince William was determined to lay his hands on his father's private papers, and for several hours officers went through the rooms ransacking tables and drawers, but nothing was found. While this was going on, a telegram arrived for William from Queen Victoria. "I am broken-hearted. Help and do all you can for your poor dear mother and try to follow in your best, noblest and kindest of father's footsteps. Grandmama."[1] One wonders if William had time to read it. He was busy walking up and down the park, fulminating against his mother to Count von Waldersee. "In spite of all assertions," he said, "she has long been prepared for my father's death; everything has most deliberately been arranged with this in sight. There is . . . nothing in writing to be seen, everything has been done away with."[2] Two days later Queen Victoria wrote in her journal: "Colonel Swaine arrived from Berlin. . . . He had brought some papers which Fritz had desired should be placed in my care."

When the Prince and Princess of Wales arrived in Berlin for the funeral they found the Empress distraught. She had left the Palace with her three daughters and taken refuge at her little country house at Bornstedt not far away. William, she declared, was doing everything to insult his father's memory. Despite her pleading he had insisted on holding a post-mortem on the body under the pretext that it was required by law, but in reality only to revive the cancer issue and further embarrass Mr. Mackenzie. She had tried to see

[1] *Letters of Queen Victoria.*

[2] *A Field Marshal's Memoirs:* Count von Waldersee.

Prince Bismarck to ask him to prevent it, but he had replied that he was too busy with his new master to spare the time. William had struck another blow by writing to Prince Alexander declaring that he would never consent to a marriage between him and Victoria. Although the dead Emperor had left a last testament, dated April 12th, saying: "I entirely acquiesce in the betrothal of your second sister with Prince Alexander of Battenberg. I charge you as a filial duty with the accomplishment of my desires . . .," he had based his refusal on the "profound conviction held by my grandfather and father."

The Prince and Princess were appalled by William's behaviour. They were shocked to learn that he even had taken the funeral arrangements out of his mother's hands and was ignoring her wishes; in the end she refused to attend the public ceremony and held a private service of her own. The Prince of Wales was doubly affected, for he was genuinely moved by the loss of his brother-in-law. Before leaving London he had written his second son: "Try, my dear Georgy, never to forget Uncle Fritz. He was one of the finest and noblest characters ever known; if he had a fault he was too good for this world."[1] He longed to talk about Frederick and hear his praises sung, but the Berlin world was cold and derisory. Count Herbert Bismarck referred to the dead man as an "incubus" and said that an Emperor "who could not speak was not fit to reign." The Prince was so outraged that he told Prince Hohenlohe he would have liked to throw him out of the room."

However, Herbert also took exception to the conversation; the Prince was indiscreet enough, or perhaps angry enough, to suggest that the Emperor Frederick might have wished to return Alsace and Lorraine to the French. Herbert repeated this remark to William who was so indignant that when he made a public speech a month later he said: "There are those people who have the audacity to maintain that my father was willing to part with what he gained on the battlefield. We, who knew him so well, cannot quietly tolerate, even for a single minute moment, such an insult to his memory. . . ." At the end of his oration he turned to the British attaché, General Blumenthal, and said: "I hope the Prince of Wales will understand that."

The Prince understood only too clearly, and the Princess as well.

[1] *King George V*: Harold Nicolson.

Alexandra had never liked the Germans anyway and now every time she thought of William's treatment of his mother she boiled with rage. "Instead of William being a comfort and a support to her," she wrote in August 1888, "he has quite gone over to Bismarck and Co. who entirely overlook and crush her. It is too infamous."

Even Queen Victoria was caught up in the storm. Very haughtily did she receive her grandson's emissary, who had been sent to announce formally the accession of a new sovereign. Soon the British Military Attaché in Berlin was writing to the Queen's secretary: "The young Emperor spoke to me this morning of the cold reception his Envoy, General von Winterfeldt, had received at Windsor. . . ." Victoria wrote on the margin: "The Queen intended it should be cold. She last saw him as her son-in-law's A.D.C. He came to her and never uttered one word of sorrow for his death, and rejoiced in the accession of his new master."[1]

The Queen recovered her composure and made a final attempt to induce William to behave "decently." "Let me . . . ask you to bear with poor Mama if she is sometimes irritated and excited. She does not mean it; think what months of agony and suspense and watching with broken and sleepless nights she had gone through and *don't mind it.* I am so anxious that all should go smoothly, that I write thus openly in the interests of both.

"There are many rumours of your going and paying visits to Sovereigns. I hope that at least you will let some months pass before anything of this kind takes place, as it is not three weeks yet since dear beloved Papa was taken, and we are all still in such deep mourning for him. . . ."[1]

William's reply was firm. He was leaving for the Baltic, "where I hope to meet the Emperor of Russia, which will be of good effect for the peace of Europe, and for the rest and quiet of my Allies. I would have gone later if possible, but State interest goes before personal feelings, and the fate which hangs over nations does not wait till the etiquette of Court mournings has been fulfilled . . . I deem it necessary that monarchs should meet often and confer together to look out for dangers which threaten the monarchical principle from democratical and republican parties in all parts of the world. . . ."[1]

[1] *Letters of Queen Victoria.*

William's jibe about democracies was not wasted on Victoria. She promptly telegraphed her Prime Minister, Lord Salisbury. "Trust that we shall be *very cool*, though civil, in our communications with my grandson and Prince Bismarck, who are bent on a return to the oldest times of government."[1]

[1] *Letters of Queen Victoria.*

4. *Dropping the Pilot*

" So we are bound together—I and the army—so we are born for one another, and so we shall hold together indissolubly, whether, as God wills, we are to have peace or storm." These were the twenty-nine-year-old Kaiser's first public words, delivered in a proclamation to the army. Europe stirred uneasily and the French paper *Figaro* commented morosely that " a prince who is an enthusiast for the army is also an enthusiast for war." Three days later William II struck a different note in a speech to the people, declaring that he had vowed to God " to be a righteous and gentle prince, to foster piety and to maintain peace ; " but the London *Times* remarked caustically that his first pronouncement seemed " more spontaneous."

What sort of a man was this new Emperor ? A religious fanatic ? A war lord ? An exhibitionist ? The chancelleries of Europe busied themselves with painstaking assessments of his character but no two opinions seemed to tally. It was known that he possessed a mercurial temperament which could plunge him from exuberance to depression, from jocular friendliness to stiff censoriousness in a matter of minutes. He was difficult to fathom ; indeed, the only facet of his character, clear to all, was his changeability. " He is rather short," wrote the British politician, Mr. John Morley, " pale, but sunburnt ; carries himself well ; walks into the room with the stiff stride of the Prussian soldier ; speaks with a good deal of intense and energetic gesture, not like a Frenchman but staccato ; his voice strong but pleasant ; his eye bright, clear and full ; mouth resolute ; the cast of face grave or stern in repose, but as he sat between two pretty women he lighted up with gaiety, and a genial laugh. Energy, rapidity, restlessness in every movement from his short, quick inclinations of the head to the planting of the foot." The author seems to have paused at this point and reread his pen portrait. Was something wrong with it ?

"I should be disposed strongly to doubt," he suddenly added, "whether it is all sound, steady, and the result of—what Herbert Spencer could call—a rightly co-ordinated organisation."[1]

The German people, on the other hand, had no such misgivings. They were thrilled by the style and dash of their twenty-nine-year-old Kaiser. Above all they liked his constant references to the Deity, his presentation of himself as the instrument of the Divine Will. This gave them confidence, and confidence was all they needed for their army of four million men was the strongest in the world. While William's flamboyant utterances disturbed the complacency of Europe his own people were brought cheering to their feet. "Dazzling" was the word most frequently used to describe the Sovereign. Even a cynical Foreign Office official was soon writing in his diary: "His liveliness is invaluable to us. . . ."

William was quick to exploit the praise that engulfed him. During the first year of his reign he demanded a huge sum of money which he spent on redecorating his palaces, smartening up his bodyguard, designing new uniforms for his officials, new standards and orders for his regiments. A royal train of twelve carriages with the saloon car magnificently upholstered in blue satin was forthcoming; also an Imperial yacht, described in State papers as "a pattern for the Grand Squadron" but, later, carelessly referred to by the Kaiser as "a pleasure boat" for himself and his family.

William liked spit and polish, and he organised his court on military lines. Forgetting God for the moment, he let it be known that the Sovereign was to be referred to in dispatches as "The Most High" or "The All Highest"; communications from the royal hand were to be carried in special blue envelopes superinscribed "Expressed by order of The All Highest,"[2] and his courtiers were never to argue or protest, merely to bow and reply: "As Your Majesty commands."

William's home life was conducted in the same brisk pattern. Here, also, there was no hint of insubordination. His dull, pious, servile wife, Dona, known to the world as the Empress Augusta Victoria, was the embodiment of devoted obedience. She fulfilled the Prussian ideal of womanhood by concerning herself mainly

[1] *Recollections:* Viscount Morley.

[2] To this day in Berlin unpleasant letters are often referred to as *Blauebriefe.*

with her kitchens and nurseries. Her spare time was dedicated to stamping out vice and raising money for ecclesiastical purposes. During the first ten years of William's reign she was instrumental in building 42 new churches. She spent many hours discussing morality with the Protestant clergy, and refused to invite any young man to Court who was suspected of having had sexual intercourse before marriage.

Dona regarded William as a demigod. She loved him and was frightened of him. His slightest wish became her heart's desire. One of her greatest joys was the intimate family breakfasts they had together. She liked to hover over her husband, buttering his toast and removing his plates. As a result she frequently got no breakfast herself, for as soon as he had finished he would jump up and announce that it was time for a walk. " Come along! No dawdling!" And Dona would hurry after him. As far as woman were concerned she had no cause for complaint. Although he liked to sit next to a pretty woman at dinner, he had no liking for balls and chaffed rather than flirted. His favourite recreation was shooting. Sometimes he went to Austria as a guest of the Emperor, but more often he graced the domain of some Prussian magnate, such as Count Eberhard Dohna, who owned a vast estate, Prokelwitz, in Silesia. These visits were quite unlike the entertainments arranged in England for the Prince of Wales. Luxury was frowned upon as being unmanly; the rooms were simple, the food plain, and no women were present. Enormous pains were taken to see that the time-table moved with military precision, and the guests spent anxious hours before the Sovereign's arrival trying to think of anecdotes and conversational gambits that might amuse him.

The host, Count Dohna, was ingenuous. William had once found a thunderbolt in the garden of a nearby estate and had talked about it for years, so the Count obligingly acquired bits of a meteorite and scattered them along his gravel path. " Life at Prokelwitz," wrote one of the guests, " is extremely easy-going and restful. One gets up about six o'clock to assemble for breakfast in the forest with the Emperor. Potatoes are roasted at a big fire, stuck on wooden spikes, and handed round by the guests' keepers. There is bread and butter, too, and various wines. The Emperor drives out there while it is still night—about two o'clock—and has a beefsteak beforehand. We lie about on the grass while breakfasting, talk about the incidents of the chase, and tell stories. The Emperor, in the highest of spirits, laughs and chaffs us all, and it is hard to remember the Imperial purple in such light-hearted moments. . . . At about eleven we are back in Prokelwitz, where in the plain, whitewashed dining-room with its hundreds of antlers on the wall, and its open doorways, a hot breakfast awaits us. After this the Emperor goes to his room to sleep until about three o'clock in the afternoon. . . . Between three and four the Emperor attends to the private letters of State which have arrived from Berlin. Dinner takes place at four. . . . We appear in morning-dress, and no luxury of any kind is displayed. . . . About six o'clock the Emperor drives out again to the chase, and those who stay behind go for a walk, until about half-past nine the Emperor's return is announced. A signal sounds when the carriage is seen approaching the village, two great torch-lights are lit in front of the house under the old linden trees, the keepers assemble, and we form a group at the door when the wagon drives in."[1]

These parties might have been on the dull side if it had not been for the presence of a man who seemed to exercise a magic spell over the Kaiser. "Meet Philip Eulenburg my bosom friend—the only one I have." Thus William presented Count Eulenburg to his tutor, George Hintzpeter, in 1887. The Count was twelve years older than William and noted for his charm, "a pale, grey-haired somewhat weary looking man with a pallid, fleeting smile, something of a visionary . . . who told his tales in a quiet, soft, subtle voice with a grave smile and a certain fascinating charm of manner."[2] He was a brilliant conversationalist, something of a rarity in Berlin, and a talented musician. He had suffered a miserable childhood under the direction of a stern Prussian father who had forced him to conform to the accepted pattern of aristocratic behaviour; first the army, then the diplomatic service. Eulenburg's real interests were music and poetry and he had loathed military life, complaining despairingly of the narrow-minded vulgarity of his fellow officers. Nevertheless he had not disgraced the family name, for he had brought back an Iron Cross from the Franco-Prussian conflict.

Eulenburg first met William at one of the Prokelwitz shooting

[1] *Philip Eulenburg: The Kaiser's Friend:* Johannes Haller.

[2] *Memoirs of the Kaiser's Court:* Anne Topham.

parties in 1886—two years before he came to the throne. After dinner the guests begged him to sit down at the piano and sing some of his own ballads. The Prince was transfixed; never had he met such a fascinating man, never had he heard such intoxicating songs. "My attitude toward Prince William," wrote Eulenburg, "was cordial yet circumspect, when in 1886 his friendship for me became ecstatic . . . my attitude was cordial, because his enthusiasm for my music and my musical performances, which almost feverishly delighted him, was congenial to my artistic soul, and very likely flattered my vanity as well. . . ."[1] There were to be many more Nordic ballads, many more thrilling moments with the Prince "always sitting beside me and turning the pages . . . and he loved to greet me, when we met on shooting-mornings in the forest, with turns and phrases from my verses. I have had many a ravished listener to my performances, but hardly ever have I inspired such ravishment as in Prince William. And as at the same time I familiarly frequented Bismarck's house, was an officer in the Prince's adored Guards, and (alas!) profoundly intitiated in the byways of politics, I can understand that the young Prince should have felt as if looking deep into a cup filled with a draught whose ingredients were delightful to his palate."[2]

The news that Eulenburg had become the favourite spread rapidly. Although he was only a minor secretary at the Munich Legation he suddenly found the Bismarcks treating him with great seriousness. "It was very useful, your going to see Prince William," wrote Herbert Bismarck on June 11, 1886. "He thinks a great deal of you and has sung your praises to me in every kind of way. You must make use of this, and at Reichenhall talk to him again and get an influence over him. For the heaven-storming strain in most of his opinions must be toned down, so that the Potsdam Lieutenant's outlook may gradually give way to statesmanlike reflections. Except for that, the Prince is really a pearl. . . ." Then again: "And so you are going to Bayreuth with Prince William to-morrow. I hope you will distract his mind, so that the Wagnerian trombones may not damage his bad ear with their discords. Six hours of the Music of the Future would inflame even my drums. I am always afraid that the Prince will do too much, so energetic

[1] *Philip Eulenburg: The Kaiser's Friend:* Johannes Haller.

[2] *Aus 50 Jahren:* Prince Philipp zu Eulenburg-Hertefeldt.

as he is in everything; and he must be prevented from that, for his health is of quite inestimable importance to the German nation."[1]

Count Eulenburg developed his friendship with great sureness of touch. Since he lived in Munich and William in Berlin most of it had to be done by post. His letters were amusing and deferential all at once, and heavily laden with rather soulful sentiments which apparently pleased his young master.

"I went one evening lately," he wrote to William in 1882, "to the great New Year's reception, where the House of Wittelsbach displayed itself in such splendour as gave a good Prussian food for reflection. I could not help thinking of my Emperor that is to be, how he avoids such pretentiousness. I thought of Potsdam, of our sledge-driving, our intimate communion, and a sense of such deep friendship came over me that all of a sudden I felt the glitter around me as an unbearable oppression. How human is our relation—and how I suffer from the thought that the social abyss between us, bridged by our friendship, must inevitably widen more and more when the Imperial Crown is on your head. . . ."[1]

This same note was sounded even more forcibly when William mounted the throne. "My Prussian heart, despite all its pain, beats joyously for the Sovereign, but my friendship's heart is filled with melancholy at the thought of the deep chasm which nevertheless separates the Sovereign from the subject. But no subject can honour his Sovereign more than I do, who have been allowed to look into the heart of the noblest of *friends*. I pray from the depths of my soul that Your Majesty will deign to preserve me the favour which has become a radiance in my life."[1]

These sentiments were not hypocrisy. If William was fascinated by the Count, the Count, on the other hand, was thrilled by the emotions he had produced. His adoring eyes, said old Prince Bismarck, were enough to spoil the best breakfast. He went on to describe him as "something of a Prussian Cagliostro . . . a mystic, a romantic rhetorician . . . particularly dangerous for the dramatic temperament of our Emperor. In that high personage's presence he assumed adoring attitudes which I believe to be perfectly

[1] *Philip Eulenburg: The Kaiser's Friend:* Johannes Haller.

sincere. The Emperor has only to look up, and he is sure to find those eyes fixed worshipfully upon him."[1]

Despite the enchantment, Count Eulenburg was worldly enough to know that the Prince's favour was bound to inspire jealousy, and even before William came to the throne dispensed with unnecessary trouble by offering himself as a tool of the Bismarcks. "I do not know whether you are aware that the Crown Prince corresponds with me?" he wrote to Herbert Bismarck in the spring of 1887. "I am sometimes uneasy at having to give him an answer to political questions, knowing pretty well that it is not generally desired. You know my sentiments, my loyal attachment to the Prince and yourself. . . ."[2] The invitation was eagerly accepted and it was intimated to Eulenburg that he would become an official Foreign Office representative attached to William. "They want to use me for a certain kind of influence on him—the Prince," he wrote in his diary. A year later the Prince was Kaiser and from then on Eulenburg sent copies of his letters, and William's replies, to Herbert; he received instructions how to handle every political occasion, what to persuade his master to do and leave undone.

The Bismarcks were not the only ones who took pains to cultivate Count Eulenburg. As soon as his friendship with William became known, he received a letter from Baron von Holstein of the German Foreign Office. This powerful, shadowy figure had a dark reputation. He had been launched into diplomacy years earlier by the old Bismarck, who always referred to him as "the man with the hyena eyes." He had no scruples, and did not hesitate to slander, bludgeon, bribe, or blackmail in carrying out Bismarck's orders. Apparently he lived in perpetual fear of assault, for he always carried a revolver in his pocket and several times a week visited a small shooting gallery for target practice. By the same token he was a dangerous enemy, often scenting hostility in imaginary actions, and hitting back mercilessly. If someone happened not to bow to him, "this was enough to institute a persecution of the enemy which never came to an end. Even a word that somebody might somewhere have let fall . . . sufficed to establish a lasting

[1] *Reflections and Memories:* Otto von Bismarck.

[2] *Aus 50 Jahren:* Prince Philipp zu Eulenburg-Hertefeldt.

enmity . . . for he was convinced that any one of them would let himself be bribed, would steal from him, or even murder him. . . . All his energies were concentrated on politics, and that in the region of intrigue."[1]

As a bachelor Holstein was able to dedicate his whole life to the Foreign Office. He shunned all publicity, never attended social functions, never travelled, and formed all his deductions from written reports. He worked so hard that he possessed an encyclopaedic knowledge of foreign treaties. He also carried on a vast correspondence with German diplomats all over the world. He often commanded them to send him private reports, over the heads of their superiors; this invariably placed them in the palm of his hand, for he could threaten to reveal their disloyalty.

He refused to take responsibility. His rank was only that of a Privy Councillor and he would not even accept a position as head of a department. It was part of his pathological nature only to exercise power in the back rooms where no one could fasten blame on him. As the years progressed he was witness to so many unsavoury transactions that even Bismarck stood in awe of the monster he had created. " A troublesome passenger," he wrote, " but if one had tried to remove him from the coach, there was the risk of his beginning to blab in foreign parts."

So Baron Holstein remained at the Foreign Office, weaving his web ever tighter. When Eulenburg sprang into prominence he wrote to him out of the blue, using the pretext of congratulating his handling of Bavarian affairs. Eulenburg understood the importance of maintaining cordial relations with the *éminence grise*; the correspondence developed, the friendship grew, the eulogies expanded. By Christmas 1890 Holstein had become " uncle " to the Eulenburg children, and the Count was writing to the Baron in a highly romantic vein. " With Mussigny's incomparable and never-fading crimson-lake I paint in my heart your name, first known to me some years ago as that of a peculiar, unapproachable personage, never likely to unveil to a young Secretary of Legation who was more occupied with poetry than with diplomacy; but who subsequently to my amazement, and at first not without a certain misgiving on my part, entered into relations with me—and now is lauded by my children as a beneficent ' uncle ' who gives

[1] *Aus 50 Jahren:* Prince Philipp zu Eulenburg-Hertefeldt.

them splendid books, and toys from Solkach's. So there is a destiny in all things; I am heartily grateful to the Giver of all good for having won you to myself. I cannot now imagine what my life would be like without you. Not only the political life that I have got into I know not how, but the private too."[1]

"As cold as a block of ice," said Count Herbert Bismarck, describing William II. "Convinced from the start that people only exist to be used—either for work or amusement—and that even then they only do duty for a given period, after which they may be cast aside."[2] Old Prince Bismarck noted his son's observations; but he had no intention of being discarded. He planned to remain in office until he died.

Despite his seventy-three years, he was in excellent health and enjoying life more than ever. So long as his son Herbert and Holstein and Eulenburg all kept a watchful eye on the Kaiser, he had nothing to worry about. At any rate he got on well with William. Although the Sovereign was impetuous and inexperienced and arrogant, he had always hero-worshipped the Chancellor, and far from quarrelling with him, was eager to earn his respect. During the first year of the new reign the Austrian Ambassador described their relationship as a "honeymoon." At the New Year of 1889 William telegraphed the old man that he was "full of joy and confidence, since you are still at my right hand, beginning the New Year with fresh vigour .... May it long be vouchsafed me to work with you." And on an imperial visit to Bismarck's country estate, Count Eulenburg noted how the Kaiser made Bismarck precede him through a doorway. Even Bismarck himself was impressed by the young ruler's respect. "So considerate. ... He was surprised that I had delayed breakfast for him until eleven o'clock . . . and has not got up before nine because he thought that I slept late."

This cordiality did not mean that Bismarck was free from trouble. The most irritating thorn in his flesh was the muddle-headed, fire-eating Field Marshal von Waldersee whom William had appointed Chief of Staff. Waldersee still exerted great influence over William and still was preaching the preventive war. He loudly criticised Bismarck's policy of trying to improve relations with Russia.

[1] *Philip Eulenburg: The Kaiser's Friend:* Johannes Haller.
[2] *The Holstein Papers:* edited by N. Rich and M. H. Fisher.

Instead of appeasing Russia Germany should attack and destroy her. She also should attack and destroy France before the latter grew too strong. War, not peace, was what was needed.

The Kaiser was dazzled by this sort of talk, and Herbert Bismarck reported anxiously that he fancied himself in the role of Frederick the Great—sometimes even of Julius Caesar! Herbert accompanied him to Italy in the summer of 1889 and was surprised to see him stop and gaze meditatively at a statue of Caesar. Later, he remarked sombrely: "I think I have a mission to destroy Gaul, like Julius Caesar."

Bismarck was amused by these stories. It showed that the Kaiser was more interested in applause than responsibility. He was an exhibitionist; therefore he would be content with uniforms and decorations and state visits, and leave authority in the hands of his Chancellor. And even if he were not content, what could he do? Was Bismarck not the most celebrated statesman in Europe? Had he not carved the German Empire and placed the imperial crown on the Hohenzollern head? Fame was security; no one would risk becoming a laughing stock by replacing a giant with a gnat. So little did Bismarck worry about William that he scarcely bothered to come to Berlin. During the first eighteen months of the reign he spent only four months in the capital. The rest of the time he relaxed at his country estate, Friedrichsruh, near Hamburg. Since almost everything required his signature, affairs of state were slowed to a snail's pace. The business of the nation was regulated by messenger boys with dispatch cases. The Chancellor did not care. There was nothing to hurry about anyway. Visitors to Friedrichsruh were struck by his amiability and contentment. His pale coughing wife was forever sewing at his side; one of his sons was always ready to spring to attention when his voice rang out: "Come here you!" At meal-times he presented the same formidable picture, eating enough for three and throwing his meat bones over his shoulder to a pair of huge, yelping dogs.

Nevertheless, Bismarck's hands were firmly on the helm. Once he had said to a friend: "I will tell you the secret of politics: friendship with Russia." This was the basis of his policy. A year before William came to the throne the Chancellor had signed an alliance with Russia which he regarded as a master-stroke. As usual it was secret, so secret that he would not even tell the new Kaiser about it. The Czar had refused to renew the Three Emperors Alliance in 1887 because of Austria's intrigues in the Balkans. Instead he had offered to sign a treaty with Germany alone. This caused Bismarck a brief moment of embarrassment because of his secret treaty with Austria;[1] but he decided that frankness was the best policy, pulled out the document and showed it to the Russian Ambassador, apologising but saying that it had been forced upon him by Russia's belligerent attitude at the time; and now it must be taken into consideration in drafting a Russo-German agreement.

The Ambassador did not take umbrage and a treaty was drawn up stating that if either Germany or Russia found themselves at war with a third power the other would preserve a benevolent neutrality. This provision would not apply if Russia attacked Austria (which allowed Bismarck to honour his Austrian treaty) or if Germany attacked France. Since Bismarck had no intention of attacking France, he was more than satisfied, for the treaty meant that if France—still crying revenge for Bismarck's seizure of Alsace-Lorraine in 1870—attacked Germany (a much more likely contingency) Russia would be obliged to remain neutral. And this was not all. To make sure that Russia did not succumb to French blandishments in other ways, he agreed to support the Czar diplomatically in the latter's efforts to gain control of the Turkish Straits—the "historic mission" of which Russia always dreamed, and which had been denied her by the Berlin Treaty of 1878.

From every angle Bismarck regarded his new treaty as a diplomatic triumph. Not only would it prevent Russia from forming an alliance with France, but it would enable Bismarck, by virtue of having treaties with both Austria and Russia, to exert pressure on each and prevent them from coming to blows in the Balkans. Bismarck called his alliance the "Reinsurance Treaty," for he seemed to have insured himself against almost every contingency.

However, Bismarck's friendly attitude towards Russia was exactly what his political opponents objected to. Although Prussia had been on close terms with Russia ever since the days of Napoleon, the German people did not like the Russians. Time and again in recent years they had strained against this unwelcome bond of amity

[1] Germany was also linked to Austria, and to Italy, by the Triple Alliance Treaty signed in Vienna in 1882.

and ached to give their support to German-speaking Austria. In 1889 Austria was pressing Germany to undertake joint military action against Russia and many of William II's intimates, including Count Waldersee, were itching to oblige. Even Baron Holstein felt that at least Germany should make it clear that Austrian ambitions were nearer to her heart than those of Russia. Bismarck scoffed at his critics for they had missed the essence of his handiwork; and in 1888 published the terms of the German-Austrian Alliance to stress the fact that the treaty was purely defensive, not otherwise.

Bismarck's opponents did not dare to attack him outright on foreign policy; he was too much respected for them to risk a challenge, so they fastened on his old age. It is surprising that he did not see how his long absences from Berlin would play into their hands; or even understand how unpopular he was. Quite apart from political differences, many members of the hierarchy felt that they had suffered his tyrannies long enough and were anxious to see him go. There were other reasons as well; Holstein wanted more power at the Foreign Office and Waldersee, now Chief of Staff, even saw himself stepping into Bismarck's shoes. "The Chancellor is showing signs of age," he wrote in October 1888. "He contradicts himself oftener than he used to do and repeats orders given a few days before. This makes co-operation with him more and more difficult. . . ." Moltke, the retiring Chief of Staff, lashed out even more bitterly. "He has intimidated nearly everyone, so that none dares to express an independent opinion. He wants to be master all round, and is no longer fit to be so. He is Foreign Minister and interferes with every one of the Home Ministers, paying no attention to the Chief's views; he is Prussian Prime Minister and Minister of Commerce, and regards the various Heads of Departments as his subjects; added to which he sits tight at Friedrichsruh, and is difficult to get at. . . . All complain of insufficient instructions, of having no real power of decision, and more particularly too of the Chancellor's publicity."[1]

Gradually Baron Holstein became the subterranean leader of the anti-Bismarck campaign. Brilliantly he played on the dissatisfaction and ambitions of those close to the Kaiser, feeding them with information designed to show that the old man was losing his grip

[1] *Memoirs, Letters and Documents:* Helmuth von Moltke.

in foreign affairs. " Our policy," he wrote in his diary, " with its criss-cross of commitments—resembles the tangle of lines at a big railway station. The chief pointsman thinks he can clock everything into its proper place and hopes particularly that the greater the confusion the more indispensable he is." Count von Waldersee was only too eager to repeat these criticisms to the Kaiser, and gleefully took note of the Sovereign's ruthless nature. " Perhaps he is not endowed with heart to an excessive degree but just that is an excellent thing. He has a will of his own and is inclined to rule by himself." The Count encouraged this inclination by whispering in William's ear that if Frederick the Great had retained a man of Bismarck's stature he would not have been " the Great." William's egotism proved fertile ground for these potent seeds. Although as a prince he had revered the Chancellor, now that he was Kaiser he did not find it amusing to be dwarfed by his celebrated minister. The name of Bismarck reverberated through Europe, and had become synonymous with the name of Germany, while the Hohenzollerns, he felt, were scarcely mentioned. He began to writhe when he heard people praising Bismarck for the unification of Germany; for had not the nation sprung into being under the rule of his grandfather, William I? Bismarck deliberately had snatched the credit to the detriment of the Sovereign. As jealousy took possession of his heart, he convinced himself that the Chancellor no longer was his servant but his rival; and that it was imperative for the dignity of his dynasty to show the world that the Hohenzollerns, and not the Bismarcks, ruled Germany.

Even during the honeymoon period, Bismarck began to have trouble with the young Emperor. For one thing the old man did not find William's family rows nearly so amusing now that they had international repercussions. A few months after the accession he provoked an incident which caused Bismarck a good deal of explaining. The Prince of Wales wrote to his nephew that he was going to Vienna to visit the Emperor Franz Joseph and hoped that he might see him there. But William had other ideas. He was determined to show the world that he was not under the thumb of his English relations as his father had been; furthermore, he was still annoyed by the Prince's remarks at his father's funeral. So he waited until his uncle had arrived in Vienna, then telegraphed to

Franz Joseph, announcing his own imminent arrival and stipulating that since he was coming to discuss "affairs of state" it would not do to have other royalties present. Poor Franz Joseph was placed in a terrible dilemma. He could not afford to offend the Kaiser at this particular juncture, for Austria was trying to persuade Germany to give up her policy of friendship with Russia and come down squarely on the Austrian side. The situation was explained to the British Ambassador who had the unpleasant task of relaying it to the Prince of Wales. Edward was amazed and indignant but gallantly offered to relieve the Emperor's embarrassment by retreating to Rumania until his nephew's visit was over. William made matters even worse by laughing about what he had done, and boasting to his Viennese friends that he preferred his "uncle's room to his company." These remarks were repeated to Edward when he returned.

Needless to say, the incident caused a storm. Queen Victoria took up the cudgels on her son's behalf and demanded an explanation from Berlin. William surprised everybody by lying his way out and denying all knowledge of the affair. How could the British Ambassador have got hold of the idea that he did not wish to see his uncle? This placed the blame squarely on Bismarck who finally wrote to Lord Salisbury explaining that the Czar of Russia might have been jealous if the Prince had been present at a meeting between the Kaiser and Franz Joseph; furthermore, the Prince had an unfortunate habit of treating William like a nephew rather than an Emperor. This was too much for Victoria. She sent a scorching reply to Salisbury pointing out that the Czar was the Prince's brother-in-law and could hardly take exception to his presence at a social gathering. As for the Prince "not treating his nephew as Emperor," she continued, "this really is *too vulgar* and too absurd, as well as untrue, almost *to be believed*. We have always been very intimate with our grandson and nephew, and to pretend that he is to be treated *in private* as well as in public as 'his Imperial Majesty' is *perfect madness*! He has been treated just as we should have treated his beloved father and even grandfather. . . . If he has *such* notions he had better *never* come *here*. . . . As regards the political relations of the two Governments, the Queen quite agrees that that should not be affected (if possible) by these miserable personal quarrels; but the Queen *fears* that, with such a hot-headed, conceited, and wrong-headed young man, devoid of all feeling, this may at ANY moment become *impossible*. . . ."[1]

The affair seemed to have reached an *impasse*, for the Prince said he would not meet the Kaiser until he apologised and the Kaiser said he could not apologise for what he had not done. However, Major-General Ellis, the Prince's equerry, inadvertently broke the tension: " No English gentleman would behave like either Emperor W. to his uncle or like Bismarck father and son. But we must not forget that they happen none of them to be *English gentlemen* and we must take them as we find them—pure Prussians. Every German and Austrian knows what that means. . . ."[2] Viewed from this perspective the Prince found himself able not to forgive but to try and forget. So when the Kaiser had the effrontery to propose himself for the Cowes Regatta in 1889, he agreed to meet him; and the Queen, urged by Lord Salisbury to restore harmonious relations, decided to try and induce more civil behaviour by giving him a magnificent reception. She arranged a Naval Review in his honour and made him an Admiral of the Fleet. " Fancy wearing the same uniform as St. Vincent and Nelson," he wrote jubilantly to Sir Edward Malet. " It is enough to make me quite giddy. . . ." Although he arrived in England in his most amiable mood, disquieting rumours from Berlin claimed that he was already talking about building a rival fleet of his own; *The Times* newspaper expressed doubts on the wisdom of allowing him so free a study of British naval organization. " I am now able," William wrote to the Queen, thanking her for her hospitality, " to take an interest in your fleet as though it were my own, and with keenest sympathy shall I watch every phase of its further development. . . ."[3]

The clash between William and his Iron Chancellor came in January 1890. The only person taken by surprise was Prince Bismarck. Indeed when Czar Alexander III had visited the capital three months earlier, he had asked the Prince point-blank: " Do you expect to remain Chancellor? " The old man had bristled with indignation and replied that he would remain at his post until he died. His first intimation of trouble came when the Kaiser

[1] *Letters of Queen Victoria.*

[2] *Henry Ponsonby, His Life from His Letters:* Arthur Ponsonby.

[3] *King Edward VII:* Sir Sidney Lee.

called a Crown Council without consulting him, and even refused to reveal the agenda. No king had behaved in such a high-handed fashion for thirty years.

Apart from Sovereign and Chancellor, eight ministers gathered around the green baize table. William opened the session by announcing that he had summoned the meeting on the anniversary of Frederick the Great's birthday, as he had momentous proposals to put forward in the field of labour legislation. The time had come to mitigate the anti-Socialist laws, and try and remedy some of the grievances of the working man. This was the only way the dangerous Social Democrats vote could be stemmed. He read out his list: shorter working hours, no child labour, no Sunday work. When he finished he turned to the Chancellor and asked for his opinion. Bismarck was not in the best of moods. He was chagrined at the scant respect being shown him; never had he taken second place at a Crown Council. Furthermore, he knew who had inspired the Kaiser's ideas: that nincompoop George Hintzpeter. Not that Bismarck was against social reform as such. During 1883 and 1884 he himself had introduced the first comprehensive social insurance scheme in history; and only the preceding year, in 1889, had rounded it off with contributory old-age pensions.

But now Bismarck had other plans. He was secretly determined to abolish universal suffrage and perhaps even do away with the Reichstag. His plan was to introduce harsh new anti-Socialist laws which would produce a wave of anarchy and give the Emperor the excuse to declare a state of siege. This would mean that the army automatically would take control of the country under the command of the Sovereign. During the interval of military dictatorship Bismarck would re-design the Constitution, and sweep away all semblance of parliamentary institutions. That was his strategy and he did not want it disturbed. So he answered the Kaiser's arguments with firmness and irony. Such liberal legislation as the Sovereign proposed, he asserted firmly, would not stem Social Democracy but give it a new impetus. "If Your Majesty attaches no weight to my counsels," he threatened, "I do not think I can remain in my place."

There was a painful silence; but the Kaiser did not try and placate him as his grandfather would have done. "That puts me in a dilemma," he said, looking round the table. "I beg these gentlemen for their opinion." The gentlemen dropped their eyes and fumbled with their papers. Although many of them agreed with the Sovereign, they were too frightened of Bismarck to oppose him. All owed their positions to him, all were acquainted with his vindictiveness; if he won the battle with the Emperor, woe to those who had crossed him. William had no choice but to adjourn the meeting. He shook hands with Bismarck and smiled, but inwardly he was smouldering. He waylaid the Minister of War in the corridor and said angrily: "Why did you leave me in the lurch? You, every one of you, looked as though you had been flogged! What had he said to you beforehand?"

Now it was the Ministers' turn to be in a dilemma. Who was going to triumph, Emperor or Chancellor? Their only concern was to place themselves on the winning side. There was no question where the ultimate power lay; the Emperor could demand Bismarck's portfolio, whereas Bismarck could not demand the Emperor's crown. But would the Emperor really assert himself? After a painful struggle, the ministers decided to back William. At the Crown Council a week later Prince Bismarck found that the wind had changed, the whole table opposed him. Triumphantly William presented a draft of his social reforms, expressing the noble but doubtful sentiment that he wished to be known as *le roi des gueux*, protector of the poor. Bismarck refused his countersignature, and the bill went forward in the Sovereign's name only —an event that had not occurred for thirty years.

This time Bismarck left in a rage. He castigated the ministers as cowardly and treacherous. Yet the truth was that they were creatures of his own making. "How utterly corrupting Bismarck's influence has been on the political life of Germany," the Empress Frederick had written in 1888. "It has made Berlin almost intolerable to live in, if one is not his abject slave!! His party, his followers and admirers are fifty times worse than he is. . . ."[1] However, Bismarck did not feel that the game was lost, for the elections were still to come. They were held on February 20th and reached his highest expectations. The National Liberals and the Bismarckian conservatives each lost over fifty per cent of their seats while the socialists, the radicals, and the Catholic centre—all opposed to Bismarck—ended with a total of nearly two-thirds of the seats.

[1] *Letters of the Empress Frederick.*

Indeed, the socialists polled more votes than any other single party although, because of the voting system, they did not receive a proportionate number of seats.

Gleefully Bismarck met a rather disconsolate Emperor and outlined his plans for a *coup d'état*. There would be no new anti-Socialist law, or for that matter not even a new army law, with such a Reichstag—or any Reichstag elected by universal suffrage. Therefore the Reich should be dissolved and the constitution rewritten. William was impressed, grasped Bismarck's hand and exclaimed: "No surrender." But he soon changed his mind. What he wanted most of all was to be his own master, and if he fell in with Bismarck's scheme the reverse would happen—the old man would be more powerful than ever. So on March 4th he turned down the Chancellor's scheme, saying that he did not wish to mar his reign with bloodshed. The ministers backed William, and this time Bismarck departed, not only angry but disturbed. It was impossible to influence the Emperor when ministers encouraged him and backed him up. This would have to be stopped; so he whipped out an Order of 1852 forbidding ministers to instruct or advise the Crown unless the Prime Minister was present.

Matters were approaching a climax. Baron Holstein attempted to induce Prince Bismarck, through the offices of Count von Kessel, a relation of the family, to modify his attitude. Not that Holstein had decided to support Bismarck. On the contrary, this was the way he worked; moving on one front but always protecting himself on another. Although he had been providing Count von Waldersee with information for months, he felt it wise to appear as a conciliator in case Prince Bismarck triumphed. "I told von Kessel . . . where in my opinion Bismarck's tactics were mistaken," he wrote in his diary. "The prime mistake was Prince Bismarck's habit of staging the *public* discomfiture of his opponents, particularly the Kaiser, instead of trying to win them over in private." Von Kessel lunched with the Chancellor at the Palace, but afterwards called on Holstein and said: "It's a waste of time. Father and son listen patiently, and then, with a rigid smile, turn down every suggestion that they should give way or behave less harshly."[1]

Holstein had an unhappy knack of reaching the wrong conclusion. It was not a question of tactics. It was a fierce battle for power.

[1] *The Holstein Papers*: edited by N. Rich and M. H. Fisher.

Bismarck recognised this at once; if he altered his tone and became more suppliant the sceptre would fall from his hands. He had always treated the Emperor harshly, and until now had been successful. When, for instance, the Emperor Frederick lay dying and William had sent the Chancellor a draft of the speech he intended to deliver to the Federal Princes upon ascending the throne, Bismarck had rebuked him for his indecent haste and advised him to burn it. Later, when William began writing comments in the margins of state papers, Bismarck asked him to refrain because of the confusion it caused. The Kaiser had taken these rebuffs meekly, and Bismarck believed that it was the right way to handle him.

But this time he had gone too far. "I have no ministers," stormed the Kaiser. "They are all Prince Bismarck's ministers!" On March 15th he decided to visit the Chancellery and have things out with the old man. Although he still had a rankling fear of Bismarck, he knew that if he did not take action he would become a laughing stock. The scene was as stormy as he envisaged. He criticised Bismarck for trying to whip up support in the Reichstag by consorting with a certain party leader whom the Chancellor knew the Kaiser particularly disliked. "Abandoning all manners and all reserve," wrote William in a letter to the Emperor of Austria, "he told me he was not going to be led by me in leading-strings, once for all he would have nothing of that sort from me, I had no notion of Parliamentary life, it was not my place to order him about in such matters. . . ."[1] Bismarck threw his dispatch case on the floor and said that if William wanted his resignation he could have it; he could not do his duty unless he saw whom he liked. "Even if your Sovereign forbids it?" asked the Kaiser. "The power of my Sovereign ceases at my wife's drawing-room," snapped the Chancellor.

Then William raised the subject of the 1852 Order, and told Bismarck he would have to withdraw it. The Chancellor shook his head. "No Premier can remain responsible if the monarch makes decisions on the advice of all and sundry." According to William, Bismarck added "that he had no trust in 'his' ministers, they had brought things to me behind his back, things with which he disagreed, and he had given them a lesson in consequence. I pointed out to him that it amounted to a deep affront to me, who

[1] *Kaiser and Chancellor:* Karl Novak.

had co-operated loyally with him as his sovereign, to accuse me of secretly intriguing against him behind his back; this he would not admit . . . I asked him to let me take a greater share in business and to initiate and include me in important decisions, but he refused with decision, saying that he must have made up his mind beforehand as to his decisions before he came to me. . . ."[1]

By this time Bismarck could scarcely control himself. But he had one last trick up his sleeve—not a particularly relevant one, but none the less satisfying. He picked up his case and pulled out a paper. The Kaiser asked him what he was looking at and he pretended to draw away in embarrassment. It was a report from London on the Czar's visit, he said, but he preferred his sovereign not to see it. William snatched it from his hand and read Alexander III's comment on himself. "*C'est un garçon mal élevé et de mauvaise foi.*" William flung down the paper and stalked out of the room.

The Kaiser was anxious for Bismarck to resign of his own accord and not to be put in the position of dismissing him. He was worried about public opinion, particularly European opinion, and did not want to arouse taunts of ingratitude—or perhaps even look ridiculous—by quarrelling openly with the famous old man. Furthermore, he was still a little frightened of Bismarck and awed by the momentous step he was taking; so he criticised the Chancellor ceaselessly to give himself confidence: "Things are at quite a bad pass with Russia at present," he told von Waldersee. "There is a strong feeling there against me, and Czar Alexander is talking against me offensively—he says among other things that I am mad. The feeling against us is increasing, and under no circumstances now shall I pay my visit to Krasnoe. Everyone recognises that at home things are in a bad way—what is the great Chancellor doing then? Where are his services?"

Waldersee did all he could to stiffen the Kaiser's resolve for he still had hopes of the Chancellorship and was afraid that Bismarck might find a way to wriggle off the hook. He declares in his diary that he was responsible for goading the Kaiser into the final, decisive action: that of sending General von Hahnke, head of the Military Cabinet, to the Chancellor and demanding either the withdrawal

[1] *Kaiser and Chancellor*: Karl Novak.

of the Order of 1852 or his resignation. "That is impossible," Bismarck replied. "If the Emperor wishes to quash the Order, he will have also to terminate the existing Presidency of the State Ministry. I have no objection to that.'

Hahnke reported Bismarck's reply and the Emperor sent him back again, this time repeating his command in even stronger language. "His Majesty," said General von Hahnke, "insists on the withdrawal of the Order in question. After yesterday's interview, His Majesty can only await Your Serene Highness's immediate resignation. Your Serene Highness will be good enough to be at the Palace at two o'clock, to hand over your office." "I am not well enough to go to the Palace," retorted Bismarck. "I will write."

The Chancellor took several days to comply with the monarch's command, partly because he knew how irritating the suspense would be, and partly because he wished to find the words that would do William most damage. He fastened the blame for his departure on the Order of 1852 and the Emperor's high-handedness in going over his Chancellor's head. However, his carefully chosen phrases presenting himself as the defender of constitutional rule against the Sovereign's arbitrary whims were not known until after his death in 1898, as the Kaiser suppressed its publication.

As far as William was concerned the next few days were filled with acute anxiety. What if the old man changed his mind? What if he had a trump card that would make them look ridiculous? While Bismarck was working on his statement the Emperor dined in company with Count Eulenburg. He was asked to calm the Sovereign's nerves with music. Obediently he played and sang while William sat next to him, turning the pages and joining in the choruses. "He was wholly absorbed," wrote Eulenburg, "thoroughly enjoying himself. His remarkably adaptable temperament did not desert him in these anxious hours. Only for a few minutes was the music interrupted by the burning political question—the Emperor, called out to hear Hahnke's answer, sat down again at once by the piano, and said softly: 'The resignation is all right.' Upon this he went on singing."[1]

Everyone behaved badly. Waldersee crowed, Holstein pretended that he had taken no part in the affair, Eulenburg tried to keep in

[1] *Aus 50 Jahren:* Prince Philipp zu Eulenburg-Hertefeldt.

with both sides. The Chancellor and Emperor behaved worst of all. Bismarck wept and thundered and criticised the Sovereign to anyone who would listen. He even called on the Empress Frederick, forgetful of his brutal behaviour to her, and with tears in his eyes said: " All I want is a little sympathy." When William awarded him a grant of money and the title " Duke of Lauenberg " he refused the money and announced caustically that he would use the title when he wished to travel incognito. When he left for his country estate several thousand people and many dignitaries gathered at the station to bid him goodbye; there was even a band which played a slow march. " A state funeral," observed Bismarck caustically, " with full honours." After that, whenever he took coins out of his pocket he made a point of turning the Imperial Eagle upwards so he would not have to see " that false face."

William used different tactics. He simply lied. He could not make up his mind what pose to adopt for the sake of public opinion, so he tried several attitudes. He informed Queen Victoria that he had dismissed Bismarck in order to force the old man to conserve his health and that they had parted with tears and embraces; he told the British Ambassador in Berlin that Bismarck had made such a violent scene that he expected an ink-pot to come hurtling at his head, and dignity had compelled him to ask for his resignation; he told the Czar's brother that Bismarck's departure had caused him almost as much sadness as his grandfather's death; and he told the Emperor of Austria that he had dismissed the Chancellor because he refused to co-operate.

He sent along a letter to Franz Joseph full of sentiment and falsehoods. " The man whom all my life I have looked upon as a demigod," he wrote to the Emperor Franz Joseph, " for whom I had endured in my parents' home a moral persecution like the pains of hell, the man for whom, after the death of the Emperor William, I had thrown myself alone into the breach in order to retain him,[1] bringing upon myself the anger of my dying father and the inextinguishable hatred of my mother, was looking on all this as nothing, striding past and ignoring me, because I was not ready to bow to his will. His boundless contempt of humanity, which he had for all, even those who were working themselves to death for him, did him a bad turn here, when he took his master for a nobody and

[1] There was no question of the stricken Frederick wishing to dismiss Bismarck.

tried to degrade him to a retainer. When he took his leave he charged me with having chased him away with insults; to this I naturally made no reply."[1]

William presented much the same version to the Czar of Russia, and was delighted by the reply. "Thou wast entirely right," said the Czar. "The Prince, though a prince, was after all only thy minister, thy servant. As such, his first duty was to obey thee. His disobedience to his Emperor brought his fall. In thy place I should have done just the same. . . ."

Count von Waldersee, despite all his machinations, did not become Chancellor. Instead, the Kaiser appointed an honest, bullet-headed soldier, General Caprivi. This poor man was not equipped for his position. Sometimes he sat with his head in his hands, and once he said: "I feel as though I were groping in a dark room. . . . The great man overshadows me completely." When he expressed his misgivings to the Kaiser, William remarked briskly: "There's no need for you to be anxious; one man's much like another, and I'll accept the responsibility for all transactions."

Bismarck could not take his successor seriously and barely alluded to him. However, when the harassed Caprivi cut down the trees in the Chancellery garden to make the rooms lighter, the old man expostulated that his confidence in the character of the general had undergone a shock. "I would pardon Herr von Caprivi many differences of political opinion rather than the ruthless destruction of trees."

The trees, however, were not the only things to go. Within ten days of the old Chancellor's departure the Kaiser and Caprivi managed, almost by whim, to kick Bismarck's main prop out from under the German Empire. The Russian Ambassador, Count Shuvalov, had called at the Chancellery on March 17th to discuss the Reinsurance Treaty, which had been signed in 1887 for three years, and which Bismarck had informed him he would like to renew. When he was told that the Chancellor was busy composing his letter of resignation he was so astonished that he wired to St. Petersburg that an explosion was taking place so strange that it made him wonder whether the young Emperor was "in a normal state." A few days later he told Count Herbert Bismarck—who had also

[1] *Kaiser and Chancellor*: Karl Novak.

handed in his resignation—that in the light of the new developments he would have to reconsider his offer. This message reached the Kaiser late at night on the 21st. He was so excited that he sent a messenger to wake up the Ambassador and ask him to come to the palace at eight the next morning. Shuvalov did as he was bid, and the Emperor received him instantly. "Sit down and listen to me," said William II. "You know how much I love and respect your Sovereign. Your Emperor has been too good to me for me to do otherwise than to inform him personally of the situation created by the events which have just taken place. . . . I beg you to tell His Majesty that on my part I am entirely disposed to renew our agreement, that my foreign policy remains and will remain the same as it was in the time of my grandfather." When the Czar read this wire he wrote on it: "Nothing more satisfactory could be looked for. We shall see by the sequel whether deeds correspond to words."[1]

At this point Baron Holstein stepped in. He was determined to establish himself as the master of the Wilhelmstrasse from the outset. Furthermore, he had been bitterly critical of Bismarck's policy in recent years, and it would scarcely stamp him as a man of independence if he tamely accepted the old man's treaty as his first act. So he began to raise objections which were echoed by other members of the Foreign Office. The treaty, he said, was not compatible with the terms of the Triple Alliance, and if it became known would damage Germany's relations with Austria. And with Bismarck in a rage, could anyone guarantee that it would not become known?

This squalid argument proved decisive with the Kaiser, and the treaty was turned down. A few weeks later the German Ambassador in St. Petersburg warned Berlin that Russia "might seek elsewhere the support she has failed to find with us;" and three months later, in June 1890, the Czar took the first step towards closer relations with France. "I could not but regard this," wrote Bismarck in 1896, "as a caprice of destiny, and history may have to call it a fatality."[2]

Meanwhile, in March 1890, the world was speculating on the departure of the most famous statesman in Europe. Bismarck had

[1] *The Origins of the World War:* Sidney Fay.

[2] *Reflections and Memories:* Otto von Bismarck.

been far from popular in England and France, but now people began to wonder if his successor would prove more troublesome. Sir William Harcourt wrote to Mr. John Morley: "What do you say to the removal of the great German panjandrum himself? It is not a pleasant prospect to have Europe left to the mercy of a hothead who seems also to be a fool."[1] The French were more analytical. The de Goncourt brothers noted in their journal: "This young German Emperor, this neurotic mystic, this enthusiast for the religious and warlike operas of Wagner, this man who, in his dreams, wears the white armour of Parsifal, with his sleepless nights, his sickly activity, his feverish brain, seems to be a monarch who will be very troublesome in the future."

[1] *Life of Sir William Harcourt*: Gardiner.

5. *Count Eulenburg*

"Pray do not believe that my son does anything for any other reason than vanity," the Empress Frederick remarked wearily. One of the vanities she most disliked was William's attitude as "head of the House of Hohenzollern." He declared that all members of the family, no matter how remotely connected, reflected the Imperial glory; therefore they must give him absolute obedience. He exercised tyrannical control, not only as custodian of their morals and religious beliefs, but in the running of their day-to-day lives. He felt free to criticise their clothes, manners, friends, and recreations. They could not engage courtiers without his approval or even travel from one city to another without his permission. The ladies and gentlemen of their households were informed that their duty lay, not with their immediate masters, but with the Emperor; consequently they must report any irregularities to The All Highest himself.

The Empress Frederick refused to heed her son's dicta. Once she sent him a message that she was leaving on a visit to England in the morning, and *not* to come to the station. William complained to Field Marshal von Waldersee that he could not understand his mother's ingratitude; had he not provided her with houses and money? "Of course it would be far better for me to go away from Berlin and not return," the Empress wrote to her daughter Sophie, eighteen months after her husband's death, "but I cannot be banished from the spot where my darling husband and two sweet children lie buried, nor leave the house for good and all where we spent so many years together, and where now recollections haunt every nook and corner, nor can I abandon the many institutions and works of charity of which I am the patroness and who constantly want me, so all these considerations make it impossible for me to leave Berlin altogether. Besides it would look as if I were afraid of them—William and Dona—if I gave up my rights, and as if they had succeeded in frightening or driving me away. . . ."[1]

So the Empress remained in Germany, sad and embittered, complaining to Queen Victoria of her son's slights. "When I was in Berlin I saw William three times. . . . The whole time he was gay and merry, but quite indifferent, never asking me one question about myself, and not one sympathising or kind word was uttered!" William probably would have been surprised if he had seen these pathetic outpourings, for he did not regard his mother as a pathetic person. He saw her as a clever, iron-willed woman with an "undeniable love of power." Indeed, he astonished the British Ambassador, Sir Edward Malet, at a dinner party by referring proudly to their likenesses. "My mother and I have the same characters. I have inherited hers. That good stubborn English blood which will not give way is in both our veins. The consequence is that, if we do not happen to agree, the situation becomes difficult."[2]

William made life difficult for his sisters as well. Princess Victoria still pined for her lover, Prince Alexander of Battenberg, and lived in the forlorn hope that her brother one day would withdraw his refusal. However, Alexander grew tired of waiting and finally married a Viennese opera singer. Victoria's sister, Sophie, was more fortunate. In 1889 she married the Duke of Sparta, Crown Prince of Greece. But even Sophie, in far-away Athens, could not escape William's interference. In 1891 she wrote her mother that she had decided to adopt the Greek Orthodox religion. When William heard of it he declared that it was a slight to German Protestantism and warned her that if she took such a step he would not allow her to set foot in Germany again. She argued that she was not changing her religion for worldly considerations but conviction. She sent the correspondence to her mother but the Empress was sceptical. "I am afraid your kind and nice words will be lost on him, as he has absolutely *no heart*. . . . He is, besides, not learned enough to understand that our Christian Religion has centuries ago divided itself into branches, of which each one naturally considers itself the true one, the purest and the best. . . . With William it is *not religion* that vexes him, it is his silly vanity and pride of being 'head of the family,' and *their* being obliged to

[1] *The Empress Frederick Writes to Sophie:* edited by Arthur Gould Lee.

[2] *Letters of Queen Victoria.*

bend to his will. . . ."[1] As the Empress predicted, William was not touched by Sophie's appeal and notified her that she was " banished " from Germany. She telegraphed the news to her mother, sending the message *en clair* so that all the officials could read it. " Received answer. Keeps to what he said at Berlin. Fixes it to three years. Mad. Never mind. Sophie."

Another target for the Kaiser's disapproval was his wife's younger sister, Princess Louise Sophie, who had married his second cousin, Prince Frederick Leopold. This little couple, young and gay, offended William by their independence. Sometimes he commanded his wife to reprimand her younger sister, sometimes he did it himself. Once, at a Court function, the Princess wore a cream-coloured satin dress with red poppies painted on it. " What ! " exclaimed the Emperor. " A perfect flower garden." Next day she received a message forbidding her to appear in such a striking frock.

The couple objected to the spying and tittle-tattle that went on between members of their own household and the Imperial Court, and the bad feeling, engendered by spiteful ladies-in-waiting, provided the background for a fantastic episode which occurred in the winter of 1895. The Princess lived at Glienecke, not far from Berlin. One day, when her husband was away, she decided to go skating. She was not supposed to leave the house without both a lady and a gentleman in attendance, and the gentleman had gone home on leave. However, since the lake was close and it was unlikely anyone would notice, she summoned her lady and set forth. They planned to skate to the other side, but the Princess had not gone more than a hundred yards before the ice broke and she fell in. Her companion tried to help her and fell in too. An old man saw them and came running to pull them out. Then he fell in.

Luckily a group of farm workers were near the bank and shouted that they would fetch a ladder. It took them nearly twenty minutes to get it, and when the three victims were finally pulled out they were more dead than alive. The Princess was given brandy, wrapped in blankets and driven home. A doctor was summoned from Berlin and while she lay in bed, still shivering convulsively, a servant announced that her sister, the Empress, had called to see her. Knowing that she would get into trouble for having gone out

[1] *The Empress Frederick Writes to Sophie :* edited by Arthur Gould Lee.

accompanied only by a lady, she sent a message that she was in bed with a cold, and begged to be excused. Unfortunately news of the adventure appeared in the evening papers. The Princess immediately scribbled a note to her sister explaining that she had felt unable to receive her as she was still suffering from shock. But the harm was done. Although the Princess woke up the next day with inflammation of the veins, there was to be no forgiveness.

Two days later the Emperor's A.D.C. appeared with a letter from his royal master to the Prince: " In spite of frequent admonitions you have not been lucky enough to guide and keep your wife in the conception of life proper to a Prussian Princess, which she has the high honour to be. I am, therefore, forced to use severe measures to make you both comprehend that, in virtue of my office as Chief and Head of the Family, I have the power to insist on the observance of laws of traditions, decency and custom.

" Your Court will be secluded from every communication from the outer world for fourteen days. You are to regard yourself as under arrest and to deliver your sword to my Adjutant. An officer will patrol Glienecke. From now onwards your wife is not allowed to leave the garden without *a Gentleman and a Lady*; the Mistress of the Robes is to be received daily by her for a short time and, as it should be, treated like *a lady*. Also, to ride without a Lady is forbidden! The arrest applies to your wife as well as yourself. I think fourteen days of quiet thinking will make clear to her that it is better to accommodate herself to the existing statutes. Wilhelm R."

" Those indeed were a sad fourteen days passed by us," wrote the Princess, " labouring under a sense of injustice for which there was no redress, days which neither my husband nor I could ever forget. I must confess that the first thing I did was to climb on a chair and take down the only portrait of the Emperor we had, tear it to pieces and throw it into the fire. After that I felt decidedly better."[1]

Once the old Chancellor had departed, William II was consumed by one overwhelming desire: to win fame for the House of Hohenzollern by overshadowing Bismarck's achievements with even more glorious achievements of his own. Bismarck had

[1] *Behind the Scenes at the Prussian Court:* Princess Frederick Leopold of Prussia.

unified Germany and forged it into the greatest power on the continent, and now William, with all the restless ambition of youth, desired to take her a step farther along the path of greatness and build her into an international power. His mother's gibes at German provincialism had not been lost on him; secretly he admired and envied the sophisticated internationalism that stemmed from Britain's world-wide authority. The great imperial capital of London, nerve-centre of trade and finance, extending like a giant web over the face of the globe, excited his imagination, and provoked a deep and painful jealousy. This is what he wanted for Germany. He had no thought of war, but aspired to a voice that could be heard across the oceans of the world. He would throw the Hohenzollern gauntlet into the arena by expanding his colonial possessions and building a navy. His first act after Bismarck's departure was to swap Germany's Zanzibar, off the coast of Africa, for Britain's Heligoland, in order to secure an important naval base. "The course remains the same," he told Eulenburg cheerfully, "'Full steam ahead' is the order."

But was the course the same? Bismarck had become cautious in his old age, and increasingly impressed by the advantages of peace and retrenchment. Germany, he decided, must remain inside the frontiers he had drawn for her, and so in his latter years he had bent all his energies to insuring and reinsuring the permanence of those frontiers. He not only had guarded himself by the treaty with Russia—abandoned by William—and by the Triple Alliance with Italy and Austria, but had built up a barricade of lesser agreements. For instance, in order to increase harmony with Britain he had persuaded Italy and Austria to sign ententes with London, pledging themselves to observe the status quo of Turkey and the Mediterranean. And he even dropped the idea of building a colonial empire because, he said, it would bring him into too much conflict with England. Although in the eighties he had acquired German New Guinea and territories in Africa known as German West Africa, German South West Africa, and the German Cameroons, he did nothing to develop them and at the end of the decade spoke of them with contempt as "a burden and an expense," not worth England's hostility. "Here is France and here is Russia with Germany in the middle," he once remarked to a famous explorer. "That is my map of Africa."

However, this careful conservative Bismarck of advanced years was not an image with which the public was familiar, for his cautious views—like many of his treaties—were cunningly hidden beneath the bluff exterior. The public only knew the Bismarck who had given Germany the finest army in Europe, the Bismarck of blood and iron, the Bismarck who as late as 1888 had thrilled the Reichstag, in his last speech, by declaring: " We Germans fear God and nothing else in the world." Even the ministers who served under him were scarcely aware of his preoccupation with safety; for had he not, only a few weeks before his resignation, been pressing the young Kaiser to tear up the Constitution, abolish universal suffrage, and, if necessary, fight the Socialists with bullets?

If William II's course was not the same as Bismarck's, at least his reign was the natural, almost inevitable result of the Bismarck philosophy and the Bismarck success. Indeed, it is doubtful whether Bismarck himself could have continued to rule by a policy of restraint, for he had kindled desires in the hearts of his countrymen which could not easily be extinguished. William II could almost be described as the Chancellor's own creation, for who but Bismarck had inflamed the young Prince's mind with the glory of monarchy, the desirability of autocracy, the power of intimidation? The Empress Frederick had foreseen the eventual consequences and for years bemoaned them to her mother. " Prince Bismarck has so much that is brutal and cynical in his nature, so little that is noble and upright, he is so completely a man of another century than ours, that as an example of an ideal he becomes very dangerous," she had written in 1887. " He is a patriot and a genius but as a school, there could not be a worse one! Opinions such as William holds are very much the fashion nowadays in Germany—they have half-created the immense power Bismarck possesses and he had half-created them. . . ."[1]

The most striking differences between the two regimes was that Bismarck's rule was competent and William's was not. Although the young Kaiser was a highly political animal—a fact that the old Chancellor had not fully appreciated—he was not capable of serious application. He disliked routine and even refused to set aside a regular day a week for consultation with his Chancellor. He preferred to rule by impulse and interference. Indeed, this was the

[1] *Letters of the Empress Frederick.*

only way he was capable of ruling, for although he had a quick mind and a wide range of interests, although he could assimilate facts with astonishing rapidity and often amazed scientists, artists, philosophers, and business men with his grasp of their problems, he lacked the patience to reflect and the power to reason. His head was full of information but he could not work out a logical course, or even adhere to one; invariably he gave way to the whim of the moment, changing his opinions with bewildering frequency. So he scribbled impetuous comments on the margins of state papers, wrote private letters to his fellow monarchs, held indiscreet conversations with foreign military attachés, and, when he felt inclined, made sensational pronouncements. He adored public ceremonies. He liked uniforms, decorations, crowds, and splendour. Best of all, he liked making speeches. Every time he unveiled a statue, inspected a regiment, or launched a ship he seized the opportunity to address his people; he made over 400 speeches during the first ten years of his reign.

The substitution of William's erratic gestures for Bismarck's purposeful grip created an uncertainty which was soon exploited by cliques and personalities vying with each other for the Kaiser's favour. The new Imperial Chancellor, General Caprivi, and the new State Secretary, Baron von Marschall, who had taken Count Herbert Bismarck's place, could do little to control events, for both were political novices. Caprivi made his position clear in his opening speech to the Reichstag when he said: "I am here by the orders of my Supreme Lord, and I will carry on the business of the Empire as he wishes, so long as I am able to enjoy his confidence and receive his commands." Marschall was scarcely more robust, for he began by ingratiating himself to the Kaiser's friend, Count Eulenburg. Despite the fact that Eulenburg, as a member of the diplomatic corps, was Marschall's direct subordinate, the latter wrote to him "with the heartfelt request that you will help me further by work and deed . . . as also by unhesitating criticism."

The most formidable figure to step into the Bismarck vacuum was Baron von Holstein of the Foreign Office. Both Caprivi and Marschall were so inexperienced that they regarded Holstein as indispensable. Although they were aware of his sinister reputation and abnormal mind, the fact that he had been trained by Bismarck and knew more about Germany's intricate network of treaties than anyone else gave him indisputed authority in their eyes. It did not seem to occur to them that a man with so twisted an outlook might draw false deductions and proffer unsound judgements. Instead they regarded him as an oracle. They accepted without demur his denunciation of the Reinsurance Treaty with Russia, and persuaded the Kaiser to do likewise. And by this act alone they handed him the mastery of the Foreign Office. No one except Bismarck—and he was not entirely objective—foresaw what a disaster he would prove for Germany. On the contrary, his benign, scholarly, bespectacled appearance, and above all his modesty, created an air of confidence. He refused promotion and continued to cling to the protective shadows of the back rooms. He even avoided meeting the Kaiser. " Only once," wrote William II, " did he consent to dine with me at the Foreign Office." Instead he worked in the devious ways congenial to him, using Philip Eulenburg to impress his views—the Government's views as he put it—upon the Emperor.

Eulenburg's magic for the Emperor was undiminished. " When he set foot in our Potsdam home," wrote William, " it was as if the common day was flooded with sunshine."[1] No one could transform the imperial spirits or smooth away the scowls as quickly as he. The Emperor referred to him as his best friend, and always begged him to accompany him on his trips. The Count had many good qualities. He had no malice, he was warm-hearted, hard-working, shrewd, and genuinely devoted to his master. Undoubtedly he was the best influence William ever had. His greatest fault was his dislike of responsibility. Like Holstein, he shrank from direct control. He might have become Foreign Secretary in 1893 but he rejected the idea, saying that " perpetual intercourse with the Emperor would impair my influence . . . only while I represent the Emperor's friend, whom he is glad to see again, whose letters he likes and attends to, am I serviceable to him and the Fatherland. . . ."[2] So he chose to work in a feminine way, delighting the Kaiser with his witty talk, wrapping his criticisms in silky words, and always watching and waiting for the right moment to cajole and persuade.

Holstein soon regarded Eulenburg as indispensable. Although

[1] *My Early Life :* William II.

[2] *Philip Eulenburg : The Kaiser's Friend :* Johannes Haller.

officially the Count performed the duty of Prussian Ambassador to Oldenburg, unofficially—as Holstein put it—he was German Ambassador to the Emperor. He must keep up a close correspondence with William; see him as much as possible; and report back every reaction. Apart from this, Holstein bombarded him with instructions. "Waldersee [Chief of the Imperial General Staff] must go. He would be an inconvenience in case of war, for the Emperor does not respect him. But he mustn't be made ambassador either, for then he would be dangerous to Caprivi. Also you must utter a warning against Count Wedel, who is trying for the Petersburg Embassy. In general, take a stand against the idea that military men are more reliable than civilians," or: "You might suggest to H.M. that he . . . should show a special mark in favour of Koch. It will gain H.M. a great deal of approbation, and give that conceited Birchov, that bull in the scientific china-shop, a nasty slap in the face," or: "Please get some shifting done—Rantzau to Stockholm, Busch to Stuttgart. You could tell Rantzau that, if he likes, he might be held en disposition for Brussels, the Hague, or Madrid."[1] On the margin on this letter Eulenburg wrote: "I should not *dream* of putting a finger against Rantzau." Eulenburg could only be pushed so far, for he was loyal to his royal master and refused to carry out instructions if he disagreed with them.

Holstein's interests were not only confined to personalities and soon he was asking Eulenburg to relay advice to the Kaiser on matters ranging from army reform to education bills, from suggestions for speeches to methods of handling the Reichstag. This may seem a curious role for a diplomat but as Germany was a federation of semi-autonomous states, ruled by hereditary princes, it had long been a tradition of the Foreign Office to consider any major issue within its province, and to meddle in anything it liked. Eulenburg's life became particularly arduous when he accompanied the Emperor abroad, for Holstein's telegrams were persistent and feverish and as the Count had no secretariat he often sat up, drafting replies, until the small hours of the morning. He had to conceal his labours from the Emperor for it would never do to allow work to interfere with the imperial pleasure; his was the role of the eternally light-hearted companion. When he travelled on the Kaiser's yacht to Italy in 1894, he wrote in his diary: "Every

[1] *Philip Eulenburg: The Kaiser's Friend:* Johannes Haller.

moment come dispatches which I have to attend to . . . and then I must go to the Emperor and change my clothes between whiles. In the morning a lounge suit; for lunch frock coat; if we are yachting, yachting dress; for dinner evening dress and a black tie. It is often such a rush that I dictate the most important dispatches while I am washing my hands. . . . I am like a wretched beetle that has fallen into an ant hill!" However, there was no escape, for Eulenburg's influence rested on always being a stimulating and agreeable companion. "Although I am pretty well fed-up with the everlasting tennis and the 'Christabel,' I should only injure myself to the Emperor's disadvantage if I insisted on working instead. That is precisely why he lets me say anything I like to him about politics . . . because I play tennis with him and in between rallies and pauses have a good-humoured ear at my disposal, ready to listen to tiresome matters because he is in high spirits."[1]

There were other aspects of his role that Eulenburg disliked. He loathed the Kaiser's entourage. Sensitive and imaginative, he found the crude, hide-bound mentality of the Prussian "Junker" almost unendurable. Yet these were the men the Emperor felt at ease with, basking in their sycophantic remarks, roaring with laughter at their coarse jokes, invariably alluding to them as "brother officers." Every July the Kaiser organised a male yachting trip to Norway with only a dozen picked men-friends on board. For Eulenburg these excursions were an ordeal. In the evening the guests were called upon to amuse the Sovereign. Count Goerz was a great success because he could make animal noises; Count Kiderlen, Holstein's adjutant at the Foreign Office, delighted the Emperor with dirty jokes; Count Hulsen did conjuring tricks, and some of the other guests performed song and dance acts, two of them dressing up as the Siamese twins, connected by an enormous sausage. In the mornings the Kaiser insisted on all his guests doing physical exercises on deck. It amused him to walk behind them when they were squatting and topple them over. "The old boys professed to be greatly delighted by this attention but clenched their fists in their pockets, and afterwards abused the Emperor like fishwives," wrote Kiderlen.

Eulenburg was not only bored by the company, but repelled by William's liking for "horseplay." This tendency grew more

[1] *Philip Eulenburg: The Kaiser's Friend:* Johannes Haller.

pronounced as the years advanced until Count Zedlitz, a Court official, was afraid it might give rise to unpleasant stories. The Emperor, he said, was "accustomed to amuse himself quite innocently, but still childishly, with certain people. He has for a long time past been treating von Neumann as a sort of Clown and Court fool, and he tickles and pinches Lieutenant Commander von H . . . until he makes the oddest noises." Almost all the members of the Kaiser's entourage had to submit to these indignities but Count Eulenburg was an exception. "The Emperor has never touched me—he knows that I would not suffer it," he wrote.

However, Eulenburg did not escape all humiliation. The Kaiser had a passion for uniform, and when he visited Eulenburg at his country estate, Liebenberg, he solemnly invested him with a "Court shooting dress" which he had designed himself and insisted that all his friends should wear. "It is quite indescribably uncomfortable," wrote the Count, "being in shape like a regular uniform coat and having a high collar. But as I am very frankly a civilian and intend to remain one, the military collar oppresses me not only because it inevitably recalls those utterly unbearable hours with foul-mouthed riding-masters and still fouler-mouthed commanding officers, but also because I feel perfectly sick when I have convulsively to fasten the infamous choker. And why, to complete the shooting-dress, *high brown boots with silver spurs*! should be worn, is to me an enigma. . . . To have to prance about in my old Liebenberg, when the Emperor visits me, got-up like that, making my reports to him in my peaceful room with clinking spurs, singing songs!! No; it is like spiritual cod-liver oil to me. And I will *not* be dressed like the 'Imperial Household.' I am something other than that."[1] Yet in the end he submitted and wore the uniform with no further grumbling.

Eulenburg's most thankless task was to try and curb the Kaiser's indiscretions. His passion for making speeches often seemed to end in trouble, for although he was a remarkable orator his pronouncements seem to stem from another century and were studded with references to the glories of monarchical rule "by the Grace of God"; to greatness, obedience, sacrifice, vengeance, and duty. "Him who opposes me will I smash," he declared on one occasion, and

[1] *Philip Eulenburg: The Kaiser's Friend:* Johannes Haller.

" I will lead you to days of glory," on another. When a newspaper referred to him disobligingly, he closed down the press. " A spirit of insubordination is abroad in the land ; it takes many glittering and alluring disguises, thus confusing the minds of my people and those who are devoted to me ; it presses into its service oceans of printers' ink and paper. . . ."

However, it was not only speech-making that got him into trouble. When he went to Munich in the autumn of 1891 he wrote his name in the Golden Book, dashing off the inscription " *Regis voluntas suprema lex*." As the King of Bavaria was mad, this drew forth sharp rebuke from Eulenburg. " The phrase has given much offence in the highest quarters because here *regis voluntas* is—insanity ! And also because the people, quite apart from this, thought to perceive as it were an Imperial will predominant over the Bavarian will. All parties without exception have been offended by Your Majesty's inscription." However, when Eulenburg wrote so sharply, he found that the Kaiser did not answer, so he tried to cloak his admonitions in flattery. After the " paths of glory " speech he wrote : " In Your Majesty's gift of eloquence there lies a danger—that Your Majesty may make too great use of it—If Your Majesty would be more economical of such a gift, it would be a hundredfold more efficacious. . . . If Your Majesty speaks on every occasion, Your Majesty squanders your advantage in having so fine a talent." Frequently the Kaiser's pronouncements brought him worldwide publicity. In 1891 he was so incensed by a few mild Socialist demonstrations that he forgot his declaration to Bismarck of only the year before, about wishing to be King of the Poor, and made an extraordinary address to a group of new army recruits. " You have sworn loyalty to me ; that means, children of my guard, that you are now my soldiers, you have given yourself to me body and soul ; there is for you but one enemy, and that is my enemy. In view of the present socialist agitations it may come to pass that I shall command you to shoot your own relatives, brothers, yes, parents—which God forbid—but even then you must follow my command without a murmur."[1] The speech created a sensation on the continent and drew from Tolstoi, the Russian novelist, the comment that the Kaiser obviously had a diseased mind.

[1] *Neisser Zeitung*.

The Emperor made disturbing mistakes in handling the members of his own entourage. In 1892 a scandal blew up at Court. All ranks of society, including the Empress, began receiving anonymous letters in the same handwriting, telling of scandals and intrigues taking place among the courtiers. Pornographic pictures were enclosed in which the heads were cut off and replaced by photographs of well-known people. Despite every effort to find the guilty party, the letters continued to arrive for two years. It was obvious that they were written by someone in the inner circle, for the allegations bore semblance to the truth. The Kaiser had two Masters of Ceremonies, Baron von Schrader and Count von Kotze. The austere Schrader hated the convivial Kotze, and one day was excited to find on Kotze's desk two sheets of blotting paper bearing handwriting which, he claimed, was identical with that of the letters. He took the blotting paper to the Kaiser and convinced him of his case. Kotze was visiting his mother at his country house. He returned to the Palace next day to find himself under arrest "in the King's name." Although he hotly asserted his innocence, he was taken to the Military Prison to await trial.

He was denied paper and pencil and kept under close guard. A few days later more anonymous letters were received at Court. The Kaiser realised that he had acted too hastily; a mistake had been made. Only then did he bother to consult a graphologist who told him that Kotze's handwriting bore no resemblance to that of the pornographic letters. Nevertheless there was no stopping the trial. "I have nothing to do with this business," said the Emperor. "The investigation is now being conducted by the Judge Advocate of the Court." By this time the scandal had spread far and wide, and the name "Kotze" had become a synonym for pornography. Although the Judge finally acquitted him, he had received a stigma which he could not shake off. Only the Kaiser could have repaired his damaged reputation by a strong public apology. But William was not so inclined. Instead he merely sent him an Easter gift—an egg, made of flowers. Kotze challenged von Schrader to a duel and killed him. Then he retired from Berlin, his career ruined, and buried himself in the country.

Eulenburg tried to counter the military influence surrounding the Kaiser by urging him to behave less autocratically and more "constitutionally." What did he mean? Was Germany not an autocracy; and what, in fact, were the Kaiser's powers? The truth was that the position was not altogether clear. Prince Bismarck had drawn up the Constitution of 1871 to suit his own requirements. He had designed it to give himself dictatorial powers in the name of the Emperor and at the same time to persuade the liberals that he was planting the seeds of parliamentary rule. Thus the result was a mixture of anomalies; an autocracy which had to keep an eye on public opinion, dominated by an ill-defined partnership between Emperor and Chancellor.

There were two separate water-tight branches of Government beneath the Emperor: military and civil. The civil head was an Imperial Chancellor, appointed by the Emperor and responsible only to the Emperor. The legislative body was a Reichstag, dominated by an Upper Chamber composed of the princely rulers of the German states. These gentlemen, presided over by the Imperial Chancellor, initiated all legislation; and since the Chancellor usually was Prime Minister of Prussia as well—and Prussia could always muster a majority vote—the German Empire plainly appeared to be a dictatorship in the hands of the Emperor. Yet it was not as simple as that. Unless the Chancellor carried the princes by persuasion there was always the danger of separatist movements. Furthermore, there was the Lower Chamber to consider.

This assembly was elected by universal male suffrage, a privilege which very few countries in Europe enjoyed. However, their powers were almost illusory. They could not initiate legislation, and had no say over such vital matters as foreign affairs or declarations of war; and although their approval was necessary before bills became law very little of importance came before them as the Government was not dependent on them for votes of money. Revenue was raised by indirect taxation fixed by royal decree. However, Bismarck had been obliged to give them one trump card. They had the right to approve or reject the military budget submitted to them every five years. Thus they could control the size of the German Army. Although the Kaiser could dissolve the Reichstag whenever he liked, and keep on dissolving it, the public could show their disapproval by sending back the same deputies. This nearly happened in 1893 when Caprivi's army estimates were rejected, a new election was held, and the bill only passed by a majority of eleven votes.

The very fact that the Reichstag, despite its limited powers, served as a mirror of public opinion caused Eulenburg to beg the Emperor not to ride over it rough-shod but to treat it with respect. "Blockheads," declared William irritably. They passed the Army Bill by the narrowest margin and refused to contemplate an increase in the navy. They could not seem to understand the necessity for a navy. Even Bismarck had shown a lack of comprehension when William, still a prince, had raised the matter with him. "I pointed out that steps must be taken towards the construction of a fleet, in order that German foreign interest should not be without protection; that since the prince had unfurled the German flag in foreign parts, and the people stood behind it, there must also be a navy behind it. But the prince turned a deaf ear to my statements and merely used his pet phrase: 'If the English should land on our soil, I should have them arrested.' His idea was that the colonies would be defended by us at home." William II felt that Bismarck's lack of understanding was simply old age; Germany was entering a new era and until his deputies grasped the necessity of a fleet and showed their willingness to pass a fleet bill, they would remain "fools and blockheads."

Eulenburg also tried to persuade the Emperor not to interfere too much in the work of his ministers. Although there was no clear division, constitutionally, between the Chancellor's authority and the royal prerogative, most Germans believed that they were treading a path towards parliamentary rule. They would be shocked if they felt that they were returning to the days of monarchical absolutism. Therefore the Kaiser must avoid all acts or even gestures which gave an impression of "personal rule."

Eulenburg's words, however, had little effect on William for they were drowned by the military environment in which the Kaiser lived. The Imperial Palace overflowed with army officers. The Kaiser's household was headed by General von Plessen and almost all the Court officials were soldiers with an occasional admiral thrown in. Under the German Constitution the army was responsible directly to the Emperor who, in time of war, automatically became Supreme War Lord. The élite Officers Corps constituted a privileged class above the law, akin in some ways to a mediaeval Order of Knighthood. Its members could not be tried by civilian courts, nor apprehended by the public police. They could be punished only by their own Court of Honour. As a result officers, and particularly Prussian officers, were inclined to regard themselves as demi-gods. They did not consider themselves servants of the State but servants of the Emperor—knightly paladins bound to their All-Highest Sovereign by the romantic, mystical oath of fealty which they swore to his person. Consequently, most of them despised civilian institutions in general and democratic institutions in particular. The Reichstag and the press aroused their deepest contempt, and they not only delighted the Kaiser but encouraged his autocratic tendencies by their eagerness for "strong action." Once, when a spate of articles critical of the Kaiser appeared in the press, General von Plessen was asked how he would handle the editors. "We must train the guns on them. Then they will shut up." The Kaiser contemplated sending his A.D.C.'s to challenge the editors, but finally thought better of it.

In his efforts to undermine A.D.C. influence, Eulenburg occasionally overstepped the mark. When Colonel Engelbrecht, the German military attaché in Rome, sent personal reports to the Emperor directly contrary to Foreign Office advice, Eulenburg protested to William but received a sharp rebuke. "As to Engelbrecht you've been mistaken all along. I expressly desire you to warn the Foreign Office against any further attacks on him. He has given me complete satisfaction . . . and is *my brother officer and A.D.C.* If there is any more of this kind of thing in the Foreign Office, I shall have something to say about it. Once and for all, I intend to have 'discipline on board;' else no useful work can possibly be done." Eulenburg commented gloomily in a memorandum: "And now comes the spectre of that monstrous Prussian Hohenzollern atavism peculiar to the First Guards Regiment, in the guise of the poor dear Emperor's letter. . . . For a Sovereign of the Emperor's impetuosity (called vigorous action) to be drawn once more into the atmosphere of guardsmen's rant, when with the infinite trouble and sacrifice of my own time and energy he had been at last in some degree removed from it, is melancholy indeed.'[1]

Eulenburg, at least, had the consolation that the fire-brand Chief

[1] *Philip Eulenburg : The Kaiser's Friend :* Johannes Haller.

of Staff, Count von Waldersee, had been removed from the scene. Waldersee had been bitterly disappointed not to receive the Chancellorship and had grown careless in his talk against the Emperor. Furthermore, when the Sovereign took part in the two-day annual manœuvres in the autumn of 1890, von Waldersee criticised the disposition of His Majesty's forces in front of all the princes. A few months later, in January 1891, William sent for the Count, decorated him with the Grand Commander of the Hohenzollern Order, and told him that he had an important new appointment for him—Command of an army corps. The fall from Chief of the german Staff to a Corps Commander was so great, Waldersee could find no words in reply. He went home fuming, talked it over with his army friend and decided to resign. William pleaded with him to reconsider. "I was not to mind what the world might say about it," wrote Waldersee in his diary, "but be satisfied with his friendship. He would give proof of it and show the world what it meant to be the friend of the German Kaiser. Whoever dared to say a word against me should be shattered; he would keep the press in order, and so on and so on. Finally he went so far as to entreat me in the tenderest tones. He took my hand and said: 'You will accept, won't you? Your Kaiser asks you.' I remained adamant, however, and I thank God that He gave me strength to do so."[1]

In the end Waldersee accepted the post of Corps Commander at Altona; he decided that the best course was to try and win back the Kaiser's favour, for no plums were to be had in Germany without the consent of The All Highest.

In the spring of 1894 General Caprivi threatened to resign. The Kaiser was trying to force him to introduce anti-Socialist legislation of which he disapproved, and he decided that he was sick of the whole business of being Chancellor. When Holstein heard rumours that he intended to go, he flew into a panic for fear Bismarck might return. Ever since he had played traitor to the Iron Chancellor, this contingency—which was only a figment of his imagination—had caused him constant anxiety, and he did everything he could to keep alive the Emperor's hostility. Events played into his hands, for Bismarck did not retire gracefully. He attacked the Emperor, the Government, and the Foreign Office in a series of anonymous

[1] *A Field Marshal's Memoirs:* Count von Waldersee.

articles which appeared in the *Hamburger Nachtrichten*. He ridiculed William for having exchanged Zanzibar for a " rock "—as he called it—in the North Sea. And he hinted darkly that things were not well with German policy, emphasising that Germany was only secure when she had a firm understanding with Russia.

The Government was flustered by the attacks, and many people urged the Emperor to silence the old man by a reconciliation. Bismarck stood for the Reichstag in 1891, then complained that he couldn't take his seat because he didn't have a house in Berlin. The Emperor was advised to offer him one of his palaces, but when Holstein heard of the plan he wrote an agitated letter to Eulenburg. " The intrigues about ' Bismarck's rehabilitation ' are being carried on with the most remarkable skill and a fair prospect of success. Just imagine that H.M. told the Chancellor, who told me to-day, that he was thinking of offering Prince Bismarck, should he be elected to the Reichstag, an abode in Bellevue Palace! . . . The moment he takes the first step toward Bismarck he ceases to be the first man in the Empire—Bismarck becomes *that*. . . . Could you not come here to warn the Emperor before he slides into the abyss? . . . Think of the consequences if H.M. lets himself be outwitted—he will never in his life recover from the effect."[1] Eulenburg obediently wrote to William pointing out the danger of such a reinstatement but apparently the Kaiser had never seriously entertained the idea, for he telegraphed breezily: " The premises are absolutely and completely false. I am steady as the Northern Star. Philip, don't you fall into every fool's trap. William."[1] The upshot of all this was that although Bismarck won his seat, he did not take it.

A year later, in 1892, Holstein seized the opportunity of striking a more resounding blow at Bismarck. The old Prince decided to travel to Vienna to attend the wedding of his son, Herbert, to an Austrian lady, and wrote to his friend, Prince Reuss, the German Ambassador, requesting an audience with the Emperor Franz Joseph. As soon as Holstein learned of this he drew up a minute for Reuss and persuaded General Caprivi to sign it. The Ambassador was not to attend the wedding ceremony and he was to let the Viennese Foreign Minister know that since Bismarck was travelling in a private capacity the German Government expected

[1] *Philip Eulenburg: The Kaiser's Friend*: Johannes Haller.

the official world to receive him with the "greatest possible reserve." Above all, the audience with the Emperor was to be prevented.

William readily lent himself to this shabby affair. "Bismarck," he wrote to Franz Joseph, "is to be in Vienna at the end of this month . . . in order to arrange for systematic ovations by his admirers. . . . You also know that one of his masterpieces was the secret treaty *à double fonds* with Russia, concluded behind your back, and abrogated by me. Ever since he retired, the Prince has waged war in the most perfidious manner against Me, Caprivi, and My Ministers. . . . The climax of his programme in this affair is the idea of an audience with you. I would therefore beg of you not to increase the difficulties in this country by receiving that disobedient subject before he has approached me with his *peccavi*."[1]

The Austrians did as they were bid. The Emperor refused to receive him, and his old acquaintances were "indisposed," "away in the country" or "not at home." Bismarck sensed what had happened and was consumed with wrath. To be insulted by a fatuous group of pygmies—the same men who by dropping the treaty with Russia were busy knocking down the walls of security which he so laboriously had erected around the Fatherland—was more than flesh and blood could stand. The Czar not only was cool towards Germany but turning towards Germany's implacable enemy France. Only twelve months earlier, in 1891, the French Fleet had visited the Russian port of Kronstadt, and the Czar had stood to attention while the hated revolutionary *Marseillaise* was played. It was obvious what was coming, but the Wilhelmstrasse, dominated by the crazy Holstein, sat back in smug contentment, unaware of the implications involved. Bismarck was so infuriated that he was stung into giving an interview to the *Neue Freie Presse* which, in an age of secret treaties, bordered on treachery. First, he took a crack at Holstein, then he hinted at the draft from Russia. ". . . In our Country such men have come to the front as I was careful to relegate to their native obscurity, precisely because they would be sure to change and upset the whole course of affairs. . . . More assuredly I am now absolved from any personal obligations whatever towards the dominating personalities of the moment, as well as towards my successor. Every bridge between us is broken

[1] *Grosse Politik.*

down. . . . In Berlin there is neither personal authority nor confidence. The Russian wire is cut—we are estranged."

The interview produced a crisis in Berlin. After several agitated meetings the Foreign Office decided to publish the instructions to Prince Reuss, restricting Bismarck's welcome, in order to show that the old man was merely lashing out in spitefulness, but this merely resulted in a boomerang. Public opinion was outraged by the meanness of the Foreign Office minute, and swung whole-heartedly behind the Prince. Overnight he achieved a popularity he had not enjoyed for years; and at last the Kaiser saw that his only course was to swallow his pride and try to make peace. A few months later Bismarck fell ill, and William offered him a palace in which to recuperate. But the Prince was not to be won so easily. "With the profoundest acknowledgement of Your Majesty's most gracious interest . . . but feel that my recovery will be best assisted by the domestic surroundings long familiar to me." The Kaiser persisted; first, a bottle of Rhine wine, then, in January 1894, an invitation to a Birthday Reception in Berlin. This time Bismarck accepted and attended the function accompanied by his son, Herbert. The reconciliation was only skin-deep. The Kaiser kissed his ex-Chancellor on both cheeks and showed him unflagging attention, but was careful to talk only of trivialities. However, as far as the world was concerned, peace was restored.

Eulenburg had played a leading part in restoring harmony, and Holstein found it hard to forgive him. His letters bristled with antagonism and Eulenburg wrote on one of them: "Smothered rage! If I were not what I am friend Holstein would throw me overboard!" Now that the Emperor was on speaking terms with Bismarck, Holstein scented his return to power in every event that took place. He drove Eulenburg nearly to distraction. The Count was not strong physically and suffered badly from nerves. At times it seemed as though he would crack under the strain. In March 1894 he wrote in his diary: "I spent literally the whole day in the Foreign Office which seems to me more and more like hell. Under old Bismarck one was disgusted by the terrifying fluttering at the thought of Jupiter's approach, and the disagreeable capricious treatment of subordinates. But now the fear of 'his' possible return and Herbert's terrorism dominated every councillor, secretary, understrapper—unity of command is lacking because H.M.

has no unity in himself. . . . Everyone snapping at everyone else, hating everyone else, lying about everyone else, betraying everyone else—they are drawing the chariot of State, indeed, but not for love of the poor Emperor who really means well, and yet is forever stirring up the State soup-kettle with his self-invented spoon, and preventing it from turning into any sort of soup at all. . . ." A month later further prods from Holstein drew a deeper cry of despair. " More frequently than ever I feel as if I were living in a mad-house. Insane narrow-mindedness—insane controversies—insane arrogance. Bedlam—Bedlam—Bedlam ! "[1]

Early in 1894 a journal called *Kladderadatsch* began to report the " bedlam " in a series of anonymous articles which proved highly diverting to its readers. Holstein was described as " Friend Oyster," his subordinate at the Foreign Office, Herr Kiderlen-Wächter, as " Cock-sparrow," and Eulenburg as " Count Troubadour." The three men were depicted as the clique that guided the Emperor's hand, and not only were held up to ridicule but many of their private conversations were reproduced. Obviously the articles were written by someone close to them. Holstein was beside himself with anger. He held repeated consultations with Eulenburg and Kiderlen and fastened his suspicions first on one person and then on another. One day it was his own chief, Baron von Marschall, then it was Herbert Bismarck, then Count Henckel, a gentleman who had invested money in a paper affiliated with the offending publication. Count Kiderlen challenged the editor of *Kladderadatsch* to a duel and wounded him but Holstein was not satisfied ; after all, the editor was not the real culprit. Instead he challenged Henckel, but the Count insisted that he was innocent and refused to fight. Holstein then put pressure on Eulenburg to ask the Emperor to interfere and force Henckel to fight. Eulenburg began to worry, fearing " that Holstein will hate the Emperor now, if His Majesty does not admit the case against Henckel, and a ' Holstein-hate ' for the Emperor would lead to very serious consequences." However, the Emperor refused to be drawn into the controversy, and the perpetrators of the attacks remained undetected. Years later, when it no longer mattered, two junior members of the Foreign Office, who had a room near Holstein, boasted that they had been the authors.

[1] *Philip Eulenburg : The Kaiser's Friend :* Johannes Haller.

Philip Eulenburg's presentiment proved correct. William's refusal to involve Count Henckel in the affair, combined with his attempts to reconcile Prince Bismarck, induced in Holstein a deep hostility for the Kaiser which later spread to the Kaiser's best friend —Count Eulenburg himself.

6. *The Kaiser, the Prince and England*

The German Emperor cut an imposing figure when he visited Cowes each summer to take part in the Regatta. "I sat next to William who made himself most agreeable," wrote Princess May, the future Queen Mary of England, in the summer of 1893. "Fancy me, little me, sitting next to William, the place of honour!"

The Emperor's arrival was always impressive. When the imperial yacht *Hohenzollern* entered the harbour, escorted by a group of German warships, the Royal Navy gave it a twenty-one-gun salute and the hundreds of private craft, lying at anchor, dipped their pennants. From then on there was an elaborate round of festivities; the Queen gave a state banquet at Osborne, the Prince entertained nightly at the Royal Yacht Club, German and British bands vied with each other to serenade the townspeople, the two navies exchanged a flow of hospitality, and hostesses fought with each other to fill the gaps.

William II enjoyed himself so much at Cowes that he attended the Regatta every summer between 1889 and 1895. When the Queen realised that his visits were becoming a yearly fixture she tried to discourage him, for she was always fearful lest too much intimacy with someone of his explosive nature might lead to unpleasant incidents. In 1892 she sent a message to the British Ambassador in Berlin, Sir Edward Malet, and asked if he could not drop a hint "that these regular annual visits are not quite desirable." Apparently Sir Edward could not, for nothing was said and the Kaiser continued to come.

The Queen's ministers were in favour of the visits. They felt it was better to know what the Kaiser was about than to be taken by surprise. Besides, the Queen had a salutary effect on her grandson. She handled him with tact and firmness and he showed more respect for her than for anyone else. Indeed, when Victoria visited Darmstadt in the early summer of 1892 Lord Salisbury asked if she could not arrange a meeting with the Emperor, for he was in a nervous excitable mood over the growing friendship between Russia and France, and might do something foolish unless the Queen calmed him down. But Victoria refused to comply. "No, no. I really cannot go about keeping everyone in order," she said.

The Prince of Wales always acted as host to the Kaiser. He received very little assistance from his wife, Alexandra, who loathed all Germans in general and William in particular. She repeatedly wrote to her sister, the Czarina of Russia, how untrustworthy he was and freely aired her opinions to her children. Ever since Frederick's funeral, she had refused to set foot in Berlin, and when the Prince was obliged to pay a state visit to Germany in 1890 he took his son George instead. "And so my Georgie boy has become a real life filthy bluecoated *Picklehaube* German soldier!!!" wrote Alexandra when she learned that George had been awarded the honorary command of a Prussian regiment. "I never thought to have lived to see *that*! But never mind; as you say, it could not have been helped—it was your misfortune and not your fault—and anything was better—even my two boys being sacrificed!!!—than Papa being made a German Admiral—that I could not have survived—you would have had to look for your poor old Mother dear at the bottom of the sea, the first time he adorned himself with it!"[1]

So the Prince of Wales bore the brunt of the Kaiser's annual trips. He had to dance constant attendance, racing with him by day and entertaining him by night. Even when his nephew was at his most affable he did not really get on with him. He found his jokes irritating and his sudden impulses disconcerting. Queen Victoria, on the other hand, was often greatly amused by William's unconventional behaviour. Once when he was lunching at Osborne with a few members of the family the Duke of Connaught asked the Queen if he could show her the new equipment that was proposed for the army. "We found the Royal Family talking together," wrote the Prince of Wales's secretary, Sir Frederick Ponsonby, "and at once the Duke of Connaught sent for the sergeant, who came in looking rather uncomfortable in his dark green full-dress

[1] *King George V:* Harold Nicolson.

uniform over which various khaki belts and straps had been put. It all looked very odd. The Duke of Connaught walked around explaining the object of the different straps to the Queen, while the German Emperor merely nodded and grunted to signify that he understood the explanations. I thought that this was all there was to be done, but the Emperor had not had his say. He called me up and asked whether I did not think the greatcoat that was rolled up was too high, and whether it would not interfere with a man firing his rifle lying down. Without waiting for an answer he told the sergeant to lie down and get into a firing position. He then proceeded to lie down alongside and point out that even with a Rifleman's head-dress, which was flat at the back, the greatcoat prevented his putting his head back far enough. He maintained that with a helmet or *Picklehaube* it would be impossible. It was a very hot afternoon and beads of perspiration broke out on the sergeant's face as he found himself lying down in front of the Queen with the German Emperor lying down beside him glaring at him and plying him with questions without ever giving him time to answer them. However, all this was intended for the Queen's edification and she seemed very much amused. . . ."[1]

The Prince of Wales resented the attention that the Kaiser always managed to attract. He found it annoying to be pushed off the centre of the stage by a nephew twenty years younger. Like most royalties he was a stickler for etiquette, and enjoyed the adulation and awe which his high position provoked; and William seemed to revel in snatching the place of honour to which his higher rank entitled him. When the Prince made him a member of the Royal Yacht Club William started to interfere in everything, including the handicapping, and Edward morosely referred to him as " The Boss of Cowes " and told a friend: " The Regatta was once a pleasant holiday for me but now that the Kaiser has taken command it is nothing but a nuisance. . . ."

The truth was that the two men were wholly incompatible. The Prince of Wales was more pompous in his public life, more unconventional in his private. The Kaiser could be almost alarmingly direct and friendly when he chose to be, but underneath he was a Prussian and a Puritan and his uncle was almost everything he disliked. He was soft and fat and self-indulgent, and even at 55

[1] *Recollections of Three Reigns:* Sir Frederick Ponsonby.

had a sharp eye for the ladies. He adored Paris because of the pleasures it offered, a city which William regarded as corrupt and immoral, and worse still, he had no military knowledge and had grown too heavy to sit upon a horse. Once William referred to him in front of a group of English dignitaries as " an old peacock," and another occasion chided him at a dinner party for never having seen active service. And when one of the Prince's friends was accused of cheating at baccarat in 1891, and the affair was aired in the press because of a libel suit and became a national scandal, William could not resist writing " Uncle Bertie " that it was not fitting for him to gamble in the company of subalterns half his age.

Most galling to William, however, was the fact that the Prince, despite his short-comings, was the darling of Europe. As Heir Apparent to the British throne he was regarded as the unofficial leader of society and was fêted and acclaimed wherever he went, often creating far more stir than a reigning sovereign. His clothes were copied, his gastronomical preferences studied, even his mannerisms were imitated. His popularity was largely due to his charm, which, according to the son of Queen Victoria's secretary, amounted to genius. " With a dignified presence, a fine profile (as his coins show) and a courtly manner, he never missed saying a word to the humblest visitor, attendant or obscure official. He would enter a room, and with the skill of an accomplished billiard player, look forward several strokes ahead, so that no one was left out. The appropriate remark, the telling phrase and the amusing joke, accompanied by a gurgling laugh to the close friend, made all delighted even to watch him. . . ."[1]

What was curious about the Kaiser's relations with his uncle was the fact that William credited him with far more brains and ability than English people did. The Kaiser saw him as a mischievous, Machiavellian figure, weaving plots against Germany because of his beloved France; and he did not doubt his shrewdness or his grasp of foreign affairs. English politicians and courtiers would have been astonished at this appraisal, for although they regarded Edward as a charming good-natured prince, they were highly critical of his frivolous nature and his mental capacity. They knew how disappointed the Queen was in her son's character and how despite his pleading she still refused to employ him in a responsible position,

[1] *Henry Ponsonby : His Life from His Letters :* Arthur Ponsonby.

or even, for that matter, to allow him to see the Cabinet papers. At Cowes in 1892 he was so depressed by his mother's disregard that his secretary sent a letter to Sir Henry Ponsonby: "The Prince of Wales writes to me that there is not much use his remaining on at Cowes as he is not the slightest use to the Queen; that everything he says or suggests is pooh-poohed and that his sisters and brothers are much more listened to than he is. All this is a pity and not very encouraging."[1]

Later the same year, when the Liberals came to power and the eighty-two-year-old Mr. Gladstone formed a government, he informed the Queen that he had arranged for the Prince to see the Cabinet papers. He was under the impression that this was normal practice, but Victoria reacted sharply. She wrote to Lord Salisbury asking if such a principle had ever been followed and when he replied in the negative she let Mr. Gladstone know that "nothing of the kind was done, or ought it to be done." Her secretary, Sir Henry Ponsonby, felt she was wise to take this stand. "With regard to public questions, the reading of confidential papers and responsible official work being found for the Prince, the Queen was undoubtedly justified," wrote Ponsonby's son and biographer. "She had measured his capacities and inclinations and knew that nothing could be expected from him in this direction."[1]

The Kaiser's appraisal of his uncle's ability was far nearer the truth than the patronising pronouncements of Victoria's officials, yet he was not the power that William imagined. It is interesting that the Kaiser had no inkling of the strained relations that often existed between mother and son and no understanding of the trepidation with which the Prince approached her. He had no fear of his grandmother himself, and it never occurred to him that the Prince felt differently. Once, through a characteristic lack of consideration, he made things awkward for his uncle. "His Imperial Majesty the German Emperor and H.R.H. the Prince of Wales were to have dined with the Queen last evening," reported *The Times* in August 1893, "but were unavoidably delayed by taking part in the race to Portland and joined Her Majesty later in the evening."

The truth of the story was that the Kaiser was racing his yacht *Meteor I* against the Prince's new cutter *Britannia*. When the

[1] *Henry Ponsonby: His Life from His Letters:* Arthur Ponsonby.

yachts were off Sandown the wind dropped and it did not look as though they would be back before midnight. Baron Eckardstein, a member of the German Embassy, was on the Prince's yacht and heard him say that since the Queen was giving a banquet in the Kaiser's honour, they must abandon the race and return to Cowes by train. The Prince signalled the *Meteor*: "Propose abandon race and return by train so as to reach Osborne in time for dinner." To which the Kaiser replied: "I object. Race must be fought out. It doesn't matter when we reach Cowes." The Prince came to Baron Eckardstein much distressed. "The Queen," he said, "will not understand the Kaiser's behaviour. Besides, he seems to have forgotten that she is giving this big dinner in his honour." "He then asked me," wrote Eckardstein, "whether I couldn't signal to the Kaiser's suite and get someone to point this out to him. Though I felt very dejected at the Kaiser's bad manners, I couldn't help smiling at this idea. The Prince understood at once and said: 'I suppose if you did what I suggest you would wake up the day after to-morrow at latest in the Legation at Timbuctoo.'"[1]

There was nothing to do but continue the race. Fortunately the breeze revived but the party did not arrive at Cowes until nine and at Osborne until ten. The Queen had finished dinner and was just coming into the reception room. "As she took her seat," wrote Eckardstein, "Prince Henry whispered to me: 'The Queen is in a very bad temper.' Soon after that the Kaiser appeared, followed by his suite, kissed hands and apologised for being so late. The Queen smiled graciously but showed by her manner she was not pleased with her grandson. A few minutes later the Prince hurried into the room in full uniform, but took cover for a moment behind a pillar, wiping the perspiration from his forehead before he could summon up courage enough to come forward and make his bow. The Queen only gave him a stiff nod, and he retreated at once behind the pillar again."[1]

William did not visit Cowes solely for pleasure. Although Holstein had dropped Bismarck's Reinsurance Treaty, he had tried to maintain Bismarck's equilibrium in the Balkans by refusing to back Austria in a preventive war against Russia, or to help Russia in an occupation of Bulgaria. However, the exchange of goodwill

[1] *Ten Years at the Court of St. James:* Baron von Eckardstein.

visits between Russia and France in 1891 and 1893, which presaged the Dual Alliance, prompted the Kaiser to concentrate his efforts on trying to persuade Britain to join the Triple Alliance of Germany, Austria-Hungary, and Italy. This plainly was the right course for Germany, for not only would it tip the balance in favour of the Central Powers but it would ensure that England did not join the opposite camp—a remote contingency in the nineties, nevertheless a permanent nightmare of the German Foreign Office.

Germany's difficulty was to convince England of the wisdom of abandoning her traditional isolationism. Although England and Germany shared common enemies in France and Russia, Britain had not been mixed up in European coalitions since the Crimean war. Her main concern was to protect and enlarge her scattered empire, which she did by skilfully playing off one country against another. When William sailed up the Solent each July the German Embassy moved from London to Cowes and arranged conversations between the Emperor and the Queen's first minister. William seized every opportunity to stress the advantages that Britain, the foremost naval power, would reap from partnership with Germany, the foremost military power. He also talked about his colonial ambitions in the hope of inducing England to part with some of her territories in exchange for German diplomatic backing, which, he declared, had been successful in restraining France from attacking Egypt, and Russia from becoming too adventurous in Persia and India. His main task, however, was to promote friendly relations, and to wait patiently until events played into his hands.

This happened, unexpectedly, in 1893. The Kaiser arrived in Cowes in the middle of a crisis precipitated by the threat of French aggression in Siam. Britain saw Russia's hand in France's territorial demands and suspected ultimate designs against India. She announced that she could not remain impassive if a conflict broke out and sent several gunboats up the river that flowed past Bangkok to strengthen her protest. The Queen telegraphed her Foreign Secretary, Lord Rosebery, and emphasised that "the honour of my Empire" depended on remaining firm, adding: "Germany, Austria and above all Italy should be urged to support us."[1]

The Kaiser sailed into Cowes on the 29th of July and the next evening, accompanied by Count Philip Eulenburg, dined with the

[1] *Letters of Queen Victoria.*

Prince on board the *Britannia*. He was in an aggressive mood and spent the evening telling his uncle that Germany was determined to expand its colonial possessions, particularly in Africa, and to increase its navy as a natural sequence, suggesting, not quite truthfully, that the fleet expansion had already begun. At midnight the conversation was interrupted by a message from the Queen's secretary, Sir Henry Ponsonby, with a startling communication for the Kaiser. It was a copy of a telegram which the Queen had received from Lord Rosebery. " French Government demand withdrawal of our gunboats from before Bangkok. I have refused this. Desire to see Count Hatzfeldt in London immediately."[1]

War was a possibility and it was obvious that Britain wished to sound German support. Germany now had the opportunity to draw Britain closer to the Triple Alliance in return for her backing. The Kaiser reacted in a curious way; he was filled with consternation. In order to conceal his panic from his uncle he laughed loudly and slapped the Prince on the back (some say on the front) and cried: " So, then, thou'lt soon be off to India to show what thou'rt good for as a soldier."[2] Then he departed for the Hohenzollern to find Hatzfeldt and send him to London.[3]

According to Count Eulenburg: " The Emperor took me into his cabin and completely broke down. I really have never seen him so overcome, and I had to bring the whole force of my mind to bear upon finding reasonable arguments which would soothe him. . . . The Emperor exclaimed that England's fleets were weaker than the Russian and French fleets in combination. Even with the aid of our little fleet, England would still be the weaker. The French (he said) wanted to drive Russia to some action—which, considering the Czar's hostile attitude towards us, they might succeed in doing. Our army was not strong enough to fight simultaneously against France and Russia. The French had chosen their moment very cleverly. It was impossible to sit still and let the tempest break on our heads. All Germany's prestige was gone, if we could not take a prominent part; and not to be a world-power was to cut a deplorable figure. What were we to do . . . ? "[4]

[1] *Letters of Queen Victoria.*

[2] *Ten Years at the Court of St. James:* Baron von Eckardstein.

[3] Count Hadzfeldt was ill, so Count Metternich was sent instead.

[4] *Philip Eulenburg: The Kaiser's Friend:* Johannes Haller.

Eulenburg soothed him by saying that England would temporise, and called in Metternich and Kiderlen to support his view. " When they went out the Emperor seemed calmer, but he looked very wretched—pale, and biting his lips nervously. I felt dreadfully sorry for him. He, coming here with his big talk about our ships, felt driven into a corner as it were, and politically put in his place. And to be put in one's place is always a bitter pill for one's poor dear vanity."[1]

It was obvious that the Kaiser had bad nerves. A curious side-light on his despair was the fact that his Chancellor, General Caprivi, did not share his pessimism about Germany's weakness or unreadiness. The following morning Count Hatzfeldt telegraphed to Berlin and asked categorically: " Does it at all suit our political and military policy for a European conflict to break out *now*, from which we could not hold aloof in the long run? " and Caprivi replied in a marginal note: " From the military point of view it is just as good now as later."[2]

Another strange aspect of the Kaiser's depressions was that they vanished for no apparent reason, as quickly as they came. The next morning, although the war threat was just as menacing as the night before, he emerged from his cabin in high spirits. Accompanied by Eulenburg he spent the day racing with his uncle on the *Britannia*. William remained on deck to take charge of the sailing himself, while the Prince and " Phili " retreated to the cabin. Eulenburg was not favourably impressed by his host. As the Prince " went on breakfasting steadily from ten to four," he wrote, " I had to sit tête-à-tête with him for hours on end. I learnt to know him thoroughly—a capable, amiable, but very crafty man, with a remarkably sinister look in his eye—*not* our friend."[3]

This opinion was formed largely because the Prince could not refrain from taking digs at his nephew. Considering that England was hoping to enlist the Kaiser's support in the event of war, it reveals a tactlessness on the part of Edward which shows that the friction between the two men was not always instigated by William. Edward attributed France's hostility towards Siam to Russia, declaring rather fatuously that it was " explicable by the antipathy

[1] *Philip Eulenburg: The Kaiser's Friend:* Johannes Haller.

[2] *German Diplomatic Documents.*

[3] *Philip Eulenburg: The Kaiser's Friend:* Johannes Haller.

of the Czar to my nephew Willy." Then he went on to criticize Willy's "colonial game," saying that he could understand anyone wanting to buy diamonds, but if one was not in a position to buy big ones he would have thought the effort not worth while. Lastly, he touched on the German Navy. "It is all very well for my nephew to be interested in ships. But when one sees him with his disabled arm, going on as he is now doing on deck, one cannot help being a little afraid he may do himself some damage." "This remark," declared Eulenburg, "was no less subtle than malicious, and his look was more malicious still."[1]

When the *Britannia* returned to harbour in the afternoon the Kaiser was informed that the crisis was over. The French and Siamese had reached agreement over the territorial dispute; and apparently the ultimatum about the British gunboats had been a mistake.

Just as Bismarck had predicted, Germany's pressure for colonies began to create trouble with England and vitiate the Kaiser's plan to draw her into the Triple Alliance. Although in November 1893 the two countries concluded an arrangement which opened the way for Germany from the Cameroons to Lake Chad, England showed no inclination to part with anything that belonged to her. William was particularly indignant that she would not allow him to gain control of the Samoan Islands over which Germany, Britain, and America exercised a joint suzerainty. America was willing to relinquish her rights, but England refused. In September 1893 Count Hatzfeldt told Lord Rosebery that Germany would be obliged to maintain "greater reserve" unless England became more obliging, and the following year hinted that "the advocacy of English interests must not be expected of us any longer."

Nevertheless the grievances continued to multiply. Germany accused England of making difficulties in Singapore over the recruitment of Chinese coolies for German New Guinea, and at Walfisch Bay over the unloading of German guns, needed for the suppression of a revolt in German South West Africa. After that came a quarrel over a British attempt to transfer Sudan territory to the Congo, which, the Germans said with justice, she had no right to do. This led to sharp practices on both sides and increased the general acrimony.

[1] *Philip Eulenburg: The Kaiser's Friend:* Johannes Haller.

Despite the friction, the Kaiser kept his sights securely fixed on partnership with England. When France and Russia concluded the Dual Alliance in 1894 he felt that his mission was more important than ever, and worked closely for an advantageous opening. It seemed to come in the summer of 1895. The situation looked more promising than it had for many months, for the African quarrels had temporarily subsided, and a conservative government had returned to power in England, which tended to favour Germany more than Mr. Gladstone's radical, " pro-French " Liberals. And for once, even the personal relations of the Kaiser and the Prince of Wales were undisturbed. They could almost be described as being on good terms, for William II had made a gesture which delighted his uncle. He had appointed him an honorary officer of the Prussian Dragoon Guards. One of the few things that the Kaiser and the Prince shared was a love of royal trappings. They adored public occasions, medals, ribbons, and above all, uniforms. Neither minded changing clothes a dozen times a day, indeed they looked upon it as a treat. The Prince was so enchanted with William's offer he did not mind when he learned that his nephew hoped for a *quid pro quo*.

William told the British military attaché in Berlin that he would " immensely like to have an English uniform, in order that, should he attend a review, he would not be obliged to mount a horse in an Admiral's garb."[1] Victoria said it was quite impossible; she had made William an admiral, that was enough. The Prince, still flushed with gratitude, weighed in. William was the Queen's eldest grandson and an Emperor; besides it was British policy to keep in well with Germany. The Queen retorted that William was too spoilt already, and she was under the impression that he had been made an admiral expressly to prevent him from interfering with the army. The whole thing annoyed her. " This fishing for uniforms on both sides is regrettable,"[1] she wrote her secretary. Lord Salisbury settled the argument. Although he was not in power he advised the Queen to humour the Emperor; so in the end she gave in and William was made Colonel-in-Chief of the 1st Royal Dragoons.

This, then, was the agreeable atmosphere which prevailed in early August while the Kaiser, aboard the *Hohenzollern*, was making

[1] *Letters of Queen Victoria.*

his way to Cowes. English newspapers, disturbed by the Franco-Russian alliance, remarked on the visit with pleasure, and more than one journal commented critically on England's policy of isolation. For the first time people were advancing the arguments so often used by the Kaiser; that Germany and England were natural partners for the simple reason that France and Russia were common enemies—threatening Germany in Europe and Britain in the East. If the two "cousins" spoke with one voice, the world would be forced to live in peaceful co-existence.

At the end of July, just before the Kaiser's arrival, Lord Salisbury made a proposal to the German Ambassador, Count Hatzfeldt, which was received with delight. Salisbury had returned to office a month earlier and during the interval had been deeply immersed in the problem of Turkey. Turkey not only sprawled across part of North Africa and the Middle East, but reached into Europe with possessions which to-day constitute Albania and large parts of Greece and Jugoslavia. Although the great Powers had agreed in the Treaty of Berlin in 1878 to guarantee the Ottoman Empire, in order not to squabble over its spoils, the Balkans remained explosive because of the unhappy minorities under both Turkish and Austrian rule, and the sharp conflicting ambitions of Russia and Austria. Lately, the situation had grown more perilous than ever, as the Sultan was resorting to such barbarous measures that Salisbury did not see how Britain, for one, could continue to support him. The previous autumn his Kurdish troops had carried out a wholesale massacre of Armenians, cutting them down with knives and burning them alive in their churches. Reports coming from Constantinople predicted that more outrages were imminent.[1]

Lord Salisbury, therefore, sounded Count Hatzfeldt about a possible partition of European Turkey. He told the Count that England would like Egypt, that he was prepared to give Russia Constantinople, and to distribute the other European spoils as Germany saw fit between her Triple Alliance partners, Austria and Italy. Hadzfeldt was dazzled. If Lord Salisbury's suggestion was taken up all friction between Austria and Russia would dis-

[1] In the autumn of 1895 seven thousand Armenians were butchered in the streets of Constantinople in broad daylight, their heads battered in by Kurdish clubs and their bodies littering the streets.

appear which was the cause of Russia's antagonism towards Germany. Germany would secure a rapprochement with Russia which would bring to an end the Franco-Russian alliance; and at the same time England and Germany would establish a working partnership which would open the way for England's accession to the Triple Alliance. From Germany's point of view it was too good to be true.

But they reckoned without Baron Holstein. The moment he received Hatzfeldt's dispatch telling him of his talk with Salisbury, he decided that it was a British plot " to relieve the unpleasant position in which England finds herself with France and Russia about Egypt, by producing complications in Asia Minor and the Balkans, into which all the continental powers, including ourselves, would be dragged, rather than England."[1] It was also a plot to break up the Triple Alliance by creating deadly enmity between Austria and Italy in the redistribution of Turkish territories. He instructed Hatzfeldt to turn it down, and sent a similar message to Herr von Kiderlen, the Foreign Office representative attached to the Imperial Suite aboard the *Hohenzollern*. " I do not think," he concluded, " that Lord Salisbury will pursue for the present his scheme for a flare-up in the Balkans—for that is what his proposals amount to—if he comes up against determined opposition from the Emperor and realises that His Majesty sees through him."[1]

Hatzfeldt was bitterly disappointed. Here was the opportunity for which Germany had been waiting dissolving in thin air. He wired Holstein on August 5th: " I must not deceive either you or myself. If we withdraw entirely, that is, if I can offer neither views nor advice, I can expect no further influence worth mentioning over Lord Salisbury's decisions in the matter . . . Lord Salisbury's plan frankly contemplated very rich satisfaction for Russia in the East. . . . The one cheated evidently was to be France. . . . I think it would scarcely be to our disadvantage if Russia, once satisfied saw no reason for keeping up the French friendship at our expense. . . ."[1]

William II was always attracted by dramatic interpretations, and found Holstein's arguments more stimulating than Hatzfeldt's. Moreover, he liked to pride himself in " not having the wool pulled over his eyes " and more than once had boasted that being " half-

[1] *German Diplomatic Documents:* E. T. S. Dugdale.

English" had given him special insight into the soul of perfidious Albion.

When he read about Lord Salisbury's scheme as depicted by Holstein he described it as "truly English" and said that he would have nothing to do with it. He saw Lord Salisbury on the day of his arrival, August 5th. Baron Eckardstein declares that the Kaiser was rude to the Prime Minister, but since his account is incorrect regarding the time, date, and circumstances of the meeting, it is impossible to give it credence. Only one thing is clear: the Kaiser discussed the Turkish problem and told Lord Salisbury flatly that Germany would have nothing to do with a partition of the Ottoman Empire. However, it is likely from remarks made later by the Emperor that he also hinted at the question of Britain joining the Triple Alliance; and that Lord Salisbury, nettled by his refusal to consider the Turkish problem, was more discouraging than usual.

There was a sequel to this interview. The next morning Salisbury obeyed etiquette by writing his name in the Kaiser's book. At 3.30 that afternoon he received a message that the Emperor would receive him at four. As he had already talked with the Kaiser he assumed that this was merely a courtesy in return for writing his name and replied that he had an audience with the Queen: and at four o'clock he left for London. The next day he received a letter from Victoria: "William is a little sore at your not coming to see him, having waited some time for you, thinking you would come after seeing me." William made great capital of the incident, declaring that since he would not fall in with Salisbury's plans the Prime Minister had slighted him. For years the German Foreign Office spoke of Salisbury's "insulting behaviour." Salisbury remarked acidly to Baron von Eckardstein some time later: "Your Kaiser seems to forget that 'I do not work for the King of Prussia,' but for the Queen of England."[1]

August 6th, the day that Salisbury missed his appointment, was a disastrous day all round. The Kaiser was supposed to race his yacht *Meteor I* against the Prince's *Britannia*, but when he was informed of the handicaps he said they were too high and refused to take part; and the Prince was obliged to sail the course alone. This was bad enough, but with the day's routine upset, William

[1] "*Travailler pour le Roi de Prusse*" is an idiom, meaning "to labour in vain."

went aboard one of the ships that had escorted him from Germany and made a speech that upset the whole of Britain. He had included in his escort two new cruisers, the *Wörth* and the *Weissenburg*, both named after important victories in the Franco-Prussian war. August 4th and 6th marked the 25th anniversaries of the battles and he seized the opportunity to address the officers and crew of the *Worth* on the invincibility of the German Army in terms that did not spare French feelings. The next day the British press deplored his taste in insulting a foreign power from English soil; and the *Standard* told him bluntly to return to his own dominions before making any more such inflammatory pronouncements.

Everything had gone wrong; the talks with Lord Salisbury, the sailing, even the public goodwill. An English-German partnership suddenly seemed a long way off. William blamed everyone but himself and decided to cut his stay short. As a parting gesture of defiance he got in touch with Mr. George Lennox Watson who had designed the Prince of Wales's *Britannia*. He ordered a new yacht to be named *Meteor II*, with one stipulation: to outbuild the *Britannia*. Then he returned to Germany and took the Empress on a tour of Alsace-Lorraine where he gave vent to his feelings by making a whole series of provocative speeches.

On his return to Berlin with the Kaiser, Count Eulenburg found the capital in a state of turmoil. General Caprivi had resigned in the autumn of 1894 and been replaced by the Kaiser's seventy-three-year-old uncle, Prince Hohenlohe, a former Governor of Alsace-Lorraine. As Hohenlohe was almost as much of a novice in foreign affairs as Caprivi, and as the Foreign Secretary, Marschall, was weak and unsure of himself, Baron Holstein remained master of the Wilhelmstrasse. Yet the Baron was full of grievances. Eulenburg knew that the *Kladderadatsch* incident had sparked off "a Holstein hate" for the Kaiser, and he recognised the dangerous fruit it was bearing when he heard him talk bitterly against His Majesty's intolerable "interferences." He also found that his own relations with Holstein were disturbed, for the latter had begun to resent the fact that Eulenburg would not support him in his vendetta against the Sovereign. "He scarcely ever writes to me—regards me as a renegade from the cause," Eulenburg wrote to von Bülow, the German Ambassador in Rome.

Bülow was in close correspondence with Holstein and tried to smooth matters over. " What is at present worrying and exasperating him [Holstein] is that he does not know everything that the Emperor writes and has in mind," he replied to Eulenburg. " He willingly granted that the Emperor is very talented, full of the best intentions and . . . of his own accord praised H.M.'s attitude during the last English visit towards Salisbury. . . . He only wishes that you would put up a still stronger opposition to the Emperor's whim for personally conducting policy."[1]

This was an attempt to interpret Holstein's actions logically, but Holstein was not a logical being. He was a psychopathic character and his dislike and jealousy of the Sovereign had swollen to such proportions that he seized any stick to beat him with. Holstein was in the happy position of wielding power without responsibility. Although almost all instructions sent abroad by the Chancellor and Foreign Secretary were drafted by himself, he did not hesitate to deny his own advice when it suited him. It soon transpired that the main reason for his stand against Salisbury's Turkish proposals was simply to deprive the Emperor of a diplomatic triumph. The fact that William II followed his recommendations did not pacify him, but merely prompted him to shift his ground.

Eulenburg was astonished when he returned to Berlin and discovered what was happening. He ran into Count Hadzfeldt, who was in the capital on a few days' leave, and asked him why he thought Holstein had taken " a negative and dilatory attitude toward the idea of a partition over Turkey." The Ambassador replied that it might have been the fear of seeming "too Bismarckian," then commented drily " that Holstein was now of a different opinion, and had expressed his dissatisfaction with the way H.M. had let Lord Salisbury down." Eulenburg indignantly passed this story on to Bülow, adding : " And I myself had later an opportunity of confirming this. Holstein actually went so far as to declare that the Emperor's independent conduct of policy had got us into another mess. But you know as well as I do that H.M. in his conversation with Salisbury was only putting forth the point of view which had formerly been suggested to him by Holstein."

Holstein could not know that war would break out in 1914 and that afterwards all the German official papers including his own

[1] *Philip Eulenburg : The Kaiser's Friend :* Johannes Haller.

private memoranda would be published. In 1908 he began to write a series of political essays for posterity in which he bitterly attacked the Emperor for mistakes and exonerated himself in every instance. In January 1909 he alluded to the Turkish affair. The dignified, controlled style and the air of detachment with which he sought to mislead his readers reveal the extent of his cunning. " Since it was of the utmost importance," he wrote, " to prepare the Kaiser for the possibility of the Eastern question being raised . . . I sent Kiderlen a personal telegram which reached him in Heligoland before he left for England with the Kaiser, whom he was accompanying as the representative of the Foreign Ministry. The Kaiser had in fact scarcely landed before Lord Salisbury broached the Eastern question. I heard no details of the discussion, but we did learn immediately afterwards that the Kaiser had 'turned him down flat.' This quite unnecessary brusqueness bore fruit. Lord Salisbury, unused to such treatment, avoided a subsequent interview requested by the Kaiser by pleading pressure of business and going to London."[1]

With the Kaiser and Baron Holstein at loggerheads, German policy was hopelessly confused. Although both men paid lip service to the idea of luring Britain into the Triple Alliance they pursued their objectives in a most peculiar way. Holstein did not regard friendliness or frankness as a policy; the only diplomatic weapons he understood were threats and blackmail. The Kaiser on the other hand simply followed his own emotional impulses and allowed them to lead him wherever they chanced. Neither man understood the meaning of the word subtlety. They failed to see that a working partnership with England over some practical matter, which might slowly develop into a larger alliance, was the only sensible way to try to reach their goal.

On the contrary, as far as practical matters were concerned they were wholly unco-operative, and repeatedly used small issues to kick up fearful rows. When the Kaiser returned to Berlin he learned that Sir Edward Malet, the retiring British Ambassador, had criticised German policy in South Africa. Still smarting with resentment at the way Lord Salisbury had " treated " him, the Emperor sent for Colonel Swaine the British Military Attaché and poured out a list of angry grievances. Malet, he said, not only had accused

[1] *The Holstein Papers*: edited by N. Rich and M. H. Fisher.

the German Foreign Office of stirring up trouble for England in South Africa, but had gone so far as to mention the "astounding word war." "For a few square miles full of niggers and palm trees, England had threatened her one true friend, the German Emperor, grandson of Her Majesty the Queen of Great Britain and Ireland, with war!"[1] The Kaiser went on to say that Britain's concern for the Armenians in Turkey was quite incomprehensible to him. Was it merely a cloak for a design to get control of the Dardanelles herself? If so, Britain should have confided frankly in him for he would have seen to it that Austria and Italy joined hands with them. However, his patience was now running out and he was toying with the idea of making a pact with France and laying the structure of a purely continental alliance which, if it came to pass, would not suit England at all. "I closed the conversation," he wrote, "with a clear warning that England could only escape from her present complete isolation, into which her policy of selfishness and bullying had plunged her, by a frank and outspoken attitude either for or against the Triple Alliance."

Holstein instantly saw something he could get his teeth into. He pounced on the Kaiser's boast that Germany would have helped England to force the Dardanelles. What would Russia say to that? Lord Salisbury would scarcely fail to bring it to the Czar's notice. Holstein worked himself into a frenzy, bombarding Eulenburg with exhortations to use his influence to subjugate the Emperor's "personal rule." Again Bülow was drawn in and wrote to Eulenburg: "I don't think that H.M.'s talk with Swaine was, in itself, such a terribly portentous event, as it seems to Holstein, or as he wants us to think it. . . . But what *is* serious, very serious, is that antagonism between Holstein and H.M. which was revealed by the incident in question. I can say to *you alone* and you will not say it to anyone else: *Can* so complete a divergence between such elemental and subjective natures—when it concerns the whole direction and conception of affairs—*ever* be reconciled? Can it even in the long run be concealed?"[2]

Eulenburg replied on December 29th: "Holstein's excitement and agitation about His Majesty keeps equal pace with his fears of a tack into Bismarckian waters. In his state of agitation he becomes

[1] *German Diplomatic Documents*: edited by E. T. S. Dugdale.
[2] *Philip Eulenburg: The Kaiser's Friend*: Johannes Haller.

unfair to our side, and on the other hand he rushes into a blind alley because he does not stop to think. The monstrous difficulty lies, at the moment, in the fact that if we want to preserve the present system—and I most decidedly do—we are without a common basis of understanding between the most important factors, i.e. the Emperor, Imperial Chancellor, Marschall, Holstein; and I doubt whether this can ever be reconstituted.

"Each of them is more or less incensed with all the others. If you think of policy (sans comparison, of course!) as a bitch in heat, you will have a vivid picture of the present aspect of affairs. The handsome Newfoundland (His Majesty) can inflict a deadly wound on each of the rest whenever it suits him. The long-legged one (Marschall) he really wants to dispose of, but he growls and snaps at all the others; and the solitary little grey terrier (Holstein) is frantically exasperated. How are we to stop his bristling, yapping, and whimpering? We cannot very well kill the bitch—and she is kept in such a continuous state of excitement!"[1]

This was the twisted, tormented atmosphere prevailing in Berlin when the Jameson Raid took place. On December 30th, 1895, the day after Eulenburg's bitter summary, news reached Berlin that 600 irregular troops employed by Cecil Rhodes's Charter Company and led by Dr. Jameson, Chief Administrator of Rhodesia, had invaded the Transvaal Republic. This small independent state in the southern part of Africa was surrounded by British-run territories. It was ruled by settlers of Dutch-German stock known as Boers; and in order to keep the government in Boer hands in the face of a flood of British adventurers in search of gold, the President, Dr. Kruger, refused to give "foreigners"—as he called them—the vote, and taxed them heavily. The raiders had launched their attack in the hope of provoking a general uprising which would lead to a new government and a fair deal for the non-Boer settlers.

German officialdom was thrown into a high state of excitement. Obviously this was a plot on the part of London to seize the Transvaal. Germany had 15,000 nationals living in the territory and extensive possessions of her own in East Africa; and she was not prepared to stand by idly in the face of British aggression. Holstein immediately put out feelers to Russia and France on the possibility

[1] *Philip Eulenburg: The Kaiser's Friend:* Johannes Haller.

of concerted action against Britain. And as he always proffered complicated motives for his actions he explained—in a dispatch which he drafted for Prince Hohenlohe to send to Count Munster in Paris—that Germany's anti-English move was merely another attempt to force Britain into the Triple Alliance! "While England finds that she can remain between the two hostile groups—the Dual Alliance and the Triple Alliance—not only quite happily, but also be able to continue expanding, she will naturally reject any suggestion to declare her solidarity with the Triple Alliance."[1]

The Kaiser on the other hand did not stop for reflection. He was still smarting with indignation against the haughty Lord Salisbury. First and foremost he saw an opportunity to humiliate the British Prime Minister; secondly a chance to lead a great continental combine that would represent a grouping far more powerful than the British Empire; and thirdly the possibility of acquiring a naval base for himself in South Africa as a reward for upholding the moral rights of the Boer Government. The first disappointment came when Lord Salisbury condemned the Jameson Raid and declared that the British Government had known nothing about it; the second blow fell when news arrived that Jameson's force had been surrounded and compelled to surrender. It looked as though William's hopes were dashed.

But the Emperor refused to be deterred. The bright role he had conjured up for himself had so completely captured his fancy that he could not bear to relinquish it. He insisted that Lord Salisbury's attitude was merely a ruse, and called a Crown Council at the Chancellery on January 3rd to discuss possible moves. The conference was attended by the Imperial Chancellor, the Foreign Secretary, Baron von Marschall, and a number of high-ranking naval and military advisers. Baron Holstein and Herr Kayser, the Colonial Secretary, waited in an adjoining ante-room to tender advice.

Although Holstein's feelers to Russia and France had produced no support, the Kaiser was in an excited state and still favoured strong action. Not only did he suggest sending a warship to Lourenço Marques but he put forward the idea of dispatching troops from German East Africa and declaring a protectorate in the Transvaal. His ministers were thunderstruck and pointed out that

[1] *German Diplomatic Documents:* edited by E. T. S. Dugdale.

this would call out the British Navy and mean war with England. William began to argue that the affair could be localised, then he hit on a better scheme; why not send a German staff officer to the Transvaal, disguised as a lion-hunter, to help the country organise its own force against England? At this point someone suggested rebuking England publicly in a telegram of congratulations from the Kaiser to President Kruger. Erich Brandenburg, the eminent German historian, claims that the idea emanated from the ante-room where Holstein and Kayser were sitting.

William II did not like the suggestion the least little bit. In the first place he favoured positive action, not pin-pricks. Secondly he recoiled from sending a telegram to Kruger signed by himself, thus drawing England's wrath inescapably on his own head. It was one thing for his government to incur odium, another for him to attract it personally. However, in the end he gave way to the opinion of his advisers, and sent the following wire. "I express my sincere congratulations that, supported by your people, without appealing for help of friendly powers, you have succeeded by your own energetic action against armed bands which invaded your country as disturbers of the peace, and have thus been enabled to restore peace and safeguard the independence of the country against attacks from the outside. William II."

The Germans were astonished by the violence of England's reaction. The British public was first amazed, then furious. Here was the Kaiser, who had been parading as England's best friend for the past seven years, turning against her at the drop of a hat, and even intimating that if the raid had not fizzled out, he would have declared war on her. The nation rose in a wave of angry resentment. The press poured out a torrent of abuse, the officers of the Royal Dragoons turned the Emperor's picture to the wall, and dozens of aristocratic old ladies picked up their pens and let the Kaiser know what they thought of him.

The Kruger telegram tore a breach in Anglo-German relations which never wholly mended. Although officially the rift lasted only three years, it encouraged the hostile elements on both sides and created a permanent feud which aggravated every international difficulty and continually fouled the atmosphere between the two nations. As soon as the Kaiser and his gentlemen saw that the intervention had achieved nothing but ill-will each hastened to blame the other. William reminded his ministers that he had been opposed to the telegram, conveniently forgetting the bellicose suggestions put forward by himself. In his memoirs he strongly criticises Marschall's ignorance of " English national psychology." Holstein, on the other hand, insists that Marschall regarded the Kruger telegram as a lightning conductor for the Kaiser's dangerous energy. In an account written in 1908 he describes sitting with Kayser, the Colonial Secretary, in the ante-room. " After a considerable time Marschall came in, and in that laconic way of his instructed Kayser to draw up a telegram to Kruger, at the same time telling him what to put in it. When I quite naturally expressed my misgivings he said: ' Oh don't you interfere; you've no idea of the suggestions being made in there. Everything else is much worse!' That is how the world-famous telegram came into being. The driving force was not reflection but the Kaiser's whim."[1]

Is it possible to believe that Holstein twiddled his thumbs while Kayser, at the next desk, drafted the explosive message? Baron von Eckardstein did not think so. Many members of the Wilhelmstrasse, he wrote in his memoirs, felt that Holstein was the true author; and even those with reservations agreed that " the influence Holstein had exercised since the dismissal of Bismarck was so unchallenged that he certainly could have prevented the mischief if he had wanted to." So we are forced to the conclusion that he did not want to. No doubt he found irresistible the pleasure of watching the Kaiser blot his copy-book with his English relations.

The Prince of Wales was convinced that William and William alone was responsible for the telegram and urged his mother to administer " a good snub " to him. But Victoria thought otherwise. " These sharp cutting answers only irritate and do harm and in Sovereigns and Princes should be most carefully guarded against. William's faults come from impetuousness (as well as conceit); and calmness and firmness are the most powerful weapons in such cases."[2] " My dear William," she wrote, " As your Grandmother to whom you have always shown so much affection and of whose example you have always spoken with so much respect, I feel I cannot refrain from expressing my deep regret at the telegram you

[1] *The Holstein Papers.*

[2] *Letters of Queen Victoria.*

sent President Kruger. It is considered very unfriendly towards this country, which I am sure it is not intended to be, and has, I grieve to say, made a very painful impression here. The action of Dr. Jameson was of course very wrong and totally unwarranted; but considering the very peculiar position in which the Transvaal stands to Great Britain, I think it would have been far better to have said nothing. Our great wish has always been to keep on the best of terms with Germany, but I fear your Agents in the Colonies do the very reverse, which deeply grieves us. Let me hope that you will try and check this. . . ."[1]

William's answer was childish, for instead of defending the position he had taken, he pretended that he had been misunderstood. "To me," he wrote, "rebels against the will of Her Most Gracious Majesty the Queen—the Jameson raiders—are the most execrable beings in the world, and I was so incensed at the idea of your orders being disobeyed, and thereby peace and the security of my subjects being endangered, that I thought it necessary to show that publicly. It has, I am sorry to say, been totally misunderstood by the British press. I was standing up for law, order and obedience to a Sovereign whom I revere and adore, and whom to obey I thought paramount for her subjects. Those were my motives and I challenge anybody who is a gentleman to point out where there is anything hostile to England in this."[2]

The Queen was rather shocked by the hypocrisy of this letter and sent it on to Lord Salisbury with the comment that his excuses were "lame and illogical." Salisbury agreed but felt it wise "fully to accept all his explanations without enquiring too narrowly into the truth of them."

There was no doubt that William regretted the rupture with England. At the moment that he was affixing his signature to the Kruger telegram he remarked to Baron von Marschall: "You have put an end to my visits to Cowes." However, he had one satisfaction. Although he was not present at the 1896 Regatta, he trounced the Prince of Wales. The *Meteor* took the waters and won the Queen's Cup. The Prince of Wales saw that the *Britannia* was hopelessly outbuilt and the following year withdrew her from racing.

[1] *Letters of Queen Victoria.*
[2] *King Edward VII:* Sir Sidney Lee.

7. *Real World Power*

" My dream is to marry Alix of Hesse," wrote Nicholas, heir to the Russian throne in 1889. His parents were against the match and would not give their consent. Although Princess Alix was a granddaughter of Queen Victoria and a first cousin of Kaiser William, the Czar thought his son should make a more brilliant alliance, while the Czarina, who shared the views of her sister, the Princess of Wales, disliked the idea of a German daughter-in-law. Nicholas, however, was steadfast. Five years later, when his father fell gravely ill and decided that it was urgent for the boy to marry, his heart was still fixed on the Hessian princess. He declared flatly that it would have to be Alix or no one, and finally his parents gave way. He was allowed to travel to Darmstadt to attend the marriage of Alix's brother, the Grand Duke of Hesse, to Victoria, daughter of the Duke of Edinburgh, with the express purpose of asking the Princess's hand in marriage.

All the relations were gathered at Coburg for the occasion, including Queen Victoria and William II; and most of them felt sorry for Nicholas. They knew why he had come, but did not believe that Alix would accept him. She was deeply religious and had declared, time and again, that nothing would induce her to give up her Protestantism for the Greek Orthodox faith. The only person who regarded it as a simple matter of persuasion was the Kaiser. He immediately took Nicholas in hand. He found him tortured with shyness and afraid to propose lest Alix should prove so adamant that it would deprive him of all hope. William spent much time trying to raise his morale, and finally " in his cheery, impulsive way took Nicholas by the arm, led him to his room, made him buckle on his sword and carry his fur cap in his hand, stuck some roses in his hand and said to him: 'Now we will go and ask for Alix.' "[1]

[1] *Memoirs :* Prince von Bülow.

As everyone had prophesied, Nicholas was not successful. "I had a long and very difficult talk with Alix," he wrote to his mother, "in which I tried to explain to her that there was no other way for her than to give her consent, and that she simply could not withhold it. She cried the whole time, and only whispered now and then 'No, I cannot!' Still I went on, repeating and insisting on what I had said before. And though this talk went on for two hours it came to nothing, because neither she nor I would give in. . . ."[1]

Everyone at Coburg was fascinated by the drama. The relations, wrote Nicky, "were very touching in their solicitude." William, however, was determined to bring the matter to a triumphant conclusion, and plunged even further into the fray by himself having a talk with Alix. It was a curious situation, for here was he using all his powers of persuasion to induce Alix to embrace the Greek Orthodox faith, when only three years before he had threatened to ban his sister Sophie from Germany for doing the same thing. However, in this case William's motives were not entirely unmixed for although he was eager to do a good turn for Nicholas, he also believed that it would be advantageous to the Fatherland to have a German princess on the Russian throne. His eloquence was successful, for on the 8th of April he drove Alix to the house where Nicholas was staying and pushed them into a room together. "We were left alone," Nicholas wrote to his mother, "and with her very first words she consented! The Almighty only knows what happened to me then. I cried like a child and she did too; but her expression had changed; her face was lit by a quiet content. . . . The whole world is changed for me; nature, mankind, everything; and all seemed to be good and lovable and happy. I couldn't even write, my hand trembled so. . . ."[1]

The first thing the engaged couple did was to go to Queen Victoria's room and tell her that they had reached an understanding. "I was quite thunderstruck," she wrote in her Journal, "as, although I knew that Nicky much wished it, I thought Alix was not sure of her mind." Although the wedding was some months off, the Queen invited them to visit her at Windsor in June. It was not a new experience for Alix, as her mother had died when she was a small child, and she had visited her grandmother nearly every

[1] *The Letters of Czar Nicholas and Empress Marie:* edited by Edward Bing.

summer; but for Nicholas it was an event. He was delighted with the invitation and, when he arrived, astonished by Queen Victoria's lack of convention. "Granny has been very friendly," he wrote his mother, "and even allowed us *to go out for drives* without a chaperone! I confess I didn't expect that." He was a little disappointed that he couldn't dine with the Coldstream Guards but "I couldn't give a definite answer because Granny loves me so and doesn't like me missing dinner."[1]

A few months later, in November 1894, the Czar died and Nicholas ascended the throne. Despite the deep mourning, his marriage to Princess Alix took place a few weeks later, and once again the couple travelled to England, this time for their honeymoon. "How impossible it seems that gentle little simple Alicky should be the great Empress of Russia," wrote Victoria in her diary. The Queen was hopeful that "Nicky" would liberalise the tyrannical Russian regime, but soon after his accession she was disappointed to read that he had made a public speech castigating liberalism as a "senseless drama" and announcing his resolve "to maintain for the good of the whole nation the principle of absolute autocracy as firmly and strongly as did my lamented father."

William II was not bothered by Russia's absolutism but by the Russo-Franco "Dual Alliance" which had been signed by Nicholas's father eleven months earlier. However, he looked upon Nicky as an unusually pliable young man, and was confident that he could exert a strong influence upon him. The right policy, he decided, was to distract Russia's attention. "We must try," he told his Foreign Office in July 1895, "to nail Russia down in Asia, so that she may occupy herself less with Europe and the Near East." This was not a hopeless aim, for Russia was greatly agitated by the ease with which Japan had invaded China twelve months earlier. The Czar declared loudly that his interests were menaced, and the Kaiser joined him in presenting Tokyo with a stiff ultimatum, secretly hoping that Nicky might involve himself in a Far Eastern war. But the Japanese prudently retreated, and William was obliged to think again. Perhaps he should inspire Nicholas with the idea of serving in the Pacific as the shield of civilization, or, better still, as the defender of the Cross.

[1] *The Letters of Czar Nicholas and Empress Marie*: edited by Edward Bing.

The Kaiser was not completely cynical in promoting this idea for he was deeply impressed by the efficiency of Japan's army and navy; he talked excitedly about the Yellow Peril, and declared with genuine conviction that one day the heathen races would unite and threaten the whole of Christendom. To make his message clear to Nicholas he ordered his Court painter, Herr Knackfuss, to compose a picture showing bloody hordes, under the leadership of Buddha, being held at bay by the Christian powers; in the vanguard were Russia and Germany symbolised by two sentinels upholding the true Gospel. Underneath this artistic curiosity he inscribed: "Nations of Europe! Guard your most sacred possessions;" then he dispatched the painting to St. Petersburg. The Czar wrote a letter expressing his delight, and saying that he had given orders to have it "specially framed." "So it worked all right," commented William. "That is very satisfactory."[1]

But Germany was not the only country to worry about Russia. While the Kaiser kept an anxious eye on his eastern frontier, England watched her Far Eastern possessions with equal concern. In 1896 Nicholas toured Europe and once again visited England. Queen Victoria asked him bluntly whether the Franco-Russian alliance constituted a threat to British overseas territories and he gave her an emphatic no; it was a protective agreement formed to counter the Triple Alliance, purely defensive and only operative on the European continent. The Queen recognised Nicholas for what he was: a charming, good-natured, weak-minded young man who was usually at the mercy of the last person with whom he talked. So a day after his departure she picked up her pen and tried to impress his words upon him. "Dearest Nicky, You will be surprised to get a letter from me already, but I could not manage to say something to you the day you left. It is, that I am sure you will kindly use your influence and let the French understand that you do not intend to support them in their constant inimicality towards England, which is a cause of much annoyance and difficulty to us, in Egypt amongst other subjects.

"I would not have written this had you not told me that the agreement or alliance, or whatever it is called, was *only* of a military nature. I am (and Lord Salisbury the same) so anxious that we, Russia and England, should understand each other, and be on the

[1] *Grosse Politik.*

most friendly terms, that I am sure you excuse my troubling you so soon. . . . V.R.I."[1]

William II watched the comings and goings between the royal families of Russia and England with a jealous eye. The Prince and Princess of Wales made innumerable trips to Russia and met the Czar and his mother, the Dowager Empress, at family gatherings in Denmark. William hoped that his successful intervention in Nicholas's courtship had given him an advantage, and in a letter written in the spring of 1896 reminded him " of two years ago when it was my good fortune to be able to help you secure that charming accomplished Angel who is your wife."[2]

William presumed rather heavily on the service he had done, assuming an intimacy which was not altogether appreciated. He wrote to Nicholas regularly and gave him a good deal of unsolicited advice. After one of the Czar's visits to Paris in 1895 he warned him against making " republicanism " respectable. " The constant appearance of Princes, Grand-dukes, Statesmen, Generals in ' full fig ' at reviews, burials, dinners, races, with the head of the Republic or in his entourage makes republicans—as such—believe that they are quite honest excellent people, with whom Princes can consort and feel at home! Now what is the consequence at home in our different countries? The republicans are revolutionists *de nature* and were treated—rightly too—as people who must be shot or hanged, and now they tell our other loyal subjects: ' Oh, we are not dangerous bad men, look at France. There you see the royalties hobnobbing with the *revolutionists*! Why should it not be the same with us? ' We Christian Kings and Emperors have one holy duty imposed on us by Heaven, that is to uphold the Principle ' by the Grace of God ' . . ."[2]

Nicholas sometimes resented these lectures, yet when he was in William's presence he invariably came under the spell of his strong personality. The two Emperors offered a striking contrast—the Kaiser spectacular, restless, boastful and the Czar shy, nervous, and unobtrusive. When Nicholas attended the Imperial German Manœuvres in Breslau in 1896 the Princess of Pless thought he looked " very ill and weak, but the Czarina looks very healthy and has a most charming and clever face with deep blue eyes, and low

[1] *Letters of Queen Victoria.*

[2] *The Kaiser's Letters to the Czar:* edited by N. F. Grant.

straight eyebrows; her head is small and her hair brushed up from her forehead, only a few curls on the temples and just twisted up in the back; she had loads of lovely diamonds and great big sapphires."[1]

The Czarina's appearance was misleading, for she was far from clever. She was making herself more disliked in Russia every day. She hated society and did her best to discourage Nicholas from taking part in any functions which could be avoided. She liked to spend her evenings sewing, while he read aloud to her. The Russian aristocracy complained to the English of her "German bourgeois mentality" and to the Germans of her "English stiffness." She had no warmth for anyone who was not part of her family circle, and far from being grateful to the Kaiser for having influenced her matrimonial decision, resented the fact that he regarded her as beholden to him; she told Nicholas that she could not abide him.

She was not alone in her dislike. The Dowager Empress had been so impressed by the stories her sister, the Princess of Wales, had told her that she could barely allude to William in a civil manner. Nicholas adored his mother but was a little frightened of her, and when William visited Russia in 1897 he scarcely knew how to break the news to her that it would be necessary to accord him a special honour. "Dear Mama," he wrote, on July 23rd 1897, "I'm sorry to tell you we shall have to give William the rank of Admiral of our navy. Uncle Alexei reminded me of it; and I think, no matter how disagreeable it may be, we are obliged to let him wear our naval uniform; particularly since he made me last year a Captain in his own navy, and, what's much worse, I'll have to greet him as such at Kronstadt. It makes me sick to think of it!" (In the original, in French, "C'est à vomir!")[2]

Nevertheless the visit went off well. William was determined to charm his host and succeeded so well that Nicholas, for once, was grave enough to mention him favourably to his mother. On the other hand, he found the German Empress and her favourite lady-in-waiting, the Countess Brockdorff, a severe trial. "On the whole William was very cheerful, calm and courteous, while she tried to be charming and looked very ugly in rich clothes chosen without

[1] *Daisy, Princess of Pless.*

[2] *The Letters of Czar Nicholas and Empress Marie.*

taste; the hats she wore in the evenings and at the performance at Olgano were particularly impossible. It was rumoured here that the Empress is very much under the influence of her ladies-in-waiting, especially Countess B., and that everything the latter disapproves of the Empress also dislikes.

"At Krasnoe, on the day of the Tattoo, *La Vie Parisienne* was performed, because nothing else was found suitable. The third act had been chosen for the purpose and it was to be followed by a short ballet. . . . The next day we learned that that idiot Countess B. had thoroughly disapproved of the play because she considered that it was a parody on the Germans. She thought that the Swiss admiral was an allusion to the Emperor, as he had been appointed Admiral of our fleet, and that *le vieux diplomate* was a caricature of Hohenlohe who has indeed deteriorated very much since last year. What do you think of that?"[1]

Before closing his letter Nicholas added that William had been so impressed by the *Standart* "that he said he would have been happy to get it as a present and that after such a yacht he was ashamed to show the *Hohenzollern*. All that was very pleasant to us, as you will understand, dear Mama." However the Dowager Empress made it plain that she did not understand. "I was sure the beautiful lines of the *Standart* would be an eyesore to William," she replied. "Still, his joke about how happy he would be if the yacht were given to him was in doubtful taste. I hope he will not have the cheek to order himself a similar one here.[2] This would really be the limit, though just like him, with the tact that distinguishes him!"[1]

William was oblivious of these criticisms and returned to Germany flushed with success. He had not yet learned that Nicholas was always ready to bend to a strong personality, and continually changing his views. He wrote to Philip Eulenburg that the visit had turned out far better than he had expected, that he had reached "complete agreement" with Nicky on all important political questions, "so that together we have, so to say, disposed of all the world." "A restoration of Alsace and Lorraine to France with Russian aid is an *absolute and downright impossibility*. Thus a war between Gaul and us, and Russia and us, is, God willing, *no longer* to be feared—Nicky and I again parted friends who are united by a

[1] *The Letters of Czar Nicholas and Empress Marie.*

[2] The *Standart* had been built in Denmark.

sincere affection and *absolute* confidence in one another. Our relations are now as they *never were under Bismarck*, perhaps what they were at first under Nicholas I and Grandpapa. . . ."[1]

The Kaiser had taken his new Secretary of State, the forty-eight-year-old Bernard von Bülow, former ambassador in Rome, to Russia with him. This appointment, made in June 1897, was due to Philip Eulenburg, who had met Bülow in 1881 when they both were attached to the German Embassy in Paris. They had much in common, for Bülow was an intellectual, witty, artistic, and worldly. Like Eulenburg he possessed charm and tact, but he had none of Philip's kindness and loyalty. His feelings were carefully regulated to serve an over-riding ambition. He made his way by simulating a warmth he did not possess, and by expressing sentiments he did not believe, for he had perceived that the most outrageous flatteries were credible to those on whom they were bestowed. As his career unfolded, his remarkable adroitness at slithering unharmed through awkward situations won him the nickname of "the eel."

Bülow and Eulenburg had only been in Paris together for a few months, and did not see each other for many years, but when Bülow learned, not long after Bismarck's departure, of the important role that Eulenburg was playing, he picked up the old threads. "I have a great longing to see you again, dearest Philip," he wrote in 1891. "A decade has been swallowed up since we were together in Paris." Eulenburg replied warmly, and the two men embarked on a correspondence which became, on Bülow's side, increasingly adulatory. In one letter he referred to Philip's "infinite delicacy of feeling" and in another compared him to "a beautiful falcon in a forest filled with foxes, bristling swine and cackling geese!" "It seems so natural so say *Du* to each other," he wrote in March 1893, "that I feel as if it could not be otherwise. Listen—outwardly unlike in so many ways, we are inwardly each other's true affinity.... Since the Heavenly Powers conferred on you the magic gift of bewildering and brilliant talents, I cannot compare with you productively; but I *can* receptively rejoice in you, drink in your flow of soul and admire you. . . ."[2]

[1] *Memoirs :* Prince von Bülow.
[2] *Philip Eulenburg : The Kaiser's Friend :* Johannes Haller.

Bülow was a close friend of Holstein; and as Holstein's quarrel with Eulenburg deepened over the latter's refusal to help him "muzzle the Emperor," it was only natural that Eulenburg should seek Bülow's services as a go-between. "What Holstein overlooks," Philip wrote, "is the obligation of friendship by which I am *bound.* I have always been a decent sort of person and . . . I very much doubt if I should be serving the Fatherland by leaving the Emperor stranded, or 'driving him to the wall.'" He told Bülow about Holstein's 'cabal against H.M.' and said he feared they would "stick at nothing." Although Bülow took pains not to offend Holstein he replied to Eulenburg with gushing sentiment. "I can only say that when I look into such an abyss, I feel but the more completely on our dear sovereign's side, and love him more fondly than ever."[1]

Eulenburg over-estimated Bülow's sincerity and was deeply grateful for his sympathy. It was understandable, therefore, in the spring of 1897 when the Kaiser confided that he intended to appoint a new Foreign Secretary in place of Baron Marschall, that Philip should suggest Bernard Bülow. The transfer took place in June so that Bülow could accompany the Emperor on the trip to Russia.

William was enchanted by his new adviser. "Bernard has done clever work and I adore him," he wrote to Eulenburg. "My God! What a pleasure to have someone who is devoted to you, body and soul, and can understand and wants to understand." Bernard also wrote to Philip and managed to be even more rapturous than the Sovereign. "As a personality His Majesty is charming, touching, irresistible, adorable. . . ." And in a letter a few months later: "I hang my heart more and more every day on the Emperor. He is so remarkable! Together with the great King and the great Elector he is far and away the most remarkable Hohenzollern that has ever existed. He combines in a manner that I have never before seen, the soundest and most original intelligence with the shrewdest good sense. He possesses imagination that can soar on eagle wings above all trivialities, and with it the soberest perception of what is possible and attainable; and—what energy into the bargain! What a memory! What swiftness and sureness of apprehension."[1]

[1] *Philip Eulenburg: The Kaiser's Friend:* Johannes Haller.

Bülow showed his suppleness from the very first. He not only dazzled the Emperor, but managed to retain Holstein's goodwill; and he not only retained Holstein, but managed to strengthen his intimacy with Eulenburg. Privately he sympathised with all of them in turn, and despite his " honeymoon " with the Kaiser took pains to see that Eulenburg was not neglected. " How constantly I am with you in thought! " he wrote in December 1897. " I say, write, and do nothing political without thinking of you. By your ideas, indeed, I measure everything that I do for the dear, dear Emperor, and he is always before me as the motive, the aim, the *raison d'être* of everything."[1] Years later, when Bülow came to write his memoirs, he had expunged these emotions from his mind and so completely forgotten his gratitude to Eulenburg that he could only assert that Philip " valued having a personal friend as his chief."

Bülow took up his duties as Secretary of State for Foreign Affairs at a crucial moment in German history. He arrived on the scene to find that the Kaiser was obsessed by one over-riding desire: to build a great navy. This wish was not new; ever since Bismarck had departed he had pressed for naval expansion, and in 1894—when he was making annual trips to Cowes to promote an alliance with Britain—he was talking in terms that agitated his mother. " William's one idea is to have a Navy which will be larger and stronger than the British Navy," she wrote to Queen Victoria, " but this is really pure madness and folly and he will see how impossible and needless it is. One large enough for German requirements and as good as possible of its kind is all that ought to be aimed at—with prudence and safety."[2]

William's naval ambitions, however, were not based on practical needs. He was obsessed by the conviction that it was impossible to be a power of the first rank without a great navy. The truth was that he was dazzled by English grandeur, and no other yardstick would satisfy him. He remembered how thrilled he had been as a child when his grandmother had taken him to a Naval Review, and he had seen the majesty and might of the British Empire spread before him in an armada of ironclads that seemed to stretch as far as

[1] *Philip Eulenburg: The Kaiser's Friend:* Johannes Haller.

[2] *Letters of the Empress Frederick.*

the eye could see. Now that he was Kaiser, ruling over a country bursting with energy, boasting a population of nearly sixty million and an industrial production that was beginning to outstrip Britain's, he was convinced that it was his duty to raise Germany to a similar, if not greater, pre-eminence. One day England would wake up to find that the Fatherland possessed a fleet as awe-inspiring as her own, and what a day that would be for the House of Hohenzollern! "What William I had done for the army, he wished to do for the navy," wrote Bülow. "If William I had been blessed with the unification of Germany, William II wanted to establish Germany at sea and so her position as a world power."

For a while the Empress's fears were put at rest as William's naval aspirations were blocked by the Reichstag. He could not build his fleet unless the lower chamber voted him the money. His Chancellors—first Caprivi and then Hohenlohe—told him that it was impossible to get the bill passed, for Germany was a land power, no one was sea-minded, and with the army being steadily enlarged, the deputies would refuse to sanction the expenditure. William did everything he could to educate his officials and make them understand that Germany could never attain true greatness without a navy. He knew Mahan's *Influence of Sea Power on History* almost by heart and in January 1895 gave an illustrated talk to a group of public men at the New Palace; and the following month lectured the Military Society in Berlin on the relations between army and navy.

William, however, made little headway with his ministers and deputies, and as the months passed became increasingly irritable. He began to blame every international happening, in which Germany did not get what she wanted, to a lack of sea-power. Sometimes he believed what he was saying, sometimes he merely exploited events to make his councillors "navy-minded." Two months before the Jameson Raid, when it became apparent that trouble was brewing between the English settlers and the Boer Government, he wrote to Prince Hohenlohe: "We must make capital vigorously out of this affair for eventual naval increases to protect our growing trade." And when, after the Kruger telegram, Britain sent a naval squadron into the Baltic to warn Germany to mind her own business, he talked loudly of the humiliation that the Fatherland had been forced to endure. The following year, in 1897, Britain refused to renew her old colonial agreements with Germany and asked for new ones to be drawn up; and this, too, was attributed to lack of sea-power. "The people will now perceive," he wrote to Prince Hohenlohe in 1897, "how much valuable time in the last ten years has been wasted, in spite of my warnings. If all ship-building had not been violently opposed for years by the Socialist party and allowed to come to nothing we should not now be practically weaponless on the sea and utterly a prey to those who attack our trade. If we had a strong watchful fleet there would have been no denunciation; our answer must be a large and speedy increase of ships."[1]

Prince Hohenlohe, however, still insisted that a Navy Bill was impossible, and prophesied that the schemes the Kaiser was drawing up would be "stillborn." This time William refused to listen. In the spring of 1897, shortly before Bülow made his appearance, the Kaiser appointed Admiral von Tirpitz as Secretary of State for the Navy. Tirpitz was a huge, black-bearded sailor, politically inexperienced and intellectually limited, but with a passion for a fleet equal to that of the Kaiser. He was a brilliant and unscrupulous organiser and rejected Prince Hohenlohe's defeatism contemptuously. If the German public was not in favour of a fleet it must be re-educated. A Navy League must be established to pour out propaganda; the professors must be indoctrinated, the press regimented, the industrialists instructed, the Princes suborned; in short, the nation aroused.

At this point Bernard von Bülow became Foreign Secretary. Before appointing him the Kaiser asked: "What about my ships?" and Bülow delighted his sovereign by telling him he thought a navy bill could be got through the Reichstag. Of course, he added, it would be necessary "to beat the national drum." "Agreed, agreed," cried William delightedly; this was just what Tirpitz had said, what he himself believed. From then on the Kaiser conferred regularly with his two new advisers, referring ecstatically to Bülow as a "glorious fellow" and to Tirpitz as "the master." They talked of nothing but the navy, planning their campaign, working out their tactics. They agreed with the Kaiser that it was impossible to be a great power without a great fleet, and that their main object was prestige. Tirpitz declared that a navy would

[1] *German Diplomatic Documents.*

demonstrate that Germany was as " well-born " as England; and Bülow later asserted in the Reichstag that the day was approaching when certain nations would no longer be able to " look down on Germany as a stuck-up aristocrat looks down on a modest tutor." Repeatedly the *parvenu* note was struck.

Yet the argument of prestige alone would not be sufficient to sway the Reichstag, and might lend itself to misinterpretation abroad. So the line agreed upon was " defence." Germany was expanding rapidly both in population and industrial production; as she became an increasingly severe competitor she was bound to arouse English jealousy. " We must never fail to insist," Bülow told the Kaiser, " that our naval construction has no offensive purpose behind it but is intended only to create a steady increase in the risk which any power threatening our peace must take to attack us."[1]

Thus the need for protection from British enmity became the key-note of Navy League propaganda. That it was never seriously believed was shown by the fact that few harbour fortresses or coastal defences were erected. Admiral Tirpitz talked about " the German people nearing the zenith of maturity " and Bülow coined the famous phrase about wanting " a place in the sun." Although they both warned the Kaiser not to refer too often to naval plans, he could not contain his enthusiasm and repeatedly made speeches declaring: " We have bitter need of a powerful German fleet," " Our future lies upon the water," " We hold the trident in our hands." On August 20, 1897, he wrote to Philip Eulenburg ecstatically: " The naval or ' Fleet Bill ' is practically ready, it has received my approval and in principle that of my Chancellor. It provides for the strength of the fleet to be attained by 1905 . . . Tirpitz has just organised a huge office which, both directly and through intermediaries, will look after maritima in some 1,000 to 1,500 newspapers and magazines. In the great university towns all over the country the professor class has met us willingly and is going to co-operate by speaking, writing, and teaching Germany's need to possess a strong fleet. . . . What a noble harvest is beginning to grow and what a reward God is giving me for all the care and anxiety that I have experienced over this business! "[1] The Navy Bill, which agreed in principle to the construction of a German

[1] *Memoirs*: Prince von Bülow.

fleet, was passed by the Reichstag on March 28th, 1898, by 212 to 139 votes.

The Empress Frederick seemed to be the only person capable of foreseeing the future. She did not regard the building of a German fleet as a natural development—as Bülow liked to put it—but as a complete departure from the policy that Germany had been pursuing for the past twenty-five years. Germany was a central power flanked on one side by a hostile France and on the other by an expansionist, shifty, aggressive Russia. Under Bismarck, Germany had prevented Russia from forming an alliance with France; and under William, Germany had managed to establish close relations with the Russian Czar which partly mitigated the effect of the Dual Alliance. But until now both Bismarck and William had accepted the necessity of drawing closer to Britain. One day Britain would abandon her policy of isolation, and when that day came she must be led into an alliance with Germany as the only logical and safe course for both nations. A rival fleet, however, was not the way to achieve this. Britain was bound to look upon it as an unfriendly provocation, for she had no army and regarded naval supremacy as a vital necessity for the safety of her island and her empire. Far from impressing her, Germany would only alienate her. If William was not careful he would find every nation in Europe lined up against him.

It was impossible for the Empress to influence her son, but she felt so strongly about the Navy Bill, now in preparation, that she called on her friend, Maria von Bülow, wife of the new Foreign Secretary. She found Bülow himself at home and told him of the dangers she saw ahead. Bülow was not in a mood to listen. Even if he had agreed with the Empress, he never would have risked his future by trying to deter the Kaiser from a course so close to his heart. So he dismissed the Empress's talk as English propaganda and wrote patronizingly in his memoirs: "She believed . . . the best Germany could do was to make herself useful to England and England's high aims and at the same time ennoble herself by keeping in the course of English policy, like a tiny boat in the wake of a great frigate. . . ."

Helplessly the Empress watched the clouding scene. Although her relationship with William had improved, peace had only been restored by rigid restraint. The Empress never interfered or criticised or even proffered an opinion unless she was pressed to do so. This was exactly what William wanted, and at last he welcomed her with genuine affability. Her opinion of him, however, had not altered. She could never forgive his behaviour at the time of his father's death, but the years had diluted the bitterness, and the maternal bond, so curiously unbreakable, now was fashioned almost wholly of pity. How naive and foolish and conceited he was! During the early nineties his brash, boastful utterances ringing with allusions to might and glory had made her writhe in anguish, and she found them almost unendurable. "If I had a shadow of influence I should implore William to make no speeches in public," she wrote to her mother, "for they are too terrible. . . ." Then again: "I wish I could put a padlock on his mouth for all the occasions where speeches are made in public. It is no use to say anything—the Bismarck education . . . has made him what he is."[1]

Gradually the Empress grew more resigned. Bismarck had ruined her son. She began to look upon him as a shell-shock case, a Bismarckian casualty, a victim for whom nothing could be done. He was thoroughly corrupted and Bismarck's coup in alienating him from his parents had made the corruption irremediable. What a difference between William's strident allusions to German might and her dead husband's high-minded sentiments! She often read the message that Frederick had sent to the Iron Chancellor at the beginning of his ninety-nine-day reign. "Not caring for the splendours of great deeds, not striving for glory, I shall be satisfied if it one day be said of my rule that it was beneficial to my people, useful to my country and a blessing to the Empire."

Bismarck had corrupted her son, yet quite unwittingly he had been instrumental in restoring the modicum of harmony between them. As William grew to loathe the old man, who spent his forced retirement in writing anonymous newspaper attacks, he found his mother's company more congenial. At least they shared a common detestation and although it sprang from different reasons the emotion drew them closer. William was enraged when Bismarck broke all rules in 1896, and revealed the details of the Reinsurance Treaty with Russia, which had been abandoned after his departure. But even from the grave the old man mocked them. A few months after his death, in July 1898, the first volume of his

[1] *Letters of the Empress Frederick.*

reminiscences was published and the Empress wrote William that she was disgusted by the tissue of lies. For once he replied warmly to his "most beloved mama;" then he poured out his heart, revealing a striking picture, not of Bismarck, but of himself. He stands before us gripped by romanticism and religious fervour, favoured by God to fulfil a special role; William II, not as the world saw him, but as he saw himself.

The letter begins with a vehement denial that Bismarck ever succeeded in alienating him from his parents. "He never dared and I never should have allowed him to talk about you or dear Papa in my presence." Then he continues: "I perfectly understood the terrible task which Heaven had shaped for me: the task of rescuing the Crown from the overwhelming shadow of its minister. . . . When the strife waxed hot and Bismarck began his most daring tricks against me, not recoiling before even High Treason, I sent a message to him saying: it seemed to me as if he was riding into the lists against the House of Hohenzollern for his own family; if it were so I warned him, that this was useless as in that case he must be the loser. The reply was what I had expected, and I felled him, stretching him in the sand, for the sake of my Crown and our House. . . . Where is he now? The storm has calmed, the standard waves high in the breeze, comforting every anxious look cast upwards; the Crown sends its rays 'by the Grace of God' into Palace and hut, and—pardon me if I say so—Europe and world listen to hear 'what does the German Emperor say or think' and not what is the will of his Chancellor. . . ."[1]

William glowed with pleasure at the thought of his great navy; but he could not make up his mind what foreign policy to pursue. In 1898 he seemed to hold all the key cards and to be faced by an almost embarrassing array of choices. Even his diplomatic support for Russia against Japan was paying off well. Not only had he managed to acquire Kiao-chou as a naval base, but his action had brought Russia and Britain to the verge of hostility over the supine body of China. Russia had seized Port Arthur as soon as the Japanese evacuated it, and after negotiating with the Chinese announced that she had obtained a concession to build a railway linking the port with her own trans-Siberian system. Britain did

[1] *Memoirs:* Prince von Bülow.

not say much, but since she had the largest trading interests of any European nation in China, she countered by sending her Far Eastern Fleet to the Gulf of Pecheli and occupying Wei-hai-wei and Kowloon. She, too, managed to wring concessions from the Chinese Government which legalised her position; nevertheless she was anxious, for it was obvious that Russia had still larger designs on China. Indeed, the Russian Foreign Secretary, Count Witte, swept his hand across a map of China and told the British Ambassador that the Northern Provinces, including Manchuria, would inevitably be absorbed by the Czardom.

William was delighted by this state of affairs for he saw himself in the balancing position, courted by both sides, able to throw his weight first one way, then another, according to what concessions were promised him. His eastern flank was free of trouble and he claimed that his relationship with the Czar was closer than Bismarck's had been; and now Britain was beginning to woo him with a gentle persistence that was entirely new. Bülow wrote his master a letter, studded with the usual adroit flattery, ending: "Your Majesty, on the eightieth birthday of Her Exalted Majesty, Queen Victoria, will be present as *arbiter mundi*."

This was a new and intoxicating position but it was not a policy. Indeed, during the year 1898 the Kaiser's diplomatic activity was so childishly excitable and so patently opportunist that it bordered on pantomime. England's first approach to Germany came in the spring. Mr. Joseph Chamberlain, the Colonial Secretary, told Count Hatzfeldt that he believed Britain's natural alliance was with Germany as both countries had reason to fear French and Russian aggression. He recognised Germany's right to colonial expansion, and pledged himself to use his influence to meet her legitimate aspirations. He did not pretend that his views represented those of the government but he was confident that before long he could persuade them to his way of thinking. "So they have come off their high horse, have they?" the Kaiser wrote delightedly on Hatzfeldt's dispatch. "No grabbing at them though—let them wait." However, after a talk with Bülow, who had been convinced by Holstein that it was all "English devilry," the Emperor became less enthusiastic. At the foot of another dispatch he wrote: "The gist of the matter is: by occupying Wei-hai-wei in a temper and so shaking her fist in front of Russia's nose, England suddenly finds herself in a very uncomfortable position. Russia has not so far struck at the fist, but is keeping that for later on; this is beginning to dawn on John Bull, and he wants someone to get him out of his dilemma. I shall certainly not do this on Chamberlain's promises! We shall see what happens later on."[1]

Chamberlain's nibble, however, gave the Kaiser the bright idea of playing off England against Russia and auctioning Germany to the highest bidder. So he sat down and wrote a letter to Nicky telling him that England had sounded Berlin for an alliance—and here he gave his imagination full play—" with enormous offers, showing a wide and great future opening for my country, that I think it my duty to Germany to reflect deeply before I answer. And before I do, I frankly and openly come to you, my esteemed friend and cousin, to inform you, as I feel it is, so to speak, a matter of life and death. . . . Now as my old and trusted friend I beg you to tell me what you can and will offer me if I refuse. Your proposals must be clear and frank and free from mental reservations so that before I give my final answer I can consider them in my heart and lay them before God, as I am bound to do, since the blessing of peace for my country and the world is at stake. By this letter, dearest Nicky, I show you that I put my entire faith in your absolute secrecy—not a word to anyone—the next generation is in our hands!"[2] But it all proved to be a damp squib. Nicky did not care to expose himself in so naive a manner, and merely wrote back that England had also approached Russia and made him, too, unprecedented offers. " Without thinking twice over it," he added mischievously, " their proposals were refused."

William was now in an awkward position, for he would have to produce something to show Nicholas that his talk was not mere invention. Yet Bülow had dampened Chamberlain's ardour by replying airily that the British Navy would not be much use if Germany was attacked on two fronts; furthermore, that the feeling between the two countries had been so bad ever since the Jameson Raid that German public opinion would not welcome an agreement, unless, of course, England demonstrated her goodwill by generosity in the colonial field. But Chamberlain did not respond, and as the weeks passed William began to fret. Finally,

[1] *Grosse Politik.*

[2] *The Kaiser's Letters to the Czar:* edited by N. F. Grant.

he turned to his mother and asked her to broach the subject to Queen Victoria. "I do know for a fact," she wrote on July 15, 1898, "that William is most anxious for a rapprochement with England and *hopes* with all his heart that England will COME forward in some sort of way, and meet him half way."[1]

At the same time that the Empress wrote the letter, William put forward a proposal that Germany should surrender her claims on Tonga Islands and the Samoan Archipelago in the Pacific in return for which Britain would cede her Nyasaland in Africa and Walfisch Bay, a strong strategic position in South West Africa. But Lord Salisbury politely replied that "the territorial demands were too extensive to be acceptable." William flew into a rage, and this time wrote Queen Victoria himself, saying that his overture had been treated "with something between a joke and a snub." Then he dashed off a letter to Nicky: "Since I communicated to you this June, England has still now and then reopened negotiations with us but has never quite uncovered its hand; they are trying hard, as far as I can make out, to find a continental army to fight for their interests! But I fancy they won't easily find one, at least not mine! Their newest move is to wish to gain France over from you, and they in consequence have suddenly decided to send the Duke of Connaught to the French Army Manœuvres. . . ."[2]

The Kaiser was out of sorts. Neither England nor Russia seemed inclined to offer him any advantages so he decided to try his hand in the Middle East. For months he had talked about a trip to Constantinople, and the Holy Land, which was under Turkish rule, and on October 12, 1898, he finally set forth, accompanied by the Empress and a suite of fifty. He sailed on the *Hohenzollern* to Constantinople and spent several days as the Sultan's guest. The English were indignant that he should consort with "the blood-stained" monster who had slain all the Armenians, but he left the capital with a contract to build a harbour in Haidar Pasha, a concession for a German cable between Constanza and Constantinople, and a plan for carrying the German-built Anatolian Railway to Baghdad.

[1] *Letters of the Empress Frederick.*

[2] *The Kaiser's Letters to the Czar:* edited by N. F. Grant.

He then took ship to Haifa, from which the imperial party proceeded to Jerusalem by horse, camping each night by the roadside. Despite the splendid tents and the many servants, the heat was so overpowering, and the flies so bad, that most of the entourage regarded the pilgrimage as a severe ordeal. The Emperor, however, remained enthusiastic, and his entrance into Jerusalem on October 29th was staged as a magnificent spectacle. Mounted on a black charger, dressed in gleaming white, with a gold eagle at the top of his helmet, William led his brilliantly arrayed Court through the gates of the Holy City. He had brought Herr Knackfuss on the journey to the Middle East, and the artist later reproduced the scene for the benefit of those at home.

The Kaiser was thrilled by everything he saw, and sent many ecstatic wires to the Turkish sultan thanking him for the arrangements. When he reached Damascus, his last stop, he was so delighted to walk on the same ground as the famous Saladin that he made a warm and eloquent speech ending with the words: "Let me assure His Majesty the Sultan and the three hundred millions of Moslems who, in whatever corner of the globe they may live, revere in him their Kalif, that the German Emperor will ever be their friend."[1] This did not please either London or St. Petersburg as both countries had a good many Moslems under their rule, and wondered what new mischief William was about. Furthermore, Russia had always regarded access to the Turkish straits as her "historic mission" and the Kaiser's interest in the Near East aroused deep misgivings. "And how did you like the German Emperor's speeches during his visit to Palestine?" the Czar wrote drily to his mother. The Empress Marie left him in no doubt about her feelings. "The pictures of the journey through the Holy Land would have made me laugh if the whole thing were not so revolting," she wrote to Nicholas. "All done out of sheer vanity, so as to be talked about! That pilgrim's cloak, that pose of Ober-pastor, preaching peace on earth in a thunderous voice as though he were commanding troops, and she wearing the Grand Cross in Jerusalem, all this is perfectly ridiculous and has no trace of religious feeling—disgusting! And further, what a pretty sight when they are both kneeling on Mount Sinai and are being blessed by their children's tutor, expressly brought along for the purpose! . . . But enough of it—it makes

[1] *Memoirs:* Prince von Bülow.

me too angry—it even gives me palpitations as I write about it, and it is not really worth it."[1]

Once the Kaiser returned to Berlin his *malaise* overtook him again, and he remembered how angry he was with England and Russia for not putting a proper value on his friendship by generous offers. Although Chamberlain had tried to placate Berlin by signing an agreement with Germany over Portugal's African colonies (an extraordinary document by which the two countries prematurely divided up Angola and Mozambique in case Lisbon had to apply for a loan and could not meet the mortgage payments) his temper did not improve. In the spring of 1899 he became so annoyed by Lord Salisbury's handling of the Anglo-German dispute over Samoa that he snapped out to the British Ambassador: "Tell your people to behave themselves properly." He made excited speeches hinting that England might have to face the German fleet one day, then wrote an irritable letter to his grandmother criticising Lord Salisbury, and describing Samoa as "a stupid island which is a hairpin to England compared to the thousands of square miles she is amassing right and left unopposed every year." The Queen replied calmly, saying that he must be a victim of a "temporary irritation," "for I do not think you otherwise would have written in such a strain, which I doubt whether any sovereign ever employed in writing to another sovereign—and that sovereign his own grandmother—about her Prime Minister."[2]

He was also offended by Nicholas's long silence and abused Russia so roundly to the British Ambassador in Berlin, accusing her of plots against England, that Queen Victoria wondered if he was abusing England in the same way to Russia. In order to protect her ministers, she wrote to Nicholas on March 2, 1899, that there was "something which you *ought* to know and perhaps do not. It is, I am sorry to say, that William takes every opportunity of impressing upon Sir F. Lascelles that Russia is doing all in her power to work against us. . . . I need not say that I do not believe a word of this, neither do Lord Salisbury or Sir F. Lascelles. But I am afraid William may go and tell things against us to you, just as he does about you to us. If so, pray tell me openly and confidentially. It is so important that we should understand each

[1] *The Letters of Czar Nicholas and Empress Marie:* edited by Edward Bing.
[2] *Letters of Queen Victoria.*

other, and that such mischievous and unstraightforward proceedings should be put a stop to. You are so true yourself, that I am sure you will be shocked at this."[1]

Queen Victoria's allusion to Russia's trustworthiness was diplomatic but scarcely true. All the great powers regarded Russia as a universal trouble-maker, stealthy and unpredictable. Because of her immense size her effectiveness was always over-estimated and she was watched with anxiety and deep suspicion. Her tactics were invariably the same; with one hand she stirred up trouble and with the other swore that idealism prompted her to intervene to put things right. She had employed these methods in the Balkans, encouraging the Slav minorities to rebel against Austrian rule; and now was threatening to do the same thing in China. Soon she would move into Manchuria to maintain order, then refuse to move out again. These tricks prompted Joseph Chamberlain to make a speech pointing out that it was wise to use a long spoon when supping with the devil.

And now in May 1899 the devil, disguised as " charming Nicky " who governed his country with harsh absolutism, was summoning the world's first disarmament conference at The Hague. What was it all about? Most of the powers came to the conclusion that Russia was in severe financial straits; that if she could persuade her neighbours to limit their arms she would be able to maintain her relative strength and at the same time lessen the strain on her economy. This undoubtedly was so, but it was also true that Nicholas II genuinely believed in peace, and would always prefer to gain an advantage by diplomatic manœuvre rather than war. Although the disarmament proposal was rejected, a Court of Arbitration was set up for disputes, " not affecting national honour or vital interests," which still exists today. Neither Queen Victoria nor the Kaiser thought much of the conference, but both decided that it was politic to try and humour Nicky. " I promised the Czar at Wiesbaden," wrote William sulkily, " to help him to a satisfactory result! So that *he* shan't make a fool of himself before Europe, I have to agree to nonsense! But for my part I'll go on trusting and appealing to God and my sharp sword! And —— the whole concern! "[2]

[1] *Letters of Queen Victoria.*

[2] *Grosse Politik.*

William had been at odds with both Russia and England for many months. Quite suddenly the clouds lifted and once again he was in harmony with the world. This was because Queen Victoria, who celebrated her eightieth birthday in May, wrote her grandson a charming letter and suggested that he should mark the occasion by paying a visit to Windsor in the autumn—his first visit since the summer of 1895 at Cowes. He accepted the invitation and asked if he might bring the Empress. On top of this came news that Bülow had completed negotiations with Spain, which gave Germany the Caroline and Marianne Islands in the western Pacific. William thanked him joyfully for acquiring " this pearl for my crown " and gave him the rank of Count.

A month before the visit to England, scheduled for November 1899, the Boer war broke out. All over the continent there was a strong reaction against British " high-handedness," and nowhere was the feeling stronger than in Germany. This was partly due to the fact that it was the policy of the German Foreign Office to encourage the periodic waves of Anglophobia which swept the country, as it was believed to add to Germany's bargaining power, but also to a genuine sympathy for the Boer Government. The Kaiser's consort, the Empress Augusta Victoria, hated England and saw a chance of avoiding the visit which she dreaded—" We really cannot go there," she wrote to Bülow. " I have done as you wished and said nothing to the Kaiser so far—but very soon now our ships will be burned. I am afraid it will do the Kaiser any amount of harm in the country if we really go. Britain is only out to make use of us. Of course, it is frightfully difficult for the Kaiser, but at bottom I think he would be glad to get out of it. I am anxiously awaiting your reply."[1]

The Empress was wrong. The Kaiser wanted to go, and go they did. His visit was immensely unpopular with his own people, and before leaving he tried to allay their passions by making a strong anti-British speech. However, for once, everyone in England was glad to have his moral support, and politely ignored the outburst.

Nothing was left undone for the comfort and entertainment of the royal visitors, who were treated to all the pomp and ceremony at the Queen's command. The Kaiser loved Windsor Castle. He

[1] *Memoirs :* Prince von Bülow.

had always been fascinated by the great battlements whose foundations had been laid nine hundred years before, and from the moment he arrived was deeply emotional. He called Bülow to him and said solemnly: "This is the finest reception and the most awe-inspiring impression of my life. Here, where as a child I went along holding my mother's hand and marvelling, modestly and timidly, at the splendour, I am now staying as King-Emperor." Every morning he annoyed the gentlemen of his military entourage by pointing to Windsor Tower and saying: "From this Tower the world is ruled."[1]

The Kaiser's silky, smiling Foreign Secretary was sympathetic to his mood, but he did nothing to clarify his royal master's conflicting ideas, nor to guide him along a path of logic. The truth was that at the turn of the century only one course was open to Germany: an alliance with England. William's spasmodic dreams of a continental combine were not within the realm of practical politics, for no matter how friendly the relations between Czar and Kaiser Russia's agreement with France precluded any worthwhile arrangement with Germany. It was also plain that if Germany came to an understanding with England, William would have difficulty in getting his navy bills through the Reichstag, for the deputies scarcely could be expected to vote huge sums for Germany's defence against the British Fleet if the two countries were partners.

These were matters that Bülow should have thrashed out with William II but he shrank from doing so. His eye was on the Chancellorship and he avoided anything that might upset his emotional sovereign. Equally important he was determined not to run foul of Baron Holstein. He was frightened of this dangerous unscrupulous man and had no wish to incur his disfavour as Philip Eulenburg had done. Indeed, he followed his advice so assiduously that the Baron dropped his vendetta against the Emperor and no longer complained of the imperial "absolutism." Although Holstein pretended to be in favour of an alliance with England he was incapable of taking a decisive step; he was so saturated with suspicion, so fearful lest Britain get the best of a bargain, that he could only conjure up the reasons for doing nothing at all. This negative policy suited Bülow for it enabled him to keep in with both Tirpitz and the Kaiser. He could champion the fleet and at

[1] *Memoirs*: Prince von Bülow.

the same time dazzle William with assurances that if he played a waiting game England would come forward with far more extensive offers.

It was a disaster of the first magnitude for Germany that Count Bülow should have been more interested in ingratiating himself with the powerful men who surrounded him than in selecting a prudent course for his country. The years between 1898 and 1902 marked a climacteric in European history, for during this period Britain approached Germany three times for an alliance and three times was rebuffed. If William II had been encouraged by Bülow in the autumn of 1899 there is little doubt but that he would have set in motion the machinery for an agreement. Instead, Bülow followed Holstein's advice, and insisted that England, with her troops committed in South Africa, was merely angling for the German Army to protect her scattered possessions from Russian and French threats. He even went so far as to draw up a memorandum advising the Kaiser how to behave towards his English relations!

It is interesting that Count Bülow dared to hand his master a document so insulting in its puerile instructions, so bare-faced in its flattery. "Beyond question," it began, "Your Majesty is more gifted than any of your relations, male or female. Your relations, however, do not extend to you a respect commensurate with the brilliance of your qualities—quite apart from the powerful position held by the German Kaiser. The reason is that Your Majesty has always met your relatives openly and honourably, has initiated them into your plans and hopes, and has thus provided them with the opportunity of putting obstacles in your way. For the most adroit of thrusts, if announced in advance, can be parried even by a weaker fencer. This English journey offers Your Majesty the opportunity of righting this topsy-turvy situation and winning for Your Majesty at a stroke the authority which is properly due to Your Majesty's high qualities and great power. All that Your Majesty need do to secure this is to avoid all political conversations."[1]

Then Holstein turned to the problem of Lord Salisbury, who would be eager to talk politics but who must be "disposed of fairly quickly and with immaculate politeness, but with everyday small talk and no more, asking how his wife is and so on;" then Mr.

[1] *Grosse Politik.*

Chamberlain, who " will try and rush matters and, while ready to offer substantial concessions, will try and push Your Majesty there and then into definite promises with their points raised against Russia.... Your Majesty will just listen politely to him and then give him the reply that his suggestion merits careful consideration and that Your Majesty will ' give full attention ' to it...." Finally, the Prince of Wales " or perhaps H.M. the Queen herself" might raise the question of an alliance. " It would be precisely at this point, in my most humble opinion, that it would then be of far-reaching influence on Germany's political future if Your Majesty were to decline to agree to anything definite, to permit no glimpse to be obtained of Your Majesty's own plans...."[1]

The Kaiser could not follow Holstein's instructions regarding Lord Salisbury, for the Prime Minister's wife had died a few days before the imperial visit, and Salisbury, eager to seize any excuse for avoiding the Emperor, was absent. However, William II and Bülow obediently followed Holstein's warnings in their meetings with Mr. Arthur Balfour—designated as the next Prime Minister—and with Mr. Joseph Chamberlain. Coyly they played the role of undecided maidens with ardent suitors, encouraging one moment, rebuffing the next. Chamberlain told them that personally he favoured an alliance including both Germany and America. If the two Anglo-Saxon nations made common cause with their Teutonic cousin, peace and order would be maintained throughout the world. He realised that Germany had colonial aspirations and believed that he could obtain the backing of his Cabinet colleagues to support her in establishing a protectorate in Morocco. Morocco was a large undeveloped country, rich in iron ore. The Sultan was unable to maintain his authority and warring tribes were threatening to overthrow his regime and plunge the inhabitants into chaos. Even now he could not protect foreign trade or foreign lives and it was plain that some European power would have to step in and restore order. The possession of Morocco, Chamberlain emphasised, would not only give Germany great trading prospects, but an opportunity to acquire important seaports on the Atlantic.

Considering Germany's persistent agitation for colonial expansion, it is curious that the bait of Morocco met with no response. Holstein was so concerned with " high policy " that he scarcely

[1] *Memoirs :* Prince von Bülow.

alluded to it while the Kaiser expressed total disinterest. This was partly due to the fact that for years Morocco had been in a state of anarchy; it was so large and wild and rocky it was difficult to police, and the Sultan had achieved even less than might have been expected. As far back as 1880 the European powers had become so alarmed by Moorish lawlessness and corruption—which made it impossible for them to do business—that they had called a conference at Madrid and forced the Sultan to sign a treaty promising protection for foreign lives, and guaranteeing equal rights in commerce. However, the situation did not improve much. "I have been in most Oriental countries but I have never seen such complete darkness as reigns here," Arthur Nicolson had written to the British Foreign Office in 1896. "The main policy and occupation of the Government is to set the tribes by the ears, to support one side, then wring money out of the victims for assistance rendered...."[1]

William II remembered Bismarck saying that Morocco was a good trap in which to lure France, for it would drain her resources and keep her quiet in Europe. He did not want Germany to carry the burden; besides, he was not interested in colonial territory as much as colonial power. He wanted land in central Africa and China, where the other great nations were competing, so that his voice might be heard in the international councils that mattered. He told Eckardstein that he had no interest in acquisition on the west coast or anywhere else in Morocco; and he had never understood why some Germans placed such emphasis on it.

So the Kaiser and Bülow listened sympathetically to Chamberlain's arguments, then gently raised obstacles that were almost insuperable. Bülow stressed the fact that Germany was on very good terms with Russia and that it would be impossible for her to jeopardize this relationship by an alliance with England unless both parties in the British Parliament endorsed it, and bound themselves to it for a number of years. On the other hand, he assured Chamberlain that an Anglo-German agreement was close to his heart; that he believed in it and would do his best to further the idea in every way possible.

Chamberlain was encouraged, and after the royal visitors departed, decided to test public opinion by flying a kite. He was aware of

[1] *Lord Carnock*: Harold Nicolson.

the hostility that the Boer war had aroused in Germany, but the Kaiser had assured him that he, and he alone, could control German emotions. " I am the sole master of German policy, and Germany must follow me wherever I go." So in a speech at Leicester, Chamberlain hinted at what was in his mind. " Every far-sighted statesman has long been anxious that we should not remain permanently isolated on the Continent and I think that the most natural alliance is between ourselves and the great German Empire. . . ."

This remark provoked a far greater storm of anger in Germany than Chamberlain had foreseen. Join hands with a bully who was beating down the helpless Boers? Never! But Bülow's reaction was even more surprising. Instead of trying to lower the temperature, he fell in with the prevailing mood, and deliberately raised it. In a speech in the Reichstag he delivered a severe rebuff to Britain, mocking her for her haughtiness and jealousy and asserting that " the days of Germany's political and economic humility were over." He ended on the triumphant note that the coming century would decide whether Germany was to be " the hammer or the anvil."

Why had Bülow delivered this surprising attack? The answer was that a new Navy Bill was coming before the Reichstag. The first bill had approved the idea of a fleet, but the second bill was the one that mattered for it determined the size and shape of the German Navy for the next seventeen years. As Holstein was opposed to the alliance with England, Bülow merely followed the course of least resistance and capitalised on the anti-British feeling. He told the Budget Committee that England was deeply jealous of Germany because she was becoming a serious competitor in world markets. " In view of our weakness at sea," he said, " the majority of people in England consider a war with Germany a relatively simple matter in which England would only need her fleet. . . ." On a wave of Anglophobia the Bill was carried through the Reichstag.

Bülow was not disturbed by the fact that Chamberlain was angry and chagrined. Time was on Germany's side; and all that really mattered to him was the Kaiser's goodwill. Near the end of the year, in October 1900, he realised his life ambition by succeeding the aged Prince Hohenlohe as Imperial Chancellor. When the moment approached, however, he suffered some anxiety, for although he had been earmarked as the next Chancellor for many months, the Kaiser hesitated and began to toy with several new names. "Candidly," he told Bülow, "for me, personally, Phil Eulenburg would be much the most acceptable successor. He is my best friend, I am his 'Highest.' But I do not know whether he is equal to it. I have the impression that he himself doubts it. Quite recently he told me that he had neither the knowledge nor the energy wanted for carrying on an important office. He has used up too much of his nervous energy in my service."[1]

[1] *Memoirs*: Prince von Bülow.

8. *Britain's Last Offer*

The German people had grown so accustomed to the Kaiser's melodramatic poses that they almost regarded his exhibitionism as an endearing characteristic. " The trouble with the Kaiser," a Hamburg lady remarked with fond indulgence, " is that he wants to be the bride at every wedding and the corpse at every funeral." Even Count von Waldersee was forced to admit that William was " quite a popular figure." " Apart from his political gambols and his speeches (which are not taken too seriously as people know his excitable temperament)," he wrote in his diary in January 1900, " his whole bearing, his animation and restless activity, impress the masses. By the feminine half of the nation the Sovereign is esteemed as a good husband and father of seven children. People recognize also that he interests himself most warmly in the growth of Germany's happiness and greatness, and devotes his life to these aims; and they are impressed moreover by the numbers of the subjects he takes up and seems to master, and by his more than ordinary capabilities."

Although the Wilhelmstrasse did not share the public estimate of the Kaiser's mental capacity many diplomats regarded his magnetism as a factor to be reckoned with. " The spell of His Majesty's personality " is a phrase that often appears in German official documents. As it was generally conceded that William could charm whomever he chose, no one was surprised when Count Paul Hatzfeldt reported to Berlin, after the imperial visit to Windsor Castle, that even the sophisticated Mr. Arthur Balfour had " never experienced a more stimulating hour " than that which he had spent with the Emperor. Unfortunately, however, William rarely sustained the effect of his stupendous first impressions. Those who came into regular contact with him soon discovered that his desire to fascinate vanished at the first twinge of boredom. Indeed, his good humour was as transient as an ocean breeze, for the smallest irritation could turn it into a tempest leaving in its wake a wreckage of wounded feelings and bitter resentment.

Philip Eulenburg was one of the few people who had nothing personally to complain about. In 1900 the Emperor made him a prince to show him his esteem. Yet even this devoted servant was deeply disillusioned by his imperial master's superficiality and frightening lack of discipline. The man whom he once had described as " that rare and talented being " had long ago become " the poor dear Emperor." Nevertheless Philip still grappled with the Sovereign's turbulent moods, still tried to restrain him from tactless and unnecessary interferences. Once, when he warned William against the use of arbitrary power, the Sovereign feigned astonishment. " I, an absolute monarch ! " he ejaculated sneeringly ; then added somewhat illogically : " When I get back to Germany I shall make Bernhard set the press on the lunatics who see in me the ' absolutist Emperor.' " However Eulenburg could have saved himself considerable anxiety on this score, for the truth was that although Bismarck's constitution had given the Kaiser fully autocratic powers he rarely over-rode the advice of the Wilhelmstrasse.

Far more dangerous was the Kaiser's temperament. Philip found the Norwegian cruises an increasing strain with each passing year, for the Kaiser's tantrums seemed to increase with the advancement of age. In 1900 almost any annoyance was sufficient to provoke a storm, a fact which Philip found alarming in a man of forty. " His Majesty cannot control himself any more when he is angry," he wrote distractedly to Bülow from the *Hohenzollern*. " Yesterday he did not even notice that there were sailors nearby, he simply raved on, so that they could hear every word. . . . I feel as if I were sitting on a powder magazine, and scarcely dare to breathe. Please let political reports be as few as possible, and ask him for none but *unavoidable* decisions."[1]

Much of the Kaiser's excitement was due to frustration. He had a deep urge to achieve great things for Germany, yet his course was never clear ; there was always a tiresome reason why he could not do what he wished, why his impulses must be stifled, his desires quelled. He could not make an alliance with England for fear of alienating

[1] *Philip Eulenburg The Kaiser's Friend :* Johannes Haller.

Russia; he could not join with Russia because of France; he could not expand his colonial empire because of England. Whatever direction he turned he always came up against the negative words and the restraining hands of his own advisers.

When the anti-foreign Boxer Rebellion broke out in China in the spring of 1900 he at last saw a chance of action. Once again he expounded on the Yellow Peril, and without consulting the Wilhelmstrasse, volunteered to send an expeditionary force of 30,000 men. A few weeks later he requested the powers to place Germany in charge of an international relieving force. There already were some thousands of European troops in the Far East—not to mention American and Japanese—for almost all the major powers were doing business in China and had their own military protection. However it was obvious that someone would have to co-ordinate the operation, and as the British Army was fully occupied in South Africa, and Russia and Japan refused to allow each other to direct an expedition, the Kaiser's request was granted. Furthermore, the German Ambassador, Baron von Ketteler, had been assassinated, which, William claimed, gave Germany a prior claim.

The Kaiser regarded the operation as an imperial prerogative and made it clear from the start that military matters were "no business of the Foreign Office," but to be directed "from the saddle as it were." Peking was under siege, and he saw Germany not only as an avenging angel, but as a pillar of Christendom. In this frame of mind he disembarked from the *Hohenzollern* at Bremerhaven on July 27th to inspect the marines about to depart for the Far East. He began by exhorting them to "open the door for culture" but in his excitement recommended very different methods. "You must know, my men, that you are about to meet a crafty, well-armed, cruel foe! Meet him and beat him! Give no quarter! Take no prisoners! Kill him when he falls into your hands! Even as, a thousand years ago, the Huns under their King Attila made such a name for themselves as still resounds in terror through legend and fable, so may the name of Germans resound through Chinese history a thousand years from now. . . ."

Both Eulenburg and Bülow—who had joined the party at Bremerhaven—did their best to suppress the speech, handing an expurgated copy to the press, but one reporter got the story and soon the Kaiser's words were ringing round the globe. When the

World War broke out fourteen years later his phrases were remembered and the word " Hun " became common usage. The Kaiser, however, appeared oblivious to the impression he was making and when he read a revised version of his oration in a German paper he protested to Bülow in dismay: " You have struck out the best parts of it."

A few weeks later William received a severe blow. Field Marshal von Waldersee, the Commander-in-Chief of the Joint Relieving Force, was still on the high seas when news arrived that the troops already in China had succeeded in relieving Peking and that the Imperial Government had fled. " Naturally," wrote Waldersee, " this was at first a great disappointment for the Emperor. He had got it firmly fixed in his head that . . . the Allied advance on Peking, till now regarded as impracticable on account of the rainy season . . . would begin under my supreme command, and mine would be the glory of capturing Peking. Now that dream was over. . . ."[1] The Emperor declared that Russia and England deliberately had " betrayed him," and once again Eulenburg's frayed nerves had to bear the brunt of royal chagrin.

Biographers of William II often attempt to explain his character in terms of his crippled arm. Emil Ludwig in his *Kaiser Wilhelm II*, published in 1923, depicts him as a psychological study, fashioned by the hatred of his mother who, he claims, was horrified at having produced a maimed son. But this accusation was found to be false when the Empress Frederick's letters were published some years later; she did not hate her son; her concern about his arm reflected the sorrow and anxiety that any mother might feel; and her relations with William were undisturbed and friendly until his manhood.

It is tempting to blame the Kaiser's affliction for a nature that swung between two extremes; to claim that his boastfulness hid an inferiority complex; that the arrogance was an attempt to conceal hysteria and timidity. However, no one can be sure that William's character would have been any different if he had had two good arms; and for the sake of the record this writer can find no evidence to suggest that in adult life he found his crippled arm an embarrassment. Almost the only allusion he ever made to it was when he landed at Tangiers and had to ride a strange horse

[1] *A Field Marshal's Memoirs:* Count von Waldersee.

with his "bad arm." He was exceptionally strong and used his one hand with great dexterity. He had a special knife and fork which enabled him to cut his food; he rode with ease; and in ordinary daily life carried himself with such ease that his affliction was scarcely noticeable. The Princess of Pless, who saw him often, wrote in her memoirs: "All the writings about the Emperor's suffering under a morbid sense of his incapacity to use his left arm and his feeling crippled is so much nonsense. Of course, like anyone else he would have preferred to have the full use of his limbs; from birth he had no useful left arm, was brought up to do without one and, I feel certain, never seriously missed it. In public and when posing for his pictures, naturally he did not stick out his ungrown arm and hand for people to wonder at; nevertheless in private he never bothered about it. I have sat next to him hundreds of times, watched him use the special combined knife and fork he always carried, or I have cut up his food for him and he never once showed the sign of any foolish sensitiveness or embarrassment."[1]

Despite the Kaiser's temperamental outbursts during 1900, he behaved extremely well to Britain throughout the Boer war, and, ironically enough, he received little credit for it. His stand was not wholly due to magnanimity, for he remembered how he had burned his fingers over the Jameson Raid. He had learned that Germany could not oppose Britain effectively in Africa without a fleet, so this time he resolved, early on, to remain strictly neutral. When, in March 1900, Queen Wilhelmina of Holland appealed to him to intervene on behalf of the Boers, he replied that he could play no part until he possessed more ships. The ships were vital. For although, he explained to the Queen, the Lord had said "Vengeance is mine," He might select William one day as "His chosen instrument." "Therefore it is in the interests of the world peace as well as the Dutch-Frisian race on the continent that a mighty German fleet shall be on the seas . . . until then Silence and Work."

Nevertheless, England was in real difficulties and the Kaiser might well have taken advantage of it. She was reviled all over the continent, and particularly in Germany, as the oppressor of a small, gallant people, yet her conventional, unimaginative generals could

[1] *Better Left Unsaid:* Daisy, Princess of Pless.

not cope with the irregular warfare waged by the Boer farmers. Early in December, only two months after the outbreak of hostilities, she suffered a series of ignominious defeats which became known as Black Week, and set foreign statesmen speculating on whether the collapse of the British Empire had begun. At this point, in January 1900, the Russian Ambassador, Count Osten-Sacken, talked to the Kaiser and touched upon the idea of a continental combine against England. Several conversations took place and although Osten-Sacken wrote to his Foreign Secretary, Count Muravieff, that the Kaiser would not be sorry to see Russia take action against Britain in the East, William assured Count Bülow that he had offered the Ambassador no encouragement.

Instead, he wrote to the Prince of Wales and gave him advice on how to win the war. He dispatched two series of " notes " summarising, he said, the expert opinion of his Field Marshals. The second series, dated February 19th, contained startling recommendations. He urged the British Army to halt its offensive until more reinforcements were sent out from England. Of course, he added, this could only be done if England was certain that foreign powers would not seize the moment to attack her, " which in the situation of the world appears doubtful." " If, therefore," he concluded, " diplomacy cannot guarantee absolutely to secure the respite just referred to, it would certainly be better to bring matters to a settlement. Even the best football club, if it is beaten notwithstanding the most gallant defence, accepts finally its defeat with equanimity. Last year in the great cricket match of England *v.* Australia the former took the victory of the latter quietly, with chivalrous acknowledgement of her opponent."[1]

The Kaiser's letter was tactless, even spiteful, but it was not menacing and it is a pity that the Prince of Wales did not ignore it. Instead he replied with a marked lack of humour : " I am afraid I am unable to share your opinions expressed in the last paragraph of your Memo, in which you liken our conflict with the Boers to our Cricket Matches with the Australians, in which the latter were victorious and we accepted our defeat. The British Empire is now fighting for its very existence, as you full well know, and for our superiority in South Africa. We must, therefore, use every effort in our power to prove victorious in the end ! "[1]

[1] *King Edward VII :* Sir Sidney Lee.

The Kaiser commented cheerfully: " My last paragraph . . . seems to have given you some umbrage! But I think I can easily dispel your doubts about it! The allusion to Football and Cricket matches was meant to show that I do not belong to those people who, when the British Army suffers reverses, or is unable at a given time to master the enemy, then immediately cry out that British prestige is in danger or lost! . . . As long as you keep your fleet in good fighting trim, and as long as it is looked upon as the first and feared as invincible, I don't care a fiddlestick for a few lost fights in Africa. . . ."[1]

William decided, however, that he might as well get some credit from his English relations for his neutral stand, so when he heard rumours of Russian and French plots he passed the information to his uncle, hinting at " surprises " and " intrigues " on the part of " Sundry People," and asserting: " I want a strong, unhampered England. It is eminently necessary for the peace of the world." On March 3rd he had something more concrete to communicate to the Prince of Wales. " My warnings have not been too soon. Yesterday evening I received a note from St. Petersburg in which Count Muravieff formally invites me to take part in a collective action with France and Russia against England for the enforcing of Peace and the help of the Boers! I have declined. . . . Sir Frank has been informed by me of this preposterous step in a *very confidential* manner."[2] He also let Queen Victoria know that he had saved her country " from a most dangerous situation in warding off a combination aiming a blow at England in a moment which was vital to her. May your Government see in my action a renewed proof of my firm friendship and a sign of my determination to see that you should have fair play. For I am sure that South Africa once under the British flag, order, thrift, life, commerce and peace, with goodwill towards all men, will be assured."[3]

Meanwhile the Russian Foreign Secretary, Count Muravieff, had got wind of what the Kaiser was saying, and instructed his ambassador in London to put it about that the initiative for a

[1] *King Edward VII:* Sir Sidney Lee.

[2] The Russians later insisted that their proposal did not envisage the use of force but was simply a suggestion for a joint protest to the British Foreign Office.

[3] *Letters of Queen Victoria.*

coalition had come from Berlin, not St. Petersburg. Although the Prince of Wales thanked William warmly for his loyal support, Lord Salisbury was sceptical of the whole business and inclined to accept the version unfavourable to the Kaiser. He therefore did not endorse the idea that William had rendered England an "historic service."[1]

William II derived little comfort from his family circle. In different ways, both his wife and mother seemed to exacerbate the nervous strain from which he suffered. His mother was dying of cancer. She confided her doom to him—the bitter climax of a bitter life—at the end of 1899, explaining that the doctors had given her only two years to live. Although she endured great pain throughout 1900 she managed to keep abreast of world affairs, and maintained a wide correspondence by the hand of one of her ladies. William called on her regularly and tried to fulfil the role of a dutiful son but he did not find it easy; despite their reconciliation and their mutual distaste for Bismarck's memory, William still detected a note of criticism in his mother's voice and felt uncomfortable in her company. She made an effort to cultivate an attitude of resignation (once she wrote to Queen Victoria that she felt like a hen who had hatched an ugly duckling) but every now and then she was stung to a protest. When her son declared in a public speech on July 3rd, 1900, that "in the future no great decisions in the world will be taken without Germany and the German Emperor," she wrote her mother wearily: "Dear William has made a new speech with much fanfaronade. I wish the German Government would give up the policy of constant fireworks. . . ."[2]

William's consort had an equally disquieting effect on him. He respected the pious, loving, narrow-minded Empress Augusta Victoria, but found her company far from diverting, for she surrounded herself with ladies even more bigoted and sanctimonious than herself, which produced a deeply oppressive atmosphere. He was amused by his young daughter who, people said, was a replica of himself, but he took little interest in his six sons except to impose

[1] The truth of these proceedings still remains a subject of controversy. For the two opposing versions see *King Edward VII* by Sir Sidney Lee, and *From Bismarck to the First World War* by Erich Brandenburg.

[2] *Letters of the Empress Frederick.*

on them a pattern of harsh discipline, while they, in turn, looked upon him as a terrifying figure to be avoided as much as possible.

The Empress, on the other hand, adored her husband and clung to him with embarrassing tenacity. Bülow describes her as a German "through and through," for despite her official duties her interest centred on her husband and children. She was uneducated, provincial, and professed the greatest disdain for foreigners; the Russians were barbarous, the French immoral, and the English selfish and hypocritical. She disliked the Prince of Wales because of his philandering. She was shocked by the stories she heard about him, and tried to discourage the male members of her family from visiting Britain for fear they might fall under his pernicious influence.

The Empress hated to let William out of her sight. He never made scenes with her, indeed he tried to avoid her, but she had a deep streak of persistence and, no matter how abrupt or indifferent he appeared, insinuated herself into his presence whenever she could. Sometimes he found her solicitude and devotion irritating. One night when he sat up late reading, she remained at his side sewing. Suddenly he said: "Do you mean to spend the night here?" "No, William, but I did not want to disturb you as you have been so busy reading the whole evening." "What else could I do?" replied William. "It is so incredibly dull here."[1]

The Emperor's entourage believed that much of his restlessness sprang from the uncongeniality of his family life. Many of his bachelor week-end parties, his cruises and trips abroad, were devised, they felt, purely to take him away from the Empress. "Every time he returns home," wrote the Controller of the Imperial Household, "I notice how the atmosphere oppresses him. He is always anxious to get away, but his wife's one desire is to keep him in sight as much as possible.... There is something really feminine and touching in the way she clings to him; but often I am inclined to think that it is not without its dangers for the surest way for a woman to make a man dislike her is to run after him too openly."[1]

In September 1900 the Emperor travelled to Rominten, the imperial shooting lodge, for a short holiday. Prince Eulenburg joined him and on this occasion the Empress was permitted to

[1] *Twelve Years at the Imperial German Court*: Count Zedlitz-Trützschler.

come too. Soon after her arrival William told her that the time had arrived to send three of their boys to the military academy at Plön. The idea of the parting, particularly from the youngest Prince, appalled the Empress. For once she lost her composure and made a fearful scene, weeping, imploring, and reproaching, the whole night long. The Kaiser, so accustomed to making scenes himself, was at a loss for what to do, and asked Philip "to come into his compartment in the train and poured out his heart to me in the most wretched and painful manner."[1] Eulenburg made a sensible suggestion; send the two eldest boys away and leave the youngest at home. Then he took his courage in his hands and advised His Majesty to surround the Empress with more educated ladies; and if she made any more scenes at night the Emperor must go into his own room, lock the door, and lie down. The Kaiser appeared to regard this simple recommendation as most ingenious. He nodded and said very thoughtfully: "The plan could be tried; it's not a bad idea."

Despite Eulenburg's solution the Empress's recriminations continued for some months. Respite for the Kaiser came sombrely. On January 18th, 1901, William received word from London that Queen Victoria was dying. He immediately departed for England, arriving at Osborne two days later. He was deeply moved, for his English grandmother not only was the symbol of majesty, the touchstone of all he revered, but had always treated him with dignity and consideration. Although the Boer war was still raging and anti-British feeling was at its height in Germany, William never hesitated. The respect due from one sovereign to another was an obligation he understood.

The Queen died on January 22nd. The scene, wrote Lord Esher, "was stately and dramatic. The Queen now and then recognised those about her, and spoke their names. Her difficulty in breathing was the only painful symptom. Reid—the doctor—passed his arm around her and supported her. The Prince of Wales knelt at the side of her bed. The German Emperor stood silently at the head, near the Queen. The other children and grandchildren were all there, all calling their names at intervals. She died quite peacefully. After the King left for London, the Emperor took charge of

[1] *Memoirs:* Prince von Bülow.

everything. His tenderness and firmness were quite extraordinary, so unlike what was expected of him. He refused to allow Banting's men to measure the Queen for her shell. He turned them out of the room. He sent for Reid and took all the measurements himself. He and the King and the Duke of Connaught lifted the Queen into her coffin."[1]

Queen Victoria's funeral did not take place until two weeks after her death. The Kaiser was so pleased by the warmth of his reception that he decided to remain in England the whole fortnight. This not only alarmed his advisers who felt that " the British " were bound to take advantage of his gullibility, but it distressed the Empress who felt that he might be seduced. She wrote to Bülow to " try and dissuade him from staying." " I think it is particularly dangerous the way everyone—especially the ladies—tries to besiege his warm, friendly nature, and turn his head (they all, of course, want to win him over for their own ends)."[2]

But William refused to budge, insisting to his consort that his aunts needed him. " I must help them with many things, I must give them my advice. . . . They are so kind to me, they treat me like a brother and a friend instead of like a nephew." He also spoke delightedly of how Baron Eckardstein had told him that " when it became known in London in the evening that I was coming to be with Grandmama, the people wept for joy and . . . my action would never be forgotten by the English people."[2]

Meanwhile, in Berlin, jealous pens were busy prophesying disaster. Anglophobia was a national pastime and spread right to the top ; it was too much to see the Kaiser, unprotected by advisers, expanding under the hypocritical kindliness of the sinister British. Even Philip Eulenburg was infected by the wave of jealousy and irritation, and wrote the most malicious letter of all—a letter which Bülow described as showing " real flair." " I am anxious when I think of the beloved Master in Osborne : I think of all the things he will say ! He will be like a child amidst these people who are crude despite their mourning. Amongst them he forgets all his ' shrewdness.' A sort of trustful embarrassment takes possession of him and any one of them could easily get at the secrets of his soul

[1] *Journals and Letters of Reginald, Viscount Esher:* edited by Maurice V. Brett.
[2] *Memoirs :* Prince von Bülow.

(and our state secrets). At the same time he is really in the way. The family scold him behind his back, and his own adjutants wring their hands and wish they could go home. Despite the seriousness of the situation and the real grief which he feels, I must smile when I think of the way in which he is 'exploiting' his deceased grandmother, so that he can avoid seeing 'mother' [Empress Augusta Victoria] as long as possible. . . ."[1]

Meanwhile "mother," as Eulenburg called her, was distracted. When she heard that the new king, Edward VII, had made his nephew an honorary "Field Marshal" she wrote Bülow indignantly that her fears had been justified. "It is supposed to be a gracious act, but I consider it tactless." She was even more annoyed when her son the Crown Prince was awarded the Garter, and the Kaiser's brother, Prince Henry, made an honorary "Vice-Admiral of the British Fleet." However, whatever the British did was bound to be wrong, for all the royalties attending the funeral were given a distinction and if the Germans had not been shown greater favour than the others even more of a storm would have arisen.

General von Plessen, the head of the Kaiser's suite, made matters worse. He sensed the apprehension in Berlin and was quick to capitalize on it, writing that "the English are unspeakably gratified by our coming and by the Kaiser's expressions of friendship at a time when they are suffering such calamities . . . and when they are so generally hated that they talk about it themselves. At the moment they are feeling so small that it will be a long time before they feel as small as this again. Our Master had given them self-assurance and they will certainly recover their historic insolence."[1]

The Kaiser was genuinely moved by the friendliness he met on all sides; yet his amiable mood did not spring only from sentiment. The moment the Dutch mailboat, which carried him and his suite across the North Sea, reached England he became involved in exciting new political developments. Baron von Eckardstein, the Chargé d'Affaires of the German Embassy, awaited His Majesty at the harbour and told him that Mr. Joseph Chamberlain once again was pressing the idea of an alliance with Germany. On the train to London he gave the Kaiser a detailed account of his conversations with Chamberlain which had taken place at a week-end

[1] *Memoirs*: Prince von Bülow.

party arranged by the Duchess of Devonshire. William II was so enthusiastic that he wired Bülow elatedly: "So 'they come' it seems, just as we expected. This is what we have waited for." In the same telegram, sent on January 20th, 1901, he emphasised that Chamberlain had warned Eckardstein that if Britain could not reach an understanding with Germany she would have to look elsewhere. "Baron von Eckardstein tells me of Chamberlain's confidential intimation that it is all over with splendid isolation; England must choose between Triple Alliance and France-Russia. He is *à tout prix* for the former, part of the Cabinet for the latter. Foreign Office for the former. Only if we are not willing, then the swing to the Dual Alliance. The understanding about Morocco again desired by him [Chamberlain] can come about as soon as Lord Salisbury goes to Cannes."[1]

It was perfectly clear to Holstein why Chamberlain again was seeking an alliance with Germany. Although it now was obvious that Britain would emerge victorious from South Africa, no one could pretend that her military performance had been impressive. The continent of Europe was still fiercely pro-Boer and France and Russia, encouraged by England's preoccupations, were looking about with greedy eyes. Indeed, Russia was doing more than looking. She had begun to penetrate Persia, and early in January rumours began to spread—which soon proved true—that the Czar had made a pact with China which virtually meant the annexation of Manchuria. Four months earlier, on September 10th, 1900, Chamberlain had written a memorandum for the Cabinet: "Both in China and elsewhere it is in our interest that Germany should throw herself across the path of Russia. An alliance between Germany and Russia, entailing, as it would, the co-operation of France, is the one thing we have to dread, and the clash of German and Russian interests, whether in China or Asia Minor, would be the greatest guarantee for our safety. I think, then, our policy clearly is to encourage good relations between ourselves and Germany, as well as between ourselves and Japan and the United States, and we should endeavour to emphasise the breach between Germany and Russia, and Russia and Japan. . . ."[2]

Chamberlain's memorandum was written to impress his Cabinet

[1] *Grosse Politik.*

[2] *Letters of Joseph Chamberlain:* Julian Amery.

colleagues and naturally did not present the whole picture. As Chamberlain told Hadzfeldt, he recognised the risk involved for Germany, and was prepared to pay handsomely for her support. He was not thinking in military terms; he believed that a political entente between the greatest sea-power and the greatest land-power would prove sufficiently formidable to hold Russia and France at bay without coming to blows. His idea was to start slowly. As a beginning Britain would support Germany diplomatically in the penetration of western Morocco, balking French designs and satisfying Germany's claims to "a place in the sun" by adding thousands of square miles to the Kaiser's Empire.[1] As confidence grew between Britain and Germany co-operation would be extended to other spheres; the ultimate goal would be Britain's accession to the Triple Alliance, which, in Chamberlain's view, might include Japan and perhaps, one day, the United States.

The Germans were right to analyse the proposals carefully, even to be suspicious of them; they were wrong to condemn them outright, dismiss Chamberlain as utterly cynical, and to refuse to contemplate the alternative. But Holstein's twisted mind threw every picture out of focus; and he seemed incapable of grasping the fact that if Germany wished to conclude a bargain she would have to give a *quid pro quo*. He was so excited by the thought that England might reap some profit from an alliance with Germany that his whole being throbbed with almost hysterical determination to spite her. On January 21st, the day before Queen Victoria died, he deluged London with telegrams. First he wired to Eckardstein to use his influence in preventing the Kaiser from discussing politics or committing Germany in any way. Then he assisted Bülow in drafting a reply to the Emperor which might damp down his ecstatic cry, "So they come it seems." "Your Majesty is quite right in the feeling that the English must come to us. South Africa has cost them dear; America shows itself uncertain; Japan unreliable; France full of hatred; Russia faithless; public opinion hostile in all countries. At the Diamond Jubilee in 1897 English self-conceit reached its highest point; the English peacock spread its proudest display, and preened itself in splendid isolation. . . . Now it begins to dawn gradually on the consciousness of the

[1] England reserved Tangier for herself, because of its position facing Gibraltar, and the control it gave of the Mediterranean seaboard.

English that, by their own strength alone, they will not be able to maintain their world-empire against so many antagonists. . . . English troubles will increase in the next months, and with them the price that we can demand will rise. . . . Your Majesty will execute a master-coup if Your All-Highest can succeed in leaving English personages with the hope of a future firm relationship with us, but without Your All-Highest being at present prematurely bound and committed."[1]

The idea that Britain might come to an understanding with Russia and France infuriated Holstein. "The whole threat," he wired to Count Hatzfeldt, "is just rubbish and humbug. If England makes large concessions in spheres of influence to Russia and France, it will only whet the appetite of its two opponents and make a struggle for life all the more inevitable—a reduced England against reinforced enemies." He also wired to Count Paul Metternich, who was ear-marked to succeed Hatzfeldt as ambassador in London, and who had accompanied the Kaiser as a member of the imperial suite. ". . . The threatened understanding with Russia and France is a patent fraud. Concessions [to France and Russia] might postpone Britain's fight for existence for a few years, but it would only make it the more inevitable by strengthening her opponents and diminishing the power and prestige of the British. We can wait. Time is on our side. . . ."[1]

It was tragic that the master mind behind German foreign policy should belong to a man described by his contemporaries, from Bismarck downwards, as "crazy." And it not only was tragic but remarkable that such an unbalanced intellect could persuade the Wilhelmstrasse that Britain was bluffing when she talked of France and Russia as a possible alternative. The German documents show that no one, with the exception of Count Hatzfeldt and Baron Eckardstein, even questioned this erroneous dictum. Hatzfeldt fought gallantly but he was like a small boat swept aside in a squall. "The English ministers and Chamberlain in particular," he wrote to Holstein on February 10th, "are not so stupid as not to recognise that Germany cannot and will not give them her help in China without the assurance of compensation elsewhere and above all of protection against the danger of a Franco-Russian attack." And he begged Holstein not to dismiss the possibility

[1] *Grosse Politik.*

of an Anglo-Russian understanding, adding that he felt it his duty to give this warning " before the door is shut."[1]

Meanwhile the Kaiser was growing restless. As he was temporarily annoyed with the Czar, he condemned Russian expansion in the Far East, and responded sympathetically to the British approach. But he shrank from the responsibility of taking matters into his own hands. He had no idea that the negative attitude of his Foreign Office stemmed almost entirely from Holstein's influence; in fact he was scarcely aware of Holstein's presence—he had only met him once and believed that with Bülow's advent he had been relegated to obscurity. Holstein's telegrams were always signed by the Chancellor or the Secretary of State, and once, when his name cropped up, William commented with relief: " Who ever hears of Holstein now? "

The Kaiser had often been criticised for flying in the face of his councillors, but the truth was that he made more mistakes by following their advice than if he had trusted his own judgement. At this critical time, instead of imposing his own will, he merely fretted. On the day after the funeral procession, when Queen Victoria's body was being lowered into the grave, he protested peevishly to Count Metternich: " I cannot wobble forever between Russia and England; I would find myself in the end sitting between two stools." And on the day of his departure, February 5th, he lost all restraint. In the morning he drove through the streets of London, and the sentimental British public, impressed by his devotion to his grandmother, gave him a rapturous ovation. The crowds were dense and one man delighted the monarch by shouting " Thank you, Kaiser." " The German Emperor had a noble reception to-day from the citizens of London, who have forgiven him his telegram to Kruger, in consideration of his behaviour during the last ten days," wrote Lord Esher. " I was in St. James's Street. The cortège was a pretty sight. The Blues splendid. Very few police. Large crowds. Much cheering. Very hearty. The Kaiser acknowledged the cheers, the King sitting quietly beside him—which showed fine taste. So the new reign starts under good auguries. . . ."[2]

The occasion ended with a large luncheon at Marlborough House,

[1] *Grosse Politik.*

[2] *Journals and Letters of Reginald, Viscount Esher.*

and William annoyed his suite (and German public opinion) by conferring the Order of the Black Eagle upon Lord Roberts, Commander-in-Chief of the British Army; then, still under the emotional impact of the morning drive, he made a speech, forgetful of the German Fleet and Tirpitz's " real world power," echoing for once the sentiments so often expressed by his father. " I believe there is a Providence which has decreed that two nations which have produced such men as Shakespeare, Schiller, Luther and Goethe must have a great future before them; I believe that the two Teutonic nations will, bit by bit, learn to know each other better, and that they will stand together to help in keeping the peace of the world. We ought to form an Anglo-German alliance, you to keep the seas while we would be responsible for the land; with such an alliance, not a mouse could stir in Europe without our permission, and the nations would, in time, come to see the necessity of reducing their armaments."

Bülow was not worried by the sentiments of his impressionable master. Although members of the Kaiser's household frequently criticised the nauseating flattery with which Bülow deluged the Sovereign, the Chancellor was adept at mixing the honey and poison that brought him to his own way of thinking. Shortly after returning to Germany the Kaiser began to shift his ground. When Baron von Eckardstein saw what was happening he was in despair. In his ardour to revive the negotiations and secure an agreement—his life's ambition—he adopted a novel procedure: he told Lord Lansdowne, the British Foreign Secretary, that Germany would be interested in " a defensive alliance," and at the same time gave Berlin to understand that the suggestion had come from London. Both sides asked the other to state their proposals in writing; after considerable confusion the Wilhelmstrasse made it clear that the only terms Germany would consider was a full defensive pact between the three members of the Triple Alliance and the British Empire. The pact would bind each group to give military aid to the other if an attack were launched by more than one major power—for example, Russia and France. The Treaty would have to be passed by the British Parliament and remain effective for five years.

The Wilhelmstrasse knew that such terms and conditions were an impossibility. No democratic government could bind its

Opposition in such a way. Apart from this, the swing from isolation to such far-reaching military commitments, with no control over actions that might provoke war, stood no chance of being accepted by Parliament. Lord Salisbury more than once had pointed out the liability of guaranteeing the Austro-Hungarian Empire with its discontented, rebellious Slav minorities. However, the very fact that Berlin's proposition was unacceptable was the reason it was proffered. It did not commit Germany, it left the door open, it kept (in Bülow's words) "hope shimmering on the surface," and it put the blame for failure on London.

Bülow and Holstein were the chief architects of Germany's refusal to reach an agreement with England. Most historians declare that through the miscalculations of these two men Germany lost an opportunity that might have won her world supremacy by peaceful means. Yet even without their particular personalities, it is questionable whether Germany would have reached an understanding, for Bülow and Holstein merely reflected popular opinion. Jealousy and hatred dominated Germany at the turn of the century. The animosity was almost chronic, for it had been carefully cultivated for twenty-five years, first by Bismarck to crush the influence of the Crown Prince Frederick and his wife, then by the Kaiser to wring concessions from England. But the ill-feeling leapt up like a flame when the Navy League was established in 1897 to persuade the people of the vital necessity for a fleet. A torrent of propaganda was unleashed, and professors, politicians, soldiers, and newspaper editors joined together from one end of the country to the other to depict Britain as wicked, malevolent, and ever watchful for an opportunity to crush Germany because of commercial rivalry. The works of Professor Heinrich von Treitschke, whose lectures had greatly influenced Admiral von Tirpitz, were introduced into German schools as standard works. The professor talked of German world domination and preached that the subordination of the individual to the State, and a mighty navy, were the two main essentials in reducing Britain to submission.[1]

[1] When Tirpitz wrote his memoirs after the war, he referred to Treitschke as "that splendid man" and declared, "I cannot understand why the spirit of Treitschke has disappeared from the teaching of German history." The omission was rectified under Hitler.

Radio Times Hulton Picture Library

With his mother, the Princess Frederick (the Princess Royal of England)

William as a young boy

The Kaiser's father

Radio Times Hulton Picture Library

The Kaiser's mother

Radio Times Hulton Picture Library

Radio Times Hulton Picture Library

Prince Otto von Bismarck

Radio Times Hulton Picture Library

Prince Philip Eulenburg

Baron Friedrich von Holstein

Radio Times Hulton Picture Library

Prince Edward von Bülow

Radio Times Hulton Picture Library

The Kaiser in a Cuirassier's uniform

Radio Times Hulton Picture Library

With his wife, the Empress Augusta Victoria, and two of their sons

Radio Times Hulton Picture Library

Radio Times Hulton Picture Library

The Kaiser's Uncle Bertie, later King Edward VII of England

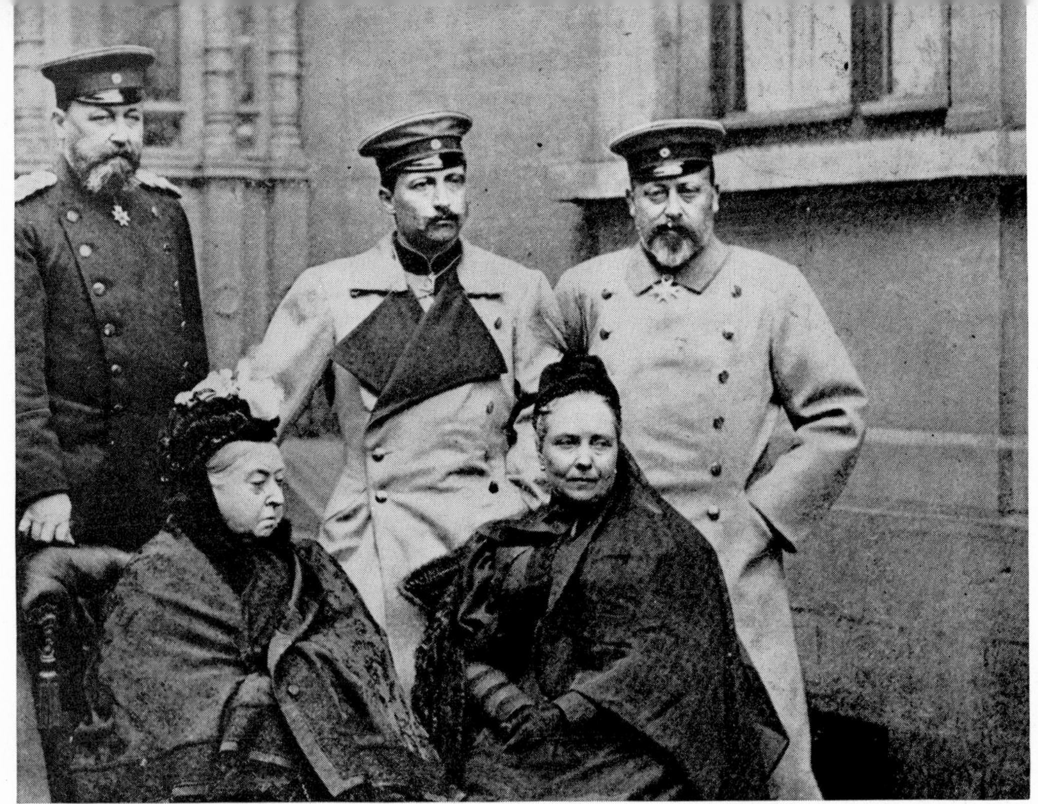

Radio Times Hulton Picture Library

Queen Victoria and the Empress Frederick with (l. to r.) Duke Albert of Coburg, the Kaiser and the Prince of Wales (later Edward VII), in 1894

Edward VII with the Kaiser, Germany, February, 1909

Radio Times Hulton Picture Library

Radio Times Hulton Picture Library

The Kaiser

The Kaiser's first wife, the Empress Augusta Victoria, from a portrait by Lazlo

Radio Times Hulton Picture Library

Czar Nicholas II of Russia (left) with his first cousin King George V of England

Imperial War Muse

The Kaiser dressed for his visit to Turkey in 1898

Imperial War Museum

Inspecting troops with Prince Rupprecht, June 1918

At the front, Cambrai, January 1918

Radio Times Hulton Picture Library

President von Hindenburg

Central Press Photos Ltd.

General von Ludendorff

Radio Times Hulton Picture Library

Radio Times Hulton Picture Library

The Kaiser with his second wife, Princess Hermine, at Doorn

With his brother, Prince Henry, during the war

Radio Times Hulton Picture Library

The Kaiser during the last days at Doorn

"The abuse poured on England by the German press day by day about everything and on every occasion is quite extraordinary," the Empress Frederick wrote to her daughter, Sophie, in the spring of 1898. "I fear that it leads to a distressing conclusion in England, which is that she has no greater enemy than Germany and no more bitter foe than William. This is *not* the case to that extent, and if it has the effect of making England draw nearer to other powers it will indeed be sad for both our countries."

By the time the Boer war broke out and envenomed the situation still further, the German people had become the victims of their own propaganda. They had such a distorted picture of Britain that they were unable to assess correctly her intentions. Even Bülow was worried by the extent of the Anglophobia. In the autumn of 1899 he wrote to Holstein from Windsor: "If the British public clearly realised the anti-British feeling which dominates Germany just now, a great revulsion would occur in its conception of the relations between Britain and Germany."[1]

King Edward sampled this animosity himself when shortly after his succession he travelled to see the Empress Frederick. He had received news that she could not live much longer, and her only wish was to see her brother. During the train journey up the Rhine to Cronberg sullen crowds were waiting at almost every station to sing the Boer National Anthem; and several times angry demonstrators shouted personal abuse to the King. Later, when Edward met Bülow at Homburg, he said: "People in this country are mad. Won't they ever quiet down? They seem to have a crack, they are quite mad."[2]

A strange happening occurred during the King's visit, not altogether irrelevant to the troubled theme of Anglo-German relations. On the third day, Edward VII's secretary, Sir Frederick Ponsonby, received a message that the Empress would like to see him. He was taken upstairs and found her in bed propped up with pillows, her face shrunken with pain. "There is something I want you to do for me," she said, "I want you to take charge of my letters and take them with you back to England."

Sir Frederick replied that he would be glad to do so and she went on: "I will send them to you at one o'clock to-night and I know I

[1] *Grosse Politik.*

[2] *Memoirs:* Prince von Bülow.

can rely on your discretion. I don't want a soul to know that they have been taken away, and certainly Willy must not have them, nor must he know that you have got them." Long after midnight there was a knock on Sir Frederick's door and to his amazement four men entered carrying three large trunks wrapped in black oilskin. He had expected a few packets of letters, but he learned later that the trunks contained all the letters which the Empress had written to her mother over the years; the Queen had returned them to her daughter so that she could look them over with a view to publication, and now she wanted them taken back to the safety of England. Sir Frederick put labels on the trunks addressing them to himself and marked them "China: Handle with Care." Although he became nervous when he saw that a party of soldiers had been employed to handle the luggage of the royal suite, the black trunks passed out of the palace doors unnoticed.

In July, Alfred Rothschild had written to Baron Eckardstein that Chamberlain was "quite disheartened" and would have "nothing more to do with the people in Berlin." "If they are so short-sighted, says he, as not to be able to see that the whole new world system depends upon it, then there is nothing to be done for them." However, the British Foreign Office made one last attempt to revive the talks. The Duke of Devonshire was convinced that the Wilhelmstrasse was sabotaging the negotiations behind the Kaiser's back. Consequently King Edward was persuaded to take the matter up with the Kaiser personally when he visited Homburg in August. Before the talks could take place, however, the Empress Frederick died and the King travelled to Friedrichshof.

It was obvious that the Kaiser's mood had changed in the six months since his visit to England. Upon his return from Queen Victoria's funeral, Bülow had found him "completely under the spell of his English impressions." "As a rule," wrote the Chancellor, "he could not change his military uniform often enough, but now he wore civilian clothes as he had done in England. He wore a tie-pin with his deceased grandmother's initial on it. The officers who were summoned to dine with him were surprised to find their 'Supreme War Lord,' as they called him, wearing civilian clothes. They did not seem to be very pleased by his constant enthusiastic allusions to England and everything English that, in his own words, 'ranked far above German habits and customs.'" However, it did not take Bülow long to alter his master's mood and soon the Kaiser was fulminating against British designs, and referring to Salisbury and Chamberlain and Lansdowne as "unmitigated noodles"—a remark that was repeated to Edward VII but did not cause him much amusement. "Whatever would the Kaiser say if I allowed myself to call his Ministers such nice names?" the Sovereign complained querulously.

The King was prepared to do his best with his nephew but the circumstances of his sister's funeral did not induce kindly emotions. Bitter memories of his brother-in-law's funeral were revived, for the same circumstances were repeated. Once again the palace was surrounded by soldiers, once again the private rooms were ransacked for papers. Sir Frederick Ponsonby watched the proceedings with a quiet smile, for the Empress's letters had arrived safely at his house in England. After the funeral Count August Eulenburg came up to him and asked him confidentially if the letters were in the Windsor archives. Sir Frederick obligingly offered to write and ask Lord Esher, the Keeper of the Archives; the latter replied truthfully that he had no idea of their whereabouts.[1]

The Kaiser's attitude did not augur success. The two monarchs arranged to meet at Wilhelmshöhe for their political conversations, and just before the King arrived William wrote to Bülow: "The building of our fleet must be expedited as quickly as possible. Who will get a nice surprise are the English, and perhaps it is aimed at them.... I am anxious for a sight of the King and Lascelles who are to dine with me on Friday."

[1] *King Edward VII:* Sir Sidney Lee.

This story had a sequel. When Emil Ludwig's biography of the Kaiser appeared after the war containing its cruel picture of the Empress, Sir Frederick felt that the time had come to let the records speak for themselves. The Kaiser, who by this time was in exile in Holland, did everything he could to prevent publication. He claimed that, as his mother's heir, he was the lawful owner of the copyright. But after a long legal argument, the lawyers decided that the Empress had given the copyright to Sir Frederick and that he could dispose of the letters as he saw fit. The Kaiser wrote a preface to the German edition of the book, in which he said that his mother "always had a strong temper" and that after her husband's tragic death "her nerves began to suffer severely." "Everywhere," he continued "she saw enemies harbouring aversion for her, hate even. She was sensitive. Anything hurt her. She was used to quick words and wrote them down...."

Everything went wrong. Lord Lansdowne had given the King a memorandum for his own use, outlining the subjects for discussion; Morocco was the chief item, but it also included China, South Africa, and Kuwait. Under a misapprehension the King had handed the memorandum to the Kaiser when they met at the Empress Frederick's funeral. William immediately sent it on to the Wilhelmstrasse and had a counter-memorandum drawn up which he now gave to his uncle. It was not very encouraging; in China Germany desired " to be conciliatory;" in Kuwait she had " no interest;" in Morocco she " reserved judgement."

However, it was not the memorandum that upset Edward VII. It was the Kaiser's veiled threats, his jovial but cutting remarks, his frequent reference to " perfidious Albion." He told his uncle that the Czar's forthcoming visit to Paris probably would be extended to Berlin and hinted that it might bring unpleasant results for Britain. England could not fail to observe, he said darkly, the strong movement among the countries of the continent towards an economic union to counter British influence, and she would do well to ponder over it.

Whatever the King felt about the meeting, it proved the last attempt to reach agreement with Germany. From then on things moved from bad to worse. The negotiations had come to an end with Germany's insistence that nothing less than Britain's accession to the Triple Alliance was acceptable to them. But Edward VII thought it wiser to inform the Kaiser in writing that the talks were over, so that there could be no misunderstanding if Britain approached other countries. He therefore sent William a message through Sir Frank Lascelles saying that he hoped Germany and England would maintain " a thorough Entente Cordiale," " but to stipulate this co-operation in a formal treaty would be difficult because of the House of Commons."

Germany was not an easy country to deal with. Although Baron Holstein was the chief wrecker of the negotiations, he immediately decided to take umbrage. He told *The Times* correspondent, Mr. Valentine Chirol, that Germany knew how to express " her thanks for our offer of marriage being rejected." He then dug up a speech that Mr. Joseph Chamberlain had made several months earlier, defending Britain against charges of cruelty in

South Africa. The Colonial Secretary claimed that Britain had never approached the examples set " in Poland, in the Caucusus, in Algeria, in Tongking, in Russia, in the Franco-Prussian war. . . ." Bülow referred to this statement in the Reichstag on January 8th, 1902, accusing Chamberlain of having " a warped mind," and delighting his colleagues by quoting Frederick the Great's reply to a criticism of the Prussian Army: " Pay no heed to the fellow and don't get excited; he is biting on granite! "

It was not wise of Bülow to antagonize the one British politician who until now had been Germany's greatest friend. The consequences were swift. " On February 8th," wrote Baron von Eckardstein, " there was a big official dinner at Marlborough House, where King Edward was still living, which was attended by all the British Ministers and the Foreign Ambassadors. As my Ambassador was at the moment ill in the country I was invited as representative of the German Embassy by the express command of King Edward. While we were smoking and drinking coffee, after dinner, I suddenly saw Chamberlain and Cambon go off into the billiard room. I watched them there and noted that they talked together for exactly 28 minutes in the most animated manner. I could not of course catch what they said and only heard two words ' Morocco ' and ' Egypt.'

" As soon as the French Ambassador had left Chamberlain I entered into conversation with the latter. He complained very much of the bad behaviour of the German press towards England and himself. He also referred to the Chancellor's speech in the Reichstag, and said: ' It is not the first time that Count Bülow has thrown me over in the Reichstag. . . . Now I have had enough of such treatment and there can be no more question of an association between Great Britain and Germany.' "[1]

Just as Eckardstein was leaving Marlborough House he was interrupted by an equerry who said that the King would like to see him in his study. Edward VII poured out a whisky and soda and told his guest gloomily that he could not look with confidence on future relations between Great Britain and Germany. " You know, of course, what has happened of late. If the Kaiser now writes me long letters assuring me of his friendship for England, I cannot, I am sorry to say, give much weight to what he says. The

[1] *Ten Years at the Court of St. James:* Baron von Eckardstein.

renewed abuse of England in the German press and the unfriendly and sarcastic remarks of Count Bülow in the Reichstag have aroused so much resentment among my Ministers and in public opinion that for a long time at least there can be no more any question of Great Britain and Germany working together in any conceivable matter. We are being urged more strongly than ever by France to come to an agreement with her in all colonial disputes, and it will probably be best in the end to make such a settlement, because England only wants peace and quiet and to live on a friendly footing with all other countries. As you very well know both I and the majority of my Ministers would very gladly have gone with Germany in all colonial and other questions, but it can't be done. In any arrangement that we may make with other countries in future, it would of course be our principle to avoid any menace against Germany. We only want, as I say, peace and quiet for ourselves and for the world."[1]

In January 1902 Britain signed a treaty with Japan. The Germans were delighted, for they believed that the alliance would bring Britain into conflict with Russia. They did not perceive that Britain had taken her first decisive step away from Germany; that her long period of isolation was at an end.

[1] *Ten Years at the Court of St. James:* Baron von Eckardstein.

9. *The Kaiser and the Czar*

" God knows everything," said Berliners, " but the Kaiser knows better." The Monarch's belief in his own infallibility was not surprising, for although criticism flowed behind his back in private letters and diaries, his person was deluged with flattery. Great officials, generals, sailors, industrialists, and princes bent their efforts to titivating the imperial fancy, feeding the imperial vanity, and bolstering the imperial will. Count Bülow continued to set the pace. " No one could fail to admire—although it shook one's confidence—the inconceivable skill with which he would almost imperceptibly shift his ground whenever he had inadvertently expressed an opinion which did not quite find favour with the Emperor, and veer to his side," wrote Count Zedlitz-Trützschler, Controller of the Royal Household, in his diary in 1903. Later, in a letter to his father he was more vehement. " What can one expect from a Chancellor like Bülow? One day the Emperor said to him on the *Hohenzollern*, ' Your light trousers are enough to upset the best weather forecast,' and he immediately retired to his cabin and put on a darker pair. At other moments he scribbles notes on his shirt cuffs, for fear of forgetting the least of His Majesty's wishes. Whenever by any oversight he expresses an opinion in direct disagreement with that of the Emperor he remains silent for a few minutes and then says the exact contrary of what he has said before, with the preface: ' As Your Majesty so wisely remarked just now, the matter stands so and so.' The policy of a Chancellor who can do such things, must, for all his brilliant gifts, and in spite of the inexhaustible resources of the country, be the worst in the world. . . ."[1]

Even the boastful dynamic Tirpitz and the modest, hard-working General Moltke, a future Chief of the German General Staff, were afraid to argue with him. When the Kaiser visited the shipbuilding

[1] *Twelve Years at the Imperial German Court:* Count Zedlitz-Trützschler.

yards in 1904 he noticed that deck semaphore, a device which he had helped to introduce into the navy as a means of communicating with other ships, was no longer being used. He demanded an explanation and four admirals, including Tirpitz, replied that newer and better methods had been discovered. The Kaiser seemed to feel that his judgement was being questioned and ordered it to be put back. After luncheon, which took place on board one of the ships, the admirals gathered in an agitated group to consider how to get round this foolish command, when the Emperor appeared on deck, sensed the criticism, and approached them angrily. "What is the meaning of all this talk? Are my commands obeyed in the Navy or not?" That evening the admirals reported that the semaphore had been re-installed in every ship in the fleet.

The industrialists and professors were even more sycophantic. Herr Ballin, head of the Hamburg-Amerika Line, and the Mendelssohn brothers, leading Berlin bankers, described the Kaiser as a "genius," while Professor Slaby, of the Charlottenburg Technical High School, frequently assured the Emperor that everybody who had ever dared to resist the All Highest had been obliged to confess himself wrong in the end. "The natural result was that the Emperor said: 'Well, that is so. My subjects ought to do what I tell them, but they always want to think for themselves, and that always leads to trouble!'"[1]

William II did not read the newspapers. He preferred to spare himself unnecessary labour by having cuttings prepared by the Foreign Office. Every day columns of newsprint were pasted on to large, gilt-edged sheets and sent to the palace. Valentine Chirol, *The Times* correspondent in Berlin, saw the Press Bureau at work when a member of the Foreign Office invited him to his office and showed him the assortment of news to be sent to the Emperor. "I observed that they did not include an important article which I had read elsewhere," wrote Chirol, "and he replied rather sententiously: 'My dear Sir, you do not seem to understand that such matters have to be laid before *Majestat* according to plan, and the article you mention might disturb the impression to be produced on the "All Highest's mind."'"[2]

William revelled in the illusion of autocracy, unaware that his

[1] *Twelve Years at the Imperial German Court:* Count Zedlitz-Trützschler.
[2] *Fifty Years in a Changing World:* Valentine Chirol.

advisers regarded him as a problem child who, with skilful handling, usually could be made to do as he was told. Count Bülow, despite his air of subservience, knew exactly how to compose the cloying phrases that brought his master into line. Nevertheless things did not always turn out as the Chancellor expected. William was so impulsive that even when he saw eye to eye with his advisers he frequently took matters into his own hands and by an impetuous speech or a sudden conversation gave events an emphasis or a startling twist that had not been planned. Furthermore, on certain subjects the Emperor was adamant; no one could advise him on his relations with the Czar. Although he was willing to accept Bülow's broad policy he would brook no interference in the execution of it, insisting that it could only be carried out by his personal impact on Nicholas.

Who, then, ruled in Berlin? Foreign governments can be forgiven for finding German policy bewildering, and for constant speculation as to who, in truth, held the reins of power. Baron von Holstein's views dominated the scene but since he had no authority he could not be held responsible; Bülow had the authority but he did not dare to claim it openly for fear of offending Holstein or the Kaiser; and when things went wrong he denied it altogether. "Bülow has often declared quite innocently in regard to measures which have called forth excitement: 'I have nothing to do with it, that is all the Kaiser's doing!' and so forth," wrote Count von Waldersee in 1902. "He admits quietly therefore that he is not Chancellor at all, but that the Kaiser is doing the work."[1]

This recognition suited the Kaiser. Very occasionally, when he was in an expansive mood he gave credit to Bülow; in July 1901 he wrote to Eulenburg: "I allow Bernard to rule. Since I have had him I can sleep in peace. I leave everything to him and know it's all right." (Eulenburg scribbled on the margin: "All very fine if the dear thing only did.") Usually, however, William took the opposite line declaring that he, and he alone, controlled the realm. In December 1901 he wrote to Edward VII: "I am the sole arbiter and master of German Foreign Policy and the Government and country *must* follow me even if I have to 'face the music.' May your government never forget this. . . ."[2] Yet when mistakes

[1] *A Field Marshal's Memoirs:* Count von Waldersee.
[2] *King Edward VII:* Sir Sidney Lee.

were made he shed responsibility as quickly as Bülow did, and fell back on the excuse that he was only a constitutional monarch. In his memoirs he explains the disastrous Kruger telegram, saying: "The Imperial Chancellor . . . remarked that I, as a constitutional ruler, must not stand out against the national consciousness and against my constitutional advisers. . . ."[1]

Who ruled in Berlin? The Kaiser ruled, swayed by Bülow, who, in turn, was directed by Holstein; and everyone blamed everyone else when things went wrong. However, all of them agreed that Britain would never succeed in reaching an understanding with the nations of the Dual Alliance; so when this proved false, no one could fasten the blunder on the other—at least not for a while.

Nineteen hundred and three. This was the year when the Kaiser referred to God as "the Great Ally." Certainly it seemed that God was smiling on Germany. This was the golden year, when there was scarcely a cloud on the horizon; the German Army stood supreme, the German Navy was expanding, German wealth multiplying, German arrogance swelling. The political situation was more than satisfactory. Germany and her two partners, Austria and Italy, were stronger than Russia and France, and the hope was growing that Russia might be drawn away from France altogether. As for Britain, she was isolated. All she had was her alliance with Japan and that was leading her towards hostility with Russia. Germany was always well off when Britain quarrelled with Russia, and the Kaiser rubbed his hands in glee. Eventually Britain would be forced to approach him cap in hand; but he would not show much enthusiasm until his fleet was built, then he might condescend to an alliance, with Germany as the dominant partner. So in June 1903 William II praised God as the champion of the German cause. "Raise your eyes! Lift up your heads! Look to the heights, bend your knee to the Great Ally, who has never forsaken the Germans and who, if He has at times allowed them to be sorely tried and discouraged, has again raised them from the dust."

Scarcely four weeks before this speech King Edward VII had paid a visit to Paris which had been hailed on both sides of the Channel as a brilliant success. Feeling in France against England was still bitterly hostile; the interests of the two countries clashed in Egypt

[1] *My Memoirs:* William II.

and the Sudan, and the subject of the Boer war continued to arouse passion. When the King entered Paris sullen crowds lined the streets and ruffians booed and catcalled, but Edward only smiled. For the next three days, wherever he went, to the races, the opera, official luncheons and dinners, he took delight in praising " French genius," " French grace," and " French spirit." By *bonhomie* and good manners alone he won over Paris; when he departed the crowds gathered again, but this time to give him an ovation. The German Ambassador described the visit in a dispatch to the Wilhelmstrasse as " a most odd affair."

The Germans had known for over a year that the French and British were holding conversations. In January 1902 Count Hatzfeldt had telegraphed: " I learn in strict confidence that for about ten days negotiations have been proceeding between Chamberlain and the French Ambassador for the settlement of all outstanding differences between France and England in colonial questions."[1] No one in Berlin worried. Although the talks had been eagerly welcomed by the French Foreign Minister, M. Delcassé (who was regarded in Berlin as Germany's arch enemy because of his desire for a rapprochement with Britain), Bülow and Holstein were confident that they would not come to anything.

It was not until the King's visit to Paris that Bülow began to take the warnings of Hatzfeldt and Eckardstein seriously. " The news received here," he wired the German Ambassador in St. Petersburg, " of a general Anglo-French understanding which, according to Baron Eckardstein, is to initiate the new Triple Entente, is by no means optimistic. . . ."[2]

However, in the next few months events took a turn which lessened German fears. Russia not only refused to move out of Manchuria but appeared to have designs on Korea as well, so Japan began to prepare for war in earnest. The Kaiser did all he could to encourage the Czar to defend his " rights," declaring that it was the duty of Holy Russia to lead a religious crusade against heathen races. He sent more paintings executed by Herr Knackfuss and designed by himself; one depicted William, dressed in glittering armour, holding a huge crucifix in his raised right arm, while the Czar crouched at his feet, clothed in a Byzantine garment that

[1] *Grosse Politik.*
[2] *German Diplomatic Documents.*

looked like a dressing-gown, gazing at him with humble admiration. German and Russian battleships cruised in the background. The Kaiser's paintings were accompanied by enthusiastic letters which were signed " Admiral of the Atlantic," and always referred to Nicholas as " Admiral of the Pacific." On December 4th, 1903, he gave the Czar technical advice about his ships and guns and enclosed a report describing the secret aid that the Japanese were receiving from the Chinese. " I hope the Admiral of the Pacific will not be angry at the signals of the Admiral of the Atlantic, who is always on the look-out. Ta, ta, best love to Alix from your devoted friend and cousin *toujours en vedette*. Willy."[1]

The Kaiser's motives in urging Russia forward were partly idealistic, for he had returned to his theme of the Yellow Peril and talked about it with deep emotion. However, he had other reasons as well. Britain was Japan's ally, pledged to help her militarily if she found herself at war with more than one power. That meant that if France came to Russia's support Britain would be obliged to aid Japan, and the two seconds, far from arriving at a permanent understanding, would be brought into conflict with one another. Britain was on the hook, and the more she struggled, the firmer she was caught; at least that is how it looked to Berlin, and that is why Baron Holstein described the situation as " highly advantageous."

The Germans may be forgiven for doubting British policy and, even more, for finding it inexplicable as it did not follow any familiar pattern. Unlike the Germans, the English had little faith in the written word; indeed they avoided it whenever possible for it meant dotting too many i's and crossing too many t's which, they had discovered, often led to unpleasant complications. They hated to tie themselves down to unforeseen commitments, preferring to improvise as they went along. That was why they had refused to join the Triple Alliance. They saw nothing illogical in their present position for they regarded their expediency as logical in itself. They were also eager to clear up colonial problems with France, so they opened talks; and if at a later date they could get on better terms with Russia, why not? None of this struck them as strange or irrational, merely as common sense.

[1] *The Kaiser's Letters to the Czar:* edited by N. F. Grant.

Britain therefore ran her two policies in separate harness. In February 1904 the Russo-Japanese war broke out, and two months later London imperturbably announced the signing of the Anglo-French entente. It was stressed that the agreement was not military, merely a settlement of disputes in Newfoundland, Siam, Africa, and the New Hebrides. The only point that attracted much attention was France's renunciation of Egypt in return for a free hand in a large part of Morocco. And since this was the same bait that Germany had turned down in 1901 Berlin could scarcely make a fuss about it. Furthermore, the German Ambassador in London, Count Metternich, was reassuring. "I am convinced that the British Government, by the progressive reconciliation with France, which has fallen so neatly into their lap, means no contrary implication as regards Germany. . . ."[1] So the German Government instructed the semi-official newspaper, *Norddeutsche Algemeine Zeitung*, to announce that there was nothing in the convention to which Germany could take umbrage. Bülow sounded the same note in the Reichstag. " From the point of view of German interest we have no objection to make against it . . . we are interested in this country, as in fact the rest of the Mediterranean, principally from the economic point of view. . . ."

This unusual docility sprang from the fact that the Germans still hoped that the entente would lead Britain, and certainly France, into trouble with Russia. Holstein wrote that it could even split the Dual Alliance. His reasoning might have proved correct if one factor had not gone wrong: the Russo-Japanese war did not proceed according to plan. Russia's huge population and unlimited resources had always induced Europe to regard her as a formidable opponent, and military experts had predicted a crushing defeat for Japan. Instead, the reverse took place. Japan began the war by a surprise attack on Russian warships lying off Port Arthur and sank three of them;[2] in August she destroyed Russia's Pacific fleet, a few weeks later her Vladivostock squadron, which left only the Baltic fleet at large; and in the autumn she scored a decisive military victory near Mukden. This situation altered the whole political

[1] *Grosse Politik.*

[2] Japan sank the Russian ships before declaring war; unlike her action at Pearl Harbour thirty-seven years later this was regarded not as a treacherous act but as a brilliant stroke of war.

outlook. There was no danger of Britain, being drawn into the conflict, and France, who had never shown any desire to become mixed up in it, was less anxious than ever to be involved. More important still, Russia was in no position to dictate to anyone.

The Kaiser, however, refused to be disheartened. Russia fought on despite her adversities, and William hoped that the situation might enable Berlin to detach her from France and draw her into the German net. This was the time to strike. Nicholas II should be made to see what an unworthy and feeble ally he had in France. If William could persuade him to sign a treaty with Germany, France would be bound to tag after him, as she would not dare to be left alone on the mainland, and the Dual Alliance would have to play the role of junior partner to the Triple Alliance. At last William would have the continental combine with which he had toyed so long, and the only isolated country would be the haughty Britain.

With this aim, the Kaiser offered to coal Russia's Baltic fleet. Since Germany officially was neutral, Britain protested sharply, mindful of her treaty obligations to Japan. This gave William an opportunity. On October 27th he wired Nicholas: "It is not impossible that the Japanese and British Governments may launch protests against our coaling your ships, coupled with a summons to stop further work. The result would be the absolute immobility of your Fleet and the inability to proceed for want of fuel. This new danger would have to be faced in common by Russia and Germany together, who would both have to remind your ally France of the obligation she took over in the treaty of the Dual Alliance. . . . In this way a powerful combination of the three strongest Continental Powers would be formed, which the Anglo-Saxon group would think twice before attacking."[1]

A week before this letter was dispatched a curious incident inadvertently played into the Kaiser's hands. The Russian Baltic fleet, on their way through the North Sea, mistook a few British trawlers fishing on Dogger Bank for Japanese torpedo boats and fired on them. One of the boats was sunk, two men were killed and others wounded. Even when the Russians saw their mistake they did not stop to rescue the wounded. The news caused consternation in London and although the Czar promptly wired the King his regrets, saying that he had received warnings that the

[1] *The Kaiser's Letters to the Czar:* edited by N.F. Grant.

Japanese " were lurking in fishing smacks for the purpose of destroying our squadron on the way out," the King was incensed by Admiral Rozhdestvensky's callous behaviour. Lord Lansdowne told the Russian Ambassador that England would demand a full apology, reparations, and the punishment of Rozhdestvensky if an inquiry proved negligence.

The Czar, greatly excited, replied to William's letter: " I have no words to express my indignation with England's conduct over the Dogger Bank incident. . . . I agree fully with your complaints about England's behaviour concerning the coaling of our ships by German steamers . . . it is certainly high time to put a stop to this. The only way, as you say, would be that Germany, Russia, and France should at once unite. . . . Would you like to lay down and frame the outlines of such a Treaty? As soon as it is accepted by us France is bound to join her ally."[1]

The very day of the Czar's reply the Kaiser and Bülow drew up a draft treaty and sent it to Russia. The most important article stated: " In the event of the two Empires being attacked by a European Power its Ally will help it with all its land and sea forces. The two Allies, in case of need, will also act in concert in order to remind France of the obligations she has assumed by the terms of the Franco-Russian Treaty of Alliance."

As soon as the draft was dispatched William began to waver. Perhaps the language was a little brusque; he wired alterations explaining that although the agreement was aimed against Britain it would not do to provoke her by speaking too bluntly. Meanwhile the Czar also had second thoughts, for the British Foreign Office, under pressure from King Edward, had suddenly modified its tone. The King, bearing in mind the future possibility of an entente with Russia, had suggested to Lord Lansdowne that he allow things to quiet down, for " perhaps we may be on a better footing with Russia later."

So the Czar now wrote William that although he was confident that France would follow his lead, he could not sign the treaty without first submitting it to Paris. The Kaiser knew this would prove fatal, as the treaty was, in fact, incompatible with the spirit of the Franco-Russian Alliance. He refused flatly to give his consent. " My opinion about the agreement is still the same: it is impossible

[1] *The Kaiser's Letters to the Czar:* edited by N. F. Grant.

to take France into our confidence before we have come to a definite arrangement. Loubet and Delcassé are no doubt experienced statesmen. But they not being Princes or Emperors I am unable to place them—in a question of confidence like this one—on the same footing as you my equal, my cousin and friend."[1] The Czar could not decide what to do, so he did nothing. For the next six months the matter lay in abeyance.

By this time, the end of 1904, Count Bülow and Baron Holstein were taking a serious view of the Anglo-French entente. Reports from the German Embassy in London persisted in suggesting that the British regarded the understanding with France as a stepping stone to a Russian agreement. Since Germany had failed to detach France by means of a special treaty with Russia Holstein decided that Germany must try and smash up the Anglo-French honeymoon by rougher methods; and Morocco appeared to offer the best opportunity. If Germany could block French expansion in Morocco, France might see that British support was worth very little, and turn towards Berlin.

Holstein worked out his Moroccan campaign on the argument that the Madrid Treaty of 1880, signed by all the major powers, guaranteed equal trading rights to all nations; France, on the other hand, always introduced a system of economic protection in her colonies so there was every reason to suppose she would try and do the same in Morocco; Germany had signed a commercial treaty with the Sultan in 1890 which gave her a special position; and although she did not do as large a business with Morocco as Great Britain, her trade was greater than France's which certainly gave her the right to be consulted before deals were made behind her back.

William II proved an embarrassment, for he did not fall in with Holstein's plan as the Wilhelmstrasse had hoped. In the first place he still believed that the more deeply France became committed in Morocco the less trouble she would prove in Europe. " In His Majesty's opinion," wrote Bülow, " all this would turn the eyes of Frenchmen away from the Vosges, and they might in time forget and forgive Alsace-Lorraine. Moreover, the conquest would weaken them militarily. . . ."[2] The Kaiser also believed that a

[1] *The Kaiser's Letters to the Czar:* edited by N. F. Grant.

[2] *Memoirs:* Prince von Bülow.

French occupation would benefit German trade, for conditions in the interior were still so lawless that it was difficult to do business. Even Bülow, in 1902, had told the French Ambassador in Berlin, M. Bilhourd, that " Germany had practically speaking no interest in Morocco, so slight and insignificant is it up to the present time."[1]

But prodded by Holstein, the Chancellor now changed his mind, and decided to transform Morocco into a major issue in an effort to drive a wedge between Paris and London. Despite the Kaiser's desire to improve relations with France, despite M. Delcassé's assurance that the free trade principle of the Madrid Treaty would be upheld, the Chancellor began to concoct a devious plan. In February an episode occurred which played into his hands. A French emissary arrived in Fez from Paris and pressed the Sultan to place his customs in French hands and to allow French officers to organise his troops. Instead of stating Germany's objections openly, Bülow asked the Kaiser, who was about to depart on a southern cruise, if His Majesty would pay a visit to Tangier.

William II was horrified. A visit by the German Emperor to the Sultan of Morocco would cause a sensation; not only would it show the world that Germany intended to thwart France and to challenge England, but it would be regarded by all foreign conservative elements as an act of treachery. That a ruler who aspired to a colonial empire should throw his weight on the side of Arabs against his European neighbours would be condemned in England as " outrageously caddish." Finally, besides hotly disapproving of this policy William II shrank from repeating the Kruger telegram episode and allowing himself to become a personal target of abuse. He flatly refused to consider it. Bülow pleaded eloquently but he remained adamant. Then the Chancellor dazzled him with a vision of the diplomatic triumph that might ensue, and William said he would " think about it." But on his way to Lisbon he hardened once more against it. " I had several talks with Freiherr von Schoen, who accompanied me as representative of the Foreign Office," he wrote in his memoirs, " as to the advisability of the visit. We agreed that it would be better to drop it." So after paying his respects to the King of Portugal at Lisbon, William II wired that Tangier was said to be full of anarchists and he could not

[1] *A History of the English People:* Elie Halévy.

possibly call there. Bülow replied emphatically, wrote the Kaiser, " that I must take into consideration the view of the German people and of the Reichstag, which had become interested in the project, and that it was necessary that I should call at Tangier. I gave in, with a heavy heart. . . ."

The Emperor's ship dropped anchor off the Moroccan coast in a heavy sea with a stiff east wind blowing, and he hoped that his suite would consider it too rough for him to land; but his equerry did a trial journey and reported, with irritating assurance, that it was not difficult at all. The episode was just as nasty as William had imagined with the street lined with " Italian and South-French anarchists, swindlers and adventurers." The Sultan's black uncle was waiting to receive him with a white Arab stallion, so high-spirited that it was difficult for the Kaiser to manage the beast with only one arm. The ride was a nightmare, for the horse reacted to the seething mass of people " who displayed their enthusiasm by rending the air with deafening shouts, and shooting wildly in every direction," wrote Baron Schoen, a member of the Kaiser's suite. " A military band sent by the Sultan, which vainly tried to drown the uproar made by the people, added to the confusion. The horse became so restive that I asked a French officer who seemed to be in command whether he could not put a stop to the firing. He replied gloomily that he had some influence over the handful of regular troops which had been entrusted to him, but none whatever over the half savage Kabyles."[1] The Kaiser did not remain long. He advised the Sultan's uncle " not to give way blindly to French pressure; " told the French representative that he had come to preserve the independence of Morocco and the principle of the " open door " policy for all nations; called at the German Legation and emphasised that Germany's commercial interests would be safeguarded; then, with considerable relief, departed.

He had not under-rated the sensation the visit would create. At first, however, the European powers were not only shocked but bewildered. What was Germany after? Until now she had raised no protest over Morocco. King Edward regarded it as " a mischievous prank " and President Loubet as " a downright insult." The pattern did not become clear until the Sultan turned down France's administrative proposals and backed Germany, who now

[1] *Memoirs of an Ambassador:* Baron Schoen.

demanded a conference of all the powers who had signed the Madrid Pact of 1880.

M. Delcassé angrily rejected the proposal and Germany countered by hinting that she was prepared to use force if France persisted in her uncompromising attitude. So here was the show-down; the Sultan backed by Germany, and France backed by Britain. But *was* France backed by Britain? What help could Britain give, if Germany's twenty-two army corps marched into Paris? And Russia was even less to be counted upon. Her troops had suffered an ignominious defeat at Mukden and only the week before, on May 27th, Japan had virtually annihilated the Russian Baltic fleet—the last of the Czar's navy—in the greatest naval battle since Trafalgar. Peace terms were now being negotiated.

France went into a panic, split between defiance and appeasement, with a majority on the side of peace at any price. President Loubet and M. Delcassé led the "stand firm" group while the Prime Minister, M. Rouvier, representing the mass of the people, begged the Cabinet to come to terms with Germany, pointing out that the British Navy did not "run on wheels" and there was nothing to stop the German Army from reaching Paris.

The British Government no longer regarded Germany's game as obscure. Morocco had little to do with the quarrel; Berlin was trying to bring about M. Delcassé's fall, and to secure a new Foreign Minister who would put an end to the Anglo-French entente. "I did not desire war with France either then or later . . . but I did not hesitate to confront France with the possibility of war, because I had confidence in my own skill and caution," wrote Bülow in his memoirs. "I felt that I could prevent matters coming to a head, cause Delcassé's fall, break the continuity of aggressive French policy, knock the continental dagger out of the hands of Edward VII and the war group in England; and simultaneously, ensure peace, preserve German honour, and improve German prestige."[1]

So German threats grew more menacing, and special emissaries from Berlin made it clear that neither M. Delcassé nor his policy could be tolerated any longer. On June 6th Prime Minister Rouvier informed President Loubet that the Cabinet would have to choose between himself or Delcassé. President Loubet's chief secretary recorded part of the conversation in his diary. "This morning

[1] *Memoirs*: Prince von Bülow.

M. Rouvier came to the President's study gravely upset," he wrote. "He had received the most startling news of the state of mind of William II. War is hanging over our heads; the Emperor can invade France within twenty-four hours; the worst eventualities are to be feared; if war breaks out, it will mean within a couple of days the outbreak of revolution in Paris and the great cities."

A cabinet meeting was held that same day, and the majority voted against Delcassé's policy. Delcassé resigned; France announced her acceptance of the conference proposed by Germany;[1] and Arthur Balfour pointed out grimly to Edward VII that the French Foreign Secretary's "dismissal or resignation under pressure from the German Government displayed a weakness on the part of France which indicated that she could not at present be counted on as an effective force in international politics. . . ."[2]

King Edward was so annoyed that when he went abroad in the summer he took pains to avoid meeting his nephew. A German comic paper showed the King leaning over a map of Europe planning a journey. "How can I reach Marienbad without running into my dear nephew?" he mused. "Flushing, Antwerp, Calais, Rouen, Madrid, Lisbon, Nice, Monaco? No. . . . Very dangerous. . . . Ah well, I'll just go by way of Berlin; there I'm sure not to find him. All right!"

The Kaiser was in a state of high excitement. He was so thrilled by Germany's triumph that he poured out his gratitude to the Wilhelmstrasse, and rewarded Bülow with the title of prince. The victory over France and England had fired him with confidence and his imagination was teeming with new ideas. He secretly resolved that while he was on his annual summer cruise in the North Sea in July he would seek a rendezvous with the Czar and push through the treaty that had nearly been signed the year before. Bülow suspected his intentions and was nettled to learn that his sovereign did not wish him to accompany him, despite his recent masterstroke. Instead, the Kaiser took with him the subservient Count Tschirschky, who was soon to become Foreign Secretary. The truth

[1] President Theodore Roosevelt congratulated the Kaiser on having got rid of "that scamp Delcassé," and praised his broad outlook in calling a conference to deal with Morocco.

[2] *King Edward VII*: Sir Sidney Lee.

was that William II believed he could do more with the Czar alone than with prominent officials around—particularly a prima donna like Bülow who only seemed to make Nicholas ill at ease.

The Kaiser believed that he was approaching Nicholas at a psychological moment. Not only had Russia lost its entire fleet in the disastrous Japanese war, but the country was disturbed by revolutionary acts. Some months earlier the peasants had declared a general strike and in January thousands had gathered outside the Winter Palace to present a petition to the Czar; the guards had fired upon them and although the massacre had cowed the nation groups of anarchists were still committing outrages. Nicholas was not likely to reject a strong, friendly hand at such a difficult moment. Apart from all this, he surely must be grateful for William's unwavering loyalty throughout his ill-starred war. When Admiral Togo had achieved his spectacular victory in May, William had written consolingly that even Frederick the Great and Napoleon had suffered defeats.

So he set out on his North Sea cruise with high hopes. He was aware that Germany was moving towards a new crisis, for only seven months earlier, in December 1904, Count Schulenburg, the German Military Attaché in London, had written that Britain's "further policy is a union with Russia which would leave Germany isolated. . . . It is altogether improbable that friendly relations will again be established between England and Germany. The only remedy against conflict with England lies in a union with Russia."[1] England and Germany were competing for Russia just as they were competing for France, and the fate of both nations depended on the outcome. That was how William saw it; and when he allowed his mind to contemplate the prospect of success he grew deeply emotional. If Russia could be persuaded to sign the treaty, France would be forced into the combine, then perhaps other continental nations would join, and in the end even America might enter. Not Germany, but haughty Britain, would be isolated; and William II would be leader of the strongest combine in the history of the world.

The Kaiser played his hand carefully. He wired the Czar casually, suggesting a friendly meeting somewhere in the Baltic; and Nicholas wired back, just as casually, naming the Bay of Björkö

[1] *Grosse Politik.*

off the coast of Finland. William then telegraphed Bülow and asked for a copy of the draft treaty which had been shelved for the past six months. He sat up that night copying the contents in his own hand. Next day, on July 23rd, the *Hohenzollern* slid into Bjorko and dropped anchor near the Czar's *Polar Star*.

It was very remote: " no human dwelling as far as the eye could reach, grey sky, grey water and an infinite loneliness." Among the members of the Kaiser's suite was General von Moltke who was amazed at how quickly the shy and reserved Nicholas succumbed to the Kaiser's rather boisterous charm. " The longer we sat at the table," he wrote, " the more he unbent; finally he was all pleasure, laughed and talked vivaciously; it was plain to see that he was happy in surroundings where he was safe. He and all his suite were of the most studied amiability; they were all suddenly able to speak German, we scarcely could recognise them."[1]

The conversation was enlivened by abuse of Edward VII. " He [the Czar] was uncommonly pleased with our Moroccan agreement, for a conference in Algeciras which would open the way for permanent good relations with France," the Kaiser wrote Bülow. " When I pointed out that in spite of egging on by England, France had downright refused to take up our challenge and therefore no longer wanted to fight, he said quickly: 'Yes, that I saw; it is quite clear that the Alsace-Lorraine question is closed once for all, thank God!' Our talk then turned on England, and it very soon appeared that the Czar feels a deep personal anger at England and the King. He called Edward VII the greatest 'mischief-maker' and the most dangerous and deceptive intriguer in the world. I could only agree with him, adding that I especially had had to suffer from his intrigues in recent years. . . . He has a passion for plotting against every power, of making 'a little agreement,' whereupon the Czar interrupted me, striking the table with his fist: 'Well, I can only say he shall not get one from me and never in my life against Germany or you, my word of honour upon it!' "[2]

The Kaiser did not mention the treaty that night, but the next morning " it came about easily, because it was God's will." William rose early, and prepared himself for his task by prayer. He opened his Bible at random and read, prophetically: " He shall reward

[1] *Erinnerungen*: H. von Moltke.
[2] *Grosse Politik*.

every man according to his works." Then as he walked the deck with Nicky he mentioned the treaty. " Oh yes, to be sure, I remember it well, but I forget the contents of it. What a pity I haven't got it here." William patted his pocket triumphantly and replied that he had it with him. " He seized me by the arm," William wrote Bülow, " and drew me out of the saloon and into his father's cabin and shut all the doors himself. 'Show it me, please!'; his dreamy eyes shone with a brilliant light.

" I drew the envelope out of my pocket, spread out the paper on the writing table of Alexander III before the picture of the Dowager Empress, among a lot of photos from Fredensborg and Copenhagen, and laid it before the Czar. Once, twice, three times he read the text I have sent you. I prayed a hasty prayer to God that He would be with us now and guide the young ruler. It was still as death; only the sea whispered; and the sun shone gaily into the dark cabin, and just in front of me lay the *Hohenzollern*, gleaming white, and the imperial standard on her fluttered high in the morning breeze; I was just reading on its black cross the letters *God with us*, when the Czar's voice said beside me: 'That is quite excellent. I quite agree!'

" My heart beat so loud that I could hear it; I pulled myself together and said quite casually: 'Should you like to sign it? It would be a very nice souvenir of our interview.' He glanced over the paper again. Then he said: 'Yes I will.' I opened the inkpot, gave him the pen and he wrote 'NICHOLAS' in a firm hand, then he gave me the pen, I signed, and when I stood up he clasped me in his arms and said: 'I thank God and I thank you; it will be of most beneficial consequences for my country and yours; you are Russia's only real friend in the whole world, I have felt that through the whole war and I know it.' The water stood in my eyes for joy—indeed it was running down my forehead and my back—and I thought, Frederick William III, Queen Louise, Grandpapa and Nicholas I were near at that moment!

" When I pointed out to the Czar that it would be well to have say two counter-signatures, it was usual with such documents, he assented and sent for Tschirschky to come over and for Admiral Bírileff to come down. . . . We gave them both a résumé of the treaty, and the old sailor mutely caught my hand and kissed it reverently. And so the morning of June 24th, 1905, at Björkö is a turning-point in the history of Europe, by the grace of God; and a great relief to my dear Fatherland, which will now be freed at last from the frightful vulture-talons of Galia-Russia."[1]

The Kaiser was not well served. However melodramatic his words, however doubtful his attempts to foil France by rushing the Czar into action, there can be no doubt that if such a treaty had become operative it would have "turned over a new leaf," as the Kaiser put it, "in the history of the world."[2] However, William had made an alteration in the text of the principal article, which declared: "If any European State attacks one of the two Empires the allied party will employ all its naval and military forces to assist its ally." After the word "ally" William had inserted "in Europe." He did not want to find himself fighting for Russia in the Far East.

The events that took place when Bülow and Holstein studied the document give the reader a penetrating glimpse of the hopeless confusion in which Germany was led. Holstein told Bülow that the words "in Europe" impaired the treaty. If Britain attacked Germany, Germany must be sure that Russia would counter-attack in Afghanistan and India. Indeed, where else could Russia help Germany against Britain? Certainly not in Europe! What escaped Holstein's attention was the fact that Britain was most unlikely to attack a German-Russian combine, and even less likely a German-Russo-Franco combine!

Bülow cynically adopted Holstein's doubts for the simple reason that they happened to suit his book. He had decided that the

[1] *Grosse Politik.*

[2] What the Kaiser thought he had achieved may be seen by a telegram which he drafted to President Roosevelt but which Bülow persuaded him not to send. "The Emperor Nicholas II and I have concluded an agreement to lend each other mutual help in case any European power should attack one of us, and France is to be co-signatory to it. In fact Germany enters the dual-alliance—originally concluded against it—as third party. So the triple-alliance and the dual-alliance—instead of glaring at each other for [no] purpose at all—join hands and the peace of Europe is guaranteed. This is the fruit of our understanding with France about Morocco, the fact, upon which you sent me so kind compliments. I am sure that this grouping of powers is leading to a general 'detente,' will be of great use in enabling you to fulfil the great mission of peace, which Providence has entrusted to your hands for the good of the world." *Origins of the Second World War:* Sidney Fay.

Kaiser's " *in Europe* " clause would serve as the grand climacteric ot his career. For years he had been subservient and sycophantic to the Emperor, not because of admiration but fear. Here was a golden opportunity to gather the sort of power that Bismarck had wielded. If he refused to countersign the treaty and proffered his resignation he would give the Kaiser a real fright and teach him that when he went off to meet the Czar it would be wiser not to exclude his Chancellor. Bülow knew his resignation would not be accepted. Basking in the triumph of his Moroccan policy he was safe; William had just shown the world his esteem for his Chancellor by making him a prince; he could scarcely drop him now without making himself ridiculous. Holstein also favoured the move. He not only disliked the Kaiser and was always ready to strike a blow at him, but for years had been urging ministers to use the threat of resignation to put an end to the exasperating interferences. So Bülow sent the Emperor a long, badly argued letter relinquishing the Chancellorship.

10. *Vendetta*

The Kaiser became hysterical when he received Bülow's resignation. He sat down at his writing table and covered sheet after sheet of paper with wild exhortations. "If Bismarck had succeeded in securing the Björkö Treaty," he declared, "he would have made all the nations acclaim him." Then he broke into a flood of lamentation and self-pity, ending with a threat to commit suicide. "To be treated like this by my best and most intimate friend . . . has dealt me such a terrible blow that I have completely collapsed, and fear that I may have a major break-down. You say the situation since the addition of 'in Europe' to the Treaty has become so serious that you cannot take the responsibility. Serious to whom? And in the same breath you believe you can be responsible to God for leaving in the lurch, in a situation which you yourself describe as peculiarly serious, your Emperor and Master to whom you have sworn fealty, who has showered affection and distinctions upon you, as I believe your most faithful friend, and your Fatherland?

"My dear Bülow, you can't do that to either of us! We have both been called by God and made for one another to work and to achieve for our German Fatherland! If it is true—which I do not think possible—that through a fault of mine, according to your opinion, a still more serious situation has been brought about, it happened with the best of intentions! You know me well enough to believe that! Your personality is worth a hundred thousand times more to me and our Fatherland than all the treaties in the world. . . . Remember that you, personally, sent me to Tangier against my will, to win a success in your Moroccan policy. I landed because you wanted me to in the interests of the Fatherland, mounted a strange horse in spite of the handicap of my bad arm, and if the ride came within an inch of costing me my life, *you* were responsible. I had to ride between Spanish anarchists because *you* wished it, and your policy was to profit by it! And now, after I have done all this, and much more for you, you want to desert me simply because a situation appears to you to be serious!

"No, Bülow, I have not deserved it of you! . . . You cannot and must not repudiate me; it would be disavowal of your own policy this year and I should be a laughing-stock for the rest of my life. This I could not survive. Let me have a few days' rest and concentration before you come, because the agitation your letter has caused me is too great; I am incapable of any calm discussion at present. Your faithful friend, William R.

"P.S. I appeal to your friendship for me, and do not let me hear any more of your intention to retire. Wire me after this letter the word 'All right' and I shall know that you will stay! For the day after I receive your resignation, your Emperor will no longer be alive! Think of my poor wife and children! W."[1]

Bülow declares in his memoirs that he was so overcome by the letter that he agreed to stay and to put his counter-signature on the treaty. The truth was that he now felt himself the master. William was so relieved by the outcome that he was as obedient as a small child. "Since Björkö," the Chancellor crowed to Holstein, "His Majesty will write to the Czar . . . exactly what we suggest to him."[2] Now he was ready to try and make the treaty operative. Nicholas had promised not to show the document to his ministers until after the Russo-Japanese peace terms had been signed, which was still a month in the offing. The reaction of the Foreign Minister, Count Lamsdorff, would be important, for he would advise the Czar on the possibility of bringing France into the agreement.

Everything depended on not allowing the Czar's enthusiasm to wane. So William sent him letters of encouragement which were screened by Bülow who apparently approved of the mixture of schoolboy fervour and malice. "The 'arch-intriguer and mischief-maker in Europe' as you so rightly called King Edward has been hard at work in the last months;" "the Continental Combine flanked by America is the only way to prevent the whole world from becoming John Bull's private property;" "Britain only wants to make France her 'catspaw' against us, as she used Japan against you." As for the British Navy's visit to Swinemunde: "I have ordered my fleet to shadow the British and when they have anchored

[1] *Furst von Bülow Denkwurdugkeiten.*

[2] *Grosse Politik.*

to lay themselves near the British Fleet, to give them dinner and make them as drunk as possible to find out what they are about."[1]

However, the Kaiser's efforts were to no avail. When the Czar showed his ministers the Bjorko Treaty in September 1905 Count Lamsdorff was appalled and " could not believe his eyes or ears." " Has His Majesty forgotten that we have a Treaty with France ? " he asked, remarking later to a colleague: " This detail no doubt escaped His Majesty in the flood of the Emperor William's eloquence." Ironically enough, Count Witte, the Finance Minister, declared that the words " *in Europe* " gave Germany a " monstrous advantage."

The Czar finally was obliged to telegraph the Kaiser that the treaty was felt to be incompatible with the terms of the Dual Alliance. On September 29th William replied : " The working of the treaty, as we agreed at Bjorko, does not collide with the Franco-Russian alliance, provided, of course, the latter is not aimed directly at my country. . . . Your Ally notoriously left you in the lurch during the whole war, whereas Germany helped you in every way as far as it could, without infringing the law of neutrality. That puts Russia morally under obligation to us. . . . I fully agree with you that it will cost time, labour and patience to induce France to join us both. . . . Our treaty is a very good base to build upon. We joined hands and signed before God, who heard our vows. I therefore think that the treaty can well come into existence. What is signed is signed ; God is our testator."[1] But the Czar buried Björkö under an oppressive silence, and refused to allude to it again.

The Kaiser did not give up hope, for he had one more string to his bow. He decided to woo France at the Algeciras Conference, scheduled to meet in the middle of January 1906, to settle the future of Morocco. His plan was to give her such a smooth passage that the pro-German element in the French Government would be strengthened. If Paris could be made to see the advantages of friendship with Germany the entente which had cracked so badly after Tangier might shatter altogether and the Bjorko Treaty spring to life in its place.

Baron Holstein, however, had a very peculiar idea of how to

[2] *The Kaiser's Letters to the Czar* : edited by N. F. Grant.

conduct a courtship. He, too, wished to draw closer to the French, but he insisted that this could only be achieved by making it clear that British support was not powerful enough to ensure France the seizure of Morocco. He favoured the bludgeoning tactics that had secured the dismissal of M. Delcassé. Consequently he dispatched two very unpleasant delegates to the Conference who spent their time whispering menacingly that if the talks broke down because of French intransigence Germany would be compelled to use force.

The Conference therefore proceeded in an atmosphere heavy with threat and foreboding. All the signatories of the Madrid Pact were present: Morocco, the three members of the Triple Alliance, the two members of the Dual Alliance, Great Britain, Spain, Portugal, Holland, Belgium, Sweden, and the United States. The English delegation was well aware that Germany's aim was to smash up the entente and wondered how the hand would be played. As the champion of Morocco's economic independence, Berlin held very strong cards, and there was considerable fear that she might command a majority following. Indeed, Bülow had instructed his two delegates, Count Tattenbach and Count von Radowitz, that whatever happened they were not to allow themselves to be shown at a disadvantage. Prestige was all-important, and they must prevent any issue being put to a vote unless they could command a majority. " If any question on which we have once taken a stand finds all the others, or a majority of them, against us," wrote Bülow, " then neither forcefulness nor threats will be of any use, as our position, after all that has passed, would be rather ridiculous."[1]

Bülow, however, had reckoned without the personality of his representatives. Count Tattenbach was hated by everyone. " Really a horrid fellow," wrote Sir Arthur Nicolson, the British delegate, " blustering, rude and mendacious. The worst type of German I have met." Although Count von Radowitz was not so aggressive, he scarcely endeared himself by declaring mournfully: " We have no wish to fight, but if we are forced to it we will crush them like flies." Therefore, when an innocent question of procedure arose on March 3rd, and the Germans asked for an adjournment, Sir Arthur Nicolson saw his opportunity. Quick as a flash he suggested putting the matter to a vote. Too late the Germans realised their

[1] *Grosse Politik.*

mistake. Every nation, except for the Austrians and the Moors, ranged itself against Germany.

Panic gripped the Wilhelmstrasse. Germany had been isolated; clearly she had no friends. The fact that even Italy, one of her partners in the Triple Alliance, had voted against her was thought to be indicative of how far feeling had swung against her.[1] The humiliation was complete. There was nothing for her to do but swallow her pride and adopt a conciliatory attitude. In the end she won enough concessions over issues involving the State Bank, customs, and port control to save her face to some extent. At any rate she impressed the Americans, who did not seem to understand the issues. They took the Conference at its face value and thought it merely involved economic questions. The fact that all the powers, including France, signed the Act of Algeciras, solemnly pledging to uphold the Sultan of Morocco's independence, and to maintain an open door policy, deeply impressed the White House. The German Ambassador in Washington wired to Berlin that President Roosevelt had asked him " to inform His Majesty the Emperor of my heartiest congratulations on this epoch-making political success at Algeciras." " Even though the foregoing does not appear to agree with the facts," commented the Ambassador ruefully, " I am convinced that the words spoken by the President come from the heart."[2]

The Kaiser was bitterly disappointed. He stormed against the handling of the Conference and told Bülow that Algeciras had reversed his Moroccan success. This was true enough, for the entente not only had been repaired but visibly strengthened.[3] Bülow was determined not to lose the Emperor's confidence, and decided that the time had come to sacrifice his friend, Baron Holstein. He told William that Holstein had deliberately disobeyed the instructions given to him, and was wholly responsible for the failure. The Emperor accepted this explanation and on April 17th wrote a minute at the bottom of a dispatch. " Herr von Holstein

[1] Italy's defection was due, in fact, to a secret agreement with France promising support on the Moroccan issue in return for French help over Italian designs on Tripoli.

[2] *Grosse Politik.*

[3] Under the stimulus of Germany's war threats Paris and London had opened secret military talks which were held regularly and continued until 1914.

in his clever way twisted my perfectly definite orders and arrangements with the Chancellor in such a manner that the exact opposite was the final outcome. He constantly stirred up poison against France anew and pressed so heavily on the Chancellor that the latter in his garden to my great astonishment repeatedly asked me the same question—whether I wished or desired war with France! Whereas my instructions . . . said expressly: 'Algeciras is to be the stepping stone of the beginning of the agreement between France and Germany.' "

If the Kaiser had understood the power that Bülow had allowed Holstein to exercise, he would not have accepted this excuse; as it was, he exonerated his Chancellor but said that he would not be sorry to see Holstein dropped from the Foreign Office. Bülow welcomed the idea, for he had begun to doubt Holstein's judgement; furthermore, Holstein was becoming almost impossible to work with. He made endless scenes and was always threatening to resign. Count Tschirschky, who had been appointed Secretary of State when Baron von Richthofen died in January, did not like the way he walked into his room unannounced, and had begun to lock his door. Holstein had taken umbrage, and placed one of his many letters of resignation on Bülow's desk. He had also quarrelled with Otto Hamman, the Head of the Foreign Office Press Bureau, demanding that the department should be brought under his authority. "I perfectly understand your moral prejudices against that blackmailer," Bülow told Hamman. "When the Conference is over I will get rid of him, but I must keep him on now, for he might seriously injure the national interests by getting up wrangles in the press."[1]

But how to get rid of Holstein, that was the question. Bismarck had been afraid to let him go because he would "blab in foreign parts" and Bülow had no wish to become a target for Holstein's psychopathic hate and vengeance. He would stop at nothing; that everyone knew. Bülow thought it out with great care, and later his friends declared that the manœuvre was his diplomatic masterpiece. On April 5th, the day that Bülow was due to address the Reichstag on the result of Algeciras, he fished Holstein's three-month old resignation out of his desk and ordered Count Tschirschky to take it to the Sovereign. The Kaiser had been forewarned

[1] *Bilder aus der Letzeten Kaiserzeit:* Otto Hamman.

and was ready to sign it; but Holstein was not to know about it for twenty-four hours.

That afternoon Bülow suddenly fainted while making his speech and was carried home. The timing of this illness was so convenient from Bülow's point of view that many people claimed it was deliberate. Not only did it relieve the Chancellor of the necessity of defending a bankrupt policy, but it spared him Holstein's fury when a few days later he learned that his resignation had been accepted. Also, it put Holstein off the track. When Bülow recovered, he assured Holstein that he had had nothing to do with the matter; how could he have done? He was ill in bed. Obviously one of Holstein's enemies had seized the moment of Bülow's incapacity to persuade the Emperor to let him go. Then Bülow consoled him; even though Holstein had lost his official position, Bülow would continue to consult him, for how could the Imperial Chancellor do without his trusted friend?

Baron Holstein had not been feared for nothing. He was enraged by his dismissal and his whole being throbbed with the determination to destroy the person responsible for his downfall. Although his smothered hatred for the Emperor burst into new flame, he knew that William would not have taken the step of his own accord. Remarkably enough, he accepted Bülow's plea of innocence, and began feverishly searching for the culprit. Who was it? Not Hamman, he was too humble to have access to the Emperor; not Tschirschky, he was too new at the Foreign Office. Someone highly placed, someone with influence, someone who hated him. When he learned that Prince Philip Eulenburg had lunched at the palace the day that the Emperor had countersigned his resignation, the search was over. Instantly, he declared that Eulenburg was the man he was after. Perhaps he really believed it; or perhaps he decided that the Emperor's best friend was too perfect a victim to overlook.

Holstein had not seen Philip for years. Their friendship had come to an end because of Eulenburg's stubborn loyalty to the Emperor and his repeated refusals to join Holstein in his intrigues to curtail " His Majesty's arbitrary power " and give more authority to the Foreign Office. One day, when Eulenburg called on Holstein, the latter made his displeasure clear by sending word that he was "not at home." This had ended the relationship. The paths of the two men did not cross again, even accidentally, for shortly afterwards Eulenburg resigned his ambassadorial post at Vienna on grounds of ill-health. Although Bülow persuaded him to remain on the Foreign Office list *en disposition*, he seldom visited the Wilhelmstrasse and took only a remote interest in the problems of the day.

Nevertheless Eulenburg remained close to the Emperor. Every year William invited him on his Baltic cruise, and scarcely an autumn passed without the Sovereign visiting Eulenburg's estate at Liebenberg. Whenever Philip was in Berlin he lunched or dined at the palace; and he was always present at the Emperor's annual shooting party at Rominten. "I can still see his pale face emerge from behind the red curtains of the gallery when he came to the tea-table of the Empress and sat down to entertain us with his store of literary and artistic reminiscences," wrote a member of the household. "One could easily understand how the robust personality of the Emperor, so frank, so generous, so open-hearted, was attracted to the somewhat reserved, mysterious, gentle nature of this brilliant man. . . ."[1] When Count Witte, the Russian Finance Minister, stopped at Rominten on his way back to St. Petersburg from the Far East, he carried away a picture of Eulenburg, suave and smiling, sitting with dignity in an imposing arm-chair, looking every inch an Emperor, while his actual Majesty perched on the arm, chattering and laughing.

Eulenburg had a love of beauty and a generosity of mind rare in Germany at this particular period. He sought nothing for himself and tried earnestly to give William wise and dispassionate advice. If anything, he was too high-minded, for the only times he threatened to bore the Kaiser was when he lectured him on the virtues of truth and nobility.

Holstein's campaign to destroy Eulenburg was not only poisonous but instructive, for it throws a searching light on the characters of the men in charge of Germany's destinies. The first indication received by Eulenburg that he had been marked down as a "victim" was on May 1st, 1906, when he received a letter from Baron Holstein which began: "My Phili—you needn't take this beginning as a compliment, since nowadays to call a man 'Phili' means—well,

[1] *Memoirs of the Kaiser's Court:* Anne Topham.

nothing very flattering. You have now attained the object for which you have been intriguing for years—my retirement." The letter went on to say that no man who valued his moral reputation would care to be seen with such a "despicable person" as Eulenburg.[1]

"Has he gone out of his senses?" Eulenburg wrote in his diary. Yet he knew at once the game that Holstein was playing. Homosexuality was widespread in Germany and Austria, and during the past few years there had been a number of scandals involving army officers and other highly placed persons; the Emperor Franz Joseph's brother had been driven into exile by such accusations; so had the brother of Prince Philip Eulenburg. Sexual abnormality, despite its prevalence, was a criminal offence and could lead to prison; even worse, it was regarded as such a moral outrage that it spelled utter social ruin. As a result, it was the most damaging charge, short of murder, that one person could make against another, and on more than one occasion unscrupulous antagonists had tried o fasten it on innocent men.

Eulenburg regarded Holstein's letter as "a matter of life and death." "I wired instantly to Axel Varnbuler, who is exceedingly punctilious in affairs of honour," he wrote in his diary, "and betook myself by the next train to Berlin, with the letter in my pocket. Varnbuler dispatched to Holstein the appropriate challenge: 'Exchange of pistol shots until disablement or death.'

"I went to the Foreign Office to give information of the proceeding, as I am *en disposition*, and therefore under the Office. Bülow is still laid by, after his slight seizure on April 5th. Tschirschky is representing him. When I told Tschirschky about the challenge, he literally collapsed upon a chair. He said that this would be one of the world's greatest scandals—for God's sake and the Emperor's couldn't I withdraw the challenge? I said I couldn't dream of doing that, and I went back to Varnbuler."[1]

As no word was heard from Holstein on May 2nd, and the Foreign Office was anxious to avoid a scandal, they begged Eulenburg to give Holstein an opportunity to apologize. On May 3rd Holstein sent the following statement: "Prince Eulenburg having assured me, on his word of honour, that he had neither hand, act, nor part in my dismissal, and has been in no way concerned

[1] *Philip Eulenburg: The Kaiser's Friend:* Johannes Haller.

in any of the attacks made upon me by the Press, I hereby withdraw the offensive remarks made upon him in my letter."[1] But Eulenburg was not reassured. He knew Holstein too well to imagine that the matter would drop. "I cannot say that I consider Holstein's attacks to be really disposed of. He will revenge himself in his wonted fashion," he wrote gloomily.

The next act in the drama was disconcerting. For years Holstein had been a bitter enemy of Maximilian Harden, the radical editor of a scurrilous newspaper *Zukunft*, but suddenly the two men exchanged open letters of friendship. "What can such a pair be brewing?" wrote Eulenburg. "I regard this Holstein-Harden alliance as an ominous development."

His forebodings were correct, for a few weeks later the paper began to refer to the "Liebenberg Round Table." Eulenburg, it told its readers, was "the leader of a sinister and effeminate camarilla, which pushed through undesirable policies and encouraged the Emperor's absolutism." At present the camarilla was working to unseat Prince Bülow and to persuade the Kaiser to appoint a Chancellor more amenable to its views. "Now I am supposed to be the arch wire-puller, the 'Chancellor-maker,' the miscreant who is turning the Emperor into an absolutist. Really, the world is *too* crazy," wrote the Prince.

Eulenburg hastened to see Bülow to assure him that the accusations were false and to ask him what he should do. The Chancellor urged him to leave Germany and remain away for some time. This was strange advice from a man who was in constant touch with Holstein and knew perfectly well that the latter's vendetta sprang from the erroneous belief that Eulenburg had caused his dismissal; if anyone could have persuaded Holstein to call off his attack, it was Bülow; but the Chancellor did not lift a finger for his friend.

By this time the press campaign had petered out, but the Prince was still racked by fear and foreboding. His letters to his friends make pitiful reading. "The feeling that a fresh storm may break out fills me with uneasiness, because I am physically too reduced to be able to act with the necessary equanimity. . . . I have never been among the strong characters who could take the bull by the horns. . . . I have worked indefatigably and faithfully for King and Country—worked until my health gave way . . . but my reward has

[1] *Philip Eulenburg: The Kaiser's Friend:* Johannes Haller.

been mud-slinging and this hunt to the death. . . . Now the poor hunted deer has had a shot through the heart and is cowering in the thicket. But his friends all cry: 'Up with you! There's no help for it. You must leap the ditches as you used to do.' "[1]

Once again his forebodings proved correct. On April 27th, 1907, *Zukunft* came out with a blistering article revealing that three elderly A.D.C.s, all members of the Emperor's entourage, were homosexuals. This was perfectly true, but it was not true that Eulenburg and Moltke were close friends of these men, as the paper alleged, and that all were members of the "Liebenberg Round Table." Needless to say, the article caused a sensation, but no one dared to show it to the Emperor. A week or two passed before General von Hülsen-Haeseler, who hated Eulenburg, hit upon the happy idea of persuading the Crown Prince to undertake the task. "Never shall I forget the pained and horrified face of my father," wrote young William, "who stared at me in dismay, when in the garden of the Marble Palace, I told him of the delinquencies of his near friends. The moral purity of the Kaiser was such that he could hardly conceive the possibility of such aberrations."[2]

The Kaiser lost his head. Although for years he had refused to read the vituperative columns of *Zukunft* and had censured people for paying attention to its outrageous assertions, he suddenly was frightened that the mud might cling to himself. He demanded the resignation of the three A.D.C.s—Count Lynar and two brothers, the Counts Hohenhau—and also of Count Kuno Moltke. Although he did not believe for a moment that Eulenburg was guilty, he sent a military aide to demand why he was taking no steps to exculpate himself. He also sent an imperial rescript to Bülow emphasising his displeasure, and ending: "I therefore insist that Philip Eulenburg shall at once ask to be retired. If this accusation against him of unnatural vice be unfounded, let him give me a plain declaration to that effect and take immediate steps against Harden. If not, then I expect him to return the Order of the Black Eagle, and avoid a scandal by forthwith leaving the country and going to reside abroad."

Eulenburg had no fight in him; although he was already taking lawyer's advice, he resigned his position and sent back his decoration. "The loss of an old imperial friendship," he wrote to Bülow,

[1] *Philip Eulenburg: The Kaiser's Friend:* Johannes Haller.
[2] *Memoirs:* William, Crown Prince.

" was not the cruel deception which perhaps you expected it to be, since I know, only too well, the character of this pilot, who shouts ' Abandon ship ' in every case long before it is necessary. I am still objective enough to realise that a monarch must be rid as quickly as possible of any friend who had got into the horrible position in which, thanks to the efforts of the Harden-Holstein clique, I find myself. . . . I know myself to be entirely innocent—but I fear false witnesses, since Holstein would not stop at having to spend ten thousand marks if he could buy some really damaging evidence."[1]

The Kaiser's harsh treatment of his devoted friend is not creditable, but Bülow's fawning acquiescence is nothing short of despicable since at this point he still believed in his innocence. " I was convinced," he wrote in his memoirs, " that the accusations of unnatural practices brought against him were unfounded. His affectionate relations with wife and children, the deep and passionate love with which his charming and distinguished wife still clung to him, made such vile assertions appear monstrous." Yet he did nothing to help his friend to whom he owed his whole public career; instead, he congratulated the Kaiser on his stand, writing that " in these painful circumstances we must see to it that the Crown is kept *ex nexu*, and completely removed from all connection with the affair." This was tantamount to endorsing Eulenburg's guilt.

Eulenburg and Count Moltke had lodged information with the Crown Prosecutor several weeks earlier, and asked him to institute proceedings against the *Zukunft*. If the Prosecutor had agreed there is no doubt but that both men would have been completely vindicated; but although the Prince was an ambassador *en disposition* and Count Moltke Commandant of Berlin, the Prosecutor declared that he was unable to grant the request as the public interest was not involved.[2] This is where Bülow could have intervened if he had wished, but the Chancellor had no intention of annoying his

[1] *Philip Eulenburg: The Kaiser's Friend:* Johannes Haller.

[2] This was not the case when Prince Bülow was accused of homosexuality by a crank named Brandt, about the same time. The Crown Prosecutor handled the proceedings and Bülow emerged with an untarnished name. He not only had the advantage of a fair hearing but his half-mad assailant could not be compared to Eulenburg's sinister enemies.

friend Holstein. Eulenburg's only recourse, therefore, was to initiate a private lawsuit against Harden. His lawyers, however, advised him against going into open court, pointing out that Harden would produce false witnesses, and the wide publicity given to the accusations, no matter how the case ended, would prove fatal to his reputation.

Count Moltke, however, refused to heed professional advice and sued Harden for libel. The case proved even more disastrous than the lawyers had predicted. It opened in the Berlin Municipal Court on October 23rd, 1907, before a young inexperienced magistrate with a butcher and a milkman as his sheriffs. Harden was represented by the Crown-Solicitor of Munich, Herr Bernstein, a clever and unscrupulous advocate who seized the offensive and, without a shred of proof, set out to implicate Moltke and Eulenburg in homosexual orgies that had taken place ten years earlier. The inexperienced magistrate failed to keep Bernstein in order, allowed him to wander far outside his brief and to call witnesses who were not subject to cross-examination. Although the hearing became a judicial farce, it was reported all over the world; even the London *Times* gave its readers full coverage under the heading PRUSSIAN COURT SCANDALS.

From the first day Bernstein's attack centred on the so-called Eulenburg "group." Harden, said Bernstein, had printed his articles in order to destroy the pernicious political influence of a degenerate coterie. He then called the divorced wife of Count Moltke, a vindictive and half-mad woman, who told the court that Prince Eulenburg had gone down on his knees and begged her to give up her husband; when she asked Moltke what the Kaiser would say to a divorce he replied that the Kaiser only knew what he wanted him to hear (sensation), for the Eulenburg group had placed an impenetrable ring around him (great sensation). Bernstein then dwelt on the notorious activities of the three Counts, the members of the imperial entourage, mentioned in *Zukunft* as perverts. Although, he said, he could not prove that either Moltke or Eulenburg had indulged in "unnatural vices" he hoped to show that they were better acquainted with the Counts, whose abnormal proclivities were beyond dispute, than they admitted. "The evidence was taken," reported *The Times* correspondent, "of a former trooper of the Gardes du Corps Regiment with regard to disgusting orgies which he described as having taken place in 1896 at the Potsdam residence of Count Lynar, who was at that time a captain in the regiment. The witness thought that he recognised Count Kuno Moltke as one of those present at these orgies. He had also believed that he recognised Philip Eulenburg."[1] Another witness told the court that he had been debauched at Count Lynar's house ten years earlier by a gentleman who *might* have been Prince Eulenburg, but he could not be sure. The witnesses that Bernstein called were not allowed to be cross-examined. He then was permitted to deliver a two-hour political attack on Eulenburg which obviously had come from the pen of Holstein. "I do not want to be King," Eulenburg was reported as saying, "I prefer to be the maker of Kings." Even *The Times* correspondent thought that Bernstein was going outside his brief. "It is strange that an indictment of this character—traversing some of the most important features of German home and foreign policy—should be delivered before a petty Court in which the bench is composed of a young judge with two lay assessors who were in this case a milkman and a butcher."

Although Bernstein had been able to produce only the flimsiest gossip to support his arguments, on the last day of the case he made great play of the fact that Moltke and Eulenburg had resigned their positions as Commandant of Berlin and Ambassador *en disposition*. If the Emperor believed in their innocence, he asked, why had His Majesty requested them to take this step? The question was unanswerable, for it was impossible to explain that the Emperor had panicked, and in order to protect himself had decided to throw his friends to the wolves. Bernstein's argument so impressed the bench that Harden was acquitted.

However, the outcome of the case was no longer important, for the public was unable to disentangle the truth from the lies, and simply fell back on the old adage "Where there's smoke there's fire." "Alas! I am still alive," the Prince wrote to his cousin, Count August Eulenburg. "I am going through tortures. Those who condemn me for not bringing an action against Harden in the summer, but merely appealing to the Crown-Prosecutor, ought to understand now why I acted as I did. . . . I agonise so deeply that I scarcely know if I shall ever stand upright again,

[1] *The Times:* October 28, 1907.

though I declare a thousand times before God that my conscience is clear."[1]

The Kaiser followed the trial with equal horror. His concern, however, did not spring from the travesty of justice or the anguish of his friends, but for fear that his own probity might be questioned —and just as he was about to depart on a state visit to England. "Suddenly," wrote Prince Bülow, "the Emperor telephoned to tell me that he had met with an accident. A sudden fit of giddiness had caused him to lie down on the sofa; there he had fainted, and rolled off his sofa to the floor. 'My head hit the ground so hard that my wife was alarmed by the noise, and came rushing in to me, quite terrified.' At present, His Majesty added, he felt too ill to think of undertaking the exhausting journey to England, and had wired King Edward to that effect. A few minutes later," Bülow continued, "the Marshal of the Court, Count August Eulenburg, arrived from the Empress to tell me that, after all, the accident had not been really so serious. The fainting fit and the bumping of the head against the floor had happened in His Majesty's fancy."[2]

The Count went on to explain that the trial had upset the Kaiser and he felt it too painful to meet his English relations at the present time. Meanwhile an indignant telegram had arrived from King Edward saying that all the preparations for the visit had been made, and demanding an explanation. Bülow wrote the Emperor begging him to reconsider, and an hour later received an invitation to accompany him to the theatre that evening. "I found him very brisk and unembarrassed: his really was an exceptionally mercurial nature! He declared that his indisposition had quite passed off; he had been able to take a refreshing gallop and had eaten a hearty meal, so that now he felt perfectly fit again . . . ready for anything . . . to go anywhere I chose to send him in the interests of our Foreign Policy."[2]

The Moltke lawsuit had been so mishandled that the Government felt obliged to step in, and ordered the Solicitor-General to hear an appeal. This time the case was conducted behind closed doors. Eulenburg testified for Moltke and declared on oath that he had

[1] *Philip Eulenburg: the Kaiser's Friend:* Johannes Haller.
[2] *Memoirs:* Prince von Bülow.

never practised any abominations. Moltke's divorced wife was shown to be a liar and the other witnesses who had testified in the previous case were torn to shreds. The hearing ended with Harden being sentenced to four months' imprisonment, but it was a hollow victory. Just as the lawyers had predicted, Count Moltke, despite a verdict of not guilty, was a ruined man; so many unpleasant accusations had been made that, although they were not proved, he was regarded as beyond the pale, and retired to his country estates.

Prince Eulenburg knew that he was the real target and that the matter would not be allowed to drop. "Harden's and Bernstein's ideal would be to have me arrested for perjury. . . . Moltke's was only the sauce for the dish. . . . Bülow has no interest in getting me out of it; he will not feel himself stronger than 'headquarters' and a short-sighted monarch, prey to utterly futile Generals. The case will last a long time and stir up endless dirt. I am to be victimised, and so are all who have stood by me. If I do not appear at the bar, I am condemned from the first day; if I *do*, they will unharness Bernstein and all his wild horses, and slay me in the gutter. So the matter stands, and yet God will not suffer me to die."[1]

The horses were unharnessed in the spring of 1908 when Bernstein found two witnesses who were willing to take the stand against the Prince. They appeared in a libel case in Munich, brought by Harden against a local paper; they testified that Eulenburg had committed acts of indecency with them when he was Ambassador in Munich nearly twenty-five years previously. Now the attack could begin again. On May 8th, the Royal Prussian Ministry, at the instigation of Prince Bülow, ordered the arrest of Eulenburg on grounds of perjury. He was so ill, partly from arthritis and partly from nerves, that he had to be carried from his house on a stretcher. It was decided to imprison him in the public hospital of the Charité in Berlin and to transport him every day to court.

Harden and Bernstein had gathered 145 witnesses. Most of them were men of the lowest class, thieves, blackmailers, perverts, and mental defectives. Dozens were brought into Eulenburg's hospital room to peer at him for identification. However, before the case opened, the witnesses had dwindled to twelve, and after the first

[1] *Philip Eulenburg: the Kaiser's Friend:* Johannes Haller.

week the twelve were reduced to two. Both of these men had been boatmen in Munich. One of them, a man called Reidl, had had thirty-two convictions; he was disqualified when it was learned that he had been convicted of accepting bribes, and had even tried to blackmail Eulenburg after the case had opened. This left only Jacob Ernst, who had been in Eulenburg's employ for many years as a general factotum. He was a middle-aged man with a family of eight. He was addicted to drink and gave his evidence haltingly. What was the truth about him? Eulenburg contended that he was a neurotic, simple-minded man who had been "worked on" by Bernstein, and, by a mixture of persuasiveness and threat, had finally become convinced that he had done something wrong. After the newspaper attacks in the spring, and before Bernstein had come into his life, he had written the Prince a letter. "Could you ever have believed, my lord Prince, that any people in this world could behave like that to such a good man as you are? I couldn't. I would have hoped the contrary. I have known you for a long time, my lord Prince. You have never shown me or my family anything but kindness, and never been the slightest trouble to any of us. Don't be afraid—it will be all right. I made someone explain the paragraph to me—it is simply shocking to say such things about you. Such a normal healthy man as you are. I will close now, hoping you will get the better of the scandal, which is not worth powder and shot, etc."[1]

Bernstein claimed that the letter had been written at the Prince's instigation. If this was so, what sort of a witness was Ernst, first supporting Eulenburg and then Harden with contradictory statements? When Ernst came into the Berlin court he began by denying what he had said in Munich and swore that he had never had indecent relations with Eulenburg; but when Bernstein cross-examined him for an hour, and threatened to send him to prison for perjury, he returned to his original story. In 1883, when the Prince was Ambassador in Munich, he was fond of going on the lake to compose his music and poetry and frequently employed Ernst as a boatman. On one occasion he had made advances to Ernst which the latter had reciprocated.

Bernstein made great play of a letter written by Eulenburg to Ernst on December 22, 1907—the day after the latter had testified

[1] *Philip Eulenburg: The Kaiser's Friend:* Johannes Haller.

against him in the Munich court—in which the Prince upbraided him for his allegations, and ended: " Besides, if anything of the kind ever *had* taken place it was such an old story that there could no longer be any question of punishment." Taken out of context the words appeared damaging, but Eulenburg pointed out that if he had intended them to carry a guilty connotation he scarcely would have put them on paper in the middle of the trial. He believed that Ernst was deranged, and was merely trying to impress on him that there was no reason to allow Bernstein to terrorise him.

Whatever the truth of the incident, alleged to have taken place twenty-five years earlier, it was obvious that Prince Eulenburg was not a homosexual in the accepted sense of the word. Despite months of investigation, Bernstein could bring no evidence against him apart from this one, doubtful episode. No one can read Eulenburg's letter without pity for his suffering. Repeatedly he declared his innocence and prayed God to relieve him from his anguish. " If only He would let me not awake! " " Oh if God would but grant me release but not in the most terrible way of all, by losing my reason." " What can be God's purpose in this? I suppose I shall understand it some day, but not here, for I am a broken man."[1]

Princess Eulenburg stood by her husband with passionate fervour, utterly convinced of his innocence. " I declare on my honour as a wife and mother that the accusations put forward are from A to Z lies invented by envious enemies and false friends; and that in the long period of the thirty-four years comprising our married life I have never perceived the smallest sign of anything but a perfectly normal emotional life or even manner of life. Nor can I understand how any reasonable person can venture to speak of abnormality in face of the fact that in the first ten years of our marriage [1876 to 1886] eight healthy children were born to us. But in Germany people have sunk so low that even the most normal and the happiest of marriages are not safe from such ' modern ' suspicions. . . . It is a convenient way of ridding one's self of a man of honour whom it is desired to ruin, and who cannot be attacked in any less decent fashion. . . ."[1]

This was part of the testimony which the Princess prepared, and

[1] *Philip Eulenburg: The Kaiser's Friend:* Johannes Haller.

waited day after day, to read out in court. But on July 13th Eulenburg was so ill that he fainted. His leg had swollen so badly that the doctors diagnosed thrombosis and refused to allow him to be moved to court. So the court moved to the hospital. Never has there been such a bizarre scene as this shameless frenzy to destroy the Emperor's favourite. Eulenburg grew steadily worse and the court adjourned; in September he was no better and the case finally was suspended indefinitely. It was believed that the jury would have returned a verdict of not guilty; but Eulenburg knew that it would not alter his position. His fall was complete. He retired to Liebenberg where he lived as a semi-invalid until his death fourteen years later.

"Rominten knew him no more," wrote the English governess employed to look after the Kaiser's daughter. "Yet probably no one was more missed than he whose name was never afterwards mentioned there."[1]

[1] *Memoirs of the Kaiser's Court*: Anne Topham.

11. *The German Fleet*

" He's a Satan. You can hardly believe what a Satan he is!" exclaimed the Kaiser about Edward VII to a startled dinner party on March 19, 1907. The outburst was caused by the knowledge that the British Government was negotiating in St. Petersburg for an agreement which would put an end to outstanding disputes between the two countries, and secondly by the announcement that King Edward, on his annual spring cruise, would meet the King of Italy at Gaeta and the King of Spain off Cartagena. The Kaiser was convinced that his uncle's main purpose was to do mischief to Germany. He was rather silent at the beginning of dinner due to indigestion, Count Zedlitz related, " but about eleven o'clock he began to talk freely about the policy of England and grew rather excited. He complained bitterly of the intrigues that his uncle, the King of England, was carrying on about him. He said he knew all about them from private letters from France, and King Edward was equally hard at work in every other country. The whole press of the world, including that of America, had already been mobilised against him by English money, and it was extraordinary how much personal animosity his uncle's attitude revealed."[1]

The truth was that the King of England was beating the Kaiser at his own game. Two years earlier, at Bjorko, William II had preached a continental combine against Britain. In the flush of triumph following his departure he had written to the Czar: " Holland, Belgium, Denmark, Sweden will all be attracted to this new centre of gravity. . . . They will revolve in the orbit of the great block of Powers (Russia, Germany, France, Austria, Italy) and feel confidence in leaning on and revolving around this mass." He had gone on to predict that even America would join, and thus John Bull would be prevented from setting " the rest of the civilised nations by each other's ears for his own personal benefit."[2]

[1] *Twelve Years at the Imperial German Court:* Count Zedlitz-Trützschler.

[2] *The Kaiser's Letters to the Czar:* edited by N. F. Grant.

But Björkö had been stillborn and Algeciras, far from prising apart England and France, had strengthened the entente. And now it looked as though Britain was making a bid for Russian friendship. It was too much. It was a sinister plot. The Fatherland was being encircled. William II's grievances found their way into the German press and soon many newspapers were attacking Edward VII and his "sinister" activities. On April 15th the *Neue Freie Presse* declared: "Who can fail to receive the impression that a diplomatic duel is being fought out between England and Germany under the eyes of the world. The King of England . . . is no longer afraid of appearing to throw the whole influence of his personality into the scales whenever it is a question of thwarting the aims of German policy. The meeting at Gaeta [with the King of Italy] is another fact connected with the burning jealousy between England and Germany. Already people are asking themselves everywhere: 'What is the meaning of this continual political labour, carried on with open recklessness, whose object is to put a close ring around Germany?'" This phrase "the ring around Germany" was picked up, and in the coming years became diplomatic jargon in the form of "encirclement."

The personality of Germany as a nation was almost perfectly represented by the personality of the Kaiser as a man. Germany was threatening and blustering one moment, pained and reproachful the next. Germany was able, tempestuous, and unwise, a country with a chip on its shoulder, longing for prestige and acclamation, prone to dark moods of dejection that turned overnight into menacing arrogance. "The majority of us Germans," explained a diplomat to his English colleague, "cannot shake off the feeling that we belong to a *parvenu* nation, and therefore we are always on the look-out to see if any other country is offering us a slight."[1] That was the Kaiser, touchy, envious, boastful, and uncertain all at the same time. Even after his triumph over Tangiers—before the defeat at Algeciras—he was bathed in self-pity because of the hostility of the British press, and nearly wept when he talked to the Princess of Pless. ". . . he got very excited and during our conversation about England he had tears in his eyes," she wrote in her diary. ". . . The two countries are of the same race, yet absolutely different in every way. . . . A nephew on one Throne, the uncle on

[1] *The Edwardian Era*: André Maurois.

the other; both countries believing themselves to be in the right and both sincerely believing that each wishes to dominate the other in the eyes of the world.... To the Emperor it is a bitter disappointment to be misjudged and to be disliked—and he wants always to be first. He is apt to rise to a pitch of excitement so difficult for his Ministers to control, that they do not tell him everything for fear of what he might do. The King simply dislikes the Emperor. I am sure he has no real and dangerous intentions towards Germany; but he just shows his teeth when a German approaches him. There are great mistakes on both sides."[1]

The " mistakes on both sides " were often ridiculous and childish and by no means only due to the Kaiser. Edward VII was so annoyed by Tangiers he refused to allow his son, Prince George, to attend the wedding of the Crown Prince in Berlin, on the grounds that he must remain at home for the visit of the King of Spain. Three months later Edward sent a letter to the Crown Prince and invited him and his bride to England. William II was furious and complained to the Czar: " He goes and invites my son behind my back to come and visit him in England. I have of course stopped that business."[2] He not only stopped it but sent a refusal on the grounds that the King of Spain would be visiting Germany! Then, to make matters worse, he informed the British Ambassador that it was usual to address such invitations to " the Head of the House of Hohenzollern," and that after the Crown Prince's last visit which had resulted " in unseemly romping in unlighted corridors " he doubted the benefits of English influences; and finally, that he suspected that the King wished " to get hold of the Crown Prince " for some abstruse purpose of his own. " The real truth," declared Edward hotly to Lord Knollys, " was that he was jealous of my asking his son at all. Of course I knew that the young man could not come over without his father's permission."[3]

The King was not as innocent as he sounded. It was not merely " jealousy." The Crown Prince was weak-minded and impressionable and whenever the King saw him he laid himself out to be as agreeable as possible, bringing the young man completely under the spell of his personality. There was nothing more annoying he

[1] *Daisy, Princess of Pless.*

[2] *Letters to the Czar.*

[3] *King Edward VII:* Sir Sidney Lee.

could do than to send him back to Berlin full of Edward's praises. "He was, as long as I can remember, extremely friendly to me," wrote the Crown Prince in his memoirs, "and took a most active interest in my development. . . . Often have we sat talking for hours in the most unconstrained fashion while he lay back in a great easy chair and smoked an enormous cigar. . . . I have scarcely ever met with any other person who understood as he did how to charm people with whom he came into contact."[1]

The Crown Prince was only one source of trouble: far more serious was the tittle-tattle which the courtiers of both monarchs picked up and reported back to their masters. The King made jokes about the Kaiser. After Algeciras he called him "the most brilliant failure in history" and the Kaiser retaliated by talking loudly on board the *Hohenzollern* in front of several Americans about the looseness of English morals and the King's relations with Mrs. Keppel. The last shaft infuriated Edward and he was determined to let his nephew know that his remarks had been reported. He instructed his secretary to write to the British Ambassador in Berlin to tell William that "His Majesty . . . does not know whether the Emperor retains any affection for him, but from one or two things which he has heard recently, he should *say not*. . . ."

However by 1906 Edward VII felt that the breach was growing too wide, and took the initiative in restoring harmony. In January he wrote the Kaiser a birthday letter saying: "We are, my dear William, such old friends and near relations that I feel sure that the affectionate feelings which have always existed may invariably continue." William responded gratefully. "The whole letter," he wrote from Berlin, "breathed such an atmosphere of kindness and warm sympathetic friendship that it constitutes the most cherished gift among my presents." But four months later when Count Metternich wrote from London suggesting that a meeting between the two monarchs would improve Anglo-German relations the Kaiser scribbled on the margin: "I don't believe it. . . . Meetings with Edward have no lasting value, because he is too envious, *propter invidiam*."[2]

Nevertheless uncle and nephew met in Germany in August, and spent three days in amiable conversation, scrupulously avoiding

[1] *My Memoirs:* William, Crown Prince.

[2] *Grosse Politik.*

politics. There were no incidents and on the surface cordial relations were restored again; but underneath the rancour persisted. Nineteen hundred and six was the year of Algeciras and in private the Emperor fulminated against Edward's "mischief-making," attributing all Germany's troubles to this one source. "He is furious at the machinations of his uncle, the King of England, against him . . ." wrote Count Zedlitz. "It was unpardonable, he says, of Russia to have ranged herself recklessly on the side of the powers hostile to Germany at Algeciras . . . and he is particularly incensed by the attitude Italy took up. He said: 'It has always been a habit of theirs to betray German Emperors and leave them in the lurch.' The explanation of it all is that the unanimous opposition of all the Powers to Germany is considered by him as a personal insult. . . ."[1]

Throughout 1907 the Kaiser's stock continued to drop while Edward VII was hailed by foreign embassies as "the most astute diplomat in Europe." That year England signed a convention with Russia which was regarded as another triumph for the King. Although the Anglo-Russian agreement was not a military alliance, only a modest, rather precarious accord over trouble spots such as Persia and Afghanistan, it was regarded quite rightly as a stepping stone to bigger things, and neutral diplomats gloated at the uneven duel being fought out between uncle and nephew. The Kaiser had failed to divide Britain and France at Algeciras, failed to ensnare the Czar at Björkö, and now Edward VII was stepping in and snatching off the prizes.

This impression was heightened in 1908 when the King paid a visit to the Czar at Reval. Although it was only a courtesy call, and nothing of political importance was discussed, the English sovereign's reputation as a master-mind had become so inflated that the Germans looked upon it as a portentous occasion. "It is amusing how England—of course it is only the King—knows how to get everything it wants," wrote Prince Gottfried Hohenlohe, an Austrian diplomat, to the Princess of Pless. "He wanted to be friends with Russia and he knew awfully well how to manage Izvolsky, the Russian Minister, who is a fearful snob and likes *de poser Anglais*. It really makes me laugh after all that the Emperor of Russia told me about, I mean *against* England. I wrote to some

[1] *Twelve Years at the Imperial German Court:* Count Zedlitz-Trützschler.

Russian ladies asking if they had already little *Saints Edouards* in the corners of their rooms. As you know, the Russian must always be putting some new saint into the corner of the walls—ceilings and so on."[1]

The Kaiser's personality which until now had been regarded as an asset, at least by the Germans, began to be widely criticised. Forgotten was " the undeniable charm " which Bülow had praised, " the great and original spirit " which the Princess of Pless had admired. Indeed, the Princess now complained that he " was terribly tactless, loud and theatrical. He has no manners," she wrote in her diary, " he cannot choose his friends . . . he is bourgeois and loud and yet sometimes he has the charm of youth. . . ."[1] Other English ladies joined the chorus, complaining that he was most frightening when he was in a jocular mood, that he gripped their hands until they winced in pain, then exclaimed merrily: " Ha Ha ! The mailed fist ! What !" Even German ladies found his jokes tiring. When his sister-in-law coughed at dinner he slapped her back so hard saying " That will cure you " that she was nearly knocked off her chair. More than ever, Count Zedlitz lamented that he offended his high dignitaries by calling them " donkeys " and " noodles " and " mutton-heads " : and when he was in a playful mood humiliated his generals by rolling them in the snow or smacking them across the backside with his Field Marshal's baton.

William II was oblivious of the effect his personality had on other people. That was the price of being a king. He moved in a world of open adulation and secret complaint. Miss Anne Topham, the English governess who joined the Kaiser's household in 1902 to tutor the nine-year-old Princess Victoria Louise, tells us that none of his courtiers really liked him or were at ease with him. They were alarmed by his explosive temperament and lived in fear of the sudden demands that he frequently put upon them. On the other hand, when he was pleased with the world no one was less pompous or more engagingly uninhibited. He often teased Miss Topham about England. He was a regular reader of *Punch* and sometimes in the evenings, when she sat sewing with the Empress, he would jump up, stride over to her with the magazine in his hand, and show her a political cartoon of himself, invariably with a spiked helmet and

[1] *Daisy, Princess of Pless.*

bristling upturned mustachios—frequently as a sea-serpent. " What do you think of that?" he would say. " Nice, isn't it? Good likeness, eh?" To which the poor woman had no answer.

The Emperor's sense of humour was always unpredictable. Once he took a walk with the Empress outside the palace grounds at Potsdam. When he returned a new sentry had been placed at the gate. The soldier addressed him as " Herr Lieutenant " and refused to let him enter. However, " Herr Lieutenant " finally persuaded the guard that he had official business with the Emperor's aide-de-camp, and the gate was opened. William II found the incident inexpressibly funny. " Considering the number of picture post-cards of the German Emperor in circulation," he laughed, " where can that man have been all his life?"

On another day, however, the same incident might infuriate him. Frequently he lost his head over unavoidable mishaps. When King Edward and Queen Alexandra visited Berlin, the horses drawing the state carriage were frightened by the gun salute and broke out of line. William was so angry that he went out of his way to introduce his Master of the Horse to the King saying: " This is the man who bungled up the procession."

The Kaiser's sons were just as frightened of him as his courtiers. Although William was often praised as a model husband and father his family life, in fact, was almost non-existent. In 1907 the Crown Prince and Prince Frederick held commissions in the army, Prince Adalbert was serving in the navy, Prince August Wilhelm and Prince Oscar were at the University, Prince Joachim finishing his military training at Plön. Only the fifteen-year-old Princess Victoria Louise could still be described as a child. Yet all six sons were tongue-tied in their father's presence. Like most Victorian parents William refused to tolerate familiarity, but it was not this—nor the religious discourses, nor the puritanical strictures—that clamped them in painful silence. It was the fact that William refused to allow them any personality. The Princess was the only exception for she idolised her " papa " and therefore managed to win a slightly favoured position. But the boys were kept in their place. If any of them ventured an opinion the Emperor was apt to rebuke them for impertinence; or worse still, to cover them with derision against which there was no redress. The Empress comforted them in private, but she never intervened for she still looked upon William as a divine oracle. He gave his views, unchallenged and expansive, on every subject under the sun from music to guns, from archaeology to plumbing. He even posed as an expert on ladies' millinery. Every year he selected a dozen hats for the Empress as a birthday present. They were large picture hats adorned with fruit and feathers, lace and flowers. Before they could be removed to her wardrobe they were placed on display in one of the reception rooms, so that the entourage could congratulate the Emperor on his exceptional taste. The submissive Empress welcomed this annual gesture as a sign of her husband's felicity.

The key-note of the Kaiser's personality was his restlessness. He seemed to burn with an all-consuming flame. Even when he carried on a trivial conversation he threw his whole body into the talk, nodding his head, rocking from one leg to another, and wagging his finger in the listener's face. His lack of repose kept him almost perpetually on the move. Although he looked upon the New Palace at Potsdam as his home, he owned over thirty castles and schlosses in Germany, and made a point of visiting a third of them every year. Sometimes it was only for a week-end, for what he seemed to like best was to climb aboard his cream and gold train and hurtle through Germany in the darkness of the night. This pleasure was not shared by his entourage who regarded the imperial train as nothing less than a form of torture. It seemed to roar and jerk and sway more than any train in the kingdom. The ladies found it so impossible to dress or undress (particularly to lace their stays or do up their hair) that most of them slept in their clothes, and faced the world wan and haggard in the morning.

Even more dreaded than the train, however, was the Emperor's annual August holiday at Wilhelmshöhe. As there was neither shooting nor sailing to occupy him, he worked off his energy in fairly rugged exercise; and as he never did anything alone, the entourage was compelled to do likewise. Everyone had to be up at 6.30 to ride with him. After breakfast there was tennis (which apparently was a severe strain, for the aides were so afraid of driving a ball into the imperial stomach that they scarcely gave him a game), and after this an hour or two of excavation in the Roman ruins near the castle. Then came lunch, always served out of doors no matter how cold the weather, and always a formal affair with the ladies in satin dresses and trains! The afternoons were even more exhausting for they were devoted to mountain-climbing or long hikes through the woods. "We are like the Israelites at the Passover," complained one of the ladies-in-waiting. "We must always have our loins girt, our shoes on our feet—shoes suitable for any and every occasion, fit for walking on palace floors or down muddy roads—our staff in our hand; nobody dare relax or settle down to be comfortable."[1]

If the Kaiser's restlessness, his nerves, his moods, bewildered the members of his own entourage it is small wonder that they puzzled and alarmed the outside world. "Sometimes," wrote the English governess, "he falls into Napoleonic attitudes, and occasionally he attempts to pinch the ear of a particular friend." This was the man with whom Europe had to deal. It is not surprising that diplomats used oceans of ink trying to analyse and fathom his being. "Too much attention cannot be paid to the character of the Emperor," wrote Mr. Cartwright, the British Minister at Munich and Stuttgart, on January 12, 1907, to his Foreign Secretary, Sir Edward Grey. "His moods and thoughts are the pivot on which German home and foreign policy turn. . . . There seems to be a conviction among well-informed people 'that the strain to which His Majesty's nervous system has been exposed during recent years has brought about a physical condition in the Kaiser which is much to be deplored and to which must be attributed the ups and downs of his moods, passing from exultant optimism to deep depression.' . . . By his habit of selecting for his entourage men of colourless opinions, he has put himself into the unfortunate position of being unable to probe seriously below the surface of questions and to learn the reality of things by encouraging contradiction. At moments, however, he begins to realise that there is danger ahead and he feels disheartened, though his confidence in himself is so great that he cannot bring himself to believe that he has really engaged on a wrong path; then, in despair, he makes speeches like the one he delivered at Breslau at the late autumn manœuvres, where in vigorous terms he denounced all those who were opposed to him as pessimists and enemies of the nation. It is this uncertainty of his moods and humours—hidden in great part from the public—which

[1] *Memories of the Kaiser's Court:* Anne Topham.

render it so difficult to follow all the turns and twists of German politics. . . ."[1]

In this atmosphere of nervousness, jealousy, and recrimination the two monarchs met twice in 1907; once in Germany, and once in England when the Kaiser and Kaiserin paid a state visit in November—the visit that William so nearly cancelled because of the Eulenburg scandal. It was something of a miracle that both meetings were harmonious for the Kaiser talked freely, in between times, of his uncle's nefarious attempts to encircle Germany. However, when he reached England he made a moving little speech at the Guildhall saying that "the main prop and base for peace in the world is the maintenance of good relations between our two countries. Blood is thicker than water. The German nation's wishes coincide with mine." Then he went to Highcliffe, near Bournemouth, to snatch a few weeks' recreation with his friend, Colonel Stuart-Wortley. While there he talked a great deal about being "misunderstood" and "the misconception of his character" and his feelings towards England. He returned to London, lunched with King Edward at Buckingham Palace, and left for Germany. The day after his departure the German Government announced its intention of replacing battleships every twenty years instead of every twenty-five, thus increasing the strength of the German Fleet by twenty per cent. The harmony induced by the Emperor's visit vanished overnight.

The Emperor knew that large naval increases were about to be announced and rejoiced in them. In the early days he had regarded his fleet as a glamorous toy, a prestige symbol that would wrest begrudging admiration from his English relations. "What William II most desired," Bülow wrote cattily, ". . . was to see himself, at the head of a glorious German fleet, starting out on a peaceful visit to England. The English Sovereign, with his fleet, would meet the German Kaiser in Portsmouth. The two fleets would file past each other, the two monarchs, each wearing the naval uniform of the other's country . . . would then stand on the bridge of their flagships. Then, after they had embraced in the prescribed manner, a gala dinner with lovely speeches would be held in Cowes."[2]

[1] *British Documents on the Origin of the War.*

[2] *Memoirs:* Prince von Bülow.

These might have been the Kaiser's emotions at the turn of the century, but in 1908 he had persuaded himself that the very dignity and future of Germany hinged upon the fleet. Every move that tightened the entente against him, every diplomatic success scored by Edward VII, convinced the Kaiser that sea-power was what really mattered. It was impossible to have an effective voice in world affairs without a navy. When he met King Victor Emmanuel of Italy in Naples he remarked sourly that his colleagues, the European monarchs, had paid little attention to what he said despite his long reign; but he was confident that a mighty German fleet would secure a proper attention for the words of the German Emperor.

Until 1908 the British Government had not tried to reach an agreement with Germany on shipbuilding. In 1906 King Edward had asked his nephew if he thought it would be possible for the two countries to reach an understanding, and William had given an unequivocal no. So the matter had not been pursued and the British Admiralty had concentrated on reorganising and strengthening its own navy. Old ships were scrapped, the Atlantic and the Channel Fleets were amalgamated into a Home Fleet and the first dreadnought, a super-battleship bigger than anything seen before, was launched. "We shall be thirty per cent more efficient," declared Sir John Fisher, the First Sea Lord, "and we shall be ready for instant war."

The German supplement of 1907, however, came as a stunning shock. Not only was Admiral Tirpitz increasing the German Fleet by twenty per cent but he was embarking on a programme of dreadnought building which threatened to equal, if not to surpass, the British effort. He would launch four dreadnoughts a year from 1908 to 1911, and after that, two a year to 1917. Suddenly the monster battleship, devised to ensure British supremacy once and for all, was recognised as a terrible mistake; for the Admiralty now declared that its appearance had made all other battleships obsolete. If this was so, and Germany and England were neck and neck in the new race, British supremacy was a thing of the past.

Panic swept the country. All the half-formed suspicions of the past few years hardened into accusations. Why, everyone asked, did Germany want a huge navy when she had an army of 4,000,000 men? Why, if she needed a navy for defence, was it designed as a fighting force? Why did it sit at home glowering at the island empire? Whom could it be directed against except Britain?[1]

The "danger-zone" that Admiral Tirpitz had predicted in 1900 had been reached, but it took a very different form than he had envisaged. Far from seizing the offensive and contemplating an attack on the German Fleet, the British public decided that Germany was planning an invasion of England and began to cry loudly for adequate defence. The Conservative opposition made impassioned speeches in Parliament, the press howled unremittingly, and even fiction writers and playrights caught the fever. The panic was extraordinary. German spies were believed to be everywhere; soon stories were going around about 40,000 trained agents disguised as waiters, about ships coming up the Humber, and a mysterious aircraft which made nightly visits to England. The cheap magazines abounded in hair-raising adventures entitled "The Swoop of the Teutonic Vulture," "The Great Raid," "The War Inevitable," "The Invaders," "How the Germans took London," "While Britain Slept," and "A Story of Invasion that will stir Britain to its Depths." Meanwhile a play appeared on the London stage entitled *An Englishman's Home*. It depicted a household where nothing but amusement and sport was discussed. "Suddenly the 'home' was surrounded by a strange army whose uniforms were taken at first for English. What army was it? The army of the 'Emperor of the North.' One of the heroes of the piece snatched a sporting rifle to defend himself and was shot on the spot for his breach of the laws of war. The territorial army came on the scene only to cover itself with ridicule. Finally, the regular army arrived and saved the situation but everyone knew that the ending was conventional and the author's real attitude one of hopeless pessimism." [2]

The Kaiser and Admiral Tirpitz genuinely were astonished by

[1] Even the German public found these questions difficult to answer. "To the man in the street the uses to which the German Navy may be put are vague," wrote the British Minister at Munich in January 1907, "but he feels more confident in the effect such a Fleet may have on foreign powers than in the capacity of the present diplomacy of the Wilhelmstrasse to protect the country. The feeling against England is to a great extent artificial but is unfortunately encouraged by the Imperial Government for the purpose of frightening the public into granting subsidies for the construction of big ships. If the Emperor asks for money for shipbuilding, he will get it." *British Documents on the Origins of the War.*

[2] *A History of the English People*: Elie Halévy.

England's fear of invasion. Invasion was not part of their programme; indeed it was regarded as an utterly absurd proposition. Tirpitz told the British military attaché that no nation in its right mind could contemplate an invasion without overwhelming sea superiority; even then, he did not see how the invading army could be supplied across miles of sea. And the Kaiser took the unusual step of picking up his pen and writing personally to Lord Tweedmouth, the British First Lord of the Admiralty. He described "this perpetual quoting of 'the German Danger'" as "something nearly ludicrous." "The foreigners in other countries," he continued, "might easily conclude that the Germans must be an exceptionally strong lot, as they seem able to strike terror into the hearts of the British, who are five times their naval superiors." He could not resist taking a crack at Lord Esher, a courtier who had been placed in charge of King Edward's royal establishments, and who had written a letter to *The Times* on naval matters. Apparently William did not know that Esher also was a member of the Committee of Imperial Defence, for he asked acidly "if the supervision of the foundations and drains of the Royal Palaces is apt to qualify somebody for the judgement of naval affairs in general?"

Lord Tweedmouth replied politely but Edward VII was outraged by the Kaiser's presumption and sent an icy letter to his nephew. "Your writing to my First Lord of the Admiralty is a 'new departure' and I do not see how he can prevent our press from calling attention to the great increase in building of German ships of war, which necessitates our increasing my own navy also! Believe me, your affectionate uncle, Edward R."[1] The Kaiser, however, was nonplussed. When he ran into Sir Frank Lascelles, the British Ambassador, at a reception, he explained cheerfully that he had felt free to write to Tweedmouth as he held the rank of "Admiral of the British Fleet."

Meanwhile, Count Metternich, the German Ambassador in London, was deeply unhappy. Repeatedly he presented the British argument to Berlin, which struck him as eminently sensible. Mr. Asquith's Liberal Government, he said, did not want to spend its money on armaments as it had been elected to carry out a large programme of social reform. However, as England possessed no army, and as her navy constituted her sole security, no British

[1] *King Edward VII:* Sir Sidney Lee.

Government could allow its naval superiority to be whittled down. For every dreadnought Germany built, England was determined to build two. But would it not be preferable for the two nations to reach an agreement on naval ratios, and save both countries ruinous and unnecessary expenditure? Metternich declared forcibly that if Germany insisted on an arms race a dangerous and permanent breach would open between the two countries which would make English hostility certain in the event of a European war.

Metternich's dispatches infuriated William II. His anger seemed to be becoming almost psychopathic, for as the weeks passed the mere mention of the word " discussion " threw him into a towering rage. He scribbled wildly over the Ambassador's reports. " We will never submit to dictation as to how our armaments are to be arranged;" " I should reply with grenades;" " That is language to be used to China or Italy or similar creatures. Unheard of!!! " " I do not wish for good relations with England at the price of not building the German Fleet. . . . The German Fleet is built against nobody, and so not against England. It is governed by our own needs. This is clearly laid down in the Naval Law and has been unchallenged for 11 years. The Law will be carried out to the last tittle, whether the Britons like it or not; it is the same to us. If they want war let them begin it; we are not afraid of it."[1]

The insistence that the German Fleet was being built in a void, irrespective of the size of anyone else's fleet, was too foolish to be countenanced. Even William did not believe it, for how was it possible to determine a " requirement " unless it was related to something? Indeed, the preamble of the German Navy Law stated clearly that the German Fleet must be so powerful that " if the strongest naval power engaged it, it would endanger its own supremacy."

The plan of William II and Admiral Tirpitz was to " neutralise " the British Navy. If they could close the gap between the two fleets, Britain would not dare to range herself against Germany, nor to thwart her will. Despite English assertions to the contrary Tirpitz was convinced that this aim could be achieved. Britain would find the financial burden too great, he argued, to maintain a wide margin of superiority. Indeed, he told the Kaiser bluntly

[1] *German Diplomatic Documents.*

that " if the English fleet is permanently and fundamentally made and maintained so strong as to make it safe to attack Germany, then German naval development from an historic standpoint would be a mistake, and Your Majesty's fleet policy an historic fiasco." And in a sentence calculated to keep the Emperor up to the mark, he added: " Germany's world position, in the existing political situation, would remain dependent on England's favour."[1]

England's favour: that was the odious factor that prompted the Kaiser's shipbuilding. He had no plan to attack the British Navy, and it never entered his head to invade the British Isles. He wanted a navy for grandeur; a navy large enough to ensure respect for the words of the German Emperor the world over; a navy powerful enough to free him from any need to consider the goodwill of England. What he failed to comprehend, however, was that a fleet strong enough to defy Britain was a fleet so strong that it would constitute a threat to the safety of the British Isles. The Kaiser flatly refused to countenance this argument, or to consider for one moment that there was anything to be said on the other side. " They will just have to get used to our fleet," he wrote haughtily, " and from time to time we must assure them it is not against them."[2]

This was the Kaiser's mood when Edward VII travelled through Germany en route to Austria in the summer of 1908. Before his departure Sir Edward Grey, the Foreign Secretary, asked him if he would bring up the subject of naval armaments when he met the German Emperor at Cronberg; the Foreign Office was anxious to know if the stone wall it had run up against was erected by Tirpitz or the Kaiser himself. Edward gave an emphatic no. Ever since his disastrous political talk with William in 1901, when he had handed his nephew the wrong Foreign Office document, he had refused to play the part of a negotiator; he was no good at it, he said, and it was not his constitutional role. Furthermore he found it impossible to carry on a rational discussion with William, and he did not want their meeting to deteriorate into a bitter scene. However he consented to take with him Sir Charles Hardinge, the Permanent Under-Secretary of the Foreign Office, and said that if the occasion presented itself Hardinge could broach the subject himself.

[1] *Dokumente:* Admiral von Tirpitz.
[2] *German Diplomatic Documents.*

Hardinge did so when the Emperor talked to him after lunch. William II appeared to be in an amiable mood, and although the Kaiser produced an entirely different set of naval figures from those the British Admiralty had given Sir Charles, the two men were soon deep in conversation. Hardinge became so interested that he lowered his guard and at one point in the argument said: " But you must build slower." The Kaiser was an expert at humiliating rebuffs. Instantly he fastened on this phrase and drew himself up stiffly, making it clear that no one used the word " must " to a German Emperor. " Then we shall fight," he retorted, " for it is a question of national honour and dignity." Gleefully he reported the scene to Prince Bülow. " I looked him straight in the eye," he wrote. " Sir Charles became scarlet, made me a bow, begged pardon for his words and urged me expressly to forgive and forget and treat them as remarks inadvertently made in private conversation." The Kaiser went on to report that after dinner, " when I conferred on him the Order of the Red Eagle, First Class, he was ready to eat out of my hand. . . . My frank words when I had showed him my teeth had not failed in their effect. You must always treat Englishmen thus. . . ."[1]

The Emperor's belief that Germany could not rank as a truly great power unless she acquired a fleet was not shared by other European rulers. The foreign guests who attended the Kaiser's annual army manœuvres usually left with a very healthy respect for the might of Germany and the majesty of William II. In 1908 Mr. Winston Churchill, the President of the Board of Trade, was one of the visitors, and the Kaiser seemed to him the very symbol of earthly splendour. " As he sat on his horse surrounded by Kings and Princes while his legions defiled before him," wrote Churchill, " he represented all that this world has to give in material things. The picture which lives the most vividly in my memory is his entry into the city of Breslau at the beginning of the manœuvres. He rode his magnificent horse at the head of a squadron of cuirassiers, wearing their white uniform and eagle-crested helmet. The streets of the Silesian capital were thronged with his enthusiastic subjects, and lined, not with soldiers, but more impressively with thousands of aged veterans in rusty black coats and stove-pipe

[1] *German Diplomatic Documents.*

hats, as if the great past of Germany saluted her more splendid future."[1]

This splendid future already was darkening; William's obsession about his fleet, combined with Prince Bülow's tortuous foreign policy, were to stamp 1908-09 as a landmark on the road leading to the holocaust of 1914. The breach with England was followed by an equally dangerous breach with Russia. When the Kaiser learned in October 1908 that Austria had announced the annexation of Bosnia and Herzegovina, he was enraged. Although the Emperor Franz Joseph had been administering these two Slav provinces for nearly thirty years, according to the provisions of the Treaty of Berlin, nominally they belonged to Turkey. William was furious that he had not been informed and furious that one of his allies had seen fit to act in so high-handed a manner to another of his allies. "Robbery and felony," he wrote on the report. "Vienna . . . has duped us in a most unheard-of fashion . . . if the Sultan in his necessity declares war, and hoists in Constantinople the green flag of the Holy War, I should not blame him."

The real clash, however, was not between Austria-Hungary and Turkey, for Franz Joseph soon managed to quiet the Sultan by paying large indemnities. The struggle was far more serious, for it heralded the dreaded conflict between Russia and Austria-Hungary that Bismarck had been so eager to avoid. Franz Joseph's Empire contained many Slav minorities, and these minorities were being encouraged by Russia to break away and link up with other Slav states. Independent Serbia (now part of Jugoslavia) was the spearhead of the attack. Backed by Russian money and influence it had cast longing eyes on Bosnia and Herzegovina for many years, hoping one day to form a Greater Serbia. Austria-Hungary had announced the annexation to forestall any such future development; but in doing so she had broken the Treaty of Berlin, and set the whole of the Balkans into a ferment.

The Kaiser's first reaction was to maintain a neutral role and to urge restraint on both sides. Although Bülow was in favour of "backing Austria-Hungary to the hilt" he played his hand prudently for several months. Meanwhile the situation worsened. Serbia was in a state of high excitement and employed agents to provoke insurrections in Bosnia. Austrian troops were sent to the

[1] *Great Contemporaries:* Winston S. Churchill.

Serbian frontier and General Conrad, the Austrian Chief of Staff, begged the Emperor Franz Joseph to allow him "to crush the dangerous little viper." St. Petersburg became alarmed that their little protégé might be attacked, and the Czar called a Crown Council to discuss possible intervention. But the generals gave an emphatic no, for Russia had not recovered from her defeat at the hands of Japan and was in no position to fight. The situation, the Czar told a friend, was frightful, "because Russia is unprepared for war, and a Russian defeat would be the ruin of Slavdom." He believed that Germany was encouraging Austria-Hungary in its belligerent attitude and even feared that Berlin might be looking for an opportunity to attack Russia.

This was not the case, and up till this moment Germany had behaved with circumspection. But as soon as Prince Bülow learned from secret service reports that the Crown Council had decided against war, no matter what the circumstances, he could not resist reaching out for a cheap victory. He allowed the Wilhelmstrasse to send Russia a stiff note—so stiff that it amounted to an ultimatum—telling her that unless she recognised the annexation of Bosnia and Herzegovina unequivocally and without further delay Berlin would not restrain Austria-Hungary from attacking Serbia. Russia had no alternative but to accept this bitter humiliation.

Prince Bülow cunningly tried to patch things up by putting about the story—which he repeats in his memoirs—that his *diktat* was a friendly gesture designed to extricate Russia from the embarrassing situation of seeing Serbia chastised by Austria-Hungary. The Czar, however, did not feel that Germany had done him a favour! On March 18th he wrote to his mother, who was visiting her sister Queen Alexandra in London, and referred bitterly to the ultimatum. "Once the matter had been put as definitely and unequivocably as that, there was nothing to do but swallow one's pride, give in and agree. The Ministers were unanimous about it. If this concession on our part can save Serbia from being crushed by Austria, it is, I firmly believe, well worth it. Our decision was the more inevitable as we were informed on all sides that Germany was absolutely ready to mobilise. Against whom? Evidently not against Austria! But our public does not realise this and it is hard to make them realise how ominous things looked a few days ago. . . ."[1] The Czar continued his letter next day. " It is quite true that the form and method of Germany's action—I mean toward us—has simply been brutal and we won't forget it. I think they were again trying to separate us from France and England—but once again they have undoubtedly failed. Such methods tend to bring about the opposite results."[1]

The Kaiser had played little part in this unfortunate drama. He met the Czar in Finnish waters in the summer and tried to smooth matters over. We do not know whether or not he succeeded; we only know that when he visited Austria-Hungary in October 1909 he made matters even worse. He delivered an inflammatory speech in which he referred to the Bosnian crisis and declared that Germany had stood behind her ally, Austria-Hungary, " in shining armour." All those who had suspected that the annexation of Bosnia and Herzegovina was a Berlin-Viennese plot were now sure of it. This conviction had far-reaching consequences. Bismarck had always stressed that the German and Austro-Hungarian alliance was purely defensive, and had laid down the axiom that Germany would not support Austria in any aggressive designs in the Balkans, as such a policy would lead her into trouble with Russia. For years the Wilhemstrasse had followed this same course, not in principle but in practice. Now, suddenly, Germany seemed to have made a new departure, and in one stroke transformed her alliance into an offensive instrument. St. Petersburg regarded it as a major event. From this moment on, Russia began to re-arm; and with the financial help of her ally, France, undertook the task of constructing strategic railways on her western frontier, necessary for a war against Germany.

[1] *The Letters of Czar Nicholas and Empress Marie.*

12. *The Interview*

In the middle of the Bosnian crisis the Kaiser committed a *gaffe* which nearly cost him his throne. It made the Fatherland the laughing stock of the world and for once the German public rose in its wrath and turned against the Crown. Forgotten was the wrangle with England over shipbuilding, forgotten the quarrel with Russia over Serbia; for weeks no one could talk of anything but the astonishing and precarious position of the German Emperor.

The story began in the middle of October 1908 when Prince Bülow, who was at his country house on Nordeney, dealing with the Bosnian affair, received a communication from Baron Jenisch, the Foreign Office representative attached to the Kaiser's suite at Rominten. Jenisch enclosed an article which had been written by Colonel Stuart-Wortley, the Emperor's host at Highcliffe, Bournemouth, the year before. The Colonel had recorded His Majesty's remarks on the "misunderstanding" between England and Germany, and now he had put them in the form of an interview with the Kaiser. He wanted permission to publish the article in an English newspaper, as the Emperor was so vehemently "pro-British" he felt sure it would alleviate suspicions and create a far healthier atmosphere.

The Kaiser approved of the idea but was sending the article to Prince Bülow to ask if he had any objections to its publication. The Chancellor tells us in his memoirs that he was too overworked to read the manuscript, for it was written on bad typing paper, was "bulky and almost illegible." "Without the slightest suspicion of the ominous contents," he writes, ". . . I sent it off at once to the Wilhelmstrasse, together with a letter to Jenisch, adding to my note to the Foreign Office the following instructions in my own hand: 'Please read the enclosed article carefully through, transcribe it in clear official script with a wide margin (or better still let it be typewritten), duplicate it, and enter, in the same hand, in the margin, such corrections, additions or deletions as may seem suitable. Further, retain a copy of the revised text for His Majesty. It is important that the utmost secrecy be observed, and that this document be returned to me as soon as possible.' The words 'carefully' and 'deletions' were both thickly underlined."[1]

Herr Stemrich, the Under-Secretary of State, was the first to read the manuscript; he thought it was too "tricky" for him to pass judgement on, so took it to Herr Klehmet who held Councillor rank; Klehmet did not gather from the instructions that he was to pass judgement on the article as a whole, but simply to make deletions, so he approved it; it then went to Baron von Schoen, the Secretary of State, who also approved it.

"A few days later, back came the article from the Foreign Office," wrote Bülow, "with the remark that only a few unimportant corrections had been found necessary—such trifles, for instance, as the correct name of the German Consular official who had been sent to Fez. Once again I had the article read, this time by the Minister von Müller, in attendance on me as Foreign Office representative.... I again asked, clearly and unmistakably, whether any possible objection could be raised against its publication. He answered me quite definitely in the negative, and I authorised him to reply in that sense to the inquiry I had received from Rominten. I had no idea that this package, from the imperial hunting-box, was a veritable charge of high explosive the detonation of which would shortly cause the most serious internal crisis I experienced during my whole term of office."[1]

It seems incredible that once the manuscript had been neatly typed Prince Bülow could not spare the time to read it. He was only too well aware of the Kaiser's penchant for sensational utterances; he knew that the article was highly political, and that it was intended for publication in a British newspaper at a time when relations between the two countries were especially delicate. Indeed, it was the first "interview" the Kaiser had ever granted. Is it possible that Bülow really neglected to look at it? This writer is inclined to think that, like the other gentlemen at the Foreign Office, he glanced through it and saw no harm in it. The Germans were not the only people guilty of insensitivity; Colonel Stuart-Wortley was certain that it could do nothing but good. When the

[1] *Memoirs:* Prince von Bülow.

interview was published, he inserted an enthusiastic foreword. " Moments sometimes occur in the history of nations when a calculated indiscretion proves of the highest public service, and it is for that reason that I have decided to make known the substance of a recent conversation which it was my privilege to have with His Majesty the German Emperor. I do so in the hope that it may help to remove the obstinate misconception of the character of the Kaiser's feelings toward England."

Bülow thought no more about the matter until October 29th when he received a press telegram from London summarising the Kaiser's remarks. " You English," the article began, " are mad, mad as march hares. What on earth has come over you that you should harbour such suspicions against us, suspicions so unworthy of a great nation ? " The German Fleet, he continued, was not being built against England ; its sole aim was to protect Germany's steadily increasing trade and her interests in the Far East ; indeed, in the face of growing Japanese power the British one day might welcome the existence of the German Fleet. The Emperor took " as a personal insult " the " distortions and misinterpretations " of the British press on his " repeated offers of friendship to England." Such an attitude made his task as a ruler—not an easy role—almost unspeakably difficult, for the great majority of people in both countries were inclined to be hostile to each other and in Germany his liking for Britain put him in a distinct minority.

He then harped back to the Boer war. At that time Russia and France had urged him to save the Boer Republics by joining a coalition which would " humiliate England to the dust ; " but he had replied that " Germany would always keep aloof from politics that could bring her into complications with a sea-power like England ; " and he had sent the text of the Russian and French notes, and his answers, to Queen Victoria, who had deposited them in the archives at Windsor Castle. Furthermore, in December 1899, when British arms were suffering severe defeats at the hands of the Boer farmers, he had tried to help his august grandmother. He had bidden one of his officers " to procure for me as exact an account as he could obtain of the numbers of combatants in South Africa on both sides, and of the actual position of the opposing forces." "With the figures before him," he had worked out what he considered to be the best plan of campaign and had submitted it for criticism to his General Staff. Then he had sent it to England, and that, too, now lay in the Windsor archives, " awaiting the serenely impartial verdict of history." It was, he continued, " a matter of curious coincidence " that the plan he had drawn up was very much the same as the one adopted by Lord Roberts which finally led him to victory. He hoped this would prove what a staunch admirer and a firm champion of Britain he was. " What more can I do? I have always stood forth as a friend of England . . . but you make it uncommonly difficult for a man to remain friendly."

The outcry was immense. The Japanese asked angrily why Germany was threatening them, and the French and Russians denied hotly, and uneasily, that they had ever proposed a coalition against England. When the British Ambassador to Russia, Sir Arthur Nicolson, called on the Czar the latter launched into a diatribe against William II. " Upon the writing table in the bow window lay a copy of the *Daily Telegraph* of October 28th heavily scored with a blue pencil. . . . The Czar was enraged by this breach of faith. He informed Nicolson that it was the Emperor William who had proposed intervention and that all that Russia had proposed was the most friendly form of mediation."[1]

The reaction in England, however, was much more devastating, for instead of being angry it was simply hilarious. It was true that the Kaiser had informed his English relations (not Queen Victoria but the Prince of Wales) that Russia was seeking a coalition against Britain, but as the reader will remember, Lord Salisbury viewed the information with scepticism; he believed that it was Germany, not Russia, who had taken the initiative against Britain and that when it failed, Berlin had the happy idea of gaining good marks at the expense of the others.

As far as the " plan of campaign " was concerned, it was also true that William had sent the Prince (not Queen Victoria) a few " aphorisms " on the Boer war, but they could scarcely be described as a plan of campaign. William had infuriated his uncle by suggesting that the best thing Britain could do was to suspend operations until reinforcements arrived from England, although of course the respite might allow time for a continental combine to form. He had ended on a cheerful note pointing out that when

[1] *Lord Carnock:* Harold Nicolson.

England lost the Test Match against Australia she had taken the latter's victory quietly " with chivalrous acknowledgement of her opponent."

Mr. Haldane, the Minister of War, was asked questions in the House of Commons about the Kaiser's " plan of campaign " and whether he intended to make it public. He replied that no such document could be found in the War Office archives or any other department. " Consequently," he said, " I am not in a position to fulfil the wish of those who want the document published. " (Loud laughter from all parts of the House.)

William II had made a complete fool of himself. How could he have allowed himself to exaggerate so wildly, when it was only too easy to disprove what he said? Eulenburg had once written Bülow that the Emperor was becoming careless about telling the truth. William did not lie intentionally, but he could not resist dressing up happenings to his own liking, altering and exaggerating them to satisfy his impulses. The more he repeated a falsified version, the more he came to believe it. For years he had been telling people about the aid he had given England during the Boer war. No one had challenged him, but even if they had, he would have sworn he was telling the truth. Indeed, only two months earlier, in the course of his famous exchange over naval plans with Sir Charles Hardinge at Cronberg, he had trotted out the same assertions. " The Emperor," Hardinge wired to London on August 16th, ". . . endeavoured to show what a good friend he had been to England in the past. Thus he repeated the statement previously made (I think) to His Majesty's Ambassador at Berlin that, during the Boer War, he had been approached by the French and Russian Governments to make a coalition against England, but that he had absolutely declined to do so, and had threatened to make war on any Power that dared to make an unprovoked attack on England at that time. I did not think it worth while to mention that this account does not tally at all with that given by M. Delcassé and the Russian Government of the transaction. So also His Majesty told me that, after our early reverses in the Boer War, he had received a letter from the late Queen Victoria, full of grief at the losses suffered by the British troops, which had touched him deeply. He had at once instructed his General Staff to draw up a plan of campaign, which he had sent to the Queen, and this plan had been followed by Lord Roberts in all its details. 'And yet,' His Majesty added, 'I am said to be the enemy of England!'"[1]

The reaction of the German press was far more violent than anything abroad. Most Germans had hotly espoused the cause of the Boers during the South African war, and were incensed to learn that the Kaiser had drawn up a "plan of campaign" for the British. Furthermore, the tactlessness of the interview had now become apparent to the most unenlightened intelligence. Why tell the Japanese that the German Fleet was being built for "eventualities" in the Far East; why tell the Russians and the French that their confidential notes had been sent to London; why tell the British that most of the Germans hated them? Each newspaper picked on the observation that it regarded as most offensive, and all of them combined in a general attack on the Emperor's "personal rule." The *Deutsche Tageszeitung* said it was time His Majesty stopped putting his fingers in the Foreign Office pie and making the nation look ridiculous; the *Börsenkurier* said the interview revealed the impossibility of controlling the Sovereign's interference and called for a constitutional change; and even the monarchical papers admitted sadly that the whole thing was "a regrettable blunder."

The cartoonists were most merciless of all. One showed the Emperor as "Little Willy" sitting at a writing table covered with ink, while Father Bülow and Mother Germania were saying: "Didn't we tell you you weren't to play at writing letters any more?" Another showed the old Emperor pleading for God's mercy on behalf of his grandson. After all he is "by the Grace of God;" and God replying: "Now you want to put the blame on me." A third showed a Court Chamberlain clasping a Bible and crying: "Oh that I could put a lock to my mouth and a seal to my lip." All sorts of jingles were put into circulation; one even arrived from England, addressed to Bülow, to be passed on to the Kaiser.

> If your lips you'd keep from slips
> Five things observe with care:
> Of whom you speak, to whom you speak
> And how, and when, and where.

. . . . .

[1] *British Documents on the Origin of the War*: Memorandum by Sir Charles Hardinge.

Bülow's immediate reaction, when he received the Wolff telegram from London on the 29th, and the sickening realisation dawned upon him that the interview alluded to was the same that had passed through his own hands, was fear for his own position. He hurried from Nordeney to Berlin, stormed into the Foreign Office, and summoned the officials who had approved the original draft. The Secretary of State, von Schoen, was not about. Instead, there was a letter from Frau von Schoen saying that her husband was ill in bed after a heart attack. Bülow claims that he immediately sent his doctor to see von Schoen, who returned smiling in half an hour. The illness of the Secretary of State was nothing graver than " nerves " brought on by fright at the difficulties his carelessness had caused. Meanwhile the other subordinates had gathered shamefacedly in Bülow's room; and when the Chancellor asked them how they possibly could have approved the manuscript, the Councillor, Herr Klehmet, replied for them all: " Because we thought the Emperor wished it." " Haven't you learned by now," rasped Prince Bülow, " that the Emperor's wishes are often sheer nonsense ? "

Bülow had no alternative but to write an abject letter to the Kaiser, telling him of the unfavourable comment the interview was provoking and explaining how it had slipped through his hands. " If Your Majesty is displeased," he ended, " with my having failed under pressure of business to go through the English manuscript in person, and blames me for the carelessness shown by the Foreign Office, I humbly beg to be relieved of my Chancellorship. But if I have not lost Your Majesty's confidence, my sole object in remaining will be to counter, publicly and emphatically, to the utmost of my ability, the unjust attacks on my Imperial Master."[1]

Bülow's nickname " the eel " was never more applicable than to the way he managed to slip and slither through the stormy, reef-ridden waters, now referred to as " the Kaiser-crisis."[2] He issued a short statement to the press in which he cleverly managed to shift the blame on to other shoulders by neglecting to say that the article had been sent to him for his personal approval, yet at the same time declaring his willingness to accept responsibility. " His

[1] *Grosse Politik.*

[2] Tirpitz once declared that " an oiled eel is a leech compared to Bülow."

Majesty forwarded the article to the Chancellor, who submitted it to the Foreign Office with the request that it should be carefully read through. Since no objection was raised and the report returned to the Foreign Office, permission to publish was given, and it appeared in the *Daily Telegraph*. When the Imperial Chancellor learned of its publication and contents he informed His Majesty that he personally had never seen the draft of the article, and that, had he seen it, he would have advised against publication, but that he considered himself solely responsible for what had occurred and absolved the officials and departments under him." However, his method of " absolving his subordinates " was original, for it was announced ten days later that the Chancellor had accepted the resignation of Herr Klehmet, and that Secretary of State Schoen had been granted leave of absence because of illness, and was being replaced, temporarily, by Herr von Kiderlen-Wächter, the German Minister at Bucharest.

Nevertheless, the statement failed to draw away the fire from the Kaiser. At first, in north Germany, where people prided themselves on the efficiency of their civil service, they were shocked by the ineptitude of the Wilhelmstrasse; but this proved to be a passing phase as it soon began to be whispered that William II had insisted on publication, and Bülow was only trying to defend him.[1] One thing was clear: Bülow himself had managed to escape untarnished. He sensed this the day after his explanation was published; and when, that same afternoon, he saw the Kaiser, who had returned to Potsdam from Rominten, he already had begun to adopt a superior air. William was completely humbled; he was so shocked and upset by the criticism that he presented a pitiable figure. For once he did not attempt to defend himself. He did not reproach Bülow for his neglect, or even refer to the Foreign Office, but simply said brokenly that the Chancellor must do or say anything necessary to mend matters. " But whatever

[1] Sir M. de C. Findlay, the British Minister-Resident at Dresden, wired the Foreign Office: "I cannot exaggerate the rage and shame caused by Prince Bülow's announcement. The German, especially the North German, prides himself on his organisation and thoroughness . . . and [yet] the Chancellor and the Ministry for Foreign Affairs have shown themselves utterly inefficient or culpably servile. All confidence was swept away. . . ." *British Documents on the Origin of the War.*

you do, get us out of this; bring us through!" he implored. Bülow told him that everything would depend on the Chancellor's speech in the Reichstag debate, scheduled for November 10th, and that he was confident he would silence the critics.

Then the Chancellor committed another blunder. He advised the Kaiser to continue with his pre-arranged plan for a visit to the Archduke Franz Ferdinand of Austria, followed by a stay at Donaueschingen with Prince Max Fürstenburg, the rich Austrian nobleman who had taken Philip Eulenburg's place as the Emperor's close friend. William II was only too glad to quit the storm and set forth next day. The Chancellor tells us that he proffered this advice because he felt that "the burdens I would have to shoulder would be easier if I were not forced to make a daily journey from Berlin to the New Palace at Potsdam"!

This caused the tension to increase rather than slacken, for the Kaiser was bitterly criticized for departing on a pleasure trip when the Reichstag debate was pending. Maximilian Harden, the man who had hounded Eulenburg to his doom, led a campaign in *Zukunft* (again believed to be inspired by Baron Holstein) which not only dwelt on the Sovereign's fecklessness but almost accused him of treachery in secretly assisting the English "enemy" while the German nation prayed for a Boer victory. Although the paper was confiscated and taken out of circulation the accusations were repeated by other papers in a veiled form. A new British Ambassador, Sir Edward Goschen, had just arrived in the capital and was amazed by the outpourings. "To a newcomer like myself," he wrote to London, "imbued with the idea that His Majesty was more or less outside public criticism, this onslaught upon him comes as a most striking surprise."[1]

The Kaiser did his best to put the affair out of his mind and to enjoy his stay abroad, but every now and then someone in his entourage showed him a selection of press cuttings which made him very unhappy. He placed all his reliance on Bülow to extricate him from the mess. "The two days here," he wired the Chancellor from Vienna, "have gone off very harmoniously and gaily. . . . The shoot went off splendidly; I brought down sixty-five stags. . . . I remember you in all my prayers morning and evening. When has He ever failed to help us, though hate and

[1] *British Documents on the Origin of the War:* Gooch & Temperley.

envy might pursue! There is a silver lining in every cloud. God be with you! Your old friend, William I.R."[1]

William II was at the Castle Fürstenburg at Donaueschingen when he read the breathlessly awaited reports of the Reichstag debate. To everyone's astonishment the proceedings turned out to be a damp squib. The deputies made it plain that they did not want any fundamental alterations. The German people were angry and humiliated but at heart intensely monarchical. They wished to let off steam but that was all. Speaker after speaker rose to attack the incompetence of the Foreign Office or the impetuousness of the Kaiser but practically no one had anything constructive to propose. One or two deputies suggested constitutional changes which would curtail the authority of the Emperor but they received no support; the Conservative Party felt "obliged to express (though most respectfully) the wish that in future the Emperor will maintain greater reserve in his conversation,"[2] but a motion by the Socialists to present an address to the Kaiser—a form of censure—was not carried, and the word "abdication" was not so much as whispered. However, they all agreed that it was wrong of the Emperor to have absented himself from Berlin at such a critical time!

But the most severe indictment of His Majesty, veiled in the faint praise so proverbially damning, came from Prince Bülow. The Prince made his master out a complete fool. He told the assembly how hard the Emperor worked for his country and how eager he was to improve relations with Britain. Then he took the interview, point by point, disowning each clause with the admission that "the colours had been laid on too thick." Finally, he came to his peroration. "Gentlemen, the knowledge that the publication of his conversations has not produced the effect which the Emperor intended in England, and has aroused deep excitement and painful regret in our country, will—and this is the firm conviction which I have gained during these days of stress—will induce His Majesty in future to observe that reserve, even in private conversations, which is equally indispensable in the interest of a uniform policy for the authority of the Crown [cheers on the right]. Were that

[1] *Grosse Politik.*

[2] This statement, on behalf of the Conservative Party, was published formally in the newspapers.

not so, neither I nor any successor of mine could bear the responsibility . . . [prolonged cheers on the right and amongst the National Liberals]. For the mistake which was made in dealing with the manuscript I take the entire responsibility. . . . It is repugnant to my personal feelings to brand as scapegoats officials who have done a life-long duty, because in a single case they relied too implicitly on the fact that I read and decide almost everything myself. . . . When the article, as to whose sinister effect there could not for a moment have been any doubts, was published, I tendered my resignation. The decision was inevitable and was not hard for me. The gravest and hardest decision I have ever taken in my political life was to remain in office, in compliance with the wish of the Emperor. I only resolved to do so because I regarded it as a behest of political duty to continue to serve Emperor and country at this time of stress." (Loud cheers.)

The Kaiser was dumbfounded. He had expected Bülow to defend him, not to apologise for him, and instead his Chancellor had chosen to save himself. Even his pretence of protecting his colleagues was nothing but a puff for his own hard work. He had told the chamber (in so many words) that any child (except the Emperor) could see that the article was bound to create a storm and that unless William II kept quiet in the future Bülow would not remain with him. There was no indication that it had been abjectly proffered as the price of his own negligence; it was presented as a protest against the Kaiser's waywardness.

What nettled the Kaiser most was the fact that Bülow had ignored and disowned his attempts to induce friendliness in the English people. He burst into tears in the forest with Prince Fürstenburg and told him that he had sent long reports from Highcliffe in which he had informed Bülow of the line he was taking, that the latter had praised his adroitness. This probably was true, for, as the reader has seen, he had recounted the services he had rendered England during the Boer war many times. What William II could not seem to understand was that there was a great difference between private remarks and those that must stand the test of public scrutiny.

The Kaiser could not decide what to do. His indignation against Bülow was tempered by the thought that perhaps the Chancellor had been driven to extremes in order to save the situation. He would wait until he returned to Berlin before passing final judgement, and in the meantime he would try to enjoy himself. But even this was doomed to failure. Although the Prince had laid on lavish entertainment, importing a cabaret show for His Majesty's pleasure, a tragedy occurred on the last night which marred the memory of the visit. The Emperor's close friend Count Hülsen-Haeseler, the Chief of the Military Cabinet (the man who had led the court attack on Eulenburg), decided to divert the assembly by dressing up like a ballet dancer and performing a *pas-seul*. It was not intended as a burlesque, for we are told that the Count " danced beautifully." " We had the usual dinner," wrote Count Zedlitz, who was in attendance, " and the ladies, Princess Fürstenburg, Princess Hohenlohe, etc., were in full evening dress with all their jewels, the gentlemen in green or black swallow tails with black shoes, and as there had been a steeplechase in the neighbourhood, some were in scarlet. This exceptionally smart and brilliant company assembled after dinner in the beautiful Great Hall of the Castle, with a band playing on the staircase. Suddenly Count Hülsen-Haeseler appeared in ballet skirts—not for the first time—and began to dance to the music. Everybody found it most entertaining, for the Count danced beautifully, and it is an unusual experience to see a Chief of the Military Cabinet capering about in the costume of a lady of the ballet."[1]

After his exhausting performance, the Count went to the Long Gallery to get his breath and suddenly dropped to the floor. Count Zedlitz saw him and hurried to his aid. From then on pandemonium reigned. The Staff physician was called and worked for an hour and a half to bring him back to consciousness. Princess Fürstenburg sat in a chair and wept, while the Kaiser paced up and down near the prone figure. Another doctor came from the town, but at eleven o'clock they both gave up their attempts at restoration and pronounced the Count dead from heart failure. " The body," wrote Zedlitz, " was then carried to the large saloon on the floor above, which was reserved for the greatest State banquets." The doctors and assistants had great difficulty in removing the General's ballet skirt and putting him back into a uniform, for by this time rigor mortis had set in. After much patience it finally was achieved, and the funeral service took place the following morning.

Meanwhile the Emperor had wired the Empress that he had lost

[1] *Twelve Years at the Imperial German Court:* Count Zedlitz-Trützschler.

" his best friend " and had decided to cancel his official trip to Kiel scheduled for the next afternoon. He suggested meeting the Empress at Baden-Baden, but after an hour or so changed his plans again and altered his time-schedule. Count Zedlitz protested that it was difficult to alter the complicated arrangements for the imperial trains twice in the same night. " The Emperor put his hand on my shoulder," wrote the Count, " and looking at me with a tragic expression, as much as to say that I was always the one to make life hard for him, exclaimed: ' Is this the time for you to want to make difficulties? ' "

Meanwhile Prince Bülow was growing uneasy. On the day of the Reichstag debate he had felt triumphant. "When amid a roar of cheering I sat down I felt that the battle had been won." He believed that he had emerged from the ordeal, saved the Emperor and, miraculously enough, increased his own prestige, and although the Emperor might not like the method he had chosen, he was scarcely in a position to object; at any rate, Bülow was confident that he could bring him round to his point of view. When he received Sir Edward Goschen that afternoon he was so self-assured that he even allowed himself to indulge in badinage at the Kaiser's expense. " The Prince was rather funny about the Plan of Campaign for the Boer War," wrote Goschen to Sir Edward Grey. " He said he had taken the trouble to fish it out of the archives. ' But,' he added, ' please do not ask me my opinion of it or I should have to tell you that it was really a very childish production, consisting partly of extracts from a well-known work on the art of war, and partly of some original thoughts on that same art which would scarcely meet with the approbation of military experts.' "[1]

Sir Edward did not feel that Bülow's speech had been as much of a success as the latter believed. He informed London that it was regarded as " unsatisfactory." " Everyone," he wired on November 13, " is angry with somebody. The general public are furious because in his speech Prince Bülow did not say enough, and . . . the Conservatives are angry with him because he said too much while not sufficiently defending the Emperor. . . ."[1] Apparently this last criticism began to spread, for a week later the Ambassador was reporting " the fairly general opinion " that the Emperor will not easily forgive " the somewhat half-hearted way " in which the

[1] *British Documents on the Origin of the War*: Gooch & Temperley.

Chancellor defended the Kaiser. "Whether Prince Bülow will remain very long in office remains to be seen." The *Berliner Tageblatt* seized upon the situation to deliver another attack on the Emperor. "We have a population of more than sixty million, a highly intelligent nation, and yet the fate of the Chancellor as well as the choice of his successor rests with one man! Such a situation is intolerable to a self-respecting nation. The events of the last few days have made it clear that the German people will not continue to allow their vital interests to depend on the mood of a single individual whose impulsiveness they have once again had the opportunity of witnessing."[1]

Despite this line of defence, the gossip began to worry Bülow and he made up his mind that he would ask the Emperor to sign a statement approving the remarks he had made in the Reichstag. This would make it impossible for William to disown him at a later date, or suddenly to demand his resignation.

The two men met at Potsdam on November 17th in an atmosphere of mutual suspicion. When Prince Bülow arrived at the Palace he was greeted by the Empress who whispered: "Be really kind and gentle with the Emperor. He is quite broken up." This was a relief to Bülow; at least he was not going to have an explosive scene with his master. On the contrary, he found the Kaiser as pained and submissive as at their last meeting. He was surprised that the press was still referring to the incident and seemed almost bemused. "But what are they so annoyed about?" he asked childishly. The Chancellor gave him a long dissertation on the imperial actions that had undermined confidence, and then told him that the public was waiting for a statement from him. He drew from his pocket the following draft: "Today His Majesty the Emperor and King received a report from Prince Bülow lasting several hours. The Imperial Chancellor described the temper roused in the German People by the *Daily Telegraph* publication and explained the position which he had adopted towards the interpolations in the Reichstag. His Majesty received the representations and explanations of the Imperial Chancellor with great seriousness, and thus announced his will: Undisturbed by the exaggerations of public opinion, which he feels to be unjustified, he regards it as his Highest Imperial duty to ensure the continuity of

[1] *British Documents on the Origin of the War:* Gooch & Temperley.

the Emperor's policy by the preservation of constitutional responsibilities. His Majesty accordingly approved the Imperial Chancellor's statements in the Reichstag and assured the Prince of his continued confidence."[1]

Prince Bülow declares in his memoirs that the Kaiser seemed relieved that so little was demanded of him, and agreed wholeheartedly to sign the document. He claims that when he took his leave William kissed him on both cheeks and said: "Thank you. Thank you with all my heart." The Emperor's memoirs, however, give a different impression. "After my return home the Chancellor appeared, read me a lecture on my political sins, and demanded the signature of the well-known document, which was afterwards communicated to the Press. I signed it in silence, as in silence I let the Press attacks on me and the Crown take their course."[2]

Whatever the truth of the two accounts, Bülow had made a mistake. In the Reichstag he had taken the middle course, so dear to his heart, and neither defended the Emperor nor thrown him over. By failing to back up his sovereign with all the skill he could summon, or alternatively to demand the constitutional changes that would have stripped the Crown of power, he had got the worst of both worlds and set the seal on his own doom.

A curious aspect of the episode was the Kaiser's delayed reaction. As soon as Bülow departed, his nerves fell to pieces and he took to his bed with "cold shiverings and hysteria." His humiliation seemed complete. After twenty years of praise and idolisation, the sudden cruel change in the temper of his people had proved too much for him. How could he ever lift up his head again? What had come over the German nation? And why was Bülow so critical? The Chancellor knew perfectly well what the Kaiser had said at Highcliffe; William remembered telling him, and he had not raised the slightest objection. The Emperor felt abandoned by everyone, and wept like a child for hours at a time. Suddenly he decided that he could endure it no longer. He would abdicate. He sent a message to the Crown Prince to come to Potsdam at once, and instructed the Court Chamberlain, Count Schulz, to get a message to Prince Bülow informing him of the decision.

[1] *Grosse Politik.*

[2] *My Memoirs:* William II.

The Empress was so shocked that she sent a footman to find Prince Bülow, asking him to come quickly and to see her first. The Chancellor received the Kaiser's message on the floor of the Reichstag just as he was rising to make a speech. Afterwards, when he was leaving the building, the royal footman caught him, and he immediately went to Potsdam. " Her Majesty the Empress received me on the ground floor. Her eyes were red with tears, but her bearing was entirely regal. She asked me at once: ' Must the Emperor abdicate? Do you wish him to abdicate? ' "[1] Bülow replied that such a thing had never occurred to him. He remained with her some time trying to calm her but she seemed at a loss to know what to do.

Meanwhile the Crown Prince had arrived. " I rushed upstairs. My mother received me immediately. She was agitated, and her eyes were red. She kissed me and held my head before her in both her hands. Then she said: ' You know, my boy, what you are here for? ' ' No, Mother.' ' Then go to your father. But sound your heart well before you decide.' Then I knew what was coming. A few minutes later I stood by my father's sick-bed. He seemed aged by years; he had lost hope, and felt himself to be deserted by everybody; he was broken down by the catastrophe which had snatched the ground from beneath his feet; his self-confidence and his trust were shattered. . . . He talked vehemently, complainingly, and hurriedly of the incidents; and the bitterness aroused by the injustice which he saw in them kept reasserting itself. . . . I stayed with him for quite an hour sitting on his bed, a thing which, so long as I can remember, had never happened before."[2]

But William II did not broach the subject of abdication; he had no real intention of taking such a plunge. Yet he found it impossible to throw off his depression. Although he rose from his bed and attended one or two small official functions, his *amour propre* had been so deeply wounded that he could not recover himself. " The gloom of the Prussian Court," wrote the English governess, ". . . can hardly be adequately pictured. The Emperor made no attempt to conceal the deep dejection of his soul, but moved about—this man usually so loquacious, so pleased with himself and the world—in a mournful silence, speaking seldom and then in an undertone,

[1] *Memoirs:* Prince von Bülow.

[2] *Memoirs:* William, Crown Prince.

as though someone he loved were dead. Everyone else, too, seemed to talk in whispers, not daring to break the ghastly silence that surrounded the Palace like a chilly winter atmosphere. . . . All the young Princes—the two at Plön, and Prince Albert from Kiel—made short, hurried visits home, in the hope of distracting their father from the brooding grief into which he appeared to have sunk."[1]

On New Year's Day, 1909, the tide turned. When the Kaiser attended a public reception in Berlin he received a tumultuous ovation. The agitation against him had come mainly from intellectuals; the prosperous middle classes had always been shocked by the criticism, and now the pendulum had swung far the other way. Sympathy for the Emperor was widespread and mounting. He had been misjudged and wronged, people said; he had been forced to take the rap for the Chancellor, who had scarcely lifted a finger in his defence. He had borne his lot with dignity and silence, and the real culprit was Bülow who had "betrayed his king." The Berlin reception was the first overt sign of sympathy for the monarch, and it was followed by many others. At the end of January the Princes came in a body to Berlin to celebrate the Emperor's fiftieth birthday, and gave a stirring demonstration of their loyalty; and at the musical festival at Frankfurt, several months later, the fervour and adulation of the crowds exceeded anything that William had experienced throughout his long reign. Even when he rode through the streets, he received cheers far more whole-hearted than ever before. "There," he exclaimed triumphantly, "I always knew the people were behind me."

The whispers about Bülow were repeated to the Kaiser, and confirmed his innermost thoughts. Suddenly his self-confidence was restored, for it was Bülow, not the Kaiser, who had committed the wrong. Soon the Kaiser was asserting that he had acted constitutionally; that everything he said had been approved. The reason for the disaster was simply that "Bülow had betrayed his king." From then on, William could say no good of his Chancellor. Probably Bülow had read the manuscript and deliberately passed it for publication in order to increase his own authority; no doubt it was a conspiracy concocted by Baron Holstein in order to get revenge for his dismissal by the Kaiser.

[1] *Memories of the Fatherland*: Anne Topham.

Nothing was too bad to think of Bülow. He fulminated against him in front of his staff, remarking bitterly that he had left him "in the lurch," and writing sarcastic minutes on the margins of dispatches. "I suppose he wants to be a Court Marshal too." The Emperor's suspicions had become accusations, and soon the accusations became monstrous facts. The following year he shocked Count Zedlitz by his "annihilating" pronouncements. "He went so far as to say that the world had not seen such a hypocrite or a liar since Caesar Borgia. He laid the whole blame for the downfall of Prince Eulenburg and the others concerned at Bülow's door. He said that he had bungled the whole business so that no other result was possible; and that quite probably the scandals had not been unwelcome to him for personal reasons."[1]

This was the unhappy background against which the affairs of Germany were conducted from January to July 1909. Every important political development bore the stamp of the strained relations between the two men at the helm of the nation's affairs, and gave each situation a twist it otherwise might not have had. Although William dealt officially with Bülow he refused to see him privately. When they met he was polite and even amiable, but he maintained a reserve which Bülow found disturbing, for, coupled with the malicious stories repeated back to the Chancellor, it left no doubt as to the Emperor's bitter displeasure. When Bülow saw public opinion swinging back to William, he became more afraid. Once again he became anxious to please, eager to impress, and loath to take any line which might exacerbate His Majesty's hostility.

In one instance, Prince Bülow's fear served Germany well. In February he reached an agreement with France, designed to put an end to the wrangle about Morocco. This was an attempt to placate William. In October, a day or two after the Austrian annexation of Bosnia had been announced, the Emperor had written the Foreign Office that if Germany was going to run into trouble with Russia, it was time she patched up things with France. He was sick and tired of the endless disputes over Morocco. Each time there was a revolt in North Africa or an outrage against Europeans, and the French landed troops to restore order, Germany accused her of breaking the terms of the Algeciras Act, and sent a threatening

[1] *Twelve Years at the Imperial German Court:* Count Zedlitz-Trützschler.

note " that Berlin could not look with indifference at possible French encroachments."

These pin-pricks not only irritated the French but William II as well. " This wretched Morocco business must be brought to a conclusion quickly and finally," he had written to Bülow. " There is nothing to be done about it. It will be French. So let us get out of the affair with dignity and be done with this friction with France, now that great issues are at stake."[1] He also wrote a similar letter to Baron von Schoen who informed M. Cambon, the French Ambassador, that it was time Germany and France shook hands over Morocco, as " the Emperor wished it." In January an agreement was drawn up in which Germany recognised Morocco as a French sphere of interest, and France reiterated her pledge to preserve Moroccan independence and promised specific economic benefits for Germany. The document was signed on February 9th, the day that King Edward VII and Queen Alexandra arrived in Berlin for a state visit—the first official visit the King had paid during the eight years of his reign.

The Kaiser was eager to flourish the agreement in his uncle's face. Although M. Cambon only arrived back in Berlin from Paris on the 9th, he was received by the Emperor within an hour of applying for an interview and the signatures were hastily affixed. William then decorated the Ambassador with the Order of the Red Eagle (which was given wide publicity) and presented him with a photograph of himself on which was written: " because the path I ordered in our Moroccan policy has had such a brilliant success in the whole world, and because we owe so much to the devoted and unselfish work of Cambon as well as to his loyalty."

Edward VII looked old and ill. He had only made the effort to come to Berlin because he wished to show the world that the *Daily Telegraph* interview had not caused any ill will. But although he was on a mission of peace, William always nettled him and he could not resist a few tart observations. After the state dinner, he congratulated the Chancellor on the agreement with France and said he hoped he would settle the Bosnian affair with equal success. " But keep a sharp look out at *him*," he added with an oblique look, " and see that he doesn't get too uppish about it." The King was well aware of the tension between Bülow and his master and

[1] *Grosse Politik.*

the next day, after the luncheon at the British Embassy, he asked the Chancellor point-blank, somewhat impudently: "How do you get on with the Emperor? It does not seem to me to be very easy for his ministers to get on with him." Bülow replied cattily that His Majesty was still very young despite his fifty years.

The Kaiser gave no indication of the strain he was undergoing. His uncle's presence always seemed to excite him and he was more voluble than he had been for weeks. "He had great fascination as a conversationalist," wrote Sir Frederick Ponsonby, one of King Edward's equerries, "as he was always so keen and interested. He practically stood on one's feet glaring into one's eyes and giving grunts of approval, which acted as a spur. . . . His sense of humour was of the blatant type and he was unable to appreciate any subtle witticism, but I have heard him tell stories which were quite funny." William II seized every opportunity to impress his visitors with his own superior knowledge of England. Ponsonby suspected that he "anticipated what subjects of conversation would crop up, then got his staff to look up statistics." The Emperor asked him across the dinner table how many people sat on the London County Council, who was qualified to vote, and how many years elapsed between elections. "I had very vague ideas on all these questions," wrote Sir Frederick, "but I bravely answered all of them, making shots at the numbers. 'I don't think you're right,' replied the Emperor, and then proceeded to give chapter and verse. I must say it was very effective and everyone present marvelled at his knowledge."[1]

At the state ball the King had such a coughing fit that the Princess of Pless thought he might pass out. He recovered himself with much difficulty, but this was proved to be the last meeting between uncle and nephew. The King died the following year.

Throughout the winter the Kaiser refused to receive Bülow in private audience. It was almost impossible to conduct the business of the nation under these circumstances, and the Chancellor pleaded repeatedly to be seen and heard. Finally, on March 11th the Kaiser agreed to receive him. The conversation took place in the Picture Gallery of the Berlin Palace. After giving William a report on foreign affairs Bülow begged to be allowed to raise a personal

[1] *Under Three Reigns:* Sir Frederick Ponsonby.

matter. "I walked up and down with him," wrote William II, "... between portraits of my ancestors and the paintings of the battles of the Seven Years War, of the proclamation of the empire at Versailles, and was amazed when the Chancellor harked back to the events of the autumn of 1908 and undertook to explain his attitude." The Kaiser told Bülow bluntly that he did not think he had defended him adequately. "Fröben," he said, "would not have spoken as you did at the Reichstag debate on November 10th." He paused before the picture of Fröben, the royal equerry who had mounted the piebald horse of the Great Elector at Fehrbellin, to attract bullets away from his master. If Fröben had been Chancellor instead of Bülow, said William, he would have declared that it was he who had advised the Emperor to speak in England as he had done. Bülow was so taken aback he could not speak. He claims in his memoirs (although it is scarcely credible) that he replied that the truth was the only possible course as no one in England or Germany could possibly believe that he was capable of advising the Kaiser to talk as he had. "Which simply means," rejoined the Emperor, "that you consider me a donkey capable of blunders that you yourself could never have committed." This exchange is most unlikely, considering the circumstances. The Kaiser's version probably comes nearer the truth. After the interview he wired his brother, Prince Henry: "Have just forgiven Bülow who begged my pardon in a flood of tears."

The Kaiser and Kaiserin dined with Prince and Princess Bülow the following night; everyone was on affectionate, almost emotional, terms, and the affair seemed patched up for good. "What a terrible winter it has been," William sighed. "But now everything is perfect again!" However, as soon as he was separated from the spell of his Chancellor's personality the old grievances overtook him. A man named Rudolph Martin published a pamphlet in which he "unmasked Prince Bülow's baseness." The Chancellor, he asserted, had deliberately encouraged the Emperor to make his "pro-English" remarks at Bournemouth, and welcomed their publication in the *Daily Telegraph*. His purpose had been to compromise the Sovereign and force him to abdicate, so that he could proclaim a republic with himself at the head. The Emperor described Martin's work as "a very good book" and loudly recommended it to everyone he met.

It was now obvious that William II would seize the first opportunity to rid himself of his Chancellor; and the opportunity was not long in coming. The Chancellor had the task of guiding the Finance Reform Bill through the Reichstag, introducing death duties for the first time. The Conservatives hotly opposed the Bill, and by May had acquired such support that Bülow's chances of success were slim. Since the Imperial Chancellor was not responsible to the Reichstag, only to the Emperor, an adverse vote would not be fatal to him if the Sovereign stood behind him. Bülow knew, however, that William would not support him if he failed; so he had no alternative but to couple the vote with his resignation. The decisive day was June 24th. Just as Bülow feared, the Chamber rejected his Bill by 195 to 187 votes. And just as he had prophesied, William II accepted his retirement.

The Kaiser dismissed Prince Bülow almost as unpleasantly as he had parted with Bismarck. After a short interview on board the *Hohenzollern*, in which he escaped from any serious talk by dragging the unhappy Chancellor along with him to a lunch on board the Prince of Monaco's yacht, he kept him in suspense by not announcing the resignation for three weeks. Bülow bitterly minded leaving. He loved the work, the power, and prestige that went with the Chancellorship, and he had the lowest opinion of Herr Bethmann-Hollweg, the Secretary of the Interior, who the Emperor had told him would take his place. It was only natural, during those agonising weeks, that he should have hoped the Kaiser would change his mind.

But William stood firm. The resignation was published on July 14th, accompanied by a handsome letter of gratitude from the Kaiser, and the announcement that the Prince had been awarded the Order of the Black Eagle in brilliants. Bülow took his official leave in the garden of the Berlin Palace, when the Kaiser surprised him by inviting himself and the Kaiserin to a farewell dinner at the Bülow's house the following night.

It was obvious that William II had an impulse to behave generously, but the darker side of his nature got the better of him. Soon he was telling his entourage, just as he had done after Bismarck's departure, that he had been forced to let Bülow go because the Chancellor had lost his memory. He was becoming so confused, almost senile, that he could not remember what he had said the day before. He had even suggested appointing as ambassador a notorious gambler and drunkard. He attributed the impairment of Bülow's faculties to overwork, and felt it his " duty as a Christian " not to oppose his return to private life.

Even the farewell dinner was marred by the Kaiser's ungraciousness. Although he arrived with a bunch of roses for Princess Bülow, which he said he had picked with his own hands, and presented her with a gold bracelet, from which dangled a portrait of himself on enamel, surrounded with brilliants, he enraged her with his conversation. When she remarked sadly that it was a pity the Death Duties had proved such a stumbling block, the Kaiser could not contain himself. " You mustn't think," he protested, " that the Bloc or the Death Duties are what made Bernard retire. The real reason was the events of last November. You see, those fellows let me know privately that they didn't really mind the Death Duties. They overthrew him because they didn't think he showed enough zeal in defending me His Imperial Master."[1]

Princess Bülow tried to argue with the Emperor, and finally said: " Your Majesty, I know nothing about politics, but I can assure you of one thing at least; that Bernard is devoted, body and soul, to Your Majesty. For twelve years he has had no other thought than the thought of serving you faithfully. He suffered very much in November and, day and night, he could think of nothing, except how to save Your Majesty, and restore your good relationship with the nation. And he succeeded. Your Majesty is as respected as ever."[1] " Yes," interrupted the Kaiser. " Now that they see they did me an injustice." " But what did Your Majesty expect Bernard to do? " " He ought to have declared in the Reichstag: ' I won't have any more of this insolent speech about the Emperor. How dare you speak like this? Quick march! Get out! ' Bernard should have declared that he stood shoulder to shoulder to me. He knew perfectly well what the article in the *Daily Telegraph* contained; I had written from Highcliffe to tell him." " But Bernard got no such letter." " Well, if I didn't write, I said it to him. I can show you the very tree in your garden under which I talked to him about it." The conversation finally ended with the Emperor advising Princess Bülow to read Rudolph Martin's book if she really wanted to know " the ins and outs " of the story!

Prince Bülow relinquished his office with a smouldering fury

[1] *Memoirs:* Prince von Bülow.

that became apparent when his memoirs were published after his death. Every page is studded with malice, and every chapter is designed to illumine his own genius and prove his infallibility. He claims to have brought Germany to the pinnacle of fame and power, and declares that if he had remained in charge the world war would have been avoided. Yet the truth is that his twelve years as Chancellor had been disastrous. His diplomatic moves had conjured into being the Triple Entente, and had left Germany and Austria-Hungary friendless and isolated. His belated agreement with France, instigated by the Kaiser, had not succeeded in erasing the hostility aroused by his repeated threats of war over Morocco. Not only was France deeply estranged, but his stinging rebuff to the Czar over Bosnia had angered Russia, and his enthusiastic support for the Kaiser's great navy, which only began to falter in the last months of his office, had alienated Britain. His public performance was unparalleled for bad relations, and his personal record was not much better. He had betrayed Holstein, Eulenburg, and the Kaiser. And now that he finally had fallen himself, accused everyone of malevolence and treachery.

He received many letters upon his resignation, among them a lone voice calling forth memories from the past—a letter of sympathy from Prince Eulenburg. Underneath the silky flattery, however, it contained such a bitter accusation that it scarcely can have been consoling. After deploring Bülow's retirement and declaring that Max Fürstenburg was " the person responsible " Philip continued with deadly innocence: " You can imagine how, in letter after letter, people have done their best to persuade me to see in you the origin and the source of all my misfortunes—all this disaster to me and mine! Many people are really annoyed by the sight of a firm and constant loyalty which will allow nothing to shake it. . . . Only one thing seemed difficult to explain: the fact that neither the official, nor even the semi-official, press cared to take up the cudgels on behalf of one of the highest German functionaries, and fight scandals and scandal-mongering newspapers."[1]

[1] *Memoirs:* Prince von Bülow.

13. *Repeat Performance*

"Everything," remarked Count Zedlitz gloomily, in February 1910, "is moving in the same groove as before." Once again the Kaiser was his old, ebullient self; once again he was taking the salute at reviews, making explosive speeches and whirling around Germany on the imperial train. Historians sometimes assert that the *Daily Telegraph* incident marked the close of an epoch by bringing to an end the Kaiser's "personal rule," but there is no evidence to support this. On the contrary, after Bülow's departure in July 1909, William II asserted himself more forcibly than he had done for a decade. This was mainly due to the fact that the new Chancellor, Herr von Bethmann-Hollweg, knew nothing about foreign affairs. He was not a clever man. A jurist by profession, he was painstaking and ponderous but slow to grasp the implications of a situation. The Kaiser did not lay down a policy, for he was incapable of working out a policy. Never once, during any of the many crises which Germany had passed through, had he contributed a serious state paper, explaining, arguing, or even outlining a consistent course of action. Instead, he contented himself by showering the Wilhelmstrasse with opinion and comment.

The Kaiser was not a statesman, but a brilliant dilettante. He was much more like his mother than people imagined, for he had the temperament of an artist rather than that of a Prussian prince. He painted, arranged ballets, occasionally wrote poetry, and was an expert on archaeology. In March he always went to Corfu, where he had bought the palace Achilleion, built by the Empress of Austria, and where he occupied himself exploring and excavating.

What the Emperor liked best was to talk and to travel. Count Zedlitz complained that he was only in Berlin (or Potsdam) two months of the year; the rest of the time he was abroad paying calls on foreign monarchs, cruising on the *Hohenzollern*, or moving around his own kingdom, visiting the imperial establishments or gracing the houses of rich noblemen who could provide suitable entertainment. One of his favourite places was the Castle Fürstenstein, the seat of the Prince of Pless. The English-born Princess found the etiquette oppressive for " every time the Emperor spoke to anyone, or even entered the room, everyone jumped up, the women curtseying and the men clicking." Furthermore there was always a martial atmosphere for the gentlemen never appeared in civilian clothes. During the day they wore the " imperial hunting costume " designed by the Emperor, and at night military regalia glittering with orders and decorations. The Emperor's delight in uniforms was a joke of long standing. The Berliners said that he would not visit an aquarium without putting on admiral's attire, and had been known to climb into the uniform of a British Field Marshal to eat a plum pudding. The Princess of Pless wondered if anyone, except the Empress in the privacy of the boudoir, had ever seen the Sovereign in mufti, and someone retorted that he obviously climbed into undress uniform for bed.

Despite the formalities, the Emperor allowed the company to relax after dinner, when he settled down to his favourite pastime. " In the evenings we talked—or rather the Emperor did," wrote the Princess in her diary. " I never met a man who can remember such millions of things at the same time, even Irish stories which I suppose he heard in England—he repeated them in German—I nearly died with laughter. And then he half acts when he tells the stories ; one evening he went on from eleven until a quarter to one. And then at tea-time he keeps on till nearly dinner time. . . ."[1]

The Kaiser always travelled with a large suite. Several members of the Foreign Office were attached permanently to him, cabinet ministers journeyed from Berlin to consult him, and every day a messenger arrived with state papers. In February 1910 he was delighted to learn that ex-President Theodore Roosevelt was planning a visit to Berlin, and astonished his suite by announcing that he would meet Mr. Roosevelt at the station in person. It was unheard of for an Emperor to pay such a mark of respect to a commoner, much less a commoner who no longer held office. " It seems to be the Emperor's intention to meet Roosevelt at the station on his arrival," wrote Sir Edward Goschen on April 23rd. " I can hardly believe it, but Stemrich says it is so. I know that His Majesty

[1] *Daisy, Princess of Pless.*

wished to do so, but I had heard that his entourage were so much against it that he had given it up. If His Majesty really does this it will be going rather far. . . . I still cannot believe it."[1]

In the end William II was dissuaded from his plan, but he gave a large dinner for Mr. Roosevelt at the New Palace in Potsdam. Ever since Björkö he had kept up a correspondence with the American President, who was impressed by William's views, and talked about an American-German-British alliance. Like William, Mr. Roosevelt was swashbuckling, provocative, and indiscreet. He lacked real understanding of international power politics, and was unaware of what the struggle in Europe was about. As the reader has seen, he had sent Germany a telegram of congratulations after Algeciras, although Europe knew that it was one of Berlin's worst failures. And now he declared loudly that it was most unlikely that Germany and Britain would go to war, for there was nothing to be gained from it; Germany could not hope to conquer Canada or India or Australia, and Britain would not be able to interrupt German trade for more than a year or two. Before he left the White House in 1909 he had disconcerted the British Ambassador in Washington, James Viscount Bryce, by telling him that " although the German Emperor was an erratic personage and had written to President Roosevelt some extraordinary letters full of alarms and wild suggestions, he did not believe he had any war-like designs, but was animated more by a sort of megalomania and by a desire to have the glory of possessing a splendid navy. So too he did not believe that the German nation was otherwise than pacific in its intentions."

What really drew the President and the Kaiser together was their common belief in " the Yellow Peril." This still remained one of William's favourite themes and he was delighted to find someone who shared his apprehensions. Mr. Roosevelt, however, went further than the Kaiser. He felt that the quarrels and bickerings in Europe were ridiculous, and that all Christians should unite against the black and yellow races. He frequently talked to German Embassy officials in Washington and the reports on his views were carefully studied and minuted by the Kaiser. " If Japan invades America using powerful forces," Roosevelt told the German Ambassador, " our army will first suffer a crushing blow. The lesson will produce a thorough military reorganisation. (The

[1] *British Documents on the Origin of the War.*

Emperor: *That is no good in a war.*) After this has been achieved, Japan's army will be annihilated if she has left it in America, and America will take her revenge." (The Emperor: *Very optimistic.*)[1]

It is obvious that if Roosevelt thought that some of the Kaiser's ideas were a bit mad, the view was reciprocated. Nevertheless Roosevelt was useful to William and he made the most of him. When the ex-President stopped in London on his way to Berlin in 1910 he told British statesmen that Germany meant no harm to anyone and was only building her fleet to protect her growing trade; the British ought to grasp her hand and keep their attention on the Far East. As Britain had a treaty of alliance with Japan, this advice was not received very warmly. Apparently Lord Londonderry, an ex-Viceroy of Ireland, made it clear that he did not share Mr. Roosevelt's views, for the latter expostulated angrily to Chancellor Bethmann-Hollweg that Londonderry had "no more brains than a guinea pig, he was as obtuse as a lamp-post; I might as well have talked to the chair opposite us. If the hereditary legislators are in the average like him in the House of Lords, then the Lord have mercy on England!"[1] Naturally, these observations were grist to the Kaiser's mill, and he was delighted that Roosevelt had defended the German Navy so strongly.

In August 1910, William II made a rash and defiant speech at Königsberg, aimed at his critics of November 1908, declaring that he ruled by "divine right." He told his audience that his grandfather, William I, had "set the Prussian crown on his head with his own hands." He had done this to emphasise that it was accorded to him by the will of God alone, and not by Parliament or by any assemblage of the people or by popular vote. Therefore he, William II, regarded himself as the chosen servant of Heaven and as such performed his duties as regent and sovereign. "Looking upon myself as the instrument of the Lord," he said, "without regard for daily opinions and intentions, I go my way, which is devoted solely and alone to the welfare and peaceful development of the Fatherland."

This was the true William speaking; the emotional mystic, the instrument of the Almighty, the passionate believer in the monarchical system. With these convictions it is not surprising that when

[1] *German Diplomatic Documents*: edited by E. T. S. Dugdale.

he learned in May 1910 that the uncle he hated so much, Edward VII, had died, he immediately made plans to attend the funeral. His reverence for kingship transcended all likes and dislikes; the death of a sovereign called for prayers from his royal colleagues, no matter how disturbed the personal relationship.

Thus once again William found himself riding through the streets of London, the centre of all eyes; and once again he found himself moved by the pageantry and continuity of his mother's land. In a letter to his new Chancellor, Herr Bethmann-Hollweg, he described the "lying in state" at Westminster, "the great old Hall," "the sunbeams falling on the dead figure and glittering crown," "the ride through solemn crowds." "It was the most impressive demonstration of the grief of a whole people for its beloved sovereign that I have ever seen."[1] He laid a wreath on the coffin, and impulsively grasped the hand of the new King, George V, as they both stood beside the catafalque. Later one of his relations said to him: "That handshake of yours is all over London; people are deeply grateful and impressed." He told this to Bethmann too, and went on to say that when he reached Windsor and spent a night at the Castle the associations "awakened the old home feelings which link me so fast with this place, and which have made these last years on the political side especially hard to bear. I am proud to call this my second home and to be a member of this Royal House—and as such I am treated with the warmest kindness." Even Buckingham Palace evoked childhood nostalgia. "I still remember a place where I was frightfully sick from eating too much plum pudding."[1]

When William II returned to Berlin he suddenly felt forlorn. The death of King Edward had marked the end of an era, for now almost all the great antagonists and friends who had been on the stage when William II ascended the throne had taken their bows and departed. Bismarck had died long ago, the evil Holstein had died in the spring of 1909, and now the treacherous Edward VII lay in state. Eulenburg was in exile, so was Count Kuno Moltke, Count Hulsen-Haeseler had dropped dead, and Bülow had been dismissed. Life seemed a little flat. King George V was not nearly so exciting an adversary as the wicked uncle, Bethmann-Hollweg not nearly so stimulating as Bernard Bülow, Prince Fürstenburg not nearly so

[1] *Grosse Politik.*

witty as Philip Eulenburg. But if life was more boring, William consoled himself that, at least, it might be less harassing. It was a good thing that the wily, hostile Edward had been replaced by a dull, plain-spoken sailor, for although the Kaiser did not believe that the new king would have much influence on policy, or be able to alter England's course in any way, events would not be inflamed by deliberate " intrigue." On the letter of condolence which the Chancellor sent him William wrote: " The system of intrigue which kept Europe on tenterhooks will come to an end. . . . I believe that European policy as a whole will be more quiescent; even if that were all it would be something."[1]

More quiescent? Herr Bethmann-Hollweg had not inherited a happy situation from Prince Bülow. " The atmosphere," he wrote, " was chilly and clouded with distrust." So chilly that almost every new political event sent a shiver of alarm across Europe; so cloudy that most of them became blurred and distorted. The Germans claimed that England had thrown a noose around their necks and was only waiting for the right moment to pull it tight. England, on the other hand, feared that Germany's repeated threats of war had started her along a path from which there might be no return. To many people the resplendent figure of the Kaiser in his eagle-crested helmet and his wonderful cloaks epitomized the bellicose spirit of the new Germany. He seemed to be a man of inordinate ambition; not content with the greatest army in the world, he now wished to rival the greatest sea-power in the world. They could not believe that the field-grey columns that defiled before him each year would be content to march forever within the boundaries of Prussia; or that the ships that slipped down the runways at Kiel, at such ruinous cost, would fulfil their purpose by remaining within the confines of the North Sea. They suspected that William II was only biding his time before making a bid for the supremacy of Europe.

Even the unskilled Bethmann-Hollweg could not fail to appreciate the perils of the situation. He was an honourable, well-intentioned man who genuinely desired to bring about an easement of the tension. His most ardent wish was to re-establish friendly relations with England. He would have liked to curtail Germany's

[1] *Grosse Politik.*

shipbuilding in return for a genuine rapprochement, but he did not dare to raise the subject with the Kaiser. The naval programme not only remained the one constant factor of William's reign but had become dangerously interwoven with the Sovereign's personal pride. More than once he told the Chancellor that the German Navy would serve as an enduring monument to the House of Hohenzollern. However, just before his departure, Bülow had persuaded him to consider a slackening of the building schedule in return for a pledge from England of unconditional neutrality in the event of war. Bethmann-Hollweg tried to negotiate on this basis, but as such a promise would have meant nothing less than handing Germany the dominance of Europe, the British Foreign Office refused to look at it.

The Kaiser saw nothing contradictory in turning out dreadnoughts and maintaining close ties with his English relations. He told his Chancellor not to heed Count Metternich's gloomy warnings from London, and assured him that feeling between the two countries would improve automatically once the German Navy was strong enough. This peculiar reasoning was based on the belief that when England saw that she could not deter Germany, she would seek her as a partner. Consequently, when cousin George V wrote to William early in 1911 inviting him to attend the unveiling of a monument to Queen Victoria, which was to be installed in front of Buckingham Palace, he accepted with genuine delight. "Let me thank you most cordially," he replied on February 15, 1911, "for the very kind letter in which you invite Dona and me to be present at dear Grandmama's unveiling. You cannot imagine how overjoyed I am at the prospect of seeing you again so soon and making a nice stay with you. You are perfectly right in alluding to my devotion & reverence for my beloved Grandmother, with whom I was on such excellent terms. I shall never forget how kindly this great lady always was to me & the relations she kept up with me, though I was so far her junior, she having carried me about in her arms! Never in my life shall I forget the solemn hours in Osborne at her deathbed when she breathed her last in my arms! These sacred hours have riveted my heart firmly to your house & family, of which I am proud to feel myself a member. And the fact that for the last hours I held the sacred burden of her—the creator of the greatness of Britain—in my arms, in my mind created an invincible special link between her country & its People & me which I fondly nurse in my heart. . . . You kindly refer to the fact of my being her eldest grandson, a fact I was always immensely proud of and never forgot."[1]

The Kaiser's visit was fixed for May: before it could take place, however, the exhausting problem of Morocco once again raised its unwelcome head, and gave the Kaiser's journey an unexpected twist. Widespread Arab insurrections had prompted the Sultan to appeal to the French for help. Early in April M. Jules Cambon informed the German Government that France was planning to send an expeditionary force to occupy Rabat, restore order at Fez and carry out a punitive expedition in the Shawia area. The Kaiser was in Corfu when he received the report, and immediately wired his approval to the Wilhelmstrasse. "It will suit us very well if the French commit themselves thoroughly with troops and money in Morocco, and in my opinion it is not in our interest to hinder them," he telegraphed to his new Foreign Secretary, Herr von Kiderlen-Wächter. "If the French violate the Act of Algeciras we can leave it to the other powers, specially Spain, to protest first. Probably people at home will again want to send a warship. But we can do nothing useful with warships, as Tangier is not threatened, and the field of action is in the interior. I beg you will, therefore. make a stand at once against warships."[2]

The Kaiser had correctly gauged the mood, not of "the people" at home, but of Kiderlen-Wächter himself. The Kaiser loathed his Foreign Secretary. Long ago this brash diplomat had been part of the backroom trio, along with Eulenburg and Holstein, which was lampooned in the press as the power behind the throne. Kiderlen was witty, loud-mouthed, and drank too much. He was nick-named "Cocksparrow," but when his self-assurance led him to mimic the Kaiser, and the stories were repeated to the Sovereign, he found himself banished to Bucharest as Minister of Legation. There he lingered for many years. Bülow sent for him when Foreign Secretary Schoen collapsed as a result of the *Daily Telegraph* interview; and he was believed to have played a decisive part in composing the disastrous ultimatum to Russia over the annexation of Bosnia. When Bethmann-Hollweg became Chancellor he

[1] *King George V:* Harold Nicolson.

[2] *Grosse Politik.*

requested the Kaiser to appoint Kiderlen as Foreign Secretary. William II protested strongly, but Bethmann argued that his own inexperience compelled him to ask for someone with expert knowledge. In the end the Kaiser agreed. " Well then, take Kiderlen," he grumbled. " But you won't know what a louse you're taking until you've got him."

If Kiderlen had been no more than a louse, his appointment would not have been so catastrophic. But he was longing to make up for his long years of exile by achieving a dramatic diplomatic *coup* that would make his name ring through Germany. Even more ominous, he had been trained in the Holstein school. " He considered that the only proper and successful way to conduct politics," wrote Erich Brandenburg, the distinguished German historian, " was to negotiate with a pistol in your hand or at least bulging out of your pocket."[1]

Bethmann-Hollweg was too naive to appreciate these finer points, and when the Kaiser returned from Corfu asked permission to bring Kiderlen to an audience so that the Foreign Secretary could outline his plan for Morocco. Kiderlen told the Kaiser that he was in full accord with the imperial view that France should be allowed to absorb Morocco; it was obvious that the Sultan could only assert his authority with French bayonets, therefore independence, as envisaged by the Algeciras Act, was a myth. But Germany must obtain compensation in return for waiving her rights. And in order to ensure that the compensation was sufficiently generous, it might be necessary to send warships to Mogador and Agadir under the pretext of protecting German nationals; just as the French " protect their subjects at Fez," he explained. The ships would help to accelerate Germany's negotiations with France; and they would show the world that she could not be fobbed off with a mere bagatelle. Indeed, Kiderlen explained that what he had in mind was the whole of the French Congo. The Kaiser was startled by the magnitude of his Foreign Secretary's scheme and pointed out, very rightly, that England might take umbrage at being excluded from this struggle of wills. He could not give an answer, he said, until he had raised the matter with King George on his forthcoming trip to England.

The visit therefore assumed an unexpected importance. Socially

[1] *From Bismarck to the World War:* Erich Brandenburg.

it was an unqualified success. As King Edward was no longer about to outrage the Kaiserin's sense of moral values, Dona consented to accompany her husband and was delighted by the warmth of their reception. The capital blazed with flags, the crowds were dense, bands played, people cheered, and hospitality flowed in every direction. King George did not share the antipathy of his father and mother towards the German Emperor and there were no irritating pin-pricks, only kindness and goodwill. Just before his departure William II raised the subject of Morocco. "I asked him," he wrote in his memoirs, "if he considered that the French methods were still in accordance with the Algeciras Agreement. The King remarked that the Agreement, to tell the truth, was no longer in force, that the best thing to do was to forget it; that the French, fundamentally, were doing nothing different in Morocco from what the English had previously done in Egypt; . . . that the only thing to do was to recognise the *fait accompli* of the occupation of Morocco and make arangements for commercial protection with France."[1] According to a note made by Bethmann-Hollweg upon the Emperor's return, William also told his cousin that Germany would "never wage a war for the sake of Morocco" but that she might seek compensations in Africa. "To this obervation," wrote Bethmann, "the monarch made no reply."[2]

The Kaiser had a childish faith in the power of kings, even constitutional kings such as George V. The fact that the English sovereign was warm and friendly apparently led him to the assumption that England would not mind if Germany bullied France into giving her what she wanted. For when Herr Kiderlen-Wächter travelled to Kiel to see William II on June 26th (where he was about to depart on his Norwegian cruise) he gave the Foreign Secretary permission to send a warship to Morocco. Kiderlen explained that he was holding talks with M. Cambon, and that the negotiations were nearly complete; the French Ambassador had suggested ceding part of the French Congo to Germany in return for Togoland. A little pressure in the shape of a German ship, Kiderlen explained, was all that was needed to bring the talks to a successful conclusion. Consequently, on July 1st, the *Panther*, a

[1] *Memoirs:* William II.
[2] *Grosse Politik.*

small gunboat with a complement of 150 men, anchored outside the harbour of Agadir.

The Kaiser had followed his usual pattern of behaviour; first a strong, clear impulse, then doubt, then capitulation. It seems astonishing that neither he nor Bethmann recognised Kiderlen's action as a replica of Tangier; nor foresaw that Holstein's legacy of blackmail would produce the same unfortunate result. This method of doing business was particularly stupid in 1911, for in the Spring the French Foreign Secretary, M. Cruppi, was talking about German participation in the Congo-Cameroon railway project; and the French Prime Minister, M. Caillaux, who took office in June, not only was known to be in favour of generous compensations but was rumoured to be an enemy of the entente.

The moment Count Metternich informed the British Foreign Office that the gunboat *Panther* had arrived at Agadir to protect German nationals Whitehall recognised the advent of a new crisis. The Permanent Under-Secretary pointed out that Germany had no nationals at Agadir; and the Foreign Secretary, Sir Edward Grey, explained in forcible language that British financial interests were larger than Germany's in Morocco and that England was not prepared to recognise any arrangement without being consulted. She demanded to know why Germany had dispatched a gunboat.

Kiderlen declined to answer. He believed that a long, brooding silence was the best way to conduct a war of nerves. He hoped that French morale would crack under the tension, and that Britain, puzzled by the situation, would not know what attitude to adopt. Just as he had envisaged, all sorts of rumours began to sweep London and Paris. "Was Germany looking for a pretext to war with France, or was she merely trying by pressure and uncertainty to improve her colonial position?" wrote Winston Churchill, the Home Secretary. "It was difficult to divine from the long string of telegrams which day after day flowed in from all the European Chancelleries what was the real purpose behind the German action."[1]

The first nerves to break were those of the Kaiser. Kiderlen had given William II to understand that the negotiations with France were nearly complete; yet when M. Cambon and Kiderlen met on July 9th the Congo and Togoland were only touched upon lightly,

[1] *World Crisis:* Winston S. Churchill.

for the German Foreign Secretary was determined to make the Frenchman speak out first. "What the devil are they at?" the Kaiser wrote angrily. "They negotiate and negotiate but no one speaks out! If we go on losing precious time like this, the Britons and Russians will stiffen the backs of the frightened Gauls, and dictate to them what is the best they can graciously concede us!! At the beginning of May in Karlsruhe the Chancellor developed to me the whole programme for our negotiations about Morocco, I said I AGREED, and now at the end of July we are exactly in the same place! This kind of diplomacy is too high and subtle for my brain!"[1]

The Kaiser's reaction forced Kiderlen-Wächter to put his cards on the table, and when he met M. Cambon on the 15th and the latter began to talk about the Congo-Cameroon railway, the Foreign Secretary drew out a map, pointed to the Congo, and said that Germany would like the whole of it. M. Cambon was so surprised that for a moment he was speechless. He said flatly that no country could give away a whole colony, but that France might be willing to cede part of it in exchange for Togoland or part of the Cameroons. Kiderlen saw that the moment for strong action, privately anticipated, had arrived. "We shall only obtain a satisfactory settlement," he wrote to Bethmann-Hollweg, "if we are prepared to face the worst, i.e. if the others feel and realise that. Those that declare in advance that they will not fight cannot expect success in politics. . . . We must have the whole French Congo. . . ."[2]

The Kaiser was horrified when he read this dispatch. He had no intention of risking a war over Morocco, and wired Bethmann from the *Hohenzollern* that no steps involving threats to France should be taken in his absence. He instructed him to open negotiations with M. Cambon along the lines suggested by the Ambassador, and announced his immediate return to Berlin. "I can't let my government act so," he wrote on the dispatch, "without being on the spot to watch the consequences and keep a hand on them! It would be unpardonable and too parliamentary! *Le roi s'amuse!* And meanwhile we are heading for mobilisation." He also noted: "London will turn nasty."[2]

When Kiderlen received these instructions he was enraged, and

[1] *German Diplomatic Documents.*

[2] *Grosse Politik.*

declared that the Kaiser was spoiling his game. He threatened to resign, but Bethmann managed to calm him down, particularly when the Emperor's prophecy about London proved correct. The British Foreign Office could not believe that the German suggestion about the Congo could be a *bona-fide* demand. It was so excessive that London decided it must have been designed purposely to provoke a refusal. Seventeen days of silence had passed since Grey had called the German Ambassador and demanded an explanation of the gunboat. Now Grey again summoned Count Metternich and asked him point-blank whether Germany was after territory in Africa or an Atlantic port. The Ambassador had received no instructions and was unable to reply.

Kiderlen's plan contained a fatal flaw. He had not taken into consideration the fact that his silence might frighten England into thinking that her interests were threatened more than those of France. By this time the British Government was gravely perturbed. Even members of the radical Liberal " peace wing " felt that if Germany thought she could brush England aside and seize an Atlantic port under her very nose she was greatly mistaken. Mr. Lloyd George, the Chancellor of the Exchequer, feared that unless Britain spoke out quickly and clearly a catastrophe might occur. That same night, July 21st, he attended a dinner at the Mansion House, and made a speech which rang round the world. " If a situation were forced upon us in which peace could only be preserved by the surrender of the great and beneficent position Britain has won by centuries of heroism and achievement, by allowing Britain to be treated where her interests were vitally affected as if she were of no account in the Cabinet of nations, then I say emphatically that peace at that price would be a humiliation intolerable for a great country like ours to endure."

The language of pre-world war diplomacy was so dignified and sedate, sometimes almost purring, that it is difficult for the present generation, nurtured on the vulgar abuse of modern dictators, to understand the sensation produced by these measured words. They blew up a storm of anger in Germany. They were a threat and an insult; an impertinent attempt by England to interfere in Franco-German affairs; and, delivered as they were by a radical who was supposed to have peaceful inclinations, they gave startling proof that Britain was far more bellicose than anyone had imagined.

Chancellor Bethmann-Hollweg sent a stiff note of remonstrance to London, so stiff that Britain ordered a concentration of the fleet. The Kaiser, still on board the *Hohenzollern*, refused to be ruffled and wired the Wilhelmstrasse that it was just " a little act of courtesy toward Paris which is simply howling for help in London."[1]

Nevertheless, Britain's action had far-reaching results; for although the German public was not clear what the Wilhelmstrasse was after, it felt with some justification that the Fatherland had suffered a humiliating defeat at England's hands. The anger in Germany was so great that the war-scare continued in Britain for two months—almost the whole time that Kiderlen and Cambon were negotiating—for Whitehall was fearful that Germany might change her mind, and make a sudden fierce gesture in order to re-establish her prestige. Agreement between the two principals, however, finally was reached on November 4th when France promised to cede 100,000 fairly worthless square miles in the Congo; nevertheless the land gave Germany two much needed river outlets for her exports from the Cameroons.

Neither country was satisfied. In France, the Prime Minister, M. Caillaux, was replaced by M. Poincaré; and in Germany the militarists poured scorn on the government for its timidity. Kiderlen put it about that Germany's failure was due to the Kaiser who had lost his nerve and " funked it." This prompted the *Berlin Post* to ask hysterically: " Are we a race of women? "; and inspired Harden's *Zukunft* to launch an attack on " Wilhelm the Peaceable," concluding with the words: " Here ends, O Zollern, thine historic glory, and here, but not in battle, fell a king."

The German Crown Prince, however, proffered no such sympathy. This foolish young man of twenty-nine added fuel to the fire by applauding in the Reichstag the warlike and anti-French speech of Herr Heydebrand, leader of the Conservative party. He was not on easy terms with his father, and except for the occasion when William II had toyed with the idea of abdication, had never had an intimate conversation with him. He spent most of his time hunting, which annoyed his father, or flirting, which upset his mother. And now he had taken to politics which angered them both. The Kaiser summoned him to the Palace and instructed Herr Bethmann to give him a dressing-down in his presence. The

[1] *Grosse Politik.*

Chancellor did as he was bid, but it did not endear him to young William who describes him in his memoirs as "sluggish and irresolute."

The Kaiser undoubtedly had prevented a war, but he had no wish that the secret should become public knowledge; no wish that the world should know that he coveted the conqueror's glory but shrank from the conqueror's risks; that he desired, in Winston Churchill's words, to be Napoleon without fighting Napoleon's battles. In order to save his face, he began to lash out wildly at England. He spread the story that when he was at Buckingham Palace he had told George V that he intended to send a warship to Morocco and the King had agreed. But when the ship arrived England deliberately had double-crossed him and tried to embroil him in a war with France. These remarks were repeated to King George, who expressed surprise. "'I will not deny that he perhaps could have said something about a ship,' the King told the Austrian Ambassador, Count Mensdorff, 'although I do not recall it. If he did, I thought of Mogador; in any case, he did not mention Agadir. And I absolutely did not express to him my own, or my Government's, consent to any such action.' The King added that it was his personal conviction that the German Emperor was a man of peace. The difficulty was that he might not for ever be strong enough to control his own militarists, since he was sensitive to their criticisms of his unwarlike hesitations."[1]

George V did not know that the pressure over Agadir had emanated from William's Foreign Secretary, not his military advisers. But the bluff unimaginative sailor-king had come closer to divining his cousin's true character than most people. "No man," he concluded to the Austrian Ambassador, "likes to be called a coward."

Agadir brought the world war immeasurably closer. First, the fact that Bethmann-Hollweg, despite his pacific reputation, had employed the same methods as Prince Bülow, disillusioned many people and made them believe that a conflict was inevitable. Second, the crisis atmosphere gave Admiral Tirpitz a perfect excuse to introduce a supplementary naval bill, greatly increasing the strength of the German Fleet. "It was a question," wrote the Admiral in

[1] *King George V*: Harold Nicolson.

his memoirs, " of our keeping our nerve, continuing to arm on a grand scale, avoiding all provocation, and waiting without anxiety until our sea power was established and forced the English to let us breathe in peace." (" Only to breathe in peace! " commented Mr. Winston Churchill. " What fearful apparatus was required to secure this simple act of respiration! ")

The Kaiser supported Tirpitz to the hilt. The fact that Britain had dared to concentrate her fleet at the height of the crisis showed, he said, that she had no value " for our friendship." " Therefore," he concluded, " we are not strong enough yet. Nothing impresses her but force and strength."[1] Although Count Metternich pointed out that if Germany went ahead with her Bill, England was bound to follow suit, and the ratio would remain the same, the Kaiser dismissed his observations with contempt. " Metternich's standpoint is exactly the same as it was over the Supplementary Laws of 1904 and 1908," he wrote on November 27th. " If I had followed him then, we should have no fleet at all now. His deduction permits a foreign power to control our naval policy, which I, as Chief War Lord and Emperor, shall not and cannot allow either now or ever! And it means humiliation for our people! We stick to our Bill! "[1]

Meanwhile, the rumours of an impending increase in the German Navy prompted Mr. Lloyd George to make an effort to remove the ill-feeling between the two nations, and to get on better terms. " We knew," wrote the newly appointed First Lord of the Admiralty, Mr. Winston Churchill, " that a formidable new Navy Law was in preparation and would be shortly declared. If Germany had definitely made up her mind to antagonise Great Britain, we must take up the challenge; but it might be possible by friendly, sincere and intimate conversation to avert this perilous development. We were no enemies to German colonial expansion, and we would even have taken active steps to further her wishes in this respect. Surely something could be done to break the chain of blind causation. . . . We therefore jointly consulted Sir Edward Grey, and then with the Prime Minister's concurrence we invited Sir Ernest Cassel to go to Berlin and get into direct touch with the Emperor. . . . We armed him with a brief but pregnant memorandum, which cannot be more tersely summarised than in von Bethmann-Hollweg's own

[1] *Grosse Politik.*

words: 'Acceptance of English superiority at sea—no augmentation of the German naval programme—and on the part of England, no impediment to our Colonial expansion—discussion and promotion of our Colonial ambitions—proposals for mutual declarations that the two powers would not take part in aggressive plans and combinations against one another.' "[1]

Cassel returned from Berlin after two days, and that night Mr. Churchill reported to Sir Edward Grey that the Emperor and the Chancellor " appeared deeply pleased by the overture. Bethmann-Hollweg earnest and cordial, the Emperor 'enchanted, almost childishly so.' . . . Cassel says they did not seem to know what they wanted in regard to colonies. They did not seem to be greatly concerned about expansion. 'There were ten large companies in Berlin importing labour *into* Germany.' Over-population was not their problem. They were delighted with Cassel's rough notes of our ideas. They are most anxious to hear from us again. . . ."[1]

Encouraged by this friendly response, the British Government decided that a cabinet minister should go to Berlin and sound the ground for an agreement. They chose Lord Haldane, the Minister of War, because he knew Germany well and spoke the language perfectly. But the Germans could not understand a Minister of War arriving to discuss naval matters, and were suspicious from the start.

As soon as the conversations developed the same familiar obstacles were struck. Britain wanted Germany to drop the new naval supplements in their entirety, and Germany wanted Britain to pledge herself to neutrality if war broke out. The Kaiser conducted the German naval talks, and the best he was prepared to offer was a slowing down of the newly planned construction, which amounted to very little. Britain, on her side, would not even consider the neutrality pledge and was amazed that Berlin should return to such a hopeless quest. Germany, however, wanted England to sacrifice the Triple Entente; and all this for a niggardly retarding of the building programme.

The truth was that the British Foreign Office would not have sacrificed the entente for half the German Fleet. Why then, the reader may ask, did the British Government send Lord Haldane to

[1] *World Crisis:* Winston S. Churchill.

Berlin? The answer was that the politicians interfered to the consternation of the diplomats. A deep schism divided the British Foreign Office and the British Cabinet. The Foreign Office contended that Germany was stronger than France and Russia combined, and that only the shadow of Britain prevented her from seizing control of Europe. It was of vital importance, therefore, to ensure the cohesion of the Triple Entente. Yet the entente was not a military alliance, only a loose partnership. The danger that it might fall apart over some disagreement haunted Sir Arthur Nicolson, the Permanent Under-Secretary of State. Ever since 1909 he had begged Sir Edward Grey to place the facts before the Cabinet and try to persuade his colleagues of the urgent necessity for changing the character of the entente and undertaking firm military commitments. This not only would weld the partnership firmly together but would leave Germany in no doubt about England's position, and prevent her from taking dangerous risks.

Grey replied, however, that the majority of his Cabinet colleagues would not face hard facts. Some were pacifists, and some were radicals who would never agree to an official alliance with such a reactionary regime as Czarist Russia. "I do not think it is practical to change our agreement into alliances," he wrote to Sir Arthur in 1909. "The feeling here about definite commitments to a continental war on unfavourable occasions would be too dubious to permit us to make an alliance. Russia too must make her internal regime less reactionary—till she does liberal sentiment here will remain very cool...."[1]

Perhaps it would have been impossible for Grey to convince the Cabinet that the best chance of peace was for Britain to state her position unequivocably; but the truth was that Grey never attempted to do so, for he himself preferred to remain in "a balancing position" or, to use his favourite expression, "to keep his hands free." By not undertaking any military commitments England could throw her weight first one way, then another. She not only could restrain Germany, but France and Russia as well. The Foreign Office countered by insisting that this was a false position. Britain's hands were not free, despite Sir Edward's illusions. Morally, Britain was deeply obligated to France. Military conversations had been going on between the General Staffs of the two countries

[1] *Lord Carnock:* Harold Nicolson.

for years, and soon there would be joint naval deployment. And even if no moral obligations existed, Britain could never allow Germany to smash France, for once she stood supreme in Europe what was to prevent her from threatening the British Empire?

Grey was not to be moved. This reasoning, he said, was sound if one believed implicitly in "the German menace;" if, on the other hand, one entertained doubts about German intentions, it was only right to try and break the deadlock. Therefore, he agreed to Lord Haldane's mission to Berlin. The Foreign Office was angry and alarmed that a cabinet minister should be sent to negotiate over the heads of the diplomats. France reacted uneasily and Russia excitedly. If Germany reached an official agreement with England, no matter how innocuous, the entente which had withstood threats of war and gunboats might fall to the ground, shattered in a hundred pieces.

But Germany failed to see her opportunity. The Kaiser and Admiral Tirpitz were just as suspicious of England as the British diplomats were of Germany. They examined the "promotion of German colonial expansion" as envisaged by Mr. Lloyd George and Mr. Winston Churchill with justifiable scepticism. Although Lord Haldane hinted that Britain might consider ceding Zanzibar and Pemba, two small islands off the east coast of Africa, he dwelt with far more enthusiasm on the Belgian Congo and Portuguese Angola! As for the neutrality pledge, all that could be offered, he said, was a promise that "England will make no unprovoked attack on Germany and pursue no aggressive policy toward her." This, the Kaiser retorted, was worthless, as who was to define an "unprovoked attack?" Germany then made it clear that she was interested in nothing else but Britain's unconditional neutrality, in return for which she would retard, but not curtail, her new programme.

The Foreign Office was delighted when Lord Haldane returned to London with this meagre proposal. Sir Edward Grey informed the German Ambassador that England could not give the desired neutrality pledge. He was aware that Bethmann-Hollweg had fought gallantly to persuade Tirpitz to forgo his fleet increases, so he tried to gild the pill by telling Count Metternich that he was confident that no quarrels would arise while the present Chancellor was at the helm. But he had to look ahead, he said, and new personalities might bring changes in German policy. When the Kaiser's eye fell on this, his indignation knew no bounds. "So he mistrusts me!!! Never have I heard of anyone concluding an agreement with . . . one particular statesman, independently of the reigning Sovereign. From the foregoing it is evident that Grey does not in the least realise who the ruler here is, and that I am the ruler. . . ."[1]

The attempts of the Foreign Office to disavow Lord Haldane's colonial offers aroused even greater ire in the Kaiser. The civil servants feared that the suggestions he had made might leak out and stir up trouble. So they drew up a memorandum emphasising that he had not made any direct offers—only offered to help in assisting Germany in her negotiations with the foreign powers concerned. "It never occurred to him," wrote the Emperor indignantly. "He made the offer *sans phrase* over the table!"[2]

The Kaiser was so annoyed by the stalemate that he made great play about perfidious Albion bargaining away other nations' possessions. "Haldane's representations were designed to induce the German Government to accept as an offering from England a trans-continental colonial Empire in Africa—consisting of a territory owned by foreign nations and not the property of England (and there was no knowledge or guarantee that those nations were prepared to renounce them in our favour)—and to drop the Supplementary Bill. In the political clause neutrality was at the same time *refused*, as being too difficult to define. Haldane was to return home with this success. The Government, which in the present uncomfortable situation in England were in urgent need of a success, wished to improve their tottering fortunes, start off with a coup, make an effect in Parliament, announce this great triumph over Germany and be praised and glorified for it. . . . This was Haldane's Mission in a nutshell."[1]

[1] *Grosse Politik.*

[2] When discussions on colonial matters were resumed a few months later, it became clear that Britain's idea was to allow Germany to get a strangle-hold on Angola by financial loans to the hard-pressed Portuguese Government, in return for mortgates on the Angola colony. It was much the same plan that had been formulated in 1898. But this time it went further. In a supplementary treaty Sir Edward Grey implicitly agreed that if Portuguese mismanagement made it necessary for an outside power to move in to restore order, Britain would not come to Portugal's aid.

In May 1912 Tirpitz introduced his new Navy Law, and in July Mr. Winston Churchill retaliated with supplementary estimates of his own which, he told Parliament, were the direct result of Germany's move. Even more important, Britain drew her battleships out of the Mediterranean to reinforce the "Home Fleet," while France transferred all heavy ships to the Mediterranean. This pooling of resources visibly tightened the entente. "But," wrote Churchill, "all was lost on Admiral Tirpitz. This sincere, wrong-headed, purblind old Prussian firmly believed that the growth of his beloved navy was inducing in British minds an increasing fear of war, whereas it simply produced naval rejoinders and diplomatic reactions which strengthened the forces and closed the ranks of the entente. . . ."[1]

Never had William II been so worried and depressed as he was during the years 1912 and 1913. Agadir had made it plain that his fleet was not yet strong enough to prevent Britain from interfering in a continental war. Peace, therefore, was essential; and yet the Balkan situation was so menacing and insoluble he feared that Germany might be dragged into a conflict by accident.

He did not know how to handle the Balkans. Bismarck, by refusing to aid Austrian expansion, had been able to maintain a treaty with Russia as well; and with his two horses in double harness had safeguarded himself, for he was able to pull first on one, then on the other, and keep them both in step. Although Baron Holstein had committed the error of refusing to renew the Russian Treaty, and Russia, as a consequence, had formed the Dual Alliance with France, Germany nevertheless had taken care to remain on a friendly footing with the Czar. The Bosnian crisis was the first instance in which Berlin had sided with Austria against Russia; and since that time the Kaiser had done his best to dispel the unfavourable impression by meeting Nicholas in person. His personality always dominated the Czar, the conversations were warm and friendly, and the Kaiser believed that he had re-established confidence.

But would events allow Germany to remain on good terms with both countries, or would Austria and Russia come to blows, and make a choice inescapable? This is what worried the Kaiser. The

[1] *World Crisis:* Winston S. Churchill.

situation was not at all what it was in Bismarck's day, for Pan-Slavism, encouraged by Russia, had become a real force; and a League of Balkan states had sprung into being with the backing of St. Petersburg. France's tightening of her hold over Morocco inspired Italy to seize Turkish-owned Tripoli, and this, in turn, soon prompted the Balkan confederation to fall upon the dying Turkish Empire in an attempt to wrest away its European possessions.

War began in the autumn of 1912 and lasted, intermittently, for a year, ending with success for the Slavs and their allies. The Bulgarians reached the defensive forts outside Constantinople, the Greeks occupied Salonika, and the Serbs flowed into the upper valley of the Vardar and the northern part of Albania. Serbia then announced that she intended to incorporate Albania into her own kingdom in order to gain a precious outlet into the Adriatic. Instantly Austria sprang to the fore. This would mean a Greater Serbia, and a Greater Serbia with its appeal to the Slav elements in the Austro-Hungarian Empire would lead to the disruption and collapse of the nation. Austria was not alone in believing that her existence was threatened; for years the Serbian Radical party had been preaching that the "liberation and union of all southern Slavs can only be attained through the destruction of the Austro-Hungarian Empire." M. Sasanov, the Russian Foreign Minister, voiced the same view to his ambassador at the Serbian capital, Belgrade, on May 6th, 1913. "Serbia's promised land," he said, "lies within the boundaries of the present Austria-Hungary. . . . It is a vital interest for Serbia . . . to prepare herself by stubborn and patient work for the unavoidable future conflict."[1] But as soon as Serbian troops began to swarm over Albania, Austria announced that she would oppose a fusion of Serbia and Albania even if it meant war.

William saw the danger and recoiled. When the German Ambassador in Vienna reported that the Emperor Franz Joseph considered the situation "worse than in 1866" the Kaiser scribbled on the margin "For us all!" "I shall not march against Paris and Moscow for the sake of Albania and Durazzo," he appended. And in a longer dispatch to his Foreign Office he argued that Austria was exaggerating the danger to herself and that Germany was not bound to support her in a Balkan dispute. "I see absolutely no risk for Austria's existence or even prestige in a Serbian port on the

[1] *Deutschland Schuldig.*

Adriatic Sea. I think it objectionable to oppose Serbia's wishes needlessly. I admit that there are many changes in the Balkans, caused by the war, which are very awkward and unwelcome for Vienna, but none are so desperate that we should be exposed to the risk of war for her sake; I could not be responsible for that either to my people or to my own conscience."[1]

However, neither the Archduke nor the Czar nor the Kaiser wanted a war, and a few weeks later they agreed to attend an Ambassadors' Conference in London, called by Sir Edward Grey. In the early summer of 1913, while the Conference was still sitting, Bulgaria fell upon Serbia; then Roumania and Greece came to Serbia's defence in order to force Bulgaria to disgorge the "lion's share" of the Turkish spoils. When peace finally was restored the map was unrecognisable. Turkey had lost almost all her European territory; Bulgaria was prostrate; Serbia and Greece were greatly enlarged; and Roumania looked likely to become the most powerful state in the Balkans. The problem of Albania, however, was still unsettled. Although the London Conference had endorsed Albanian independence, Serbian troops stubbornly remained in occupation of the northern part of the country. Austria finally decided to take matters in her own hands, and in the autumn threatened Serbia with war unless she withdrew within eight days. Russia was not prepared to intervene, and once again Serbia was obliged to retreat. The Ambassadors' Conference was criticised for its lack of firmness but Europe remained at peace.

The Kaiser was tormented by doubt as to the role England would play if Germany became embroiled in a war with Russia, and France came to Russia's aid. Sir Edward Grey repeatedly assured the House of Commons that Britain had no commitments on the continent; that if a catastrophe occurred she could be free to consider neutrality in the light of her own interests. Sometimes William II professed to believe in Britain's cool detachment; sometimes he declared that she was playing a double game and trying to entice him into a trap, so that the entente could fall upon him. In the autumn of 1912 the Kaiser asked his brother, Prince Henry, who was about to visit England, to sound King George on the matter. "Prince Henry . . . asked me point blank," the King

[1] *German Diplomatic Documents:* edited by E. T. S. Dugdale.

wrote to Sir Edward Grey, " whether, in the event of Germany and Austria going to war with Russia and France, England would come to the assistance of the two latter powers. I answered ' undoubtedly, yes . . . under certain circumstances.' He expressed surprise and regret, but did not ask what the certain circumstances were. He said he would tell the Emperor what I had told him. Of course Germany must know that we would not allow either of our friends to be crippled. . . ."[1]

Prince Henry tried not to ruffle his brother's feelings, and softened the message by saying that Germany could reckon " perhaps on English neutrality, certainly not on her taking the part of Germany, and probably on her throwing her weight on the weaker side."[1] However, that same week Prince Lichnowsky, the new German Ambassador to London, disturbed the Emperor by declaring that Sir Edward Grey had told Lord Haldane that he desired a strictly non-partisan solution to the Balkan problem; but that if war broke out Britain might find herself obliged to go to the aid of France. " He is nevertheless a partisan of the Gallo-Slavs against the Germanic race," wrote William heatedly. " Since England is too cowardly to drop France and Russia publicly in this case and hates and envies us too much, the other powers [Austria] are not to defend their own interests with the sword because England means to go against us. . . . A real nation of shopkeepers! They call it a policy of peace! Balance of Power! The final struggle between the Slav and Germanic races finds the Anglo-Saxons on the side of the Slavs!" And to the Foreign Office he wrote: " We must make a military agreement with Bulgaria and Turkey, also with Roumania. Any power we can get is good enough to help us. This is Germany's ' to be or not to be.' "

The Kaiser began to look upon Sir Edward Grey as a villain of the deepest dye. " Liar," " Hypocrite," " Sanctimonious ass," he wrote on dispatches from London. The Foreign Office were more polite but no less critical, deploring the Foreign Secretary's " false position." Grey was a humbug but not a conscious humbug. He was one of those Englishman that foreigners find impossible to understand. A high-minded man of scrupulous principle, he managed to be intellectually dishonest because he was intellectually lazy. Liberal sentiment did not like the Triple Entente. The

[1] *King George V*: Harold Nicolson.

Manchester Guardian loudly condemned supporting French interests to defeat German imperialism, and the *Westminster Gazette* championed an Anglo-German alliance to counter the reactionary Russian regime. Although the Foreign Office upheld the opposite point of view, and Sir Edward minuted his approval of the powerful anti-German theme running through diplomatic dispatches, he did not care to subject his liberal impulses to a douche of cold reason, so he simply kept the two apart. In his memoirs he seeks to justify his action with the distressing argument that " momentous British decisions are not to be found in the far-sighted views, or large conceptions or great schemes," but in the " immediate interest of this country without making elaborate calculations for the future."[1]

A reappraisal of the position, and an effort to alter Liberal opinion, would have required considerable mental exertion, and Grey was not a man who liked hard work. He loved his country house and his birds and spoke fretfully of his high position as " a duty." Foreign ambassadors were always puzzled by the time he spent in official interviews, discussing his favourite relaxation, fishing. Some diplomats felt that it must be a subtle British pose. They could not believe that a man whose decisions affected nations all over the world could so easily slide away from stirring political events into the delights of the countryside. But it was not a pose. In the middle of the Balkan crisis of 1913 Sir Edward simply disappeared for a few days. He wrote to Sir Arthur Nicolson : " There is some prospect of rain and if so the sport will be very good. It seems almost too much to expect that everything including both Balkan crises and salmon should go well simultaneously, but things seem to prosper so well in my absence that it would not be in the public interest for me to curtail it. I am in rude health with an appetite for everything except office work."[2]

Despite the Kaiser's dislike of Grey, Anglo-German relations began to improve, and on the surface were better in the last months of 1913 and the first half of 1914 than they had been for many years. This was mainly due to Chancellor Bethmann-Hollweg's friendliness and co-operation throughout the London Conference. Although Mr. Winston Churchill several times suggested that the two

[1] *Twenty-five Years :* Viscount Grey of Fallodon.

[2] *British Documents on the Origin of the War.*

countries take "a naval holiday" for one year, the fleet-building question had reached such an impasse that it ceased to be an issue. The Kaiser did not reply to Churchill's invitations and the matter was dropped. In December 1913 Bethmann told the Reichstag of the "improvement of our relations with England which is progressing so satisfactorily" and held out hope "of a permanent rapprochement between nations of the same stock." The Prime Minister, Mr. Asquith, spoke in the same vein, Sir Edward Grey described Anglo-German co-operation as "excellent," and Mr. Winston Churchill referred to a "thoroughly peaceful basis" of understanding. Professor Hans Delbrück said that neither economic competition nor shipbuilding made any difference in the relationship between Germany and England, and Admiral Tirpitz declared that the growing German Fleet had "improved the prospects of peace." The Kaiser did not know what to think. He swung from one mood to another, sometimes confident and flamboyant, sometimes gripped by deep despair. "He was quite cordial," wrote Bishop Boyd Carpenter after a visit to Berlin in June 1913. "But he spoke with a note which was new to me. He seemed apprehensive. He spoke of the dangerous position in which Germany was placed between two powers which might prove hostile. When I left him I felt that he was under the influence of a great fear."[1] "From the beginning of 1913," declared Bethmann-Hollweg, "he spoke to me of the coalition which, like that of Kaunitz, was joining against us and could fall on us."[2]

William II did not want a war. Germany was more prosperous than at any time in her history. Although the population had increased during the twenty-six years of the Kaiser's reign from 41 to 66 million, Germany's wealth had risen far more rapidly. Her manufacturing output had trebled and her national income doubled. She led all Europe in chemistry and applied science; her railway system was the best in the world; she had surpassed Britain in the production of pig-iron, was close behind her in coal and had beaten all competitors in the supply of potash. Her emigration had become a mere trickle, and as the Kaiser had informed Haldane in 1912, many German firms were importing labour from abroad. The pressure for colonies, once believed to be a necessity

[1] *Further Pages of My Life:* Bishop Boyd Carpenter.

[2] *Betrachtungen zum Weltkriege:* T. von Bethmann-Hollweg.

in order to absorb the rising population, was now solely a question of prestige. Germany was rich and powerful, justly proud of the brains and energy that had given her people such golden years. The Kaiser was certain that Germany could achieve the supremacy he coveted for her by peaceful means; but would the peace be kept?

Russia was the danger, as William II saw it. Whereas Anglo-German relations had improved, Russo-German relations were worsening each month. In December 1913 the Russians were furious when Berlin announced that General Liman von Sanders would re-organise the Turkish Army—in response to a request from the Turkish Sultan—which was in sad disarray since its defeat at the hands of the Balkan Confederation. M. Sasanov, the Russian Foreign Minister, saw the move as an effort to thwart Russia's "historic mission" of obtaining control of the Straits, and raised a violent protest. The German Government pointed out that General von Sanders's position was no more dominant than that enjoyed by Admiral Limpus, the English instructor to the Turkish Navy. Although this argument was unanswerable, M. Sasanov tried to make the appointment an international issue, and told the British that "this question must be the test of the value of the Triple Entente." But the British refused to play; and the Kaiser made an effort to pacify Russian feeling by transferring von Sanders from his command of the First Corps, an operational position, to that of General-Inspector of the Turkish Army.

This did little to diminish Russian excitement. On New Year's Day, 1914, an article appeared in a Russian military paper expressing views that had become widespread among Russian officers. "We all know we are preparing for a war in the west. Not only the troops, but the whole nation must accustom itself to the idea that we arm ourselves for a war of annihilation against the Germans. . . ." However, the German General Staff did not believe that Russia would be ready to fight before 1916; and the German Ambassador in St. Petersburg, Count Pourtalès, clung to the opinion that Russia's talk was mainly boastfulness and that, even then, her role would be defensive. The Kaiser disagreed. "As a soldier," he wrote on March 11th, "I feel, from all the information received, not the slightest doubt that Russia is systematically preparing war against us and I shape my plans accordingly."[1]

Relations with Russia continued to deteriorate, and in May 1914

[1] *Grosse Politik.*

a new crisis threatened the Balkans. Once again William II displayed the strictest caution. Serbia, still financed by Russia, still the spearhead of the Czardom's Pan-Slav ambitions, was talking of a fusion with Montenegro which would give her an outlet to the sea. Austria intervened with a peremptory "no." When the Kaiser read the dispatch he wrote on it angrily: "Unbelievable! This union is absolutely not to be prevented, and if Vienna attempts it she will commit a great stupidity, and stir up the danger of a war with the Slavs, which would leave us quite cold."[1] The leader of Austrian intransigence was the rich, aristocratic Austrian Foreign Secretary, Count Berchtold, a man of charm but limited ability, who was dominated by the fire-brand Chief of Staff, Field-Marshal Conrad von Hötzendorf. "It is absolutely necessary," the Kaiser cabled to Count Berchtold and the Emperor Franz Joseph, "that the people of Vienna should face the possibility of union (of Serbia and Montenegro) seriously. . . . There must be found a *modus vivendi* with the Dual Monarchy which will be attractive to Serbia."[1] Talk of the fusion died down, but William II was still nervous. In June 1914 he wrote: "The III chapter of the Balkan war is coming soon, in which we shall all be involved, hence the active and colossal Russ.Fr. preparations. Find out how we stand with England."[1]

Was the Kaiser in any real doubt about England? Despite Sir Edward Grey's ambivalent position, the Foreign Office left no German Ambassador in confusion as to where England stood. Sir Arthur Nicolson, the Permanent Under-Secretary, declared repeatedly—perhaps deliberately to counteract Grey's vagueness—that if a European war broke out Britain was bound to range herself beside France and Russia. For years Count Metternich had reported faithfully these sentiments; and when he retired in 1911 Baron Marschall began to echo the same views, and after Marschall, Lichnowsky, who took up his post in 1913.

The new German Secretary of State, Herr Jagow, who had succeeded Herr Kiderlen-Wächter upon the latter's death in 1912, asked Prince Lichnowsky in May 1914 how he reconciled his belief that Britain would intervene in a European war with Grey's assurances that Britain was not committed to any definite line of action. "England's principle in her foreign policy, as far as European Powers are concerned," the Prince replied, "is too well

[1] *Grosse Politik.*

known and transparent for there to be any doubts about it. It rests first and foremost on the balance of power between the groups. It is as little to England's interests that a single Power should be predominant on the Continent as that a group should prevail. . . . As most questions in politics have not one but several sides, the development of our sea-power had undoubtedly helped on the desire in England to live at peace with us, but it has also helped them to realise that it is to British interests to support the group opposed to us. It is obvious therefore that any further weakening of France, especially by defeat in war—which would moreover free us from the future necessity for great armaments on land and enable us to spend even more on our sea-power—is not to the interest of England. . . ."[1]

Bethmann-Hollweg was not disturbed. He believed implicitly that he, personally, had changed the atmosphere and established such close relations with England that the latter was no longer to be feared. If war broke out in the Balkans, he wrote to Lichnowsky on June 16th, 1914, Germany and Britain must "stand resolute as guardians of the peace of Europe" which "neither the obligations toward the Triple Alliance nor the Entente will prevent us from doing, if from the start we pursue this aim according to a concerted plan."[2]

William II wavered about England. Occasionally he echoed his Chancellor's reassuring views, but far more often talked of London's hostile machinations. When Colonel House came to Europe in May 1914, as President Wilson's representative, to see if America could lessen the tension accentuated by the feverish arms race, the Kaiser told him that Germany had been "encircled" by England; that she was menaced on every side; "that the bayonets of Europe were directed against her." He was in such a state of tension that he poured scorn on any optimistic utterances. When one of his ambassadors told him that he did not believe that war with Russia was inevitable, remarking cheerfully that no one could see three or four years into the future, the Kaiser commented drily: "The gift sometimes occurs. Among Sovereigns frequently, among Statesmen seldom, among Diplomats almost never!"

Alas, the Kaiser not only lacked the second sight of which he boasted, but within a matter of days cast to the winds the prudence which until now had been his shield.

[1] *German Diplomatic Documents:* edited by E. T. S. Dugdale.
[2] *Grosse Politik.*

14. *Sarajevo*

In June 1914 the weather was unusually fine. On the continent thousands of holiday-makers warmed themselves in the sun and forgot their anxieties about war. Only in London was the atmosphere grim and troubled, and this had nothing to do with the arms race in Europe. The Government had drawn up the Irish Home Rule Bill, bitter divisions had arisen in Parliament, and Ireland was on the verge of a civil war. Complications with Germany had been driven into the background.

On the twelfth of June the Kaiser travelled to Konopischt to spend a few days with the Archduke Franz Ferdinand, heir to the Austrian throne, to see his wonderful roses. William always enjoyed his trips to Austria; he had first visited Vienna as a small boy with his mother, and could never forget his delight at the marvellous Schönbrunn Palace, or his first sight of the Empress Elizabeth whom he always regarded as the most beautiful woman in the world. The old Emperor, now in his eighty-fifth year, had always been a firm friend to William; never had Austria's loyalty for her German ally flagged, never had a harsh word passed between the two sovereigns. William not only revered the Emperor but admired the fortitude with which he had borne the heavy trials of his life. His brother Maximilian had been shot on a hillside in Mexico; his only son and heir, Crown Prince Rudolf, had been found dead with his mistress, presumably as the result of a love-pact, at the shooting lodge at Mayerling, the year after William came to the throne; his wife, the Empress Elizabeth, had been struck down by an Italian assassin's knife in Geneva, in 1898.

The present heir to the Austrian throne was the Emperor's nephew, a morose, shy, middle-aged man whom nobody liked. Indeed, Franz Ferdinand had deeply offended his relations by marrying a commoner, Countess Sophie Chotek. Austrian society was the most exclusive and snobbish in Europe, and although the Archduke's wife came from an ancient Czech family, the union was regarded as a shocking mésalliance. "Was I not to be spared even this?" the Emperor sighed, when he was told of the engagement.

The marriage could only take place morganatically, and the Archduke was forced to renounce the throne for his heirs. Although the Countess was granted the title of Duchess of Hohenberg, she was regarded as inferior in rank to the youngest archduchess. At Court functions she was always placed at the end of the table and made to enter the room last. She was a proud, self-willed woman who found the humiliations heaped upon her unbearable. Franz Ferdinand made violent scenes with his family, but their attitude remained severe and unyielding. Gradually the couple absented themselves from the Court.

The Kaiser won the Archduke's gratitude by making a point of showing his esteem for the Duchess. Whenever the couple came to Berlin the banqueting table was moved out of the dining room and small tables put in its place. The Archduke and his wife dined at a table *à quatre* with the Kaiser and Kaiserin; thus no royal princess could complain of her placement *vis-à-vis* the Duchess.

During the Kaiser's visit to Konopischt, the Archduke told him that he and his wife were planning a visit to Sarajevo, the chief city in the province of Bosnia, to attend the military manœuvres of the Austrian Army. Since Vienna's high-handed annexation six years earlier there had been much unrest in the area. Politically Franz Ferdinand was an enlightened man who realised that Slav nationalism could not be held down indefinitely and favoured the idea that Austro-Hungarian "dualism" should expand into a form of "trialism," in which German, Magyar, and Slav nationalities would all have equal representation.

The Kaiser returned to Berlin on the 16th, and eight days later arrived at Kiel for the Regatta, which this year was attended by a British naval squadron. The Kaiser, as an admiral, directed the proceedings under the ensign of the *Hohenzollern*. On the afternoon of Sunday, June 28th, he put to sea in the *Meteor* to take part in a race. Suddenly a motor launch approached the yacht, and the Emperor saw his Chief of Naval Cabinet, Admiral Müller, waving a slip of paper. The Kaiser leaned over the stern and Müller called out that he was "the bearer of grave news" and would throw the communication aboard. But the Emperor insisted on knowing immediately what it was about; so Müller shouted out his message; three hours earlier the Archduke and his wife had been killed by the bullets of a Serbian assassin while riding in an open car through the streets of Sarajevo.

The Kaiser was appalled. "The cowardly detestable crime . . . has shaken me to the depths of my soul," he wired to Chancellor Bethmann-Hollweg. And to the Grand Duchess Louise: "The unutterable misfortune has shaken me to the very depths. Only fourteen days ago I was with him and saw him in his happy family circle. God comfort the unfortunate children and the poor old Emperor."[1]

It was not only that William II had lost a friend under shocking circumstances, not only that Germany's ally, Austria-Hungary, had been delivered a blow, but above all that a prince of the blood royal had been struck down; through his person the monarchical principle had been attacked, representing all that the Kaiser held most sacred. To him, regicide was the most heinous and unpardonable of all crimes.

He abandoned the Regatta and hurried back to Berlin. He was still in a highly emotional state when, on June 30th, he read a dispatch from his Ambassador in Vienna, Count von Tschirschky, who reported that he was trying to keep the authorities in Vienna from acting too impulsively *vis-à-vis* Serbia. Tschirschky, of course, was only carrying out the policy of restraint which had been laid down and followed by the Kaiser in the handling of Austro-Serbian affairs for the past two years. But now William II had changed. He seemed to have lost all control. He threw caution to the winds, and allowed a sense of outrage to direct everything he thought and said. "I frequently hear expressed," wrote Tschirschky, ". . . the wish that a last and final reckoning should be had with the Serbs. The Serbs should first be presented with a number of demands, and in case they should not accept these, energetic measures should be taken. *I take the opportunity on every such occasion to advise quietly but very impressively and seriously against too hasty steps* . . . the chances of every kind of action should be carefully weighed, and it should be kept in mind that Austria-Hungary does not stand alone in the world, that it is her duty to think not only of her allies, but to take into consideration the entire European situation. . . ." "Now or

[1] *Der Potsdamer Kronat:* Kurt Jagow.

never," the Kaiser scribbled furiously on the margin. "Who authorised him to act that way? That is very stupid! It is none of his business, as it is solely the affair of Austria what she plans to do in this case. Later, if plans go wrong it will be said that Germany did not want it! Let Tschirschky be good enough to drop this nonsense. The Serbs must be disposed of, and that right soon!"[1]

The Kaiser's interjections were telegraphed to Count von Tschirschky, who was forced to alter his tone. Until now he had supported Count Tisza, the powerful Minister-President of Hungary, who was having a hard battle with Count Berchtold, the Foreign Secretary. Berchtold was in favour of a military invasion of Serbia, while Tisza declared that it would be "a fatal mistake" to make "the horrible Sarajevo crime the occasion of a final reckoning with Serbia." It would, he said, "pillory Austrians before the whole world as disturbers of the peace, besides beginning a great war under unfavourable circumstances."[2] Berchtold was delighted by Tschirschky's change of attitude. As Austria could do nothing without German support, he decided to drop the argument with Tisza and before pressing his views any further to find out exactly how far the Kaiser was prepared to go. He drafted a letter for the Emperor Franz Joseph to send to William II. It was dispatched to Berlin by messenger and delivered to the Austrian Ambassador, Count Szögyény. Szögyény took it to the Kaiser at Potsdam on Sunday morning, July 5th.

The communication opened sedately. "The attack on my poor nephew," it began, "is the direct result of the agitation of the Russian and Serbian Pan-Slavs, whose single aim is the weakening of the Triple Alliance and the disruption of my Empire. . . . According to all indications, the crime of Sarajevo is not the deed of a single individual, but the result of a well-arranged plot whose threads reach to Belgrade;[3] and though presumably it will be

[1] *Kautsky Documents.*

[2] *Austrian Red Book.*

[3] This assumption was correct. In after years it came to light that the assassination of the Archduke was organised by Colonel Dimitrijević, Chief of the Intelligence Department of the Serbian General Staff, and head of the terrorist organisation *The Black Hand.* The Colonel recruited a group of poor, sickly teen-aged Serbian youths from Bosnia to kill the Archduke as an oppressor of the Serb people. Ironically enough, however, it was not the Archduke's harshness but his leniency which induced the Colonel to mark him down as a victim. Dimitrijević knew

impossible to prove the complicity of the Serbian Government, there can be no doubt that its policy of uniting all the South Slavs under the Serbian flag promotes such crimes, and that a continuation of this situation spells lasting danger for my dynasty and for my territories." The dynamite was reserved for the last paragraph. As Serbia was " the pivot of the Pan-Slav policy, " the Emperor concluded, she " must be eliminated as a political factor in the Balkans."[1]

The significance of this observation did not escape the Kaiser. By now he was beginning to recover a modicum of balance, and responded guardedly. Since the proposed " action " raised " the prospect of serious complications," he could not reply until he had consulted his Chancellor. Poor William II! His character was so unstable that within an hour Count Szögyény, who remained for luncheon, had managed to rekindle his moral indignation and rash resolves. " After luncheon, when I again emphasised the seriousness of the situation," Szögyény wired to Vienna, " His Majesty authorised me to report that in this case also we could reckon on Germany's full support. . . . His Majesty said he understood how hard Francis Joseph, with his well-known love of peace, would find it to invade Serbia; but if we had really decided that military action against Serbia was necessary, he would be sorry if we left unused the present moment which was so favourable to us."[2]

Chancellor Bethmann-Hollweg arrived in the afternoon and, as the Kaiser had predicted, offered no opposition to William's " blank cheque." " Austria must judge what is to be done to clear up her relations with Serbia," Szögyény informed Vienna in his confirmatory telegram. " Whatever Austria's decision may turn out to be, Austria can count with certainty upon it that Germany will stand by her friend and ally."[2]

What influenced the Kaiser to take this reckless plunge? First of all, both he and Chancellor Bethmann-Hollweg allowed themselves to be persuaded that Germany's vital interests were concerned.

---

that the Heir-Apparent wished to give the Slavs a large share in the Austro-Hungarian Government and feared that his liberal attitude would deal a mortal blow to the movement for a Greater Serbia. He did not bother to acquaint his naive young assassins with the intricacies of his mind.

[1] *Kautsky Documents.*

[2] *Austrian Red Book.*

Unless Serbia was subjugated, the Slav minorities under the rule of the Emperor Franz Joseph would become too strong and irrepressible that the Austro-Hungarian Empire would fall to pieces. As Austria was Germany's only sure ally he could not allow this to happen. Secondly he decided that the odds were against a Russian declaration of war.

William II had a distressing habit of believing what he wanted to believe. With scarcely a moment's hesitation he managed to shed his anxieties of the past two years. He forgot his preoccupation with the perilous balance of Europe, forgot his theory of encirclement, forgot his suspicion that Russia was arming for an encounter with Germany, forgot his warning that Austria must not come into headlong collision with the Czardom's protégé, Serbia. Russia was unlikely to fight, he argued, because her military preparations would not be complete for two years; and even more significant, because the Czar would not care to condone regicide any more than did the German Emperor. William II's views were supported by Bethmann-Hollweg, who put forward the belief that Germany's harmonious relations with England would induce London to damp down any bellicosity that might emanate from St. Petersburg. He also pointed out that Nicolas II would hesitate before offending European opinion, which was firmly on the side of Austria and expected Serbia to be punished.

Germany's incomprehension invariably stemmed from a lack of sensitivity. What neither the Kaiser nor the Chancellor appreciated was that Europe might draw a line between punishing Serbia and annihilating Serbia. Although this idea apparently did not occur to Bethmann-Hollweg, William II had a slight twinge of uneasiness. War was most improbable, but he could not wholly rule out the possibility. No matter how small the risk, he admitted that a risk was involved. Consequently on Sunday afternoon, after Szogyeny had departed, he summoned to Potsdam his Minister of War, General Falkenhayn, and Captain Zenker of the Navy Staff. He told Zenker that Austria was planning to take decisive action against Serbia but "that the Czar would refrain from supporting the Serbian regicides because he was surrounded by regicides himself."[1] He instructed both men to inform their chiefs, but did not think it necessary for them to curtail their holidays. General

[1] *The Kaiser and His Court:* Admiral von Müller.

Falkenhayn wrote that evening to General von Moltke, the Chief of the General Staff, who was taking a cure at Karlsruhe. " This afternoon His Majesty commanded me to the New Palace to inform me that Austria-Hungary appeared determined to tolerate no longer the intrigues stirred up against Austria in the Balkans, and with this in view to invade Serbia soon in case it should be necessary; should Russia not be willing to consent to this, even then Austria would not be willing to give in. His Majesty believed this was the view to be gathered from what the Austro Ambassador had said when he delivered to-day at noon a memorandum from the Government at Vienna and a letter from Francis Joseph."[1]

For months the Kaiser had planned to leave on his annual Scandinavian cruise on Monday July 6th. He wished to cancel it but Bethmann-Hollweg begged him not to do so. The Emperor protested hotly and several hours of argument followed; in the end Bethmann-Hollweg got his way on the grounds that Germany must at all costs avoid the impression of collusion. She must insist that Austria would have to deal with Serbia as she saw fit, and that Berlin could not interfere, as Austria's vital interests were at stake. Chiefs of Staff must continue their holidays and the Secretary of State for Foreign Affairs, Herr Jagow, must not be summoned home from his honeymoon. And if an Austro-Serbian military conflict began, Germany then would be in a strong position to localise it.

So at 9.15 a.m. on July 6th, William II reluctantly left for his cruise, with instructions that all dispatches be relayed to the *Hohenzollern*.

On July 10th Count von Tschirschky, the German Ambassador in Vienna, telegraphed to Berlin that Count Berchtold planned to send Serbia an ultimatum so harsh that she could not possibly accept it, thus providing Austria-Hungary with an excuse to invade. The time limit for Serbia's reply would be limited to forty-eight hours so that she would not have time to get advice from St. Petersburg. Count Berchtold told Tschirschky that if the Serbs should accept all the demands made on them, it would prove a solution which would be " very disagreeable to him," and he was still considering what *demands* could be put that would

[1] *Leitfaden* : Montgalas.

be *wholly impossible for the Serbs to accept.* " Finally," wired Tschirschky, " the Minister complained again about the attitude of Count Tisza, which made energetic procedure against Serbia difficult for him. Count Tisza asserted that they must proceed ' like gentlemen,' but that this was scarcely possible when such important national interests were concerned and *especially against such an opponent as Serbia.*" When this telegram reached the *Hohenzollern* the Kaiser wrote on the margin : " To act like a gentleman to murderers, after what has happened ! Idiocy ! " And at the bottom he appended : " I am against all councils of war and conferences, since the more timid party always has the upper hand. . . . Frederick the Great."[1]

Until now Count Tisza had fought a gallant battle. He had remained impervious to Berchtold's insistence that as " the Emperor William had given emphatic assurances of unconditional German support " Austria must seize the moment to strike. " It was not Germany's affair," he said tartly, " to decide whether we should attack Serbia now or not." Austria-Hungary should not aim for war but be content with a notable diplomatic success. Of course demands must be made on Serbia, but they should be the sort of demands that could be complied with ; not the impossible demands favoured by Count Berchtold that would deliberately provoke war.

We do not know who persuaded Count Tisza to change his mind, but at the Council of Ministers on July 14th he withdrew his opposition. The Kaiser was delighted when he read Tschirschky's report, quoting Tisza as saying : " It was very hard for me to come to the decision to give my advice for war, but I am now firmly convinced of its necessity and I shall stand up for the greatness of the Monarchy to the best of my ability." " Fortunately," the German Ambassador continued, " *full agreement and determination prevail* among the authorities here. His Majesty Franz Joseph judges very calmly of the situation, as Baron Burian, too, who has talked with His Majesty at Ischl during the last day or two, reports, and will certainly hold out to the bitter end. Count Tisza added that *Germany's* unconditional assumption of a stand *by the side of the Monarchy* had a great influence on the firm attitude of the Emperor.

" The note to be forwarded to Serbia has not yet been completed to-day in its final wording. This will not be done before Sunday.

[1] *Kautsky Documents.*

With regard to the time of its delivery to Serbia, it was decided to-day that it would be better to wait until Poincaré's departure from Petersburg, that is until the twenty-fifth." (" *Too bad*," commented the Kaiser.) " Then, however, immediately upon the expiration of the respite granted Serbia, in case the latter should not submit to all the demands, *mobilization* would follow. The note is being composed so that the possibility of its acceptance is practically excluded. . . ." (' Excluded ' twice underlined by the Kaiser.)

" In conclusion Count Tisza pressed my hand warmly, and said: ' Together we shall now look the future calmly and firmly in the face.' " (' *Well, a real man at last!*' wrote the Kaiser.)[1]

" I have my doubts," wrote Sir Arthur Nicolson, the head of the British Foreign Office, on July 9th, " as to whether Austria will take any action of a serious character, and I expect the storm will blow over."[2] England knew that Austria could do nothing without German consent, and since Germany had restrained Austria for the past two years, there was no reason to suppose that she would encourage her now. On July 17th Lloyd George made a speech at the Mansion House, urging disarmament, declaring that the international situation had been more serious in 1913 and assuring his audience that " you never get a perfectly blue sky in foreign affairs." Even as late as July 20th Sir Edward Grey was taking an optimistic line. Everything, he told the German Ambassador, Prince von Lichnowsky, would " depend on the form of satisfaction that Austria demanded, and . . . he hoped that the quarrel might be settled and localised, for the idea of a war between the great powers of Europe must be repelled under all circumstances."[1]

Lichnowsky was deeply worried. He knew that Austria's demands would be framed to provoke a conflict; indeed, members of the Austrian Embassy in London were talking most indiscreetly. The Ambassador, Count Mensdorff, predicted the complete dismemberment of Serbia, with part going to Roumania, part to Bulgaria, and a slice to Austria itself. On the 16th Lichnowsky had taken his career in his hands and written Secretary of State Jagow a

[1] *Kautsky Documents.*

[2] *British Documents on the Origin of the War.*

long letter asking bluntly what Germany hoped to gain from supporting Austria in such a hazardous undertaking. Personally, he did not believe that the smashing of Serbia would end the aspirations of the Slavs in Austria; in fact he thought that an Austrian invasion would only fan the flames of Slav nationalism throughout the Balkans and make the problem more acute.

"There may be," Jagow replied on the 18th, "different opinions as to whether we get all our money's worth from an alliance with that ever increasingly disintegrating composition of nations beside the Danube, but you will undoubtedly agree with me that the absolute establishment of the Russian hegemony in the Balkans is, indirectly, not permissible, even for us. The maintenance of Austria, and, in fact, of the most powerful Austria possible, is a necessity for us both for internal and external reasons. That she cannot be maintained forever, I willingly admit. But in the meantime we may perhaps be able to arrange other combinations."[1]

Prince Lichnowsky's anxiety was justified, for on July 22nd Sir Edward Grey received a telegram from the British Ambassador in Vienna forecasting that Austria's ultimatum to Serbia would be framed deliberately to provoke war. The Foreign Secretary was deeply perturbed. He called Lichnowsky and gave him a coldly polite warning. Britain, he said, would try to restrain Russia if Austria's demands were moderate, and reconcilable with Serbian independence. He trusted that Germany would see that this was so. "I meet with the expectation," Lichnowsky telegraphed unhappily to Berlin, "that our influence at Vienna has been successful in suppressing demands that cannot be met. They are counting with certainty on the fact that we shall not identify ourselves with demands that are plainly intended to bring on war, and that we will not support any policy which makes use of the murder at Sarajevo merely as an excuse for carrying out Austrian desires in the Balkans, and for the annulment of the Peace of Bucharest."

Lichnowsky's dispatch was re-telegraphed to the Kaiser. When the latter read Grey's courteous, double-edged observations he reacted with angry excitement that was sharpened by fear. Influence Vienna? "Why should I do any such thing?" he scribbled. "None of my business! What does 'cannot be met' mean? The rascals have added murder to agitation and must be humbled.

[1] *Kautsky Documents.*

That is a tremendous piece of British insolence. I am not called upon to prescribe à la Grey to His Majesty now to preserve his honour! So that he will see that I am not fooling. Grey is committing the error of setting Serbia on the same plane with Austria and other Great Powers! That is unheard of! Serbia is nothing but a band of robbers that must be seized for its crimes! I will meddle in nothing of which the Emperor is alone competent to judge! I expected this dispatch, and am not surprised by it! Real British reasoning and condescending way of giving orders, which I insist on having rebuffed! William I.R."[1]

The Emperor then instructed his military aide to telegraph his comments to Berlin. This was done on the night of the 23rd. Earlier that same evening the Austrian ultimatum was presented at Belgrade.

The Kaiser's cruise on board the *Hohenzollern* now became a nightmare. His absence from Berlin, due entirely to Bethmann-Hollweg's insistence that his presence would only excite European opinion, suddenly was unbearable to him. He was furious at his Chancellor for not supplying him with a general appreciation of the situation, and even worse, for neglecting to send the text of the Austrian ultimatum. Although the note was delivered on the evening of the 23rd, with a forty-eight-hour limit attached, he only learned the details from the *Norddeutsch News Agency* on the evening of the 25th. The main points demanded severe penalties for anyone working for the disintegration of the Austro-Hungarian monarchy; the suppression of all hostile propaganda with particular emphasis on the schools; the disbandment of the Pan-Slav society " Narodna Odbrana "; the disclosure of hostile remarks made by highly placed Serbian officials; the dismissal of Austrian and civilian officials indicted by Austria; and the permission for Austrian agents to take part in fighting propaganda, and for conducting the judicial search for members of the conspiracy that led to the assassination. The demands meant nothing less than the establishment of a police state in Belgrade dedicated to fighting the Pan-Slav movement which was the breath of life to Serbia.

William II, however, professed to be delighted by the vigour of

[1] *Kautsky Documents.*

the Austrian note; when he received a report from Belgrade telling him that the "energetic tone" of the Austrians was "absolutely unexpected by the Serbian Government," he wrote in the margin: "Bravo! One would not have believed it of the Viennese Government."[1]

That same day, the 25th, the Emperor received many more dispatches, forwarded from Berlin, reporting the reaction of the great powers. He was in a highly excitable mood, pacing the deck, talking endlessly, then breaking off to seize a newly arrived communication and disappearing into his cabin where he could study it and write his comments in the margin. He was like a man possessed. In order to stifle his mounting anxiety he adopted a protective bravado that was impervious to outside reason. "Sir Edward Grey," telegraphed Lichnowsky from London, "was evidently greatly affected by the Austrian note, which, according to his view, exceeded anything he had ever seen of this sort before. . . . Any nation that accepted conditions like that would really cease to count as an independent nation." ("This would be very desirable," wrote the Kaiser. "It is not a nation in the European sense, but a band of robbers!") ". . . The danger of a European war, should Austria invade Serbian territory, would become immediate. . . . What Sir Edward Grey most deplored, beside the tone of the note, was the brief time-limit, which made war almost unavoidable. He told me that he would be willing to join with us in pleading for a prolongation of the time-limit at Vienna, as in that way perhaps a way out might be found. . . . He further suggested that in the event of a dangerous tension between Russia and Austria, the four nations not immediately concerned—England, Germany, France, and Italy—should undertake to mediate between Russia and Austria." ("Superfluous," wrote the Kaiser, "as Austria has already made matters plain to Russia, and Grey has nothing else to propose. I will not join in it unless Austria expressly asks me to, which is not likely. In vital questions and those of honour, one does not consult with others.")[1]

Other dispatches written on the 24th were forwarded to the Kaiser on the 25th. From Paris came Ambassador Schoen's statement: ". . . the view is held here that Austria-Hungary would do well, in case Serbia might not agree to all the demands at once but

[1] *Kautsky Documents.*

should wish to discuss individual points, not to refuse. . . ." (" Ultimata are accepted or not!" wrote William II. " But one does not discuss any longer! Thence the name.") And on the other side of the margin: (" It is rubbish clad in stately phrases.")[1]

The report which annoyed the Kaiser most of all, however, came from Tschirschy in Vienna. " Count Berchtold requested the Russian Chargé d'Affaires to call on him in order to make exhaustive explanations of Austria-Hungary's position with regard to Serbia." ("Absolutely superfluous," exploded the Kaiser. " Will give the impression of weakness and the impression of an apology, which, in connection with Russia, is unconditionally false and must be avoided. Austria has her good reasons, has made a move on the strength of them; now it cannot later be made the subject of a quasi-decision!") " Austria," Berchtold told the Russians, " would not lay the least claim to any Serbian territory. . . ." (" Ass! She must take back the Sanjac, else the Serbians will reach the Adriatic.") " He, Berchtold, was far from wishing to upset the balance of power either in the Balkans or in Europe . . . the monarchistically ruled nations should show a solid front in their united opposition to the Serbian policy conducted with revolver and with bomb." (" That will come entirely of its own accord, and must come. Austria must become preponderant in the Balkans as compared with the little ones, and at Russia's expense; otherwise there will be no peace. Feeble!")

Was there ever any possibility that German policy, which did not seek to *avoid* an Austro-Serbian conflict, but merely to *localise* it, could succeed? On the twenty-third of July Lichnowsky had written from London that " localisation in the event of a passage of arms with Serbia belongs in the realm of pious wishes."[1] And a few days later Sir Arthur Nicolson had observed to his colleague in St. Petersburg that " localising the war merely means that all the powers are to hold the ring while Austria quietly strangles Serbia. This to my mind is quite preposterous, not to say iniquitous."[2]

Yet the Kaiser clung to the view that the Czar would not intervene on the side of " regicide;" that Russia and France were not ready for a war; and that Britain would urge moderation in order

[1] *Kautsky Documents.*

[2] *British Documents on the Origin of the War.*

to preserve the *status quo*. Even the violent reaction of the Russian Foreign Minister, M. Sazanov, when he read the Austrian ultimatum, did not serve as a warning. Sasanov greeted his Assistant, Baron Schilling, at the Foreign Office with the grim pronouncement "C'est la guerre Europèanne;" and when the Austrian Ambassador, M. Szápáry, arrived to explain the ultimatum, he said excitedly: "The fact is you want war, and have burned your bridges." Szápáry insisted that Austria was a peace-loving country only acting in self-defence. "One sees how pacific you are now that you are setting Europe on fire."[1]

In the afternoon Sazanov received the German Ambassador, Pourtales. When the latter urged that the Austro-Serbian conflict be "localised" Sazanov, "who was very much excited and gave vent to boundless reproaches against Austria-Hungary, stated in the most determined manner that it would be impossible for Russia to admit that the Austro-Serbian quarrel could be settled between the two parties concerned." He waved aside Pourtales's assertion that Austria merely wished to "chastise" Serbia. "First Serbia will be gobbled up," he said, "then will come Bulgaria's turn; and then we shall have her on the Black Sea." He ended by saying: "Austria is seeking a pretext to gobble up Serbia; but in that case Russia will make war on Austria."[2]

A report of this conversation reached the Kaiser on the 25th, and when he read the last sentence he wrote, in Berlin slang: "Well, come on then."[2] That same evening he learned that Austria had rejected Serbia's reply as unsatisfactory, that diplomatic relations had been broken off, and that both countries were mobilising. He instructed the *Hohenzollern* to head for home (despite Bethmann-Hollweg's efforts to keep him away) and issued an order to the German Fleet, part of which was scattered in Norwegian waters and the other part anchored in Norwegian ports: "Coaling to be hastened. Fleet to be held in readiness to run out."

Bethmann-Hollweg was alarmed by the Emperor's action. His policy was based on presenting Germany as a disinterested partner; he not only had prevented the Kaiser from returning to Berlin but Admiral von Tirpitz, General von Moltke, and many other high-ranking officials as well. He was frightened that changes in

[1] *Austrian Red Book.*
[2] *Kautsky Documents.*

Germany's fleet movements might destroy the innocent picture he was eager to maintain. He telegraphed the Kaiser that although His Majesty had given the order to the fleet "on the strength of a Wolff telegram," he would like to point out that "the British Navy is taking no unusual measures of any sort. . . ." The Kaiser was enraged by the reference to the Wolff telegram. "Unbelievable assumption," he wrote on the margin. "Unheard of! It never entered my mind!!! On the report of my Ministers about the mobilization at Belgrade! This may result in mobilisation by Russia; will result in mobilisation by Austria. . . . I am not accustomed to undertake military measures on the strength of a single Wolff telegram but on that of the general situation, and that situation the civil Chancellor does not yet comprehend! When Russia mobilises my fleet must be ready in the Baltic, so it is going home. W."[1]

The Chancellor's priggish, soothing attitude continued to be annoying. "I think that our attitude must be calm and aimed at localisation," he wired the Emperor the following day. "Calmness is the first duty of a citizen," jeered William. "Keep calm... only keep calm! But a calm mobilisation is something new indeed."

The Kaiser's sense of danger was more acute than Bethmann-Hollweg's, for when the Russian Foreign Minister, M. Sazanov, read the Austrian ultimatum he asked the Czar to call a Crown Council. This was held on the 25th, the same afternoon that the *Hohenzollern* headed for home. The Austrian ultimatum was due to expire in a few hours and the Russian generals were in a state of excitement; they were sure that Austrian troops would stream into Serbia when the time-limit expired. One officer looked at his watch at six o'clock and said: "The cannon on the Danube will have begun to fire by now, for one doesn't send such an ultimatum except when the cannon are loaded." (This officer had not made allowances for Austrian inefficiency; although the Austrians intended their ultimatum to provoke a conflict the fact was that they would not be ready to send their army into Serbia for another two weeks.)

Those present at the Crown Council were unanimous in their

[1] *Kautsky Documents.*

opinion that it was politically and morally impossible for Serbia to be crushed, but they disagreed on the steps to be taken. The generals wanted the Czar to sign a general mobilisation order, but M. Sazanov did not want a European war if he could avoid it, and insisted that every effort should be made first to make Austria capitulate by diplomacy; he therefore managed to persuade the Czar to sign an order for " partial " mobilisation only, which meant calling up the army corps in the southern districts, and even this was only to go into operation if Austrian troops crossed the frontier. The generals were horrified at this decision for the army blue-print did not allow a partial mobilisation; the plans had been drawn up for a general mobilisation or nothing, and if they were altered the result might be widespread confusion. Nevertheless M. Sazanov got his way, but in order to placate the generals the Czar also agreed that the " Period Preparatory to War " should secretly be put into immediate operation. This meant cancelling all leave, manning the frontier posts, breaking up the summer camps, " shoeing the horses and locking up the spies."

There is little doubt that when the Kaiser arrived back in Potsdam at noon on July 27th he was still angry with his Chancellor. However, there is no truth in Bülow's story that Bethmann-Hollweg met him at the station and offered to resign; and that the Emperor replied: " You have cooked this broth; now you can stay and eat it." Until now the Kaiser had not been critical of the way his Chancellor had handled the situation, but he was irritated by his patronising manner; by his insistence that so many important officials should remain away from the capital; by his ignorance of military matters; and most of all by his reluctance to consult his sovereign. Furthermore, the Kaiser had an uneasy feeling that Bethmann-Hollweg lacked the quickness and the skill to grasp the full implications of what he was doing or to adapt himself to new developments as they arose.

Bethmann, on the other hand, was alarmed by the Kaiser's sudden appearance. He let the British Embassy know, through Jagow, that the Emperor's return was regretted for fear it might " cause speculation and excitement," but that it had been taken on " His Majesty's own initiative." What he really feared was that the Kaiser might inflame the situation by some reckless move.

Consequently, when Bethmann attended a meeting at Potsdam in the afternoon of the 27th, at which the Kaiser, General von Moltke, and Herr Jagow were present, he took pains to give the Emperor a sanguine picture. The Serbian reply was said " to agree to almost all the Austrian demands; " and although Austria had rejected it because it did not acquiesce in " unconditional acceptance," Russia was about to enter into direct talks with Vienna in the hope of reaching a compromise on the one or two remaining points of issue. Meanwhile Britain, France, and Italy were all showing a strong desire for peace. And as Austria had stated categorically to Russia, only yesterday, that she had no territorial designs on Serbia, he was sure that the policy of " localisation " was succeeding.

Bethmann also showed the Kaiser a telegram from London in which Sir Edward Grey once again suggested a meeting of ambassadors, representing Britain, Germany, Italy, and France, to be held in London. Lichnowsky's telegram was couched in strong words. The only possibility of avoiding a general war lay " in the acceptance of Sir Edward Grey's proposal to hold a conference *à quatre* here; " and " the localisation of the conflict as hoped for in Berlin was wholly impossible and must be dropped from the calculations of practical politics." Lichnowsky ended on a personal note. " I would like to offer an urgent warning against believing any further in the possibility of localisation, and to express the humble wish that our policy be guided solely and alone by the need of sparing the German nation a struggle which it has nothing to gain from and everything to lose."[1]

This telegram did not quite square with Bethmann's rosy optimism so he deleted this last sentence from the dispatch before showing it to the Emperor; and no doubt he murmured something about the Ambassador's " emotional approach," for he afterwards annotated the document: " Submitted to His Majesty. His Majesty disapproved of Lichnowsky's point of view." After this it was not difficult for the Chancellor to show the Kaiser the reply he had sent Lichnowsky in the morning. " We would not be able to summon Austria before a European court of justice in her case with Serbia.... Our mediation activities must be confined to a possible Austro-Russian clash. . . ." Bethmann's negative stand, of course, was

[1] *Kautsky Documents.*

due to the fact that mediation of any kind was bound to restrain Austria in her " final reckoning with Serbia." But in order not to annoy Britain he suggested direct conversations between Austria and Russia, and ended with a rebuke for Lichnowsky. " I therefore request you most urgently to advocate in London the necessity and the possibility of localisation."[1]

There is no indication that the Kaiser criticised Bethmann's actions but his misgivings were well founded; for the Chancellor took his leave about 7 p.m. to hurry back to Berlin, where he spent the evening committing irretrievable blunders. As a result July 27th was fated to go down into history as a turning point in the events leading to the first world war.

Bethmann-Hollweg failed to perceive that the severity of Austria's demands had begun to arouse suspicion as to Germany's intentions in the Balkans. He therefore was blind to the dangers stemming from the altered climate. Awaiting him on his desk was the Serbian reply to the Austrian ultimatum. As this document had been presented to the Austrian authorities thirty-six hours earlier, and promptly rejected by them as " inadequate," he scarcely glanced at it. The Serbian Legation had been so slow to decode and translate the communication that only now was a copy available. It was even more conciliatory than Tschirschky had predicted. Indeed, Serbia had practically swallowed the whole of Austria's impossible demands. Even when she demurred over the establishment of an Austrian agency in Belgrade, on the grounds that this would constitute an infringement of sovereignty, her tone was accommodating. " If the Imperial and Royal Government is not satisfied with this reply, the Serbian Government, considering that it is not in the common interest to precipitate the solution of this question, is ready, as always, to accept a pacific understanding, either by referring this question to the decision of the International Tribunal of The Hague, or to the Great Powers."

The well-meaning Bethmann-Hollweg was every bit as disastrous as the unscrupulous Prince Bülow. He was utterly unable to grasp the significance of the Serbian reply. Its compliance had changed everything. Austria's demands had been framed to provoke a refusal; the fact that the Serbs had virtually accepted them had thrown a spanner into the works, destroying all possibility of

[1] *Kautsky Documents.*

localising the quarrel. The suspicions that had been rising in Europe now seemed wholly justified. If Austria-Hungary could reject such a yielding reply and order mobilisation, it proved that she was not interested in redressing a wrong, but in extending her influence in the Balkans; and, since she would not dare to behave in such a high-handed way without the backing of Berlin, it was obvious that Germany was on the move.

The crisis immediately took on a sinister aspect. Men of moderate opinion, such as Sir Francis Bertie, the British Ambassador in Paris, who on the morning of the 27th had been urging " pressure on the Russian Government not to assume the absurd and obsolete attitude of Russia being the protectress of all Slav states no matter what their conduct," suddenly found the ground cut from beneath his feet; while men like Sir Eyre Crowe, the Assistant Under-Secretary at the Foreign Office, a rabid Germanophobe who for years had been talking about " the German menace," moved into the ascendancy. It looked as though Germany was ready to provoke war in order to secure the supremacy of Europe.

The obtuse Bethmann-Hollweg remained oblivious to the revulsion of feeling that had taken place against Germany. Although the red lights were flashing wildly he saw none of them. Even a chilling communication from London did not induce him to alter his course. The peaceable Serbian reply, Sir Edward Grey had told Prince Lichnowsky angrily, was due to Russian pressure and should it not be " accepted by Vienna as a foundation for peaceful negotiations . . . it would be absolutely evident that Austria was only seeking an excuse for crushing Serbia. It was plain that Russia could not regard such action with equanimity, and would have to accept it as a direct challenge. The result would be the most frightful war that Europe had ever seen, and no one could tell to what such a war might lead. . . ." " I found the Minister irritated for the first time," ended Lichnowsky. ". . . everybody here is convinced that the key to the situation is to be found in Berlin, and that, if peace is seriously desired . . . Austria can be restrained from prosecuting, as Sir Edward Grey expressed it, a fool-hardy policy."[1]

Bethmann-Hollweg remained inflexible. Germany had promised to support Austria-Hungary whatever action she saw fit to take and Germany could not break her word. He not only failed to see that

[1] *Kautsky Documents.*

the Serbian reply had created new circumstances, but that it offered Germany a heaven-sent opportunity to extricate herself from a perilous situation. The only compromise he made was to forward Sir Edward Grey's telegram to Vienna, apologetically asking Count Berchtold to consider it in order to humour London.

But he made no effort to prevent Berchtold from taking the fateful step of declaring war on Serbia. Lying on his desk was a telegram from Tschirschky advising him that Berchtold planned to make this move within the next forty-eight hours so as to put an end to the mounting pressure for mediation. Bethmann-Hollweg still clung to the fantasy that localisation was possible.

15. *Armageddon*

The Kaiser reacted quite differently from his Chancellor when he read the Serbian reply, which did not reach him until the following day, the 28th. " A brilliant performance for a time-limit of only 48 hours. This is more than one could have expected! A great moral success for Vienna; but with it every reason for war drops away, and Giesl ought to have remained quietly in Belgrade! After such a thing, I should never have ordered mobilisation."[1]

William II always reacted emotionally, and because he was not troubled by the wooden logic that plagued Bethmann-Hollweg, he was far more perceptive. He saw at once that Germany and Austria were being placed in an invidious position by their uncompromising attitude towards the Serbian note. Even more significant, he once again was seized by fright. He had in front of him Grey's icy interview with Prince Lichnowsky, in which the Foreign Secretary insisted that the key to the situation lay in Berlin and that if Germany desired peace he was convinced that she could restrain Austria. Apparently Bethmann had hesitated before sending this alarming dispatch to the Kaiser, for at the bottom Jagow had written: " Shall this telegram be submitted to His Majesty?" and Bethmann had replied: " Early to-morrow morning to the New Palace by messenger."

The dispatch made a profound effect on William II. He did not want a European war, only a European victory. And he suddenly saw that he was standing far closer to the edge of the precipice than he had imagined. In a flash all his martial ardour vanished. The dozens of marginal annotations he had made, with their peremptory demands and their fierce bravado, were instantly forgotten. From now onwards the Kaiser was interested only in maintaining peace. From now on, everything he did was born of a frantic effort to stop the cumbersome machine in time to

[1] *Grosse Politik.*

avoid a crash. An overpowering fear had taken possession of his soul.

At 10 a.m. he sat down and wrote Bethmann-Hollweg a memorandum; the first memorandum that he penned since the beginning of the crisis. "After reading over the Serbian reply . . . I am convinced that on the whole the wishes of the Danube Monarchy have been acceded to. The few reservations that Serbia makes . . . could be settled by negotiation. It contains the announcement *orbi* and *urbi* of a capitulation of the most humiliating kind, and as a result *every cause for war* falls to the ground.

"Nevertheless, the piece of paper, like its contents, can be considered as of little value so long as it is not translated into *deeds*. The Serbs are Orientals, therefore liars, tricksters and masters of evasion. In order that these beautiful promises may be turned to truth and facts, a *douce violence* must be exercised. This should be so arranged that Austria would receive a HOSTAGE [Belgrade] as a guarantee for the enforcement and carrying out of the promises. . . . In case Your Excellency shares my views, I propose that we say to Austria: Serbia has been forced to retreat in a very humiliating manner, and we offer our congratulations; naturally, as a result, EVERY CAUSE FOR WAR HAS VANISHED. But a GUARANTY that the promises WILL BE CARRIED OUT is unquestionably necessary. That could be secured by means of the TEMPORARY military occupation of a portion of Serbia. . . . Your Excellency will submit a proposal to me along the lines sketched out; which shall be communicated to Vienna."[1]

Thus William II, for the first time since the crisis had begun, made a move to restrain Vienna. Bethmann-Hollweg did not receive the Kaiser's message until early afternoon, and by this time he, too, was growing worried. Austria had declared war at 11 a.m. and already there had been repercussions from Russia. At 1 p.m. a report was received from St. Petersburg saying that reservists were being called to the colours. He therefore did not demur at the Emperor's instructions and drafted a telegram for Vienna. But he could not bring himself to use the Kaiser's strong language. There was no sentence saying bluntly, "every cause for war has vanished." The message was toned down and softened, until it became a series of suggestions rather than a command. Apart from this, he even managed to shift the emphasis so that the suggested peace move,

[1] *Kautsky Documents.*

instead of being a matter of necessity and common sense, was presented as a question of tactic so "that responsibility for the extension of the war" should "fall on Russia." And finally, although he warned the German Ambassador to discuss the plan "thoroughly and impressively with Count Berchtold," he reduced the urgency by warning him : "You will have to avoid very carefully giving rise to the impression that we wish to hold Austria back."

What was Bethmann-Hollweg playing at? He was so mesmerised by detail that his chief concern was to save face with Austria. Perturbed though he was, he did not realise, even at this late hour, that he was standing on the brink of war. Privately he still believed that his good relations with Sir Edward Grey would save the situation. "Bethmann's and Berchtold's policy of invading Serbia," wrote Admiral Tirpitz, "was based on the expectation that the love of peace shown by England in recent years would go so far as to cause the Czar, if the worst came to the worst, to refuse his patronage to the Serbs, or to leave him to fight a continental war without England's help."[1]

The German Chancellor's picture of himself riding on a noisy but fairly safe train driven by England, was far from reality. The truth was that the engine driver had jumped off three days earlier, and the train was hurtling blindly through Europe dependent for its salvation on pure chance. On July 25th, the day that Austria rejected the Serbian reply, Sir Eyre Crowe had written a Foreign Office minute that had been adopted as British policy. "The moment has passed when it might have been possible to enlist French support in an effort to hold back Russia. It is clear that France and Russia are decided to accept the challenge thrown down to them. Whatever we may think of the merits of the Austrian charges against Serbia, France and Russia consider that these are the pretext, and that the bigger cause of Triple Alliance versus Triple Entente is definitely engaged. I think it would be impolitic, not to say dangerous, for England to attempt to controvert this opinion, or to endeavour to obscure the plain issue, by any representation at St. Petersburg and Paris. . . ."[2]

[1] *Memoirs :* Admiral von Tirpitz.

[2] *British Documents on the Origins of the War.* When the British Blue Book was published in 1914 in order to reveal the part played by England in the negotiations

Although Sir Edward Grey continued to work for a peaceable solution he accepted this crucial dictum and made no attempt to influence or restrain Russia. And by doing so he relinquished control of the European crisis. He allowed Britain to be towed in Russia's wake in exactly the same way that Germany permitted itself to be dragged after Austria. Neither nation had the least idea that the other was not in the operator's seat. Thus Europe lurched and jolted towards war.

Rumours of troop movements in Russia began to trickle into Berlin, late on the night of the 28th, while Bethmann-Hollweg was pressing the idea of mediation on Austria. The Chancellor became uneasy and suggested that the Kaiser send a personal telegram to the Czar. "It is with the gravest concern," wired William, "that I hear of the impression which the action of Austria against Serbia is creating in your country. The unscrupulous agitation that has been going on in Serbia for years has resulted in the outrageous crime to which Archduke Franz Ferdinand fell a victim. The spirit that led Serbians to murder their own king and his wife still dominates the country.[1] You will doubtless agree with me that we both, you and me, have a common interest, as well as all Sovereigns, to insist that all the persons morally responsible for the dastardly murder should receive their deserved punishment. In this politics play no part at all.

"On the other hand I fully understand how difficult it is for you and your Government to face the drift of your public opinion. Therefore, with regard to the hearty and tender friendship which binds us both from long ago with firm ties, I am exerting my utmost influence to induce the Austrians to deal straightly to arrive at a satisfactory understanding with you. I confidently hope you will help me in my efforts to smooth over difficulties that may still arise. Your very sincere and devoted friend and cousin. Willy."[2]

Strangely enough the Kaiser's telegram, dispatched around midnight, was crossed by an urgent appeal from the Czar—two cries for help passing each other in the darkness.

---

leading to the war, this minute was expunged. However a reference to it inadvertently was left in the table of contents. A German scholar wrote to the Foreign Office in the spring of 1924, and asked for the missing passage. It was communicated to him with the permission of the Secretary of State.

[1] This was a reference to the assassination of King Alexander and Queen Draga of Serbia in 1903. [2] *Kautsky Documents.*

The Czar to the Emperor
Peterhof Palace, *July 29, 1914*

HIS MAJESTY THE EMPEROR, NEW PALACE

Am glad you are back. In this most serious moment I appeal to you to help me. An *ignoble* war has been declared to a *weak* country. The *indignation* in Russia, *shared fully by me*, is *enormous*. I foresee that very soon I shall be *overwhelmed* by the *pressure* brought upon me, and be forced to take extreme measures which *will lead to war*. To try and avoid such a calamity as a European war, I beg you in the name of our old friendship to do what you can to *stop* your allies from *going too far*.

NICKY[1]

The Czar's telegram was sent at two in the morning. The "pressure" to which he referred was the desire of his military advisers for general mobilisation—even though the order would make a European war almost a certainty. They argued that the Austrian declaration against Serbia had already rendered a conflict inevitable, and that since Russian mobilisation was slower than anyone else's it ought not to be delayed. But although fear provided the main impetus, there were aggressive voices as well: voices that scorned the talk of self-defence and openly favoured war with Germany. These were the ultra-conservative army leaders who believed that only the battlefield could cure Russia's deep social unrest; and the Pan-Slav school who talked of the glittering prizes the Balkans would offer when Germany was defeated. Whatever the argument, almost everyone agreed that although Russia was not fully prepared the moment was right for a showdown: France would stand by her ally, and it seemed likely that England would stand by France.

Until now M. Sazanov had refused to listen to the military. Although he had persuaded the Czar to agree to a partial mobilisation order against Austria, he was so eager to give mediation a chance he had not put the edict into operation. He had requested direct talks with Vienna and was still waiting for a reply. But when he heard of the Austrian declaration of war against Serbia, he threw in his hand and no longer opposed the High Command.

[1] *Kautsky Documents.*

The Czar knew from Sazanov's attitude that the request for general mobilisation would soon be put before him. It was delivered, in fact, nine hours after his telegram to the Kaiser, and he reluctantly and sadly gave his assent to it. Before the order could become effective, however, the signatures of three other ministers were necessary; and one of them, the Minister of Marine, could not be found, and would not be back in the capital until evening. Meanwhile, the Russian Foreign Secretary received a message from Vienna, flatly refusing the Russian invitation which had been made four days earlier to hold direct talks on the Austro-Serbian conflict. The Austrian Ambassador, M. Szápáry, called on Sasanov to try and explain his country's point of view. "While we were thus engaged in a confidential exchange of views," said Szápáry, "Sazanov heard by telephone that we had bombarded Belgrade. He became like a man beside himself. . . . 'You only wish to gain time by negotiation, but you go ahead and bombard an unprotected city!'[1] He went on to denounce Austria in the most excited fashion."[2]

By nightfall the military had received the third signature and one of the officers left for the Post Office to send the fatal message. Just as he was setting out, however, the Czar received a second telegram from the Kaiser. "It would be quite possible for Russia to remain a spectator of the Austro-Serbian conflict," wrote William II, "without involving Europe in the most horrible war she ever witnessed. I think a direct understanding between your Government and Vienna possible and desirable, and as I already telegraphed you my Government is continuing its exertions to promote it. Of course, military measures on the part of Russia, which would be looked upon by Austria as threatening, would precipitate a calamity we both wish to avoid, and jeopardise my position as mediator which I readily accepted on your appeal to my friendship and my help."[3]

The peace-loving Czar promptly telephoned two of his generals and in a three-cornered conversation cancelled the order for general mobilisation, insisting instead on partial mobilisation which meant only calling up the troops in the four southern districts. A messenger

[1] This bombardment was carried out by artillery from Austrian territory, which extended to within a few miles of the Serbian capital.

[2] *Austrian Red Book.*

[3] *Kautsky Documents.*

was rushed to the Post Office and at 9 p.m. managed to stave off the fateful telegram which was on the verge of being dispatched to the far-flung Russian Empire. Once again Europe tottered back from the precipice.

That same day, July 29th, the Kaiser and Bethmann-Hollweg waited all day for an answer to their " peace-pledge " proposal of the night before. Telegrams, however, took many hours to go and come, for they had to be put into cypher, transmitted, and decoded the other end. By the end of the day the only news from Vienna was a dispatch from Count Tschirschky, written the day before, which ended: " Count Berchtold is in very good spirits, and is proud of the countless telegrams of congratulations that are coming to him from every portion of *Germany* ! "

The Kaiser's nerves were nearly at breaking point. All day he had paced the floor at the New Palace. As the tension mounted he began to lash out wildly against his Chancellor for his incompetent handling of the crisis; now that things were going wrong he blamed him bitterly for allowing the Austrians to get the bit between their teeth, and for not having kept control in German hands. When Admiral von Tirpitz visited him that evening he found him complaining excitedly that he did not know what Austria wanted; the Serbs had conceded everything but a few bagatelles; since July 5th the Austrians had refused repeatedly to declare their aims. Admiral Tirpitz agreed that Bethmann was at fault and advised the Emperor, even at this late date, to appoint a new Chancellor, but William II replied that it would be a mistake as Bethmann enjoyed the confidence of Europe. The truth was that the Kaiser was so rattled he did not know what to do.

However, there was one bright spot on the horizon. The Emperor's brother, Prince Henry, had arrived at Kiel the day before from a short stay in London. He sent the Kaiser a letter telling him that he had had a conversation with George V. " Georgie," he wrote, was eager to see the struggle between Austria and Serbia localised and hoped that Germany could accept the mediation of the four powers " in order to restrain Russia." The Prince continued: " He said further, to quote his own words, ' we shall try all we can to keep out of this and shall remain neutral.' I am convinced that this statement was made in all seriousness, as was also that to the effect that England would remain neutral at the start; but whether she will be able to keep so permanently I am not able to judge, but doubt it on account of her relations with France."[1]

A fierce new hope leapt up within the Kaiser's breast. It may seem extraordinary that William II, the son of an English princess who prided herself on her knowledge of British parliamentary rule, could have placed such reliance on the casual remark of a constitutional monarch made three days earlier. One must remember, however, that the Kaiser had looked upon Edward VII as a political force, not as a figurehead, and no one could say that he was wrong; but as a result he made the mistake of exaggerating the role of George V. When Admiral Tirpitz cautioned against placing too much reliance on the monarch's remark, the Kaiser drew himself up and replied: "I have the word of a king; and that is sufficient for me."[2]

George V would have been amazed if he had known the commotion his brief conversation with Prince Henry was causing at Potsdam. Before he went to bed on the night of July 26th he had written laconically in his diary: "Prince Henry of Prussia came to see me on Sunday July 26 at 9.30 a.m. and asked me if there was any news. I said the news was very bad and it looked like a European war and that he better go back to Germany at once. He said he would go down to Eastbourne to see his sister [The Queen of Greece] and he would return to Germany that evening. He then asked what England would do if there was a European war. I said: 'I don't know what we shall do, we have no quarrel with anyone and I hope we shall remain neutral. But if Germany declared war on Russia, and France joins Russia, then I am afraid we shall be dragged into it. But you can be sure that I and my Government will do all we can to prevent a European war.' He then said—'Well, if our two countries shall be fighting on opposite sides, I trust that it will not affect our own personal friendship.' He then shook hands and left the room, having been with me about eight minutes."[3]

[1] *Kautsky Documents.*

[2] *My Memoirs:* Admiral von Tirpitz.

[3] According to Harold Nicolson: "Prince Henry, in after years himself admitted that, in the excitement of the moment, he may well have interpreted as a definite assurance what was no more than an incidental expression of an anxious hope."—*King George V.*

That night, while the Kaiser's head was full of George V's "promise of neutrality" as he now called it, Bethmann-Hollweg arrived at the New Palace. According to Admiral Tirpitz he, too, was nearing a state of collapse, for at last he realised that his policy of localisation would not work. At 9 p.m. a telegram had arrived from London couched in the strongest terms, clearly indicating that if a European war broke out it was improbable that England would stay out. Sir Edward Grey had called Prince Lichnowsky to him and told him that he did not want their warm personal relations to lead the Ambassador astray; he also wished to spare himself later the reproach of bad faith by making the position as clear as possible. Opinion in London, he said, which at first had been favourable to Austria and recognised that she must have satisfaction, now had altered because of Austria's stubbornness and turned "completely to the other side." Nevertheless, Britain probably would continue to be neutral if the conflict remained confined to Austria and Russia. But if Germany and France should be drawn in, as was much more likely, "then the situation would immediately be altered, and the British Government would, under the circumstances, find itself forced to make up its mind quickly. In that event it would not be practicable to stand aside and wait for any length of time. . . ."

Although Bethmann apparently did not bring a copy of Grey's telegram with him, he informed the Kaiser of its contents.[1] Admiral Tirpitz says that he "utterly collapsed" and suggested sacrificing the German Fleet in order to keep England out of the conflict. However, we have no accurate report of what went on at Potsdam. All we know is that when Bethmann returned to Berlin he summoned the English Ambassador, Sir Edward Goschen, and made a desperate bid for British neutrality. "Chancellor having just returned from Potsdam," wired Goschen to London at midnight, "sent for me again tonight and made the following strong bid for British neutrality. . . . as far as he was able to judge the key-note of British policy, it was evident that Great Britain would never allow France to be crushed. The Imperial Government was ready to give every assurance to the British Government provided that Great Britain remained neutral that in the event of a victorous war Germany aimed at no territorial acquisitions at the expense of France. In answer to a question from me, His Excellency said it

[1] The Kaiser's annotations on Grey's telegram are dated July 30th.

would not be possible for him to give such an assurance as regards colonies. . . ."[1]

London was astonished by this proposition. Bethmann's assurance that although France's territorial integrity would be guaranteed, no similar guarantees could be given about her colonial possessions, struck the British Foreign Office as incredible. "For Britain to make this bargain with Germany at the expense of France," Sir Edward Grey wired Goschen, "would be a disgrace from which the good name of this country would never recover." Not only did Bethmann's suggestion shock London, but it seemed to be the final proof that Germany was determined to go to war.

The situation in Berlin, however, was one of fear and confusion. For the first time Bethmann-Hollweg earnestly endeavoured to apply the brakes to Austria. Between eleven and three in the morning he sent a spate of telegrams; one demanded an instant reply to the peace-pledge proposal; another, based on an earlier communication from Sir Edward Grey, who had passed on news that the Serbians might be willing to swallow all the points in the Austrian ultimatum, said: "Please show this to Berchtold immediately, and add that we regard such a yielding on Serbia's part as a suitable basis for negotiation along with an occupation of a part of Serbian territory as pledge." The fourth telegram was sharper. It was in answer to a report from St. Petersburg that Count Berchtold had turned down the idea of direct talks with Russia. "We are ready, to be sure, to fulfil our obligations as an ally but must refuse to allow ourselves to be drawn into a world conflagration frivolously and in disregard of our advice. Please say this to Count Berchtold at once with all emphasis and with great seriousness."

The final telegram sent at three in the morning was the strongest of all. Bethmann came to the conclusion that he must put his pride in his pocket and let Austria know that despite all Germany's bravado and boastfulness she was afraid of a European war. "If Austria refuses all negotiations," he wired, "we are face to face with a conflagration in which England will be against us; Roumania and Italy according to all indications will not be for us, and we shall stand two against four Powers. Through England's opposition the main blow will fall on Germany. Austria's political prestige, the military honour of her army, as well as her just claims against

[1] *British Documents on the Origins of the War.*

Serbia, can be adequately satisfied by her occupation of Belgrade or other places. Through her humiliation of Serbia she will make her position in the Balkans, as well as in her relation to Russia, strong again. Under these circumstances we must urgently and emphatically urge upon the consideration of the Vienna Cabinet the adoption of mediation in accordance with the above honourable conditions. The responsibility for the consequences which would otherwise follow would be, for Austria and for us, an uncommonly heavy one."[1]

But it was all too late. If Bethmann had followed the Kaiser's instructions thirty hours earlier and told the Austrians bluntly that " no more cause for war exists " his intervention might have been effective. Now, however, the irresponsible Count Berchtold was intoxicated by the role he was playing and refused to take Bethmann's remonstrations seriously. He replied with almost unbelievable levity that it did not matter whether or not Belgrade swallowed all the points of the ultimatum, it was no longer possible for Austria to negotiate on the basis of the Serbian reply. " It might have been satisfactory before hostilities [the Austrian declaration of war] had begun," he explained airily, " but now Austria's conditions must take another tone." As for the peace-pledge plan, the Count required more time for reflection.

While Bethmann was sending his frenzied and ineffective messages the Kaiser was having an equally harassing time at the New Palace. At one-thirty in the morning of the 30th, before he had gone to bed, he received a letter from the Czar announcing partial mobilisation against Austria. " The military measures which have now come into force," wrote Nicholas, " were decided five days ago for reasons of defence on account of Austria's preparations. I hope with all my heart that these measures won't in any way interfere with your part as mediator which I greatly value. We need your strong pressure on Austria to come to an understanding with us. Nicky."[1]

William II did not know, of course, how close Russia had come to general mobilisation ; how the Czar had intervened just as the order was about to be sent over the wires and stopped it. Instead of being grateful to Nicholas he flew into one of his rages. " And these measures are for *defence* against *Austria*, which is in *no way* attacking him ! ! ! I can not agree to any more mediation, since the Czar

[1] *Kautsky Documents.*

who requested it has at the same time secretly mobilised behind my back. It is only a manœuvre in order to hold us back and to increase the start they have already got. My work is at an end."[1]

This news was bad enough; but when he read Sir Edward Grey's warning telegram forwarded by the Chancellor at eleven o'clock in the morning, his indignation mounted even higher. Grey's assertion that "it would not be practicable for Britain to stand aside for any length of time" was not at all what the King had said to Prince Henry. The remark that he was speaking plainly "to spare himself the reproach of bad faith" drew from the Kaiser, "Aha, the common cheat." "England reveals herself in her true colours," he wrote at the bottom, "at a moment when she thinks that we are caught in the toils and, so to speak, disposed of! That common crew of shopkeepers has tried to trick us with dinners and speeches. The boldest deception, the words of the King to Henry for me. 'We shall remain neutral and try to keep out of this as long as possible.' Grey proves the King a liar, and his words to Lichnowsky are the outcome of an evil conscience, because he feels that he has deceived us. At that, it is as a matter of fact a threat combined with a bluff, in order to separate us from Austria and to prevent us from mobilising, and to shift the responsibility for the war. He knows perfectly well that if he were to say one single serious sharp and warning word at Paris and Petersburg, and were to warn them to remain neutral, both would become quiet at once. But he takes care not to speak the word, and threatens us instead! Common cur! England *alone* bears the responsibility for peace and war, and not we any longer! That must also be made clear to the world. W."[1]

These outpourings only emphasize that William II, who had the power to rule, was incapable of exercising it; while Bethmann-Hollweg, who had been given the authority to rule, shrank from decisive action. Instead, they both sat back, the one given up to vituperative abuse and the other to futile gestures, and let events take their course. On July 30th, which proved to be the last day that peace might have been preserved, both men knew that Austria was unlikely to agree to mediation; that Russia was determined to fight if Serbia was attacked; and that Germany, France, and Britain would all be drawn into the conflict once it began. Germany

[1] *Kautsky Documents.*

did not want a world war. She knew that Vienna could get what it wanted by mediation. Why, then, did she not take matters into her own hand and force Austria to compromise? "Even now," wrote the famous German historian, Erich Brandenburg, "the decisive word was not spoken, viz. that the terms of the alliance were not considered operative if Austria, by rejecting intervention, appeared the aggressor."[1]

The truth was that the Kaiser was too hysterical and the Chancellor too incompetent to take charge of the situation. Although the Kaiser had forced Bethmann to urge mediation on Austria he lacked the capacity to follow up his impulse and to see that the command not only was delivered but accepted. He had never really ruled, only interfered, and it was too late for him to alter the habit of a life-time. Bethmann, on the other hand, was too rigid to meet new circumstances. According to Erich Brandenburg he did not dare reverse his stand for fear of alienating Austria. "It was the danger of losing our last ally, which had been like a burden on our statesmen since the formation of the entente. . . ." This argument, however, is not convincing. If Germany needed Austria, surely Austria needed Germany even more. Where was Austria to go? Into the entente, which meant into the arms of Russia? Austria had no alternative but partnership with Germany.

A clever diplomat not only could have saved the faces of both Austria and Germany but exploited the situation to their advantage, because of the infinite relief that would have been felt in Britain and France. Instead German diplomacy failed miserably and catastrophically. Escape equipment had been handed to Germany more than once by both Britain and Russia. On July 28th Prince Troubetskoi begged the Kaiser's personal military representative, General von Chelins, to urge his imperial master to take the dispute to The Hague Court of Arbitration. And the following day, the 29th, the Czar himself wired the Kaiser: "It would be right to give over the Austro-Serbian problem to The Hague Conference. Trust in your wisdom and friendship. Your loving Nicky."

The fact that The Hague was an untried tribunal and had not yet acquired prestige was beside the point; as we know, the Serbs had already agreed to submit the dispute to The Hague, but far more significant was the fact that since the Court of Arbitration was the

[1] *From Bismarck to the World War*: Erich Brandenburg.

Czar's own creation, it was the one sure way to stop Russian military intervention. William II, however, considered the suggestion almost insulting; that a great power should allow a tribunal to determine its vital interests was ludicrous. "Well, well! Thanks all the same," he wrote in the margin; and Bethmann-Hollweg commented tersely: "The idea of The Hague Conference will be naturally excluded in this case." The Kaiser wanted to find a solution, but only on his own terms.

On that same afternoon, the 30th, M. Sazanov drove to the Czar's palace to urge his imperial master to re-issue the general mobilisation order which had been quashed the night before in favour of partial mobilisation. The generals were in a state of great agitation for they maintained that it was impossible to call up only the four southern districts and that the whole mobilisation plan would be endangered if the Czar did not change his mind. The artillery bombardment of Belgrade which had taken place the day before had incensed M. Sazanov, and he told General Ianuschkevich, the Chief of Staff, that he would support any military requests he made. Consequently the General telephoned the Czar and tried to persuade him to return to the general mobilisation order. But the Czar was adamant and threatened to break off the conversation; General Ianuschkevich prevented this by saying that M. Sazanov was beside him and had something to ask. Sazanov then requested an immediate audience but the Czar replied that he was "too busy." After a pause he added: "Is it all the same to you if I receive you at the same time with Tatischchev at 3 o'clock, because otherwise I have not a minute of free time today?" Sazanov thanked the Czar and said that he would arrive at the time suggested.[1]

The generals begged Sazanov to use every argument he could conjure up, both political and military. If he was successful, he was to telephone General Ianushkevich from the Palace, so that he immediately could convert the partial mobilisation into general mobilisation. "After this," added the Chief of Staff, "I will retire from sight, smash the telephone, and generally take all measures so that I cannot be found to give any contrary orders for a new postponement of general mobilisation."[1]

[1] *Schilling's Diary.*

Sazanov found the Czar pale and nervous, fully conscious of the awful responsibility resting upon him, for it was understood by all military men that mobilisation meant war.[1] Furthermore, it was bound to provoke similar measures in Germany and once the machine began to move nothing would be able to stop it. " Think of the responsibility which you are advising me to take!" said the Czar. " Think of the thousands and thousands of men who will be sent to their deaths." Sazanov argued that he would have nothing with which to reproach his conscience as war clearly had become inevitable. Diplomacy had finished its work. It was time for His Majesty to think of the safety of his Empire. The refusal to order general mobilisation would only dislocate the whole Russian military organisation and disconcert Russia's allies. " It only remains to do everything necessary to meet war fully armed and under the conditions most favourable to us. Therefore it is better without fear to call forth a war by our preparations for it, and to continue these preparations carefully, rather than out of fear to give an inducement for war and be taken unawares."

The Czar sat silently staring into space, and could not bring himself to speak the decisive word. After an hour General Tatishchev said: " Yes, it is hard to decide." In a burst of irritability the Czar said: " I will decide," and immediately gave the order for general mobilisation. Sazanov hurried to the telephone, notified General Ianuschkevich and said: " Now you can smash the telephone. Give your orders, General, and then—disappear for the rest of the day."[2]

If England had retained control of the crisis, the world war might have been avoided. The truth was, however, that Sir Edward Grey misjudged the situation in Berlin, just as Berlin had misjudged the mood in London. " My reading of the situation at the time," he wrote in his memoirs, " was that Austria had gone recklessly ahead against Serbia, believing that the history of the annexation of Bosnia and Herzegovina would be repeated. . . . When Austria

[1] " The whole plan of mobilisation is worked out ahead to its final conclusion and in all its details," wrote General Dobrorolski, Chief of the Mobilisation Section of the Russian General Staff, in his memoirs. ". . . Once the moment is chosen, everything is settled; there is no going back; it determines mechanically the beginning of war."

[2] *Schilling's Diary.*

found that the parallel of 1909 was not to be repeated and that things were serious, she began to try and get out of it. Germany then precipitated war and told Austria that, as an Ally, she could not get out of it . . . it seemed impossible to come to any other conclusion. That was, then, to me, the true account of how war was brought about."[1]

Notwithstanding his suspicions, if Sir Edward Grey had been a more decisive personality and had refused to abandon the driver's seat he might have secured a peaceable solution. Both sides recognised England as the key country. If Grey had warned Russia not to mobilise until every hope of mediation was exhausted, and Austrian troops actually began to cross the Serbian frontier, the war would have been postponed until August 12th as that was the earliest date by which Austrian mobilisation could be completed. Germany had moved from localisation to mediation in four days; would she have moved from suggesting mediation to commanding it in another four days? The answer is hidden from us. Certainly on July 30th, when Russia was about to explode in flames, there was little sign of it. That afternoon, when the Kaiser read the message from the Czar which ended: "We need your strong pressure on Austria to come to an understanding with us," he scribbled: "No, there is no thought of anything of that sort!!!"

One thing, however, is certain: that unless Germany had dropped persuasion for compulsion and made it clear to Austria that the terms of the alliance would not operate unless she agreed to mediation, Vienna would not have given in. Berlin's urgent entreaties fell on completely deaf ears. When the German Ambassador presented Bethmann-Hollweg's strongly worded plea to Count Berchtold at lunch-time on the 30th he wired Berlin that "the Minister, who listened pale and silent, while it was read twice . . . said at the conclusion that he would report to the Emperor at once about it." However, the official documents show that the impression he gave was deceptive; when he had his audience with Francis Joseph immediately after luncheon (at almost the same moment that Sazanov was pleading with the Czar for general mobilisation) he expressed himself in complete accord with Field-Marshal Conrad von Hötzendorf the Austrian Chief of Staff. Together they secured the Emperor's agreement on two points: (a) that the war would be

[1] *Twenty-five Years:* Viscount Grey of Falloden.

carried out against Serbia, and (b) that general mobilisation would be declared on August 1st. Berchtold's conciliatory talk with the German Ambassador in the morning, which gave the Kaiser the impression that Austria would agree to the " Hostage Plan " and abandon the idea of dismembering Serbia, was merely a ruse to keep Germany quiet until it was too late for interference.

Why was Austria so recalcitrant? After years of being referred to as a weakling Austria was thrilled by her own spirit. When she broke off relations with Serbia Vienna burst into a frenzy of joy, and huge crowds roamed the streets all night singing patriotic songs. Even the old Emperor, so timid at first, was now so buoyed up by the warm response of his people that he was not even deterred by a personal telegram from the Kaiser asking him earnestly to reconsider his decision. Indeed, the tables had been turned so completely that now the Austrians were beginning to jeer at the Germans for having cold feet. " While the Emperor, Francis Joseph, at this hardest moment in his life, was taking with deep solemnity and calm resolution the step whose heavy consequences were as clear to him as its inevitability, it seemed as if the Emperor William was thinking of retreat . . ." wrote Field-Marshal Conrad von Hötzendorf. The General therefore decided to put general mobilisation a day ahead in order to forestall any weakening.

Meanwhile, in Berlin, General Moltke, the Chief of the General Staff, was having a fierce argument with Bethmann-Hollweg. Moltke was a nephew of the great commander who had won fame in the Franco-Prussian war, but he had little in common with his uncle except for his name. He was a nervous, diffident man; when the Kaiser offered him the post of Chief of Staff in 1906, upon Count Schlieffen's retirement, he had shrunk from the responsibility, and begged Prince Bülow to dissuade the Emperor from pressing the appointment on him. " I lack the power of rapid decision; I am too reflective. . . ." But the Kaiser would not listen and for eight years Moltke had fulfilled his tasks with conscientiousness. He was adequate enough in ordinary times but when a crisis blew up he was tortured by uncertainty. Now he was convinced that war was coming, and was in an agony of fear lest the German Army should be caught at a fatal disadvantage. For the past thirty-six hours he had been urging the Kaiser and Bethmann-Hollweg to declare a state of " Threatening Danger of War," but they refused on the grounds that it might jeopardise negotiations. On the night of the 30th, the same night that Russia ordered general mobilisation, Moltke panicked and took matters into his own hands. He feared that Austria's delay in mobilising against Russia would leave Germany to bear the brunt of the Russian attack, so he wired Vienna: "Stand firm to Russian mobilisation. Austria-Hungary must be preserved. Mobilise at once against Russia. Germany will mobilise."[1] At the same time the Austrian military attaché telegraphed Field-Marshal Conrad von Hötzendorf: "Moltke said that he regards the situation as critical if the Austro-Hungarian Monarchy does not mobilise immediately against Russia. . . . Decline the renewed advances made by England for the maintenance of peace. The standing firm in a European war is the last chance of saving Austria-Hungary. Germany will go with her unconditionally."[1]

Count Berchtold was holding a meeting of ministers when Conrad von Hötzendorf entered the room with these telegrams. When the Count read them he exclaimed in surprise: "Who rules in Berlin? Bethmann or Moltke? He then turned to his colleagues and said: "I called you together because I had the impression that Germany was drawing back; now I have the most satisfactory assurances from the highest military authority."

Who ruled in Berlin? Moltke or Bethmann or the Kaiser? The truth was that no one ruled in Berlin.

At seven that evening, while Berchtold was holding his council, the Kaiser received an alarming dispatch from Count Pourtalès in St. Petersburg. It did not mention the order for general mobilisation—for news of that decision did not reach the outside world until the next day—but referred to the partial mobilisation of which the Czar had already informed the Kaiser by telegram. Sasanov had told the German Ambassador that Russia's military measures could not possibly be retracted and "he was not to be diverted from the idea that Russia could not leave Serbia in the lurch."

The interview with Sazanov had such a menacing tone that all William's optimism melted away. Now he was fully aware that the drama was reaching its terrible climax; but it was not Russia that drew forth his wrath, nor Austria, nor France. All his bitterness was directed at Britain. Britain was the key to the situation; she

[1] *Aus meiner Dienstzeit:* Baron Conrad von Hötzendorf.

could have restrained Russia if she had wished; she had deliberately trapped and betrayed him. In a flood of fury and self-pity he poured out his heart. "England, Russia and France have agreed among themselves . . . after laying the foundations of the *casus foederis* for us through Austria . . . to take the Austro-Serbian conflict for an *excuse* for waging a *war of extermination* against us.... That is the real naked situation slowly and cleverly set going by Edward VII and . . . finally brought to a conclusion by George V.... So the famous encirclement of Germany has finally become a fact, despite every effort of our politicians and diplomats to prevent it. The net has been suddenly thrown over our head, and England sneeringly reaps the most brilliant success of her persistently prosecuted purely *anti-German world policy* against which we have proved ourselves helpless, while she twists the noose of our political and economic destruction out of our fidelity to Austria, as we squirm isolated in the net. A great achievement, which arouses the admiration even of him who is to be destroyed as its result! Edward VII is stronger after his death than I who am still alive! And there have been people who believed that England could be won over or pacified, by this or that puny measure!!!... Our consuls in Turkey and India, agents etc. must fire the whole Mohammedan world to fierce rebellion against this hated, lying, conscienceless nation of shopkeepers; for if we are to be bled to death, England shall at least lose India. W."[1]

The certain news of Russia's general mobilisation did not reach Berlin until noon on July 31st. Although General Moltke was now frantic, Germany still did not order general mobilisation, but instituted a "Threatening Danger of War" period, while Bethmann-Hollweg telegraphed Count Pourtalès in St. Petersburg to inform Russia that unless she halted her mobilisation Germany would take retaliatory measures. This message was transmitted to M. Sazanov at midnight. He did not reply to it, and at 5 p.m. on August 1st the Kaiser ordered general mobilisation. An hour later Count Pourtalès called on M. Sazanov to hand him a declaration of war. Three times the German Ambassador asked the Russian Foreign Minister if he could not give him a favourable answer to his request of the night before, and three times Sazanov answered in the negative. "In that case, Sir," said Pourtalès, drawing a

[1] *Kautsky Documents.*

document from his pocket, " I am instructed to hand you this note." The Ambassador then walked to the window and wept, saying: " I never could have believed that I could quit St. Petersburg under such conditions." He embraced M. Sazanov and departed.

In the late afternoon of August 1st Germany and Russia were at war and France was mobilising. But the drama only now was approaching its climax, for the eyes of Europe were on England, the country that would tip the balance one way or the other. Was William II right in his fears, or would England remain uncommitted as Chancellor Bethmann-Hollweg still hoped? At 5 p.m. a sensational telegram arrived in Berlin from Prince Lichnowsky. The Ambassador reported that Sir Edward Grey had called him on the telephone and asked whether " if France agreed to remain neutral in a Russo-German war, we would not attack the French. I assured him that I could take the responsibility for such a guarantee and he is to use this assurance at today's Cabinet session."[1]

Amazed and overjoyed, like man reprieved from a death sentence, the Kaiser called General Moltke, explained the situation, and commanded him to isssue new orders ; the advance would take place not in the west, but in the east. The highly strung Moltke was as appalled as the Russians had been at the idea of partial mobilisation ; the army was a vast and intricate machine that could not be tampered with. " That is impossible, Your Majesty," he protested. " An army of a million cannot be improvised. It would be nothing but a rabble of undisciplined armed men, without a commissariat." " Your uncle," replied the Kaiser angrily," would have given me a different answer." But the present Moltke clung stubbornly to his view. " It is utterly impossible to advance except according to plan ; strong in the west, weak in the east."[2] So William telegraphed to King George V : " On technical grounds my mobilisation which has already been proclaimed this afternoon must proceed against two fronts east and west as prepared. This cannot be countermanded because I am sorry your telegram came too late. . . . I hope that France will not become nervous."

Despite General Moltke, the Kaiser gave orders to his aide-de-camp : " The 16th Division at Trier will not be transferred to

[1] *Kautsky Documents.*

[2] *Erinnerungen :* H. von Moltke.

Luxemburg." The General wrote that when he heard this news he felt as though his heart would break. " Here was yet another risk of complications in advance. When I got home, I was like a broken man, and shed tears of despair . . . I sat in my room, doing nothing, utterly dejected, until at eleven o'clock I was again summoned to His Majesty."

Meanwhile, at the New Palace in Potsdam, the Kaiser and his Chancellor were in transports of delight. England had drawn back at the last moment; Austria could settle her affair with Serbia; Germany had a free hand to deal with France and Russia. Miraculously all had been saved! Then the blow fell. A telegram arrived from King George saying that Prince Lichnowsky must have misunderstood Sir Edward Grey who apparently had been merely speculating as to what Britain's position would be if the German and French armies faced each other without fighting.[1] The Kaiser sent for Moltke and said grimly: " Now you can do what you like." But the General was so shocked by the Kaiser's earlier demand that he found it difficult to compose himself. " I have not been able to get over this experience," he wrote in his diary. " It was as though something in me had been irretrievably shaken. My confidence and self-reliance were destroyed."

Earlier in the day the British Government had sent notes to Paris and Berlin asking whether the respective countries would observe Belgian neutrality. France gave an unconditional assent, and, as England expected, Germany was evasive. The military leaders of all countries believed that Germany would attack France through Belgium.[2] Long ago the German General Staff had accepted Count Schlieffen's thesis, that in a war on two fronts Germany must strike at France with lightning speed and knock her out of the war in the first few weeks, so that the German Army could turn back to stem the huge man-power of Russia. Everything depended, so the generals argued, on the rapidity with which Germany could strike; therefore the passage to France could not be through the heavily

[1] In Lichnowsky's *Mission to London* he explains that the misunderstanding arose because Grey's suggestion involved not only Germany's neutrality towards France but towards Russia as well.

[2] General Sir Henry Wilson outlined the Schlieffen plan to the British Cabinet in 1911, and the same year the plan was discussed at a Franco-Russian military conference.

fortified zones of the Franco-German frontier but through Belgium where the French border was almost undefended.

When Sir Edward Grey received Germany's unsatisfactory answer, he summoned Prince Lichnowsky and read him a unanimous warning from the British Cabinet that if Germany violated Belgian territory, " it would make it difficult for the Government here to adopt an attitude of friendly neutrality." Lichnowsky then asked Sir Edward whether, if Germany gave a promise not to violate Belgian neutrality, Britain would remain neutral. "I replied," wrote Grey, " that I could not say that: our hands were still free, and we were considering what our attitude should be." The Ambassador then asked Grey if he could formulate any conditions on which Britain would remain neutral. " He even suggested," wrote Grey, " that the integrity of France and her colonies might be guaranteed. I said that I felt obliged to refuse definitely any promises to remain neutral on similar terms, and I could only say that we must keep our hands free."[1] " For the present," Lichnowsky wired, Grey had assured him " there was not the slightest intention of proceeding to hostilities against us." " He lies," wrote the Kaiser. " He told Lichnowsky so himself four days ago."

It was clear to William II that the invasion of Belgium would be the *casus belli*. " It is on this that England's going in against us will depend," he wrote on a message from Brussels. Yet he knew that it would not be the true cause; even if he observed Belgian neutrality he was certain that Britain would only find another issue on which to enter the conflict. Indeed, she was already partly committed, for on August 2nd Britain announced that she would defend the French coast against any attacks by the German Navy. That same day, an ultimatum, which had been sent to Brussels in a sealed envelope four days earlier, was delivered to Belgium by the German Ambassador. It demanded a free passage for the German Army, promising that Germany would pay indemnities, repair all damage at the end of the war, and guarantee Belgium's sovereignty and independence. Belgium rejected the ultimatum on August 3rd and appealed to England for diplomatic intervention.

That same day Germany declared war on France, and Sir Edward Grey made a stirring speech in the House of Commons, stressing

[1] *British Documents on the Origin of the War.*

Belgium's gallant stand, pointing out the dangers of allowing the channel ports to fall into German hands, emphasising Britain's close association with France, and intimating that honour would not allow England to stand aside and see her friends destroyed. He received an ovation which gave him the authority to take the final steps. The next day, August 4th, German troops crossed the Belgian frontier, and that evening at 7 p.m. Sir Edward Goschen called on Chancellor Bethmann-Hollweg and told him that unless Germany withdrew its ultimatum and stopped its troops from violating Belgium territory, peaceable relations between Germany and Britain would end at midnight.

That same evening excited crowds gathered outside the Kaiser's Berlin palace. William II came on to the balcony looking white and strained. "I know no parties any more. Only Germans." Then he told them to go home and pray.

16. *Supreme War Lord*

Never, wrote Admiral Tirpitz, had people seen the Kaiser " so tragic and disturbed " as during the first weeks of the war. Prince Bülow was moved by " his pallor, his haggard, almost un-nerved look . . . he might have been quite ten years older." William II nursed a premonition of disaster in his heart; every comment, every marginal annotation, every emotional outpouring during the last three days in July reveal his uncertainty and despair, yet he did not have the courage to retreat. When, in the opening days of August, Italy and Roumania found ways to excuse themselves from honouring their treaty obligations, and declared neutrality, he wrote bitterly: " Our allies are already before the war falling away from us like rotten apples! A total collapse of both German and Austrian foreign diplomacy. This should and could have been avoided. W."[1]

This was one of the few occasions on which the Kaiser blamed his own officials. As he was the supreme ruler, all failures, logically, must rest with him. Therefore he did not allow himself to reflect on Count Metternich's warnings, over the years, that the German Fleet was locking England into the tight embrace of France and Russia; or on Prince Lichnowsky's repeated assertions that if Russia became involved in a European war France was bound to support her, and England equally certain to side with France. Nor did he dwell on the indignation and alarm that Germany had provoked in France and Russia by her action over Tangiers, Algeciras, and Bosnia. Nor to the inescapable fact that on July 5, 1914, he had given Austria *carte blanche* to take violent measures against Serbia, and had informed his army and navy officials that the action incurred the risk of a general war.

Instead, he returned to his original theme that England had plotted Germany's downfall. His expression grew calmer and his

[1] Roumania had secret commitments to the Triple Alliance.

spirits lifted, for soon his conscience was absolved of all responsibility. Russia had mobilised while he was exchanging telegrams with the Czar and mediating at Vienna, because England, far from trying to restrain St. Petersburg, had flashed the signal for hostilities to open. Edward VII had laid the trap but George V had sprung it. He had lied to Prince Henry about Britain's neutrality, and pretended, in his telegram to William, that his government was exerting pressure on Russia to accept the " hostage " plan; and all the while his Foreign Office was preparing the issue of Belgian neutrality, not mentioned until August 1st, as a *casus belli*. Soon the Kaiser was telling his entourage that George V and Nicholas II had plotted the attack against Germany when they met in Berlin in 1913 to attend the wedding of the Kaiser's daughter, Princess Victoria Louise, to the Duke of Brunswick. William remembered walking into King George's apartment and finding them locked in close conversation; they had broken off, and jumped to their feet in embarrassment, and now he understood the reason. He told Bülow that history showed no greater perfidy than that his " cousins and colleagues " had led his own daughter, poor child, to her marriage altar " with guile and treachery in their hearts! " And that Queen Victoria must have turned in her grave when the British grandson flung down the gauntlet of war to the German grandson.

The Kaiser was not the only one tc place the blame on England. Soon all Germany rang with tales of England's villainy. A White Paper was published with selected dispatches, showing the Kaiser's efforts to keep the peace, which inflamed scholars and intellectuals and convinced them that Britain had entered the conflict from greed and jealousy. Germany, they argued, was fighting a defensive war, for Russia had stepped into a quarrel which did not concern her, in order to smash Germany and advance her own interests in the Balkans and Turkey. But why should England, Teutonic in blood and language, wish to stab her kinsfolk in the back? Why should she help the savage Slav to destroy the great civilisation of Luther and Kant, Goethe and Beethoven? " England," declared Professor Harnack of Berlin University, one of Germany's leading academicians, " cut the dyke which has preserved Western Europe and its civilisation from the encroaching desert of Russia and Pan-Slavism. We must hold out, for we defend the work of fifteen hundred years for all Europe and for Great Britain herself . . . the cause of the trouble is envy, envy of our fleet, our industry, our trade."[1] The Hellenist scholar, Professor Wilamowitz, described England as " the evil spirit which had conjured up this war from hell;" and the greatest of all German jurists, Gierke, cried out: " Storm on with thy Slav and Gallic accomplices, thou low-minded nation. Thou shalt never falsify the judgement of God, perfidious Albion."

The Kaiser was Supreme War Lord and Supreme Authority. No decision could be taken, no plan introduced, without his sanction. Although the civil power of the State, as well as the military, was centred in his person, it was thought proper for a Prussian king to lead his soldiers—a conception that proved to be a century out of date. On August 16th William II quitted his capital and, accompanied by a large retinue, travelled to Coblentz, where he installed himself at Great Army Headquarters. " No other course is open to a sovereign in the prime of life," the aged Franz Joseph remarked to Chancellor Bethmann-Hollweg.

The Kaiser arrived at a critical moment. The Schlieffen plan, the blue-print for rapid victory on which all the hopes of the General Staff were pinned, was in full operation. The design called for a huge turning movement through Belgium, which was to strike France in the form of a " great right wheel." The whole German Army was to be flung into the battle; it did not matter if the Russians penetrated East Prussia, or the French drove their way into Lorraine. Every available division was to be thrown into the supreme battle which would knock France out of the war in six weeks' time, and bring the whole Allied structure crashing to the ground. Russia would be unable to stand alone on the continent and England would be forced to make peace. The British General Staff had surmised the German plan as early as 1911 and had outlined it to the Cabinet almost exactly as it was put into operation in 1914. The French, however, did not believe that the Germans would be able to accomplish their turning movement and, consequently, left the France-Belgium frontier largely undefended while they launched an offensive in Lorraine.

The German attack began with an assault on Liège, under the

[1] *Germany:* G. P. Gooch.

command of General Ludendorff. The heavily defended city fell in two days, and ten days later all the outlying fortresses were in the invader's hands. The Belgians retreated to their principal bastion at Antwerp, while the German Army, consisting of 35 army corps, poured through the south-eastern corner into France.

Despite this momentous news, the Kaiser's presence had a dampening effect on Headquarters, for William was obsessed by the grim reports coming in from the east. The German Commander on this front, General Prittwitz, had been allotted only 14 divisions to stem the Russian tide. And now two Russian generals, Rennenkampf and Samsonov, were advancing into East Prussia, each with an army larger than that of Prittwitz. Although the Schlieffen plan demanded utter concentration on the western front the Kaiser talked indignantly of the violation " of our lovely Masurian Lakes." On August 20th, four days after the Emperor's arrival, General von Prittwitz telephoned Great Headquarters in a state of agitation and so upset General Moltke that the latter sacked him on the spot. Moltke then telegraphed General von Hindenburg, a retired commander who possessed an unrivalled knowledge of the treacherous terrain around the Masurian Lakes, and Major-General Ludendorff, who had covered himself with glory in the storming of Liège, and ordered them to take charge of the eastern army.

All Germany was bewailing the fire and sword that was sweeping East Prussia, and William II's pride was deeply stung. He felt that it reflected on his personal leadership, and on the morning of the 21st was plunged in gloom. When he went for a walk in the garden with two of his Cabinet chiefs, Müller and Lyncker, he suggested resting a moment on a bench. As the seat was too small for three people the officer went to fetch a chair. " Am I already such a figure of contempt," said the Emperor icily, " that no one wants to sit next to me? " " This," wrote Müller, " was symptomatic of his whole outlook. He already imagined himself being cold-shouldered because his policy had resulted in a great part of his country being over-run."[1]

While the Kaiser was bathed in self-pity the first great splintering clash between the German and French forces—numbering 2,000,000 men on one side, 1,300,000 on the other—took place near Metz in the Battle of the Frontiers. Three hundred thousand French soldiers

[1] *The Kaiser and His Court:* Admiral von Müller.

were killed, wounded, or taken prisoner; the stronghold of Namur capitulated; the British, who had taken up positions at Mons, retreated; and soon the whole Allied Army was in retreat with the Germans in close pursuit. "The Kaiser is radiant," wrote Müller. "He told everyone here the news during his ride and even informed the recruits exercising on Rheininsel."

We do not know how much pressure, if any, the Kaiser exerted on General Moltke to transfer divisions from the west to the east. All we know is that William II was affronted by the Russian invasion of Prussia, and exultant at the German advance in France. Moltke was so highly strung that he found the Sovereign's exuberance unbearable and referred scathingly to His Majesty's "hurray-mood." "It is heart-rending," he confided to Müller, "to see how entirely he fails to see the gravity of the situation."

Yet on August 25th the nervous, unsure Commander-in-Chief, chosen by the Kaiser for his modesty and courtier-like qualities, forgot the gravity of the stuation and appears to have humoured the wishes of his Supreme War Lord. With the French and British armies in full retreat, Moltke allowed himself to be diverted from his main objective and ordered the transfer of two army corps to East Prussia. General Ludendorff cautioned him against weakening the western front, pointing out that the reinforcements could not arrive in time for the impending battle. Indeed, five days later—just as the General Staff was about to move to Luxemburg—news came in that the engagement had been fought. Hindenburg had won a smashing victory over the Russians at Tannenberg with the slaughter and capture of 1,000,000 men. This was one of the great actions of the war, overnight transforming Hindenburg and Ludendorff into national heroes.[1]

Although fortune seemed to be smiling on Germany, the Kaiser and Moltke were to pay dearly for their defection. Throughout the train journey to Luxemburg William II, in a state of elation, related blood-thirsty tales of German feats at the front which sickened the neurotic Moltke, who once again was tormented by doubt. "We have driven the French back but they're not defeated yet," the General protested to Müller. Nevertheless it looked more

[1] The battle of the Masurian Lakes, fought from September 5th to 15th, was also a great victory, inflicting an equally decisive defeat on General Rennenkampf's army.

than promising; the French Army was nearly at the gates of Paris; the French Government was making plans to quit the capital for Bordeaux; and the leading scout patrols of the invading army could see the Eiffel tower. The Germans, however, were not interested in the capital. Their objective was the final destruction of the French field armies; so the two leading German armies, under General Bülow and General Kluck, began to swing left and move between Paris and Verdun.

On the morning of September 7th the Kaiser drove many miles in an attempt to reach General Bülow's headquarters. As he neared Châlons he was told that French cavalry might break across the road at any moment. "The route was not safe for the Kaiser," wrote Müller in his diary. "At 5.15 back in Luxemburg after a fruitless 480 kilometre drive."

The Kaiser found bad news upon his return. His 2nd and 3rd Armies had met unexpected resistance, and were making no progress. The next morning it was learned that the remaining three armies, commanded by the Crown Prince, the Duke of Wurtemberg, and Crown Prince Rupprecht of Bavaria, had also been halted. Great Headquarters soon discovered what was happening. Around noon a courier came dashing in with a copy of General Joffre's battle orders. The whole French Army had done a right-about face and the Battle of the Marne had begun.

The General Staff was not dismayed by the battle; what concerned them was the fact that General Bülow and Kluck, in turning to present a flank guard to Paris, had left a gap of thirty miles between them; and into that gap the British Expeditionary Force of 120,000 men was marching![1] The German armies were in danger of being cut in half. Where were the reinforcements to plug the hole? At this very moment two army corps, fresh from the western front, were detraining in East Prussia hundreds of miles away. "Desperate panic seized severely the entire army, or to be more correct the greater part of it," wrote Colonel Bauer, a Staff Officer at Headquarters. "It looked at its worst at the supreme command. Moltke completely collapsed. He sat with a pallid face gazing at the map, dead to all feeling, a broken man. General von Stein, Moltke's deputy, certainly said, 'We must not

[1] The German General Staff could not know that the British were marching into the gap by accident!

lose our heads,' but he did not take charge. He was himself without confidence and gave expression to his feelings by saying: 'We cannot tell how things will go'... We younger people could not get a hearing."[1]

The Kaiser was at Headquarters. Here was the Supreme War Lord's opportunity to take charge of the situation. General Moltke was weeping openly, and was quite unfit to carry on. It was William II's duty to call his staff officers together to survey the situation coolly and to decide, after listening to the arguments, the best course to follow. But the Kaiser seemed paralysed. He refused to intervene because he could not bear to shoulder the responsibility. The distraught Moltke, therefore, remained in charge. He summoned Lt.-Colonel Hentsch, the Intelligence Officer, and told him to proceed to the armies of Kluck, Bülow, and the Crown Prince; and if he found that the British Army was across the Marne in any strength to co-ordinate a general retreat to the River Aisne. Hentsch found that the British indeed were across the Marne so he ordered all five armies to retreat. The Crown Prince was so indignant that he refused to obey the command until he received it in writing. The next day a telegram was sent to him.

"Majesty," Moltke is reported to have said to the Kaiser, "the war is lost." His loss of nerve had prompted him to take the worst possible decision. If the Germans had dug in they might easily have retrieved the situation. Indeed, the British Army might have found itself in a trap, and been annihilated by the cross-fire of the two armies. But if Moltke had failed, so had William II. The fact that he was incapable of exerting his authority in a crisis did not escape the notice of his service chiefs. "The Kaiser endeavours to express his own excitement," wrote Admiral Tirpitz on September 11th, "but he is, from a military point of view, out of it. When one thinks of 1870—the dignity, the earnestness, the clear-headed man who could make up his mind and dare to carry through his decisions, and finally of the 'Iron' man—one is filled with fears and anxiety."[2] A few days later he wrote: "The frightful sacrifices have been in vain . . . all is to be ultimately attributed to tomfoolery."

William II, however, took one decision; he relieved Moltke and

[1] *World Crisis:* Winston S. Churchill.
[2] *Memoirs:* Admiral von Tirpitz.

appointed General Falkenhayn in his stead. The latter made a valiant effort to retrieve the situation by a huge drive towards the Channel ports. Antwerp fell on the 10th, but the British forces which had been transferred from the Marne and the remnants of the Belgian Army stood firm and the first Battle of Ypres yielded little to the invaders, but huge casualties on both sides. By November the German attack had spent its force and the Battle of the Marne was over. The quick victory prescribed by the Schlieffen plan had not been achieved, and Germany's calculations, based on a short incisive war, would have to be revised. The Allies knew that they had been saved from certain and swift destruction and spoke of "the miracle of the Marne."

This famous battle brought the war of manœuvre to an end until 1918. For the next three years the two sides remained locked in a stalemate which they tried repeatedly to break, resulting in the greatest letting of blood ever seen. Already, the opening weeks of the war had taken a frightful toll. The French losses in dead, wounded, and captured were over 850,000; the British 85,000; and the Germans 650,000: more than a million and a half men, not counting the sacrifices on the eastern front, in eight weeks' time!

The Kaiser established himself at Great Army Headquarters which had moved to Charleville-Mézières in France. The generals were astonished by their Supreme War Lord. Many of them had never seen him at close quarters before, never worked with him on day-to-day business as his political advisers had done. They knew he was temperamental and restless, but they imagined him to be a man of brilliant talents. Although they had been dismayed by his lack of leadership during the Moltke crisis, they were even more perturbed to discover that he was incapable of serious thought. When they dined with him and tried to talk shop he interrupted the conversation with a flow of irrelevant chatter and anecdote. Even at a Crown Council he would not sit still for more than a short while. He not only failed to give the conference any sense of direction but began drumming on the table if the discussion bored him. Sometimes he broke off an argument of urgent importance by standing up suddenly and saying: "Gentlemen, we must not be late for luncheon."

Some of his officers believed that the war had wrought an appalling change in him, while others seized on the Crown Prince's explanation that the *Daily Telegraph* incident had destroyed his self-confidence. The truth was that he was the same man that he had always been but since the demands made upon him were greater than in peacetime, his faults stood out in sharper outline; unstable, excitable, egotistical, in fact wholly unfitted for the critical position in which he found himself. "The contrast," wrote General Freytag-Loringhoven, the Quarter-Master General, "between the masterful personality which he tried to assume (and indeed was obliged to assume) and the absence of any real force of character, grew daily more glaring until the bitter end. It was his and Germany's misfortune that it could not be said of him as of his grandfather that he was no mere War Lord but a true soldier."[1]

Yet William II insisted on being treated as a soldier. Although he recoiled from responsibility, he could not bear to shed the illusion of himself as a great generalissimo. He play-acted tirelessly as Supreme War Lord, visiting the front, bestowing medals, and travelling backwards and forwards in his cream and gold train, accompanied by a glittering retinue, between eastern and western headquarters. As his generals began to take his measure, they quietly went about their business and consulted him less and less. Although no decision could be taken without him, they presented him with completed plans and requested his signature as a formality. The Kaiser did not wish to be faced with difficult decisions; on the other hand he was quick to notice any circumvention of his authority, and began to complain that proper deference was not being shown to him as supreme commander.

The army, however, was fighting for its life, and Headquarters, buzzing with staff officers, was far too harassed to pay lip-service to the Emperor in order to sooth his ego. William openly mourned his old friend, General Moltke; and although he had installed the breezy Falkenhayn in his stead, began to complain of his off-hand manner. "This evening," wrote Admiral Müller on November 6th, "Prince Max of Baden came to dinner. Remarkable frankness on the part of His Majesty. A great many stories of the war in the air were told. The Kaiser had not heard them before and said

[1] *Menschen und Bilder:* General Freytag-Loringhoven.

to the Prince: 'You see I only hear such things purely by chance. The General Staff tells me nothing and never asks my advice. If people in Germany think that I am the Supreme Commander they are grossly mistaken. I drink tea, saw wood and go for walks, which pleases the gentlemen. The only one who is a bit kind to me is the Chief of the Field Railway Department who tells me all he does and intends to do.' This was of course said as a joke but it was none the less true."[1]

The Kaiser's three Cabinet chiefs whose duty it was to keep him in touch with civil, military, and naval affairs had the worst task of all. They not only discovered that they were dealing with a man who was unable and unwilling to apply himself to urgent problems, but to whom it was dangerous to supply too much information. He exaggerated good news out of all proportion, and allowed bad news to unnerve him for days. The Cabinet chiefs, locked in daily and inescapable contact with him, began to find his lack of balance not only distressing but repellent. Admiral Müller, the chief of the naval Cabinet, kept a day-by-day diary and sourly recorded the Sovereign's change of moods.

"Oct. 26, 1914. His Majesty returned this evening at 6 p.m. He had seen Heeringen and Kluck (First Army), spoken to many senior officers and visited the 12th Grenadier Regiment (Frankfurt-on-Oder). He was in excellent fettle . . . full of lust for battle."

"Oct. 28, 1914. The Kaiser looked very ill and depressed. He said, amongst other things: 'No one comes to our aid. We stand completely alone and must suffer defeat with dignity."

"Nov. 8, 1914. The Kaiser, with a small escort, attended Divine Service in the field on Sunday with the Crown Prince. He was very depressed by the news reported to him yesterday evening of the fall of Tsingtau."

"Dec. 1, 1914. The Kaiser very depressed at not receiving the expected news of victories in the East and West. 'Where are we heading?' he asked. 'Never a victory, always defeat.'"

"December 17, 1914. 1 p.m. lunch with the Kaiser who had just received from Hindenburg final confirmation of our victory. Flags are to be put out! . . . The Kaiser is elated. . . ."

"February 15, 1915. Lotzen. His Majesty has decided to remain for the moment in East Prussia, giving as his reason that 'I wish to

[1] *The Kaiser and His Court:* Admiral von Müller.

be considered the liberator of East Prussia, otherwise it will be merely looked upon as another triumph for Hindenburg.' "[1]

The Kaiser was determined not to let the control of the navy slip out of his grasp as he felt that of the army had done. "I will not have anyone," he told Admiral Tirpitz at the outbreak of war, "come between me and my navy." He made it clear that neither Admiral Tirpitz, as Secretary of State, nor Admiral Pohl as Naval Chief of Staff, had the authority to issue operational commands. "I need no chief," he told Admiral Müller. "I can do this myself."

The Kaiser's object, however, was not to employ the navy but to preserve it. His first order to his fleet was to wage "only guerilla warfare against the English until we have achieved such a weakening of their fleet that we could safely send out our own." This decision not only surprised Admiral Tirpitz but the British Admiralty. Although Germany possessed only 16 super-dreadnoughts compared with England's immediately available 24, the German Naval Staff knew that never again would it have such a favourable moment in which to attack the British Navy. Not only was England transporting a steady flow of troops across the Channel which made them particularly vulnerable, but by requisitioning the ships building for foreign powers in British yards, plus her own construction, she would have in three months' time seven new dreadnoughts, and in six months' time twelve new dreadnoughts. This would put the ratio at 34 to 19, and 39 to 21. "We therefore looked for open battle . . . we expected it," wrote the First Lord of the Admiralty, Mr. Winston Churchill, "and we courted it . . . and nothing happened. The Grand Fleet remained at sea: the German Fleet did not quit the shelter of its harbours. . . ." Even when, on August 28th, units of the British Navy broke into the Heligoland Bight in a daring raid and went "rampaging about" the Emperor was furious to learn that his ships had struck back. Several German cruisers proceeded to the assistance of the flotillas under attack and suffered severe damage. The Kaiser did not congratulate them on their gallantry. He would not tolerate, he said, losses of this kind, and immediately issued orders, restricting still further the initiative of the Commander-in-Chief. In future, even fleet sallies would have to be approved by His Majesty. "I

[1] *The Kaiser and His Court:* Admiral von Müller.

learned of this orally," wrote Tirpitz, " and took the first opportunity to explain to the Emperor the fundamental error of such a muzzling policy. This step had no success, but on the contrary there sprang up from that day forth an estrangement between the Emperor and myself, which steadily increased. . . ."[1]

This was an understatement; Tirpitz argued and fought and raged. On September 16th, 1914, he wrote to the Naval Chief of Staff: " I cannot see the use of preserving the fleet intact until the declaration of peace;" and on October 1st: " If the fleet remains in its withdrawn position its moral strength and capacity will deteriorate;" and on October 11th: " The instruction that the fleet is to be held back . . . will result in the fleet never having an opportunity of a decision by battle."[1]

William II was adamant. The German Battle Fleet had been built as a tribute to his reign and he could not bear to risk it against far superior forces. Politically, it was the most expensive fleet ever constructed. It had cost Germany the friendship of England, and, without question, was the most important single factor in convincing the British Foreign Office that England could not stand aside in a European war. Yet, except for occasional " fleet sallies " and the Battle of Jutland in 1916, which in no way affected Britain's control of the seas, the great monster dreadnoughts lay in harbour throughout the war. This was more than ironic. Why had Britain been so frightened? Why had she believed in the possibility of an invasion throughout 1908? Why had she guarded herself against a German naval attack after Agadir?[2] The answer was that although the British had an immediate superiority in home waters of eight dreadnoughts, " there was not," as Winston Churchill points out, " much margin here for mischance, nor for the percentage of mechanical defects which in so large a fleet has to be expected, and no margin whatever for a disaster occasioned by surprise had we been unready. To a superficial observer who from the cliffs of Dover and Portland had looked down upon a Battle Squadron of

[1] *Memoirs:* Admiral von Tirpitz.

[2] " It was not known," wrote Harold Nicolson, whose father, Sir Arthur Nicolson, was head of the Foreign Office from 1910 to 1916, " that from September 8 to September 22, 1911, we were in constant expectation of hostilities, and that tunnels and bridges on the South Eastern Railway were being patrolled day and night." *Lord Carnock.*

six or seven ships, lying in distant miniature below, the foundation upon which the British world floated would have presented itself in a painfully definite form."[1]

Furthermore, how could England know that the feverish, glittering, arrogant Kaiser had fear in his heart? For thirty years he had stormed and threatened, and although no one doubted that the German Army was the most formidable machine in the world, his war-like posturing had finally persuaded the British that his fleet was a mortal danger as well as his legions. Although the British Admiralty knew the approximate strength of the German Navy, they feared surprise, or misadventure, or new and unforeseen weapons. " None of the gloomy prophecies," wrote the First Lord cheerfully, " which had formed the staple of so many debates and articles . . . materialised."

When Admiral Tirpitz realised that his imperial master did not intend to risk his dreadnoughts in any important engagement with the British Navy, he began to champion the idea of submarine warfare as the only means by which England's tight naval blockade could be broken. However, Tirpitz had neglected to build submarines in peacetime and in 1915 Germany possessed only 25 of these vessels, which meant that no more than seven could be in continuous use. The German Admiralty now initiated a huge submarine-building programme which would give the navy 50 U-boats by 1916 and 200 by 1917.

Despite the paucity of U-boats Tirpitz was in favour of launching a campaign immediately, while the Kaiser was against unrestricted submarine warfare either now or in the future. William II was right about this, and was strongly supported by Chancellor Bethmann-Hollweg. They justly feared that indiscriminate sinkings not only would endanger their relations with Holland and the Scandinavian countries, but might bring them into conflict with America as well. The cold, immaculate President Wilson, who had declared that the United States was " above battle," was greatly concerned with the freedom of the seas. In November 1914 he had protested to Britain against searching of ships for contraband, and seizing foodstuffs destined for Germany, both of which were an infringement of the Declaration of London, an agreement on the rules of sea blockade signed by the European powers and the United States in 1909.

[1] *World Crisis:* Winston S. Churchill.

Germany intervened by announcing on February 4, 1915, that as a retaliatory measure she would sink enemy merchantmen in the waters around the British Isles. This, in turn, gave the English a trump card; because of Germany's proclamation, said Mr. Asquith, Britain would maintain a total blockade against Germany, intercepting all imports or exports no matter what they were.

President Wilson was annoyed with both countries, but, as Winston Churchill points out, "between taking a ship and sinking a ship there was a gulf." Therefore, when the giant liner *Lusitania* was sent to the bottom of the sea off the coast of Ireland in May 1915, and 1,200 passengers were drowned, the civilised world was stunned and horrified. 124 Americans lost their lives, and the United States was brought to the brink of war. The fact that the German Government pointed out that the ship was carrying munitions had little effect, and the American Secretary of State made it clear that a repetition of the act would mean hostilities.

Consequently, the Kaiser and Bethmann-Hollweg refused to authorise the "unrestricted" warfare for which Tirpitz was pressing. The old Admiral was incensed; indeed, he had been in a continuous rage ever since the outbreak of war. Even before the *Lusitania* was sunk he was complaining of the Kaiser's timidity, and Bethmann's flabby outlook. "Really it is hopeless," he wrote to a friend on March 22nd. "There's a fleet of forty armoured ships more than half super-dreadnoughts, and over 100 torpedo boats lying rusting in harbour,[1] while Germany is engaged in a struggle for her very existence, and I have to sit here, powerless. . . . In the navy, in the army, in politics, no co-operation, nearly everyone trying to keep one eye on the Kaiser, who is surrounded with weak people. . . ." And five days later: "I see only one way out: the Kaiser must give out that he is on the sick list for eight weeks or more, Hindenburg must come and take Bethmann's place, and take control of everything including the army and navy."[2]

Admiral Tirpitz won the support of the Crown Prince to the idea of making General von Hindenburg a "dictator," mainly because the Prince loathed Bethmann-Hollweg, but no doubt because he also saw an opportunity for himself if his father retired for several months. But Tirpitz soon learned that young William was a doubtful asset. His reputation among members of the military

[1] These figures were greatly exaggerated. [2] *My Memoirs*: Admiral Tirpitz.

hierarchy lay in shreds. Although His Royal Highness commanded an army group, everyone knew that his Chief of Staff did all the work, and that the Prince was pleasure-loving and woman-mad. " He often shocked soldiers returning from the front," writes his biographer, Klaus Jonas, " when he greeted them in his extravagant clothing, with a narrow riding whip in his hands, surrounded by Indian whippets. If now and then, in his white uniform, he threw them cigarettes, many of them indignantly thought that he had just come back from playing tennis. Whenever young French girls waved to him, he stopped his bright red car in the streets, picked them up and listened with a great deal of interest to their worries about their husbands or sweethearts. Often he promised to make inquiries for them at Supreme Headquarters, and by doing so he completely ruined his reputation at the German High Command."[1] Not only this, but the Crown Prince took one French woman after another for his mistress, and even moved into the house of a widow at Stenay. He tried to telegraph General Joffre to ask news of the lady's father, but the telegram was intercepted and sent to Bethmann-Hollweg, who protested angrily to the Prince that his irresponsible action might have enabled the Allies to make harmful propaganda.

Tirpitz's plan with the Crown Prince, therefore, did not get far, but he managed to win a good many recruits to the idea of unrestricted U-boat warfare. The Admiral who, in peacetime, had insisted that the building of the German Navy was not the cause of England's antagonism, now was unperturbed at the idea of bringing the United States into the conflict. He disapproved hotly of " kowtowing " to anyone, and was highly indignant at the conciliatory tone of the German note after the sinking of the *Lusitania*. " America is so shamelessly, so barefacedly pro-English," he wrote on July 25th, 1915, " that it is hard to credit that we shall eat humble pie. Yet in this connection I believe nothing to be impossible. A remark in the Note indicates that we have already made promises privately to limit the submarine activity. . . . I, for my part, will not join in a formal renunciation of the submarine warfare, whereby we should abandon the only weapon we have in our hands against England in the future."[2]

[1] *The Life of Crown Prince William :* Klaus Jonas.

[2] *My Memoirs :* Admiral Tirpitz.

Admiral Tirpitz managed to convince General Falkenhayn and Admiral Holtzendorff, the new naval Chief of Staff, of the necessity for submarine warfare. But Tirpitz got nowhere with his attempt to make Hindenburg Chancellor, and the Kaiser and Bethmann-Hollweg continued to block his submarine plans. Nevertheless, at the beginning of 1916 he succeeded in bringing the issue to the forefront once again. In January, Admiral Müller, as the Kaiser's personal adviser, found himself caught between a cross-fire of opinion. Bethmann-Hollweg told him that if Germany embarked on this type of warfare the neutrals would band together and launch a crusade depicting her as the "mad dog" among the civilised peoples of the world. Holtzendorff, on the other hand, insisted that England would be obliged to sue for peace within six months—and once England was knocked out American help would not be effective, no matter whether or not she declared war.

William II began to waver. On January 15th Müller wrote in his diary: "His Majesty took the humane standpoint that the drowning of innocent passengers was an idea that appalled him. He also bore a responsibiilty before God for the manner of waging war. On the other hand he must ask himself: could he go against the counsel of his military advisers, and from humane considerations prolong the war at the cost of so many brave men who were defending the Fatherland?"

The Kaiser finally reached a compromise. On March 6th he held a meeting in which it was decided to initiate submarine warfare against "armed merchantmen," and to study the effect on the neutrals before embarking in an all-out attempt to cut Britain off from vital supplies by sinking everything approaching her shores. Tirpitz was so disgusted that he handed in his resignation which was accepted. However, a few weeks later the passenger steamer *Sussex*, with a few Americans aboard, was torpedoed in the Channel; once again the United States threatened to break off relations, and once again Germany abandoned U-boat warfare.

The Kaiser's quarrel with Admiral Tirpitz did not create much stir, for on the whole the first eighteen months of the war were fairly satisfactory for Germany, and Berlin remained in the grip of optimism. "Our first demand in peace," wrote Professor Delbruck, "will be for a great colonial empire, a German India, big enough to defend itself in war, consisting of the Belgian and the French Congo and English tropical Africa. If that is not enough we can develop Turkey with capital and advice. . . ." Belgium, of course, would remain German, and many intellectuals were in favour of retaining northern France as well.

The Professor's sanguine outlook sprang from the fact that although Germany had not been able to deliver a decisive blow, neither had the Entente; and Germany had more than held her own in the feverish scramble for allies. In almost every case, participation in the struggle by uncommitted countries revolved around the question of material gain. In August 1914 Japan joined Britain and France and seized Germany's Far Eastern bases, but in October of the same year Turkey joined the Central Powers because of her enmity to Russia. Greece wobbled precariously but remained neutral. Italy joined the Allies in 1915 after months of cynical bargaining with both sides, finally settling for the huge territorial acquisitions promised by London at the expense of Austria, Turkey, and even (secretly) Serbia. Bulgaria, on the other hand, coveted Serbia and joined Germany.

Germany's policy throughout 1915 was to keep her armies in France on the defensive while the Allies drenched themselves in blood by launching gigantic and abortive offensives at Champagne, Artois, Ypres, and Loos.[1] Meanwhile, Falkenhayn sent reinforcements to the east, enabling Hindenburg and Ludendorff, now firmly entrenched as national heroes, to drive the Russians out of Poland, Lithuania, and Courland. Austria, the country which had been the most reckless in provoking the European war, had been partially over-run in 1914 both by Russia and Serbia; now Falkenhayn rid Galicia of the Russians, while Bulgaria, who entered the contest when the British failed to force the Dardanelles, smashed Serbia and Montenegro. This enabled Germany to establish rail communications with Turkey, and gave her mastery of the Balkans.

In 1916, however, Falkenhayn made a serious mistake. He believed that he could break the deadlock in the west by launching a prolonged offensive at Verdun, with such a concentration of artillery fire that the French Army, forbidden by pride to abandon the historic fortress, would be "bled white." Falkenhayn's forces would

[1] During 1915 the approximate total of dead, wounded, and captured was: French 1,300,000; German 600,000; British 400,000.

advance step by step under protection of cannon, exacting two or three lives for every German, until the enemy's will to resist was broken and a total collapse occurred.

The attack opened on February 21st and although the first and most terrible onslaught ended by the first of March, the battle continued, except for brief intervals, for nearly six months. But long before the autumn leaves had fallen it was apparent that Falkenhayn was unlikely to achieve his objective. Although the Allied losses were one and a half times as great as those of the Germans, French morale had weathered the Verdun storm and British soldiers had shown themselves unflinching on the Somme. 1916 ended with the number of dead, wounded, and captured exceeding a total of two million men: German 964,000; French 876,000; British 621,000.

Hindenburg and Ludendorff began to have doubts about Falkenhayn's plan as early as March, when the first shattering drive had spent itself. The Kaiser was deeply dejected. "One must not utter it," he confided to Admiral Müller on March 11th, "nor shall I admit it to Falkenhayn, but this war will not end with a great victory." The general public were slower to doubt, but by May rumours were sweeping Berlin that Verdun was a costly failure, and for the first time the public began to have gnawing doubts about Germany's ability to win the war. The sacrifices had been tremendous. The merciless grip of the British sea blockade had put the country on an austere rationing system from the early days of the struggle; the roll of killed, wounded, and missing mounted daily and by the middle of 1916 Germany's total losses approached two and a half million men. Were these terrible demands being made for nothing? An agonising reappraisal slowly forced itself upon the nation. The cold scrutiny of the public gaze centred on the Kaiser, and the imperial leadership, until now accepted with pride and confidence, began to be questioned with startling candour.

The criticism was overdue, for it would be difficult to imagine a great power governed in a more bizarre way than Germany during the war years. Although William II was the supreme authority of the State, civil as well as military, he did nothing to co-ordinate the nation's efforts or to impose any overall plan. The army had no inkling as to what the politicians were doing, while the Chancellor often learned of the army's plans by pure accident. "During my whole tenure," wrote Bethmann-Hollweg, "no kind of war council was held in which the political and military agreed the issue."

The Kaiser insisted that political matters were of secondary importance, and continued to try and foster the ridiculous impression that he was in command of his army. He had grown more restless than ever, and now the imperial train not only took him across Germany to military headquarters but to Cadinen for a look at his farm; to Homburg for rest-cures; to Potsdam to see the Empress. A steady flow of couriers pursued him around the countryside trying to get answers to urgent questions. Intermittently, almost fitfully, he held Crown Councils at Army Headquarters; but more often he informed the emissaries that he was "holding the matter in abeyance" or referred them to his Cabinet chiefs. The navy made the most urgent representations, for the fleet could not move without the Emperor's consent. Sometimes William took umbrage at these intrusions. Once, when the Commander-in-Chief of the Fleet asked permission to send a squadron into the Baltic to attack Russian shipping at Riga, he snapped back that he refused to concern himself with such details; the Baltic Commander could use his own initiative. "And yet," Müller wrote in his diary, "he insists that he himself is the Supreme Commander...."

But it was on the civilian front that the Emperor's omissions were most glaring. There were vital problems that needed careful thought and delicate handling: propaganda, diplomatic strategy *vis-à-vis* the neutrals, industrial co-ordination, finance, food, civilian morale. Yet William II, posturing childishly as a war lord, refused to spend any time in his capital. He talked contemptuously of "civilians" and referred scathingly to the Reichstag, which was becoming increasingly important as a sounding board of public opinion, as "that monkey-house." "I cannot understand," wrote Herr Ballin, the great ship-owner: to Admiral Müller on May 12, 1916, "why His Majesty does not send for men like Wangenheim and Count Schwerin-Lowitz etc. to see him at Headquarters and discuss their wishes and anxieties with him.[1] I cannot conceal from

[1] Wangenheim was the President of the Farmers' Union, and Count Schwerin-Lowitz President of the Prussian Chamber of Deputies; both men were Conservative members of the Reichstag.

you that the Kaiser's aloofness has had a very bad effect upon the nation.... I consider it essential in the interest of The All Highest that he should take a more active part in the leadership and a more personal interest, so that the people will refrain from questioning the usefulness of their Emperor. A communiqué from Headquarters that the Kaiser had received this or that high official in a long audience, that he had given a full report on the present situation, etc., would suffice to lead patriotic feelings back into the right channels and prevent them flowing unnaturally to Eastern Headquarters...."[1]

Admiral Müller repeated the contents of Ballin's letter to the Emperor. "Just as I was beginning to pick up again in health," the Sovereign protested. "He also pleaded," wrote Müller, "that Schloss Bellevue was not yet ready and that all the carpets had been removed etc. I spoke immediately to Gontard [Controller of the Royal Household] and ordered him to see that the castle was put in order overnight and to inform the Emperor forthwith."[1] William II finally said curtly that he would leave on the 19th "unless anything of military importance happened in the meantime."

William II did not understand that even in an autocracy power springs from the will, or at least the obedience, of the people. His authority had never been questioned, and he believed that the strength of Germany and the security of his dynasty emanated solely from the army. It never occurred to him that the war might be won in other ways as well: by outwitting the enemy in diplomacy, by inventiveness and cunning, by utilising the brains and energy of civilians. Nor did it occur to him that civilian anxieties could sap the vitality of his wonderful military machine. But even if he had understood all this, he would not have known how to gather the reins in his hands and direct a concentrated war effort. He had been born to his position, not struggled for it, and was scarcely aware of the reinforcements which kept it in place. It would have been impossible for him to break away from monarchical traditions, and suddenly to become accessible to men in all walks of life; to discard his autocratic paternalism, and to woo and convince his subjects as a politician might have done. Although he acceded to Admiral Müller's request and spent several days in Berlin, receiving important members of the Reichstag, he did not

[1] *The Kaiser and His Court:* Admiral von Müller.

seem to know what was expected of him, and made little impression on them.

Perhaps all that was needed was the application to formulate a policy, and the will to enforce it, but this was beyond the Emperor's capacity. He had never been able to resist the contagion of ideas. So he toyed long over decisions, often ending by taking them haphazardly on the advice of his subordinates. He was always looking for an escape from his anxieties and he derived much joy from the Battle of Skagerrak, known in England as the Battle of Jutland. This episode marked the principal encounter of the war between the British and German navies. The British Admiralty learned that the German High Seas Fleet was planning to leave harbour on a " fleet sally " and ordered Admiral Jellicoe to sail forth and engage it. The Admiral blundered and never managed to bring his super-dreadnoughts into serious action; as a result the Germans sank three British battle-cruisers, as well as three cruisers and eight smaller vessels, while the English destroyed only one German battle-cruiser, one old battleship, and nine smaller ships. Neither side lost any dreadnoughts, but the fact that the German Navy, with greatly inferior forces, had sunk a much larger tonnage than the British prompted well-justified jubilation inside Germany. "The spell of Trafalgar has been broken," the Kaiser declared at Wilhelmshaven. However, the event had little bearing on the course of the war.

Meanwhile in Berlin morale continued to decline. By the summer the news that Roumania would enter the war on the side of the Allies, hard on the heels of the appalling casualty lists stemming from Verdun, produced a dangerous frame of mind. " How badly we are led " became a universal cry and the Kaiser was condemned loudly for not making drastic changes. The Reichstag deputies demanded that Falkenhayn should be replaced by Hindenburg and Ludendorff, while the service chiefs attacked Bethmann-Hollweg for timidity and weakness. Although the Emperor was informed of the growing dissatisfaction, he refused to concern himself; when Bethmann asked to see him urgently he sent word that he was too busy. " Political questions are of no importance now."

He finally was prevailed upon to receive his Chancellor at Pless, and agreed to attend a meeting with his ministers in Berlin. The conference, however, was an utter failure, for the Kaiser refused to spare more than three-quarters of an hour for the session and monopolised the conversation with "stories of the harvesting at Pless, the birth of a zebu calf at Cadinen and the instructions he had given to Hindenburg." "The company was flabbergasted," wrote Müller. One of the Cabinet chiefs declared that in future the Kaiser should not be asked to make visits to Berlin; but Müller, who did not understand the material he was dealing with, insisted that the Sovereign must be forced to fulfil his duties. The Court Marshal, Freiherr von Reichach, tried to convince the Admiral "that if we wished to avoid the Kaiser's complete breakdown His Majesty must be allowed a long convalescence at Homburg," but Müller remained adamant. "I stood by my guns," he wrote, "and insisted that the Kaiser did not need any physical cure but that we must work on his temperament by giving him some responsible work to do to jolt him out of his lethargy. Soon after this," continued Müller, "I was given an audience by His Majesty and I must confess I was horrified to notice how worn and ill he looked. Violent and unpredictable, dominated by a single thought: 'Leave me in peace.' Occasionally this changed to: 'The Chancellor must make up his own mind.'"[1]

At the end of August Roumania entered the conflict, and Bethmann-Hollweg told William that he must dispense with Falkenhayn and appoint Hindenburg Chief of the General Staff and Ludendorff First Quartermaster-General. Otherwise the Chancellor could not guarantee "the dynasty." Although in some ways the Emperor was thankful to have strong hands take charge, he wept openly, for he could not bear the thought of being over-shadowed in the public eye by the great war leaders. When the announcement was made Bethmann tried to console him by pointing out the enthusiasm of the population, but William replied stonily: "I do not care." However Hindenburg managed to handle his imperial master with considerable tact for in October the Kaiser told Admiral Müller calmly that "he, the Supreme War Lord, was not for the moment the ruler. During the war he had to take a back seat. Hindenburg had said that politics had no place at Headquarters."[1]

Although for twenty-five years William II had posed as a warrior king, exciting his people with romantic references to "shining

[1] *The Kaiser and His Court*: Admiral von Müller.

armour" and "gleaming swords," this grim struggle was not at all what he had envisaged. He had thought of a short, sharp conflict ending with the German Kaiser leading his triumphant army through the Brandenburg Gate as his father and grandfather had done before him. Instead, the army scored successes but not victories, and the generals were pushing the Sovereign aside. Worst of all, he could not see an end to it. No matter what successes Germany had in the east, how was she to break the deadlock in the west? William II had spent most of the war fighting against a premonition of defeat. Now he eagerly encouraged the Chancellor to put out peace-feelers.

Bethmann-Hollweg and most of the Foreign Office had been in favour of a negotiated peace for many months. Indeed, the main reason that the Chancellor had installed Hindenburg as Chief of the Great General Staff was because he believed that the Field Marshal's stature and prestige were necessary to shield the monarchy against the criticism that might arise. He had told Hindenburg his plan, and the Field Marshal had given the Chancellor his tacit consent. However, Bethmann-Hollweg soon discovered that Ludendorff still believed fiercely in total victory and was exercising an ever-increasing influence over the old man; and the only peace that Ludendorff desired was a conqueror's peace.

Nevertheless William II stood by his Chancellor and encouraged him to make overtures to the Allies. "Such an initiative as this," he wrote to Bethmann-Hollweg on October 31st, 1916, "needs a Monarch whose conscience is awake, one who knows himself responsible to God, who acknowledges his duty to all men—even his enemies; a Monarch who feels no fear because his intentions may be misinterpreted; who has in him the will to deliver the world from its agony. I have the courage; I can dare this thing, with God. Quick, Mr. Chancellor. Submit me the notes. Make everything ready."

It was decided, however, that the peace move would have a better chance of success if it were not dispatched until after the defeat of Roumania. This did not take long. Roumania entered the war on the 28th of August, and by December 6th German and Austrian troops were marching into Bucharest. A week later the Chancellor forwarded a brief note to the enemy powers. The latest events, he said, showed that the resistance of the Central Powers was unbreakable; but since they did not seek to annihilate their opponents, they proposed negotiations. "They feel sure that the propositions which they would bring forward would serve as a basis for the restoration of a lasting peace. If, notwithstanding this offer of peace and conciliation, the struggle should continue, the four Allied powers [the Central Powers] are resolved to carry it on to the end, while solemnly disclaiming all responsibility before mankind and history." Ludendorff, however, drew up such a flamboyant army order, which was made public the same day, that Bethmann-Hollweg's note had little chance of success: "Soldiers! in the consciousness of victory which you have won, the rulers of the Allied States have made an offer of peace. We shall see if the object is achieved. Meanwhile you have with God's help to stand fast against the enemy and defeat him."

Mr. Lloyd George, who had overthrown Mr. Asquith as Prime Minister only a few days earlier, was not favourably impressed by Ludendorff's extravagant claims, nor even by Bethmann-Hollweg's self-confident assertions. "To enter into a conference," he told a large London audience, "on the invitation of Germany, proclaiming herself victorious, without any knowledge of the proposals she has to make, is to put our heads in a noose. . . . What hope is there in the Chancellor's speech that the arrogant spirit of the Prussian military caste will not be as dominant as ever if we patch up peace now?" Ten days later, on December 30th, the Allies sent a formal rejection.

Meanwhile President Wilson had stepped into the picture. Before Germany received the Allied reply, he requested the belligerents to announce the terms on which they thought the war could be ended. Germany did not comply at once, but the Allies sent a blustering note which could only mean war to the bitter end; the return of Alsace-Lorraine, the dissolution of Austria, the partition of Turkey, the cessation to Russia of Austrian and German Poland. At the end there was an attempt to drive a wedge between the German people and their leaders. "There is no need to say that if the Allies desire to shield Europe from the covetous brutality of Prussian militarism, the extermination and the political disappearance of the German people have never formed part of their design." President Wilson was shocked by the Allied note. For months he had been talking about moderation and "peace without victory," and London's only response was a series of impossible demands. On January 6th, 1917, the American Ambassador to Germany, Mr. Gerard, was instructed to give the Allies a rap over the knuckles. "Our relations have never been better," he told the American Chamber of Commerce in Berlin, "and their continuance is guaranteed so long as men like Bethmann-Hollweg, Helfferich, and Zimmermann, Hindenburg and Ludendorff remain."[1]

Here was Germany's golden opportunity, but neither the Kaiser nor the Chancellor, neither diplomats nor deputies nor service chiefs, were shrewd enough to see it, much less to grasp it. President Wilson wished to bring the war to an end, and the United States was the only power in a position to exercise influence on Britain. Britain could not continue to fight without the food and munitions flowing across the Atlantic. If the Germans had responded to Wilson's invitation, and sent reasonable peace terms, the President would have put pressure on England to enter into negotiations; and England could not have refused. "There was one mistake in diplomacy that, if it had been made, would have been fatal to the cause of the Allies," wrote Sir Edward Grey in his memoirs. "It was carefully avoided. The cardinal mistake would have been a breach with the United States, not necessarily a rupture, but a state of things that would have provoked American interference with the blockade, or led to an embargo on exports of munitions from the United States. Germany on the other hand did make this cardinal mistake."[2]

The reason that the Kaiser and Bethmann-Hollweg failed to grasp the significance of Wilson's intervention was because they looked upon the American President as "pro-English." He had done nothing more than censure Britain when she insisted upon a total blockade and refused to allow foodstuffs to reach Germany in flagrant violation of the Declaration of London. Ludendorff, on the other hand, was strongly opposed to a negotiated peace, and not in the least afraid of bringing America into the war. He still had a burning faith that German arms would triumph, and alluded to the almost non-existent American army with derision. He made great play of the Allied rejection of Bethmann's peace-feelers, referring to it as "a contemptuous rebuff." After Lloyd George's speech he

[1] *My Four Years in Germany:* James Gerard.
[2] *Twenty-five Years:* Viscount Grey of Fallodon.

telegraphed the Kaiser urging him to sanction submarine warfare without delay.

Although William II stubbornly had opposed the suggestion for eighteen months, he now felt the ground cut from under his feet. He dreaded bringing more neutrals into the war, yet he could see no alternative. His navy was so confident of results it assured him that England would be brought to the peace table by the summer. Lastly, and perhaps most decisive, he feared running into a headlong clash with Hindenburg and Ludendorff. So he did what he had often done before; instead of insisting that the political views should be put strongly to the military, he avoided an encounter by "suddenly coming round to the idea." "He is definitely in favour of it," wrote Müller on January 5th, "even if the Chancellor is opposed to it. He voiced the very curious viewpoint that the U-boat question was a purely military affair which did not concern the Chancellor in any way."[1]

What were the arguments in favour of the U-boats? The British blockade had been tightly maintained for over two years and the cumulative effect was producing widespread suffering among the civilian population. The winter of 1916–17 was known as "the *ruben* winter" for there was almost nothing to eat but swedes, and bread riots had become a common occurrence. "We are all gaunt and bony now," wrote the English-born Princess Blücher, "and have dark shadows around our eyes, and our thoughts are chiefly taken up with wondering what our next meal will be. . . ."

The hunger was bad enough, but the bitterly cold weather increased the misery. There was no coal to be had, and "a perfect epidemic of burst water pipes all over Berlin." "And as there are no plumbers to repair the damage," wrote the Princess, "people are beginning to think that the torments of Dante's inferno are capped by the hardships of this deadly winter. . . . There are practically no motors to be had, and the few antediluvian droshkies are being dragged wearily along by half-starved beasts who, if they happen to fall, don't even attempt to rise, but lie still, humbly grateful for the respite from work on the cold, frozen ground. As for the mood of the people the heroic attitude has entirely disappeared. Now one sees faces like masks, blue with cold and drawn by hunger, with the harassed

[1] *The Kaiser and His Court:* Admiral von Müller.

expression common to all those who are continually speculating about the possibility of another meal."[1]

Hindenburg believed that unless measures were taken to strike against the hated English, he would not be able to maintain the morale of his army. Furthermore, the navy had convinced him that the submarine was a winning card. Britain imported nearly seventy per cent of her food, and as she already was on strict rationing, the German Admiralty estimated that if they sank even twenty-five per cent of the merchant ships supplying her needs, they would bring her to starvation point in a few months. As the United States scarcely possessed an army it would take at least eighteen months for the Americans to assemble, train, and equip sufficient soldiers to be of use, and by that time the war would be over; furthermore, if Germany sank the shipping how would America get her troops across the Atlantic?

The critical decision was taken at a Crown Council held at Pless on January 9th. Those present were the Emperor, the Chancellor, Hindenburg and Ludendorff, and the three Cabinet chiefs. The Chancellor and Rudolf von Valentini, the Civil Chief, were the only two opposed to the submarine campaign. But Admiral Müller tells us that although Bethmann-Hollweg was "agitated and depressed" he did not defend his convictions. "... The crux of the Chancellor's speech," wrote Müller, "was that in view of the opinions of the General Staff and the Admiralty he could not oppose unrestricted U-boat warfare.... Holtzendorff then spoke very enthusiastically on the subject, and was followed by the Field Marshal who stated that the soldier in the trenches was waiting for the U-boat war.... Then His Majesty replied, giving statistics of corn and shipping markets from a newspaper article by Newman, very much in favour of unrestricted U-boat warfare, and upon this signed the decree laid before him. He remarked in passing that he expected a declaration of war from America. If it came—and the Chancellor should if necessary make concessions to American passenger liners to avoid it—so much the better...."[2]

President Wilson did not know of the German decision to start U-boat warfare on February 1st, and on January 22nd made a

[1] *An English Wife in Berlin:* Princess Blücher.

[2] *The Kaiser and His Court:* Admiral von Müller.

speech to the Senate emphasising his belief in " peace without victory " and stressing the rights of " self-determination," ideas which were to form the basis of his famous Fourteen Points. Four days later he sent a message to the belligerents offering to act as a mediator. Meanwhile the German Ambassador in Washington, Count Bernstorff, like many other German Ambassadors before him, was frantic. He had been instructed by the Wilhelmstrasse to inform the President of the resolve to begin unrestricted U-boat warfare. He sent agitated telegrams begging for a postponement. " Wilson thinks the Entente terms impossible . . . if we only have confidence in him, the President is convinced that he could bring about both peace conferences. . . . If submarine war is now begun without further ado, the President would regard this as a further slap in the face, and war with the United States is inevitable. . . . On the other hand, if we accept Wilson's proposal and plans come to grief on the obstinacy of our opponents, it will become very difficult for the President to enter the war against us even if we then begin unrestricted submarine war. . . . What is in question, is, therefore, only a postponement of short duration."

Nevertheless, Wilson's services were scorned. German writers frequently declare that since 21 U-boats had already gone to their stations, the offer came too late. This is a foolish argument, for Germany was to send 200 U-boats into the seas to take part in the operation. It would have been perfectly easy to inform the President that the 21 submarines had been dispatched before his offer had been received, and would be recalled as quickly as possible. But William II had deserted Bethmann-Hollweg and thrown in his lot with the military in order to avoid a crisis; and the military did not want peace but victory. Surely this of all moments was the time for a Crown Council, where the political considerations at least could have been placed before the High Command.

If the Kaiser had rescinded the submarine decree at the eleventh hour would his throne have been in danger? He would have had the Chancellor and the Foreign Office with him, and judging from reports on the temper of his people, not only would have commanded wide popular support among the civilian population but ordinary soldiers as well. Furthermore, the army was an imperial institution; and Field Marshal von Hindenburg, like every member of the Officer Corps, was a fervent supporter of the monarchical principle. It would have been unthinkable for the High Command to remove the dynasty: and who was there to replace William II? Not the Crown Prince, for he had put himself beyond the pale by his feckless behaviour and amorous proclivities. There is little doubt, therefore, but what the Sovereign's will would have prevailed. It was the Kaiser's tragedy that he always succumbed to the loudest voice; and it was Germany's tragedy that she never knew when to strike a bargain. "If she had accepted the Wilson policy," wrote Sir Edward Grey after the war, ". . . the allies could not have refused. They were dependent on American supplies; they could not have risked the ill-will of the Government of the United States, still less a *rapprochement* between the United States and Germany."[1]

Instead, the Kaiser approved Secretary of State Zimmermann's reply: "Delay impracticable." "The Kaiser thinks," wrote Müller, "that Wilson only asked for a postponement in the interest of England, knowing of the hardship resulting from her serious food shortage. He is confirmed in his view by a letter received to-day from the Hamburg corn merchant Newman to his aide . . . who had shown it to His Majesty."

Thus William II took the most crucial decision of the war. Like a drowning man Bethmann-Hollweg sent Germany's peace aims to Washington for the private information of the President. They were fairly moderate, promising to restore occupied territory, but insisting on "colonial territory commensurate with Germany's population and economic interest," and compensation for damage to "German undertakings." However when the German Ambassador informed Wilson that the U-boat campaign would begin on the following day, the President no longer was interested. He broke off diplomatic relations with Germany, and two months later America entered the war.[2]

[1] *Twenty-five Years:* Viscount Grey of Fallodon.

[2] It was not only "freedom of the seas" that pushed America into the war. The British Secret Service managed to get hold of a document revealing the attempt of Herr Zimmermann, the German Foreign Secretary, to secure an alliance with Mexico, in the event of the United States and Germany going to war; as inducements he was offering Mexico Texas, Arizona, and New Mexico. This document, which also mentioned the possibilities of persuading Japan to take action against the United States, was published by the American Government on March 1st.

17. *King of Prussia*

The Kaiser realised too late that by failing to support his Chancellor over the U-boat war he had weakened his hand still further with the army. He became consumed with anxiety about his own position, for General Ludendorff drove the lesson home by treating him in a patronising manner that was entirely new to him. In February, when William II was at the New Palace, and the High Command visited Berlin, Ludendorff informed His Majesty that Field Marshal von Hindenburg would not be able to spare the time to make daily trips to Potsdam to report to him. The Kaiser suggested that Ludendorff come instead, but the latter replied that he, also, was "too busy." Finally it was agreed that a staff officer would make the journey.

William's perturbation increased when he learned that an "anti-Chancellor" meeting had taken place at the Hotel Adlon, organised by big industrialists who claimed that they had the support of the High Command. It was perfectly true that the generals had no use for Bethmann-Hollweg. Although the Chancellor had been instrumental in persuading the Kaiser to give Hindenburg and Ludendorff control of the army, they branded him as a defeatist. The fact that he had not even summoned sufficient spirit to resign on the submarine war only increased their contempt and strengthened their determination to get rid of him at the earliest opportunity. "I prefer a man with a little more strength," Hindenburg remarked.

William II feared that Ludendorff was trying to impose Tirpitz on him as Chancellor, and told his entourage excitedly that he would never give his consent. "His Majesty is very angry at the treacherous baiting of the Chancellor which he sees as a threat to the right of monarchs to choose their own ministers. . . ." Yet he still declined to take charge of the home front, still clung to military headquarters. Although he knew that his role as Supreme Commander was illusory, he did not know that his subjects knew it, fondly

17

imagining that the public looked upon him as a great war lord. This was far from the case, for by January 1917 criticism of the Sovereign had swollen to new proportions. "I think people in England hardly realise the covert scorn with which people speak of him here," wrote Princess Blücher. "The remarks often made astonish me. 'Let him talk as if he had won these victories, and let him believe he is running the whole army.' 'Send him to the East where there are some prisoners to march past and he will be pleased; and again to the West when there is a little success to show him and he will be as pleased as ever.' "[1]

The Kaiser was so pitifully inadequate that he verges on tragedy. Although as a Prussian prince he had been taught that in time of war his duty lay with his soldiers, the fundamental truth was that the army, no matter how high-handed, offered him a haven, cushioning him against the problems of the outside world. He had no real faith in the U-boat campaign. Indeed he had no real faith that Germany could win the war. He struggled bravely against his defeatism but lacked any conception of what was required of him. In place of the leadership that was demanded, all he could give was showmanship.

Yet he presented a paradox, for he clung feverishly to every scrap of power, refusing to delegate the authority rusting under his control and bewailing any infringement of the imperial prerogative. Admiral Tirpitz put his finger on the Sovereign's dilemma when he wrote that "His Majesty prays for a release by the shifting of his responsibilities to others: then he comes up against the wall with which he has surrounded himself, and against his self-conceit."[2]

The Kaiser's advisers marvelled at his lonely isolation. However, he showed no desire to shed his dynastic personality, or to lower the barriers that made intimacy impossible. The only visible change in him was his dependence on the Kaiserin. The Empress devoted herself tirelessly to works of charity and displayed a strength of character that seemed to breathe confidence into William II when he was with her. In March 1917 he came more nearly to breaking point than at any time in the two and a half years of war, and retreated to his castle at Homburg where the Empress joined him. Despite the protests of the Cabinet chiefs he refused to move

[1] *An English Wife in Berlin*: Princess Blücher.

[2] *Memoirs*: Admiral von Tirpitz.

for a month. It was here that he heard the stupendous news that a revolution had broken out in Russia and that the Czar had been forced to abdicate. He was too dejected to rejoice, and put the most pessimistic interpretation on it. "His Majesty is convinced that this will prolong the war because it was engineered by the Entente and England in particular," wrote Müller. For several months no one knew what to make of the situation. The new Russian Government was a coalition of Conservatives, Liberals, and Socialists, and also included the first Soviet, a committee of workers and soldiers. The Conservative Prince Lvov was Prime Minister and the Socialist Kerensky Minister of Justice. Gradually it emerged that the Government intended carrying on the war, and was planning a new offensive in the direction of Lemburg.

Meanwhile on April 3rd the new Emperor of Austria arrived at Homburg, accompanied by his Foreign Secretary, Count Czernin. Old Franz Joseph had died in November 1916, and had been succeeded by the Archduke Karl, a nephew of Franz Ferdinand whose assassination had sparked off the holocaust. This young man had no stomach for the war, and told William II bluntly that Austria was on its last legs and could not hold out beyond the autumn; that if peace negotiations revolved around the cession of Alsace-Lorraine to the French, Austria would balance the German sacrifice by ceding Galicia to the part of Poland that would come under German jurisdiction. The Kaiser, however, replied that as the Allies had rejected his offer of negotiations in December there was nothing he could do. "I long for peace," he told Czernin, "but I cannot beg for it." Czernin prophesied to Müller that unless the war ended within three months the people would end it without their governments. "I can't have a wager with you," he said to the Admiral, "because should this happen it will be impossible to pay the bet."

Count Czernin's hint of revolutionary action was not entirely a flight of fancy. In January one of Germany's socialist deputies had shouted out to the Reichstag: "The people don't want war; what they want is peace and bread and work;" in February and March there were food riots and scuffles with the police in which people were killed; and in April a protest strike of half a million men in Berlin. Behind the agitation there was mounting resentment of the Junkers whose estates cushioned them against starvation. Even soldiers returning from the front complained of the superior food given to officers. "Everywhere," wrote Princess Blücher, "you hear it murmured: 'We are forced to keep silent now: but wait until after the war is over then our turn will come.'" The fact that America entered the world struggle on April 6th was scarcely noticed.

The Kaiser was disconcerted by Czernin's statements, and on April 5th told Müller that the people "must be given assurance of His Majesty's liberal sentiments." He intended to announce a reform of the Prussian Lower Chamber without delay. This body was elected by a three-tiered voting system which always enabled the largest tax-payers—or the richest men—to elect a majority. A plan of reform, said the Kaiser, had been drawn up some years before, and was favoured by Bethmann-Hollweg. Three days later, on Easter Sunday, April 8th, the Kaiser announced his concessions as "an Easter egg" to his people, and told them that they would come into effect at the end of the war.

This gesture, however, did little to raise morale, and throughout May and June the Emperor's advisers begged him to take up residence in Berlin. By this time even the navy had become disillusioned about the submarine campaign, for England had introduced a convoy system that seemed to be triumphing over the torpedo attacks. On June 20th, Herr Ballin wrote Müller a despairing letter in which "he cursed the Chancellor for weakening on the question of unrestricted U-boat warfare, cursed Holtzendorff who, by waging this type of warfare, had alienated more and more of the neutrals, cursed Helffrich who could not get away from the shipping compensation law, and finally cursed the Kaiser who was always in Cloud Cuckoo Land. . . ." A week later William II continued to insist that his place was at the front, and assailed Müller for having "twice forced him" to visit the capital. "And what did we get out of it? He had no intention of going to that —— place again. When I replied that everyone in Berlin was very gratified by his visit he merely said: 'Not a soul is grateful to me.'"[1]

But in the end he gave in, and agreed to arrive in Berlin on July 7th. As chance would have it, this turned out to be the day after the Catholic Reichstag deputy, Erzberger, had made a sensational speech to his Centre Party behind closed doors. Erzberger had got hold of the despairing memorandum which Count Czernin had

[1] *The Kaiser and His Court:* Admiral von Müller.

sent to the Kaiser upon his return to Austria, and he read it out to his Committee. " Our military resources," said Czernin, " are coming to an end. We must begin negotiations before our enemies are fully conscious of our exhaustion. Another winter campaign is absolutely out of the question. The basis of my argument is the danger of revolution. The burden on our people is intolerable. The bow is so taut that it may snap at any moment. It is no good telling me that the monarchical idea is too firmly rooted in Berlin and Vienna for the monarchy to be overthrown. This war has no precedent. If the monarchs do not make peace in the next few months their people will make it over their heads, and then the waves of revolution will sweep over everything for which our sons are fighting to-day."

It was obvious that there was no hope of peace unless a policy of " no annexations " was proclaimed. For months the Social Democrats had been advocating this course, and the fact that Erzberger, a bourgeois deputy, now was prepared to forgo all conquests had a profound effect on the Reichstag. It also made a deep impression on Hindenburg and Ludendorff, who decided that the defeatists were getting dangerously out of hand. They blamed Bethmann-Hollweg for not maintaining a tighter control; first the democratisation of the Prussian Lower House and now this. They decided that only drastic action could save the situation, hurried to Berlin and informed the Kaiser that unless he dismissed his Chancellor they would hand in their resignations. William II had no choice but to comply. He told Müller indignantly that " this behaviour on the part of Prussian generals had never been heard of before in the history of Prussia."

He was so piqued by the audacity of his High Command that he refused to take any interest in the selection of a new Chancellor. It did not much matter who was chosen, anyway, as it was obvious to the Sovereign's advisers that from now on pressure from the generals would decide important issues. The Kaiser's Cabinet chiefs spent several hours thumbing through the Gotha Almanack and the Official Directory looking for a suitable candidate. But there seemed to be no one talented enough to please everyone and at the same time innocuous enough to avoid offence. They were in despair when General Plessen, the Kaiser's Adjutant-General, burst into the room and suggested Michaelis, who was not even an imperial minister, only a Prussian minister in charge of agriculture. The Cabinet chiefs were relieved, and presented his name to the Kaiser who observed laconically that he was " a rather insignificant little man," but at the same time assented. He was so insignificant, however, that in three months' time everyone agreed that he would not do, and the seventy-three-year-old Count Hertling, Minister-President of Bavaria, was appointed in his place

Michaelis did not stem the tide that Erzberger had set in motion. On July 19th the Reichstag passed a " Peace Resolution," renouncing all conquests, by 212 votes to 126. However, by this time the opinions of the Reichstag had ceased to be of much importance.

" The Kaiser is daily growing more and more the shadow of a king," wrote Princess Blücher in July 1917, " and people talk openly of his abdication. . . ." " He is out in the cold," wrote Müller, " not because he has abandoned his rights but because he has failed in his duty." Duty was not the right word, for the Kaiser had given every scrap of his nervous energy to the war. He simply was unequal to the task. Field Marshal von Hindenburg had not " imprisoned " him, as many people suggested, but merely stepped into a perilous gap. There could be no intermediary course. Either peace must be made or the war prosecuted with the utmost vigour. The Kaiser's inability to make up his mind, and throw his weight firmly on one side or the other, had brought Germany to a dangerous pass, and Hindenburg, in seizing the initiative, had done the only thing possible. As he was a loyal monarchist, he had no intention of replacing the Kaiser, but had felt it essential to grasp the helm of a foundering ship.

Although William II chafed at the impudence of his generals he experienced a sense of deep relief. A few weeks earlier he had been in such a state of agitation that Müller had consulted the Staff Physician and asked if His Majesty should be treated with greater consideration. Niedener had replied in the affirmative, warning the Admiral that " there was the possibility of a complete breakdown for this highly nervous man of whom before the war we had all entertained an entirely false impression. It would have been a different matter had he worked, but this he never did. . . ."

The breakdown came in July, but in a different form than that which the doctor had envisaged. Once Hindenburg had taken matters into his own hands the Kaiser stopped fretting and escaped into a world of fantasy. From July 22nd 1917 to July 22nd 1918 he was more cheerful and composed than at any time in the war. He no longer lived with the nightmare of defeat, for he refused to contemplate the scene as a whole. The fact that the British convoy system was beating the U-boat war, that American reinforcements would be arriving within twelve months, that the deadlock on the western front appeared unbreakable, no longer tormented him. Instead he ignored the overall picture and concentrated on the victories of the German Army in the east.

His jubilation began with the news of Germany's midsummer offensive against Russia which was to lead to the latter's final defeat. "His Majesty," wrote Müller on July 22nd, "is once more in his well-known, impossible victory mood." From then on the Kaiser lived in a whirl of intoxicating pretension. He visited the scenes of Germany's successful battles, Tarnopol and Courland, and once again began to make bold speeches. "Where my bayonets are on guard the land will under no circumstances be returned." In September he visited Roumania; in October Bulgaria and Turkey; in November the north of Italy. He told his Chancellor, Count Hertling, that he was so enchanted with Roumania that he intended to keep it after the war. And when Müller referred to the Reichstag's Peace Resolution with its emphasis on no annexations he replied: "It couldn't matter less. The Reichstag can do what it likes. I have the nation and the army behind me and Michaelis has the revolver, my final decree, in his pocket."

Underneath the surface there was a steady buzz of peace talk. The Reichstag Peace Resolution had induced the Pope to try to bring the belligerents to the conference table, and in August he sent his Nuncio, Pacelli, to Berlin. But the Germans refused to state precise terms and the Entente showed no eagerness to enter discussions. Herr Kühlmann, who had succeeded Zimmermann as Foreign Secretary in the spring of 1917, put out feelers of his own, and tried to establish contact in Paris and London, but each time he came up against the stone wall of French *revanche*. France insisted on the restoration of Alsace-Lorraine, while Germany insisted on the integrity of her Empire. In October Kulhmann said bitterly: "The quarrel for which Europe is gradually being transformed into a rubbish heap is the future of Alsace-Lorraine."

The Kaiser, however, had lost interest in the peace moves. At the end of October the Italians suffered a stunning defeat at Caporetto at the hands of the great German General von Mackensen, which practically knocked them out of the war. And far more significant, in November the Bolshevists overthrew Kerensky (who had succeeded Prince Lvov as President in July) and declared Russia's intention to withdraw from the war. Negotiations opened at Brest-Litovsk on December 22nd.

Signs of softening on the part of the Allies were ignored by the Kaiser. The French and British had suffered enormous casualties during the year 1917. In the spring they once again had tried to achieve a breakthrough by launching huge offensives, the British at Arras and the French between Soissons and Champagne. Although the Canadians had taken Vimy Ridge, the French had suffered one of their heaviest defeats at Chemins des Dames. The number of wounded had been so great the field dressing stations could not cope with them and mutiny broke out in ten divisions. By the close of the year, after more fighting at Paschendaele and Cambrai, French and British casualties numbered nearly 1,400,000 men compared with Germany's 850,000. And no decisive result had been achieved.

At the end of November Lord Lansdowne, the former British Foreign Secretary, who had been responsible for forging the Entente, wrote a letter to the *Daily Telegraph*. "We are not going to lose this war; but its prolongation will spell ruin for the civilised world . . . what will be the value of the blessings of peace to nations so exhausted that they can scarcely stretch out a hand with which to grasp them? If the war is to be brought to a close in time to avert a world-wide catastrophe, it will be because on both sides people realise that it has already lasted too long." And in January President Wilson outlined his fourteen points, which stressed freedom and self-determination for all people, and seemed to suggest a basis of negotiation.

But while these speeches were being made the Germans and Austrians were parleying with the Russians. Although the talks opened on the acceptance of "no annexations and no indemnities," the Germans suddenly announced that Poland, Lithuania, Courland, parts of Estonia and Latvia, desired separation from Russia under German protection. Trotsky protested, and asked for a plebiscite, but the Germans answered by breaking off the talks and advancing towards Petrograd. Trotsky capitulated and peace was signed on March 3rd. At the same time a separate peace was concluded with the Ukraine and Roumania.

Although the Kaiser had retired to Homburg at the end of January, and refused to move for six weeks to the disgust of his advisers, he lived in his dream world poring over reports and press cuttings with great excitement. " Very disagreeable outbursts of megalomania," wrote Müller on February 20th, " which always ensue when things are going well for us."[1] When the Kaiser was asked by the newspaper *Kölnische Zeitung* whether a plebiscite would be held in Courland he replied proudly: " I will take the Duchy of Courland, I, the victor by the strength of my sword, but not from the hand of the assembly."

The climax of the first world war came in the spring and early summer of 1918 when Hindenburg and Ludendorff hurled four thunderbolts at the Allied lines in a last desperate attempt to secure a decisive victory. Now that peace had been signed with Russia they were able to transfer 1,000,000 men and 3,000 guns to the western front. The first offensive opened in March on the St. Quentin sector of the British line, and the initial battle, in which the Germans outnumbered their opponents three to one, resulted in the capture of 90,000 British soldiers and 1,300 guns.[2] The Kaiser was at Hindenburg's Headquarters at Avesnes when the first news came in; and upon his return that night on the imperial train to Charleville he was so excited that he shouted to the guard on the platform: " The battle is won, the English have been utterly defeated." The fighting continued for some days and the Emperor visited von Hindenburg's headquarters each morning. He took such childish delight in the victory that the Field Marshal issued a communiqué beginning: " Under the personal command of His Majesty the Emperor . . ." This caused the *Kölnische Zeitung* to refer to " the Kaiser's Battle," which upset the Emperor for he protested to Herr Berg that it made it seem as though none of the other battles had had anything to do with him.

[1] *The Kaiser and His Court:* Admiral von Müller.

[2] The Germans also captured 2,000,000 bottles of whisky.

However, Ludendorff did not achieve his objective. The British Army, described at German Headquarters as "lions led by donkeys," put up a furious resistance; this tenacity, coupled with the general exhaustion of the German soldiers, finally brought the drive to a halt. A second attack against the British front at Armentières in April, designed to reach the Channel ports, also failed after bitter fighting for the same reasons. The third German offensive was launched against the French at Soissons in May. The town was captured, and in three days the Germans advanced thirty miles and crossed the Marne near Château Thierry. Five British divisions, who were supposed to be refitting and recuperating, were caught up in the fighting and displayed almost incredible valour. The Kaiser visited the sector where the English were engaged in the opening days of the battle. He was in high spirits, but at lunch, wrote Müller, "spoke very harshly of the brutality of our men, who made no effort to help badly wounded English soldiers, although right in their path. He had seen to it personally that they were bandaged and carried down the line." However, the German troops were so underfed and weary that they could barely look after their own wounded, much less the enemy. Their poor physical stamina prevented them from exploiting their initial success, and once again their offensive petered out.

Meanwhile the news from Austria was chilling. In June the Emperor Karl's army struck against the Italians on the Piave. They crossed the river but floods destroyed the bridges and 100,000 Austrian soldiers were drowned or captured. This disaster, coupled with the fact that no matter how many battles were won, none were decisive, produced a sobering effect on the German Foreign Office. On June 25th Herr Kühlmann delivered a speech to the Reichstag in which he said that although the integrity of the German Empire was a basic condition of peace, "a conclusion by military decision without diplomatic negotiations is improbable. . . . The eye therefore must seek for political factors, which might eventually open possibilities. . . ."[1] Kühlmann's statement was nothing less than a blunt announcement that the German Army could not win the war, and that peace would have to be negotiated. "It has fallen like a bomb," wrote Princess Blücher. "Everyone seems to agree that what he has said is the truth, and nothing but the truth,

[1] *The Kaiser and His Court:* Admiral von Müller.

but that it was a heinous offence to say it."[1] Up till now the population had been willing to put up with appalling hardships for the sake of ultimate victory. But if Germany was spilling its blood for nothing, why was the carnage not brought to an end? Conditions in Berlin were almost as bad as in the winter of 1916–17. "We ourselves have little to eat but smoked meat and dried peas and beans, but in the towns they are considerably worse off," wrote Princess Blücher. "The potatoes have come to a premature end, and in Berlin the population have now a portion of 1 lb. per head a week, and even these are bad. The cold winds of this wintry June have retarded the growth of vegetables, and there is almost nothing to be had. We are all waiting hungrily for the harvest and the prospect of at least more bread and flour."[1]

General Ludendorff was so angry at Kühlmann's speech that he persuaded the Kaiser to dismiss him, and to appoint Herr Hintze in his place. Ludendorff then turned his attention to his fourth and greatest attack which was under preparation and would be launched in the middle of July in the vicinity of Rheims. "If my offensive at Rheims succeeds," he observed, "we have won the war." "If the German offensive at Rheims succeeds," said Marshal Foch, "the Germans have won the war." The attack opened on July 15th with a barrage from 8,000 guns. It was the largest bombardment of the war, but it was too late. Half a million Americans had landed in France in April, May, and June, and the Entente now had the reserves they needed to pit against German soldiers almost at the end of their resources. Within a week the Allies had stopped the giant attack, and the Kaiser's world of illusion, which had lasted one year to the day, finally broke into pieces. Müller's diary gives a laconic account of His Majesty's reaction. "July 22, 1918. This afternoon the Kaiser drove over to Avesnes to hear a report. He was told the bitter truth which conflicts with the optimistic communiqués. The Field Marshal admitted total failure . . . we left Bosmont late in the evening for Spa. After dinner His Majesty spoke of himself to a small circle . . . as a defeated War Lord for whom we must show consideration. . . . July 23, 1918. After lunch in the train the Kaiser admitted that he had not closed an eye all night. He had seen visions of all the English and Russian relatives and all the ministers and generals of his own reign marching past

[1] *An English Wife in Berlin:* Princess Blücher.

and mocking him. Only the little Queen of Norway had been friendly to him. . . ."[1]

During the last week in July, General Foch launched a long-prepared counter-offensive, and started an advance that was not to stop until Germany laid down its arms four months later. The Marne was crossed once again and Soissons recaptured. On August 8th a combined Franco-British attack supported by several hundred tanks—used for the first time in large numbers—broke the spirit of the German defence. It seems incredible to-day that anyone could have expected troops to stand up against tanks, but Ludendorff lamented the loss of morale and named August 8th " the black day of the German Army." " Disastrous day on the Somme," wrote Müller. " The French, British and Canadians have broken through our front to a depth of 12km. The Kaiser was very low in spirits this evening. He said: ' It's very strange that our men cannot get used to tanks.' "

Privately Hindenburg and Ludendorff faced reality. Two days later they left the Kaiser in no doubt about the gravity of the situation. " Naturally," William II replied calmly, " things cannot go on like this indefinitely and we must find a way to end it all." On September 13th a meeting was held at Great Headquarters—which were now at Spa in Belgium—attended by the Kaiser, the Crown Prince, the Chancellor, and Foreign Secretary Hintze. The Kaiser favoured the communication of German conditions through the Queen of Holland, and Chancellor Hertling was given permission to act when he saw fit, though it was generally agreed that it would be best to wait until the Allied offensive had died down. Apparently the Emperor believed that he had some weeks in hand, for he suggested setting up a Commission of Propaganda for " reducing the enemy's confidence and enhancing that of the German people." His proposal came to nothing, for the war was nearly over; but it is interesting to notice that only now, when the German Army was facing defeat, did he begin to understand that power could reside somewhere else than with the military.

The armistice did not come for another two months, but everyone at the meeting in Spa knew that Germany was doomed. What did the Kaiser do during these days so crucial for the fate of his

[1] *The Kaiser and His Court*: Admiral von Müller.

country? He retired to his private castle at Wilhelmshöhe near Kiel "to await the holding up of the enemy." The Empress had suffered a mild heart attack, and William II seized the excuse to remain three weeks at Wilhelmshöhe pursuing mild diversions. "We behave here as though nothing had happened," Müller wrote acidly on August 20th. "For example this afternoon we set out in five cars to visit a picture gallery at Kassel . . . ;" and on the 24th: "This evening Gontard brought the Kaiser a pencil sketch which had been found in the castle and was thought to be the Kaiser's work, although in actual fact it was by an Italian seascape painter Marino, now living in London. His Majesty commented: 'You know, if I had that man's talents I should have been a seascape painter and not an Emperor and I shouldn't be in such a horrifying position to-day.'"

The Kaiser recognised the position as horrifying; he knew that the end was approaching but he could not bring himself to initiate the moves that would bring his world crashing around his head; so the war proceeded, and the slaughter continued. Meanwhile Princess Blücher was writing in her diary: "The whole political situation is so perilous at the moment that everyone feels something momentous must be going to take place. . . . Capitalists and large landowners are beginning to talk in earnest about their land being confiscated and their property divided up in the Bolshevik manner. The whole public spirit is so depressed and the universal suffering so great that the people are threatening to take matters into their own hands. . . . Wounded men refuse to consent to operations which might heal an injured limb, on the ground that they would then be sent back to the front, and they have no intention of going there."[1]

The Empress was rapidly improving but after eight days at Wilhelmshöhe the Emperor complained of the state of his own health and summoned Dr. Kraus for consultation. His advisers knew their imperial master so well that they warned Kraus beforehand that if he found nothing wrong with the Emperor to say so with great firmness. But Kraus slipped up, for in answer to a question from the Kaiser he said that it would be a good thing if His Majesty was to supervise the diet and prescriptions given by the doctors to the Empress. "And this was distorted to mean that His Majesty must remain with the Empress. And out there on the

[1] *An English Wife in Berlin*: Princess Blücher.

Western Front blood is flowing in streams and one strip after another is being given up."[1]

On September 2nd the news became infinitely worse. The English broke through in strength at Cambrai and the Kaiser was in such a state of agitation that Admiral Müller departed from his usual role and tried to comfort him; whereupon William II retired to bed. Meanwhile the High Command was growing desperate. Hindenburg had told the Kaiser on August 14th that peace would have to be made, but nothing had been done beyond asking the Queen of Holland if a conference could be held in The Hague. On September 4th Ludendorff got in touch with Herr Ballin and asked him if he would go immediately to Wilhelmshöhe and urge the Kaiser to set peace negotiations in motion. Ballin complied but he was only permitted to see the Kaiser in the presence of his chief of the military cabinet, Herr von Berg, who kept interrupting the conversation in order to soften Ballin's message. When the latter suggested mediation on the basis of President Wilson's fourteen points, Berg deliberately changed the subject. He later explained to Ballin that he must not make the Kaiser " too pessimistic." " The Emperor talked about a Second Punic War," wrote Ballin. " I thought he seemed very much misled, and in the arrogant mood which he affects in the presence of the third person. . . . The poor monarch is so humbugged that he has no idea how catastrophic things have become."[1] " It was infinitely difficult," wrote Lt.-Colonel Niemann, who was attached to the Kaiser as military aide, " to give the Emperor a clear idea of the situation without disturbing his equilibrium."[1]

We know from Müller's diary that this was not true; that the Kaiser had a perfectly clear idea of the situation; but that he did not want to face up to it. The slaughter on the western front continued, and he remained at Wilhelmshöhe (except for a brief trip to Essen to talk to the workers) for another six days. On the eleventh of September he went to Great Headquarters at Spa. His Chancellor also had been informed by the High Command of the urgency of the situation which was deteriorating each day. By now Austria was trying to make a separate peace. On the 25th of September the Kaiser travelled to Kiel to inspect the submarine school. As he was about to depart he received news of Bulgaria's

[1] *The Kaiser and His Court:* Admiral von Müller.

collapse which, everyone knew, meant the finish of Turkey's resistance as well. "His Majesty commented: 'This can bring the war to an end, but not in the way we wanted.'" "Even now," added Müller, "he did not find the courage to travel to Berlin or even to Spa; instead he returned to Wilhelmshöhe."

The Kaiser's advisers enlisted the Empress's help, however, and told her that William II was doing himself harm by remaining with her. On the 29th of September he arrived back in Spa. This time Hindenburg and Ludendorff allowed no doubt to linger in his mind. They told him that Germany must seek an armistice immediately; the army was at the end of its tether; they no longer could hold even the Flemish coast. Afterwards Müller remarked: "However the war ends, our people have behaved most gallantly." "Yes," replied the Kaiser, "but our politicians have fallen down appallingly on the job."[1]

Now everything came in a rush. A new Chancellor would have to be found to make the peace; and a new Government would have to be formed representing all parties, even the Social Democrats. This meant the "modernisation" of the Constitution (the word democratisation was avoided to spare the Emperor's sensibilities) and a severe curtailment of monarchical authority. William II offered no resistance but by this time Ludendorff was at his wit's end. While the Kaiser and Chancellor Hertling were conferring on October 1st he burst into the room. "Is the new Government formed?" "I cannot work miracles," replied the Kaiser. "It must be formed at once," said Ludendorff. "The request for peace must go to-day." Six precious weeks had slipped by, and now there was not a minute to be lost or the whole German front might split wide open, and allow the enemy to pour into the country.

On October 3rd Prince Max of Baden, the Kaiser's cousin, was appointed Chancellor and that same night a request for an armistice on the basis of the fourteen points was sent to the American President. Four days later, on the 8th, Wilson replied, demanding an evacuation of enemy territory, and asking whom he was dealing with. The Kaiser spotted the implication. "Don't you see?" he said excitedly to Colonel Niemann. "The object of this is to bring down my House, to set the monarchy aside." On October 14th a second

[1] *The Kaiser and His Court:* Admiral von Müller.

note arrived, demanding the abandonment of the U-boat war, and insisting that " the arbitrary power " which had governed Germany up till now must be removed, or rendered harmless.

This time the Kaiser did not refer to Wilson's pointed demand; instead he pretended he did not understand, and much to Müller's surprise said he would like to associate himself with Berlin's response which assured the American President that a democratic government controlled the destinies of Germany. The population, however, understood only too clearly; the Kaiser was an obstacle to peace. The people had no hatred for William II, but no love for him either. He seemed a remote, far-away figure, and if his presence meant that Germany could not get a good peace, then he must go. " Now that his time has come," wrote Princess Blücher, " one pities him. A deplorable position for a great king to be the object of pity. Why has he let things go so far? Why has he not already abdicated, instead of waiting until he is forced to do so? Every child in the street is saying, 'The Kaiser must go.' He absolutely seems to cling to his shadow of a throne, and people say, curiously enough, it is the Kaiserin who is advising him and begging him not to go."[1]

It was not the Kaiserin. It was William II who stubbornly refused to hear. On October 21st he summoned the members of his new Government to the Schloss Bellevue in Berlin and said: " I feel myself one with you in the sacred purpose of leading back the German Empire out of the present distress to tranquil and peaceful development." On October 24th, however, Wilson's voice spoke out with unmistakable clarity. The power of the King of Prussia appeared to be unbroken; and if the United States had to deal with " military leaders and monarchical autocracy . . . it must demand not peace negotiations but surrender." This clearly was a call not only for the abdication of the Kaiser, but for the resignation of Hindenburg and Ludendorff as well. Ludendorff made things easy for the Emperor, although he issued a manifesto to the army describing Wilson's terms as " unacceptable to us soldiers." Prince Max threatened to resign unless he was dismissed; and on October 27th the Kaiser had a stormy scene with the General which ended with the latter handing in his resignation.

But what about the Kaiser? Public pressure was increasing and most German officials regarded his abdication as inevitable. The

[1] *An English Wife in Berlin:* Princess Blücher.

monarchists felt that the only hope for the dynasty lay in the establishment of a Regency, for no one believed that the country would stand for the Crown Prince. For years Berlin had been repeating a *bon mot* uttered by Herr Kiderlen at a shooting party: " Be careful not to shoot the Kaiser, or we'll get something much worse." " Not only Wilson but the whole German nation would willingly renounce the Crown Prince," wrote Müller on October 10th.

Admiral Müller was astonished by the Kaiser's resilience. Although he looked " hollow-eyed " he was surprisingly cheerful as the tension mounted. He continued to talk about a Second Punic War, and his imagination already had conjured up exciting new circumstances. " The Kaiser," wrote Müller on the 29th, " painted a very bold picture in conclusion: an agreement with England to include a treaty with Japan to fling the Americans out of Europe. ' A European Monroe Doctrine therefore which I outlined to Hintze at Spa as the policy to be followed in the future.' The Kaiser already envisaged Japanese Divisions arriving via Serbia on the Western Front to help throw out the Americans. In this way we could obtain a good peace, for the English had no interest in weakening us and would gladly see us in possession of a strong fleet and an even stronger submarine force."[1]

The Kaiser announced his intention of leaving Berlin for Spa that same evening. Prince Max was distraught when he learned of this plan. He could not bring himself to tell William II that the question of his abdication was on everyone's lips; that the public were convinced that he alone stood in the way of " a good peace;" and that the Social Democrats, who were willing to support a Regency in favour of one of the Kaiser's grandsons, were threatening to withdraw their support from the Government unless he gave up the throne. The reason given by the Social Democrats was that they could not continue to restrain their pro-Communist colleagues from establishing a republic unless the Kaiser sacrificed himself without delay.

Although Prince Max saw clearly that the continuance of the monarchy was at stake he was too frightened to present the Kaiser with the facts. For the past week he had been hoping that William would renounce the throne of his own accord. But now all that

[1] *The Kaiser and His Court:* Admiral von Müller.

he could summon the courage to do was to beg the Kaiser not to leave the capital and to ask him why he wished to go to Spa. "I said," wrote William in his memoirs, "that I considered my return to the front to be my duty as Commander-in-Chief, after I had been nearly a month away from the desperately struggling army. To the Chancellor's objection that I was wanted at home I answered that there was a war on, and that the Emperor belonged to his soldiers."[1]

This was not the whole truth; although the Kaiser feigned innocence, he was well aware that pressure for his abdication was mounting. His officers, who had taken an oath of fealty to him personally, scarcely could ask him to give up his throne. They had sworn to defend him to the end. William II had been weak and vacillating about many things but not this; he sat on his throne by the grace of God and he would not renounce it without a bitter struggle. Indeed, he had taken the pains to extract a promise from each one of his six sons not to precipitate his abdication by agreeing to accept a regency. If William II was to be deposed it would mean the end of the monarchy. The German people were not to have their cake and to eat it too.

Prince Max was becoming desperate. He was not a coward, but the mystical bond between the Sovereign and those who served him was so strong that a straight request to the Emperor to abdicate seemed to smack of high treason. So he tried to find other people to broach the subject. No sooner had the Emperor departed than he asked one of the Kaiser's sons, Prince August Wilhelm, if he would go after his father and persuade him to abdicate, but the young man refused indignantly. On October 31st Max wired to the Kaiser asking him to return to Berlin, but this time William refused. The next day, November 1st, the Chancellor sent the Home Secretary, Herr Drews, to Spa to put the matter clearly before the Kaiser. Drews did so in the presence of Hindenburg and General Gröner. The Emperor felt warm and secure at Spa, for his two generals expressed shocked indignation, and Hindenburg told Drews "in the strongest words possible" that the army would not hold together if the Emperor went, "but would simply stream back home, like a horde of marauding bandits."

But would the army hold together if he stayed? On November

[1] *My Memoirs:* William II.

2nd news arrived in Berlin that the navy had mutinied. On the 29th and 30th of October the Third Squadron of the High Seas Fleet had been assembled on the Schilling quay at Kiel in preparation for a raid to force the exit to the Channel, to relieve the evacuation operations in Flanders and Belgium. The crews, however, believed that the officers were planning a decisive battle with the British Fleet and refused to obey. " If the English attack us," they declared in a proclamation, " we will defend our coasts to the last, but we will not ourselves attack. Further than Heligoland we will not go."

There were wholesale arrests, but the mutiny was spreading so fast that discipline could not be restored. On November 1st the seamen held a meeting at the Kiel Town Hall and demanded the release of their comrades; on the 3rd a monster demonstration of sailors and workmen took place, with cheers for " the Republic;" on the 4th the Red Flag was hoisted on all the warships; and on the 5th the whole working population joined the insurrectionists, red badges appeared by the thousands, and it was apparent that the mutiny had become a revolution. Not only Kiel but Hamburg, Lübeck, and Bremen had passed into the hands of Soldier and Worker Councils. On this same day, November 5th, a message from President Wilson reached Berlin announcing that the Allies had agreed to an armistice. The following morning Germany's representatives, headed by Deputy Erzberger, were conducted through the enemy lines and received by General Foch with the brutal words: " What do you want? "

By November 7th almost all the cities of Germany were in the hands of the insurrectionists. They were not revolutionaries in the true sense, for the mass of the people who had thronged to the red banner did not favour Bolshevism or even Socialism. They merely were people determined to bring the war to an end, an impossibility, they believed, as long as the Kaiser remained on the throne. On the morning of the 7th the Social Democrat members of the Government, led by Herr Scheidemann, informed Prince Max that unless the Kaiser abdicated by noon the following day, they would walk out of the Government and organise the revolutionaries. Dr. Gwinner, a member of the Prussian upper chamber, called on Admiral Müller, who was working at Naval Headquarters in Berlin, and asked if he would travel to Spa and persuade the Kaiser to abdicate. Müller replied that he had no authority to do so, and Gwinner told him that if the Social Democrats quit the Government and organised the insurrectionists " it would mean the scaffold for the Kaiser."

Prince Max telegraphed Spa informing the Emperor of the Socialists' ultimatum. He said that since he could not ask his sovereign to abdicate he must offer his resignation. That night, however, he partially overcame his scruples and telegraphed again saying that civil war would develop unless the Kaiser went. No, replied William II; and Prince Max must not go either. To avoid misunderstanding the Kaiser put his commands into written messages ending: " His Majesty emphatically declines to consider the dynastic question raised in Your Grand Ducal Highness's proposals, and considers it as much as ever his duty to remain at his post."[1] So at midday on November 8th the Socialists left the Government, and on the same day Bavaria split away from the German Empire and proclaimed itself a free state. The Munich Palace guard was disarmed as the population cried: " Down with the Kaiser, long live the Republic." In Berlin the Social Democrats were busy organising the masses to take part in a giant rally. The atmosphere was electric.

While all this was going on the Kaiser was talking of leading his troops against the revolutionaries. He called a Crown Council for the morning of the 9th to discuss " the operation in the interior commanded by the Emperor." On the night of the 8th however Hindenburg and Gröner at last realised that they had been far too optimistic. Reports were flowing into Great Headquarters showing that even the army was disintegrating. That night they asked sixteen officers in Schulenburg's Army Group whether the troops would follow the Kaiser into Berlin to re-establish monarchical control, and twelve replied no.

Hindenburg admitted to Gröner that the Kaiser's plan was hopeless. As the two generals set out from their headquarters at the Hotel Britannique to attend the Emperor's Crown Council in the Château de la Fraineuse, Hindenburg was in the grip of a fierce emotion. He wept freely and when he arrived for the historic meeting he was unable to speak. The Council was held in the large

[1] *Memoirs :* Max, Prince of Baden.

cold garden house at the back of the Château. Among those present was Field Marshal von Hindenburg, Generals Gröner and Plessen, Count von der Schulenburg the Crown Prince's Chief of Staff, Freiherr von Grunau, and Lt.-Colonel Niemann. The only heat in the room was a dimly burning wood fire and the Emperor leaned against the chimney-piece and shivered. As it was too painful for von Hindenburg to disillusion his Emperor, General Gröner was obliged to do the speaking. In sombre tones he told the Kaiser that an operation against the interior was out of the question. It was no longer a matter of suppressing an insurrection but of civil war. The rebels controlled most of the key points on the Rhine and troops in many parts of the country were joining the revolutionaries. Count von der Schulenburg was furious at Gröner's estimate and began to argue wildly. He said that in a week's time it would be possible to gather a force of picked men on the Rhine upon whom the Emperor could rely. But the Emperor was beginning to waver. He had been prepared for a fight until he had seen from von Hindenburg's attitude that the old Field Marshal did not believe it could succeed. Now he groped for a compromise. He would not ask the troops to fire on their comrades. " I want to spare the Fatherland a civil war; but after the armistice it is my desire to come home to peace at the head of my army."

The generals were not to be spared embarrassment. The Kaiser still had not grasped the full significance of the situation. The moment had come to tell him plainly that the revolution was not organised by a handful of Communists, but that it had become a nation-wide rebellion, born of an anguished desire for peace, and that no one felt this peace would be procured unless the Kaiser gave up his throne. Hindenburg remained silent, only General Gröner had the courage to utter the fateful words. " Sire, you no longer have an army. The army will march home in peace and order under its leaders and commanding generals, but not under the command of Your Majesty, for it no longer stands behind Your Majesty."

The Kaiser's face turned scarlet and he started towards General Gröner in a movement of rage. " Your Excellency! I demand a written statement of this opinion! I will have an announcement in black and white from all the generals commanding that the army is no longer behind its Supreme War Lord. Have they not sworn it to me in their military oath?" " In the present situation, Sire," replied Gröner sadly, " the oath is mere fiction."

The Kaiser's world had collapsed. As though to emphasise it, a laconic message arrived from the Commandant of Berlin: " All troops deserted—completely out of hand." William II adjourned his Council and walked through the French windows of the lodge into the garden, where he talked for a few minutes with Freiherr von Grunau, the Foreign Office representative at Great Headquarters. He " spoke with bitterness of the way in which the Democratic Government, in spite of his ready acquiescence in all the reforms and changes of personnel, had neglected to take any effective steps to counter the attacks which had been directed against his person and which aimed ultimately at destroying the institution of the Monarchy itself; it had allowed itself to be taken in tow by the Social Democrats, who were only concerned to establish their own supremacy. Finally the Kaiser expressed his willingness to abdicate, if that was what the German people really wanted; he had reigned long enough to know what a thankless business it was; far from clinging to his imperial position, he had only done his duty in remaining at his post and not deserting army and people at such a time as the present. Now the others might show whether they would manage things any better."[1]

Meanwhile the Crown Prince had arrived and the deliberations were resumed. More army corps commanders had been asked if they could rely on their troops and the answer was no. But Count von der Schulenburg still retained hope and gave the Kaiser new courage; perhaps if His Majesty resigned as Emperor but remaned King of Prussia his authority could be re-imposed; the Prussian troops undoubtedly would remain loyal and their example might turn the tide. At this moment Prince Max got through on the telephone and implored the Emperor to give his decision to abdicate; nothing else could save the monarchy and avert civil war. A huge strike had been proclaimed, thousands of workmen were gathering together, and tension was such that at any moment the mob might come flowing down the Wilhelmstrasse with machine guns. Schulenburg refused to be hurried, for the Kaiser had been won to his suggestions of " partial abdication." A few minites later the telephone rang again. " It is a question of minutes," said Berlin.

[1] *Memoirs:* Max, Prince of Baden.

This time Schulenburg replied: "His Majesty is resolved; he is at this moment formulating his resolve on paper; it will be in the hands of the Imperial Government in half an hour."

Prince Max and his Cabinet could not wait. The vast throngs needed only a spark to set them off. In his memoirs the Prince declared that Schulenburg had neglected to mention William II's fantastic intention to remain as King of Prussia; so that when he stepped on to the balcony of the Chancellery and announced, prematurely, the abdication of the Kaiser and the Crown Prince, he believed that he was only anticipating the resolve of his Emperor. The monarchy, Prince Max told the people, would remain, for the Social Democrat Deputy Herr Ebert had agreed to serve as Imperial Chancellor under a Regency which was now in the process of being set up.

It was not until Hindenburg and his generals had taken their leave of the Kaiser and returned to the Hotel Britannique, and until William II had led his dispirited entourage in to luncheon at the Château, that telegrams began to arrive informing them of the Chancellor's action. "Treason!" cried the Kaiser. "Barefaced, outrageous treason!" He leapt up from the table and went into the hall, where he feverishly began filling in telegraph forms, insisting that he still remained King of Prussia. But even worse news was in store for him. Prince Max's move had come too late to be effective. The Communists—or Spartacists as they were called—had seized the imperial palace, and proclaimed the Soviet Republic from its steps. This act had thrown Chancellor Ebert's Social Democrat supporters into a panic, and he was unable to restrain the hysterical Scheidemann from proclaiming a Socialist Republic from the portico of the Reichstag. So now, not only was William II deposed, but the monarchy had collapsed.

The Kaiser fumed and stormed. He was so emotionally upset that it was impossible to talk to him calmly. Suddenly Hindenburg and Gröner were announced. "My God," he cried, "are you back here again already?" Then he gave Gröner an annihilating look and said: "You no longer have a War Lord," and refused to address him again. Hindenburg was now fully in control of himself. The problem no longer was a dynastic question—but a struggle between Bolshevism and Socialism. The only question that remained was what to do with William II. The roads to Berlin were blocked;

so was the road to the front; and he could not guarantee the Emperor's safety at Spa. "I cannot accept the responsibility," he said, "of seeing the Emperor haled to Berlin by insurgent troops and delivered over as a prisoner to the revolutionary Government. I must advise Your Majesty to abdicate and to proceed to Holland."

"Do you think that I am afraid to remain with my troops?" William II flung back furiously. No one answered and he paced up and down the room in a frightening silence. Finally he signalled one of his entourage to make preparations for the journey. At this point Admiral von Scheer was announced. "Field Marshal," said the Emperor, turning to von Hindenburg, "will you please repeat to Admiral Scheer what you have said to me." Hindenburg repeated solemnly: "The army and the troops are no longer behind Your Majesty. There are no loyal troops left. Would to God, Your Majesty, that it were otherwise." The Emperor then began to storm once again; he told Scheer that because of this state of affairs he had been forced to resign as Emperor; but his intention had been to remain as King of Prussia. "But that the gentlemen may learn how I am served by my Chancellor—Prince Max of Baden proclaimed my abdication both as Emperor and King this morning without my knowledge and without my authority. That is the way I am served by my last Chancellor!" Scheer groped for words and said rather lamely that it was no longer possible to rely on the navy. "I have no navy," snapped the Emperor.[1]

The generals and the Admiral took their leave and for the next five hours the Kaiser struggled with himself for the right thing to do. He told the Crown Prince that he might not go to Holland at all; that whatever he did he would not make a decision until the following morning. Later in the afternoon he received a telephone call from Berlin telling him that the Empress was remaining quietly at the New Palace at Potsdam. This decided him to cancel his flight. "My wife is sticking it out—and they want to persuade me to go to Holland. I never will. It would be like a captain deserting the sinking ship." Nevertheless he moved to the imperial train; and when Colonel Niemann arrived with his baggage at nine o'clock summoned by General Plessen "in case they left that evening," the Kaiser's mood had altered completely. "In the

[1] The authority for the agitated scenes on the morning of November 9th is *Hindenburg: The Wooden Titan* by Sir John Wheeler-Bennett.

train I found the Emperor already at dinner with his suite. I had been afraid that the excitement of the previous hours had made him lethargic. But not at all. He looked at me with all his animation; his face calm and resolute . . . The Emperor had quite changed his mind about going to Holland. 'Well if it must be so,' he said, '. . . but not before tomorrow morning.' "[1]

Field Marshal von Hindenburg expected to take his leave of his sovereign at breakfast time. But at dawn, before anyone was up at Great Headquarters, the gold and white imperial train slid out of the station and gathered speed for the Dutch frontier. The Kaiser wrote no farewell message to his generals but before leaving scribbled a letter to the Crown Prince. "Dear Boy," it began, "Since the Field Marshal can no longer guarantee my security here, and since he also will no longer take the responsibility for the loyalty of the troops, I have decided, after severe inward struggle, to leave the collapsed army. Berlin is totally lost in the hands of the Socialists, and two governments have already been formed there, one by Ebert as Reich's Chancellor, and another at the same time by the Independents. I recommend that you remain at your post and hold the troops together until they start the march back home. As God wills auf Wiedersehen. General von Marschall will keep you informed. Your stricken father, William."[2]

William II crossed the Belgian-Dutch frontier at Eysen. He gave up his sword to an astonished Dutch sentry, who thought for a moment he must be dreaming, and wondered wildly what he had better do. He telephoned The Hague. Queen Wilhelmina received the news in a business-like way and summoned her Cabinet. Meanwhile the Kaiser waited at the border. Six hours later he was told that he might enter Holland. A special train was on its way to the frontier to provide accommodation for His Majesty and his entourage until more definite arrangements could be made. The next day, November 11th, word arrived that Count Godard Bentinck, a Dutch-English Count of the Empire and a hereditary Knight of the Order of St. John, would put his house at Amerongen at the German monarch's disposal. "Who is this Bentinck? I don't think I know him," said William II. They met for the first

[1] *Kaiser und Revolution:* Colonel A. Niemann.

[2] *The Life of Crown Prince William:* Klaus Jonas.

time at Maarn station the next afternoon. "Now," said the Kaiser to his host, as they drove across the bridge leading to the Bentincks' seventeenth-century, moated house, "for a cup of real good English tea!"

November 11th. On that same day, at five-twenty in the morning, the armistice was signed, bringing an end to the war in which ten million men had laid down their lives.

18. *Epilogue at Doorn*

" A friend came in to spend the evening with us yesterday, and had come straight from Amerongen, where he had spent two hours with the Emperor," wrote Princess Blücher from Berlin, in February 1919, three months after William's flight. ". . . He was taken down to the gallery in which the Emperor takes his exercise daily, and there he walked with him for two hours. He told us the first sight of him was a great shock. The Emperor has grown a long white beard ; he brushes his now quite white hair straight back, and his complexion is sallow and unhealthy. But he bore himself with great dignity and spoke quickly and with reserve. . . . He had tried from the moment he came to the throne to assert his own authority, but he was too young and perhaps too impulsive. . . . He said that he had enough English blood in his veins to know that the only thing was to go in with England, but he was always talked over by his military authorities and diplomats. . . . He complained most bitterly that he was deceived and lied to from the outset of his reign, and especially throughout the war. I did not give my opinion," observed Princess Blücher, " but I cannot help thinking that if a man is an Emperor one of his chief aims should be to employ every person and every method by which he can arrive at the truth."[1]

William II's desire to excuse himself was heightened by the campaign which had sprung up in England to bring him to trial as a " war criminal." The fact that millions of people in Britain, France, and America held him personally responsible for the war came as a genuine shock to him, for long ago he had convinced himself that the conflict had been thrust upon him by the Entente. He did not seem to realise that for four years Allied propaganda had laid atrocities of every kind at his door, and that cartoonists usually drew him as a butcher brandishing a huge knife with the blood running down his arms and dripping off his hands.

[1] *An English Wife in Berlin* : Princess Blücher.

Indeed, the British public was enraged when it learned of his "escape" to Holland. On November 10th the English poet, Alfred Noyes, lashed out against Holland to a huge audience at Carnegie Hall in New York. "These people would permit the Emperor to retire to his yacht and his champagne dinners while 10 million men he has murdered lie rotting in the ground." Two days later the London *Times* printed a letter from Arthur Conan Doyle urging that the neutrals should be warned "that we certainly shall not recognise any rights of asylum for those whom we regard as murderers." And four days later, on November 16th, *The Times* published an article by Sir Valentine Chirol (who had been knighted for his services as a correspondent in Berlin) which purported to be a "character-sketch" of William II, but would have astonished the fallen monarch's advisers. "Only a man," wrote Chirol, "possessed of ruthless energy and untiring industry, who combined the most extraordinary versatility of methods with a fixity of purpose that amounted almost to an obsession, would have exploited as he did all the material and intellectual forces of a gifted . . . nation. He built up the fleet to destroy the British Empire. He lied and deceived. Then when trickery and deceit had done their work, the last word belonged to him who wielded the mightiest sword . . . and what sword could have seemed to him mightier in August 1914?"

The Kaiser found the anger of the British people incomprehensible. "Why do the English hate me so? Why do they hate me so?" he repeatedly asked his host as he paced up and down the Long Gallery of the Bentinck house. When the latter explained that they held him responsible for the death of women and children during the U-boat war he replied hotly that the British blockade had killed far more women and children than those who had died at sea. Furthermore, the British were still maintaining the blockade, despite the armistice, and thousands were dying in Germany at this very moment. He could not believe, he said, that this was the real reason for the campaign against him; it was too illogical, there must be a hidden motive.

If he was perplexed by the English attitude he was even more disturbed and wounded by the temper of his own people. Although he had left Germany because von Hindenburg had told him that it would be intolerable for the ex-Sovereign to fall into the hands of the Communists, he now was excoriated by all classes. He was astonished that von Hindenburg did not step forward and tell the German people that the Emperor had departed, much against his will, on the urgent advice of the High Command. Although William II had left after the Republic had been declared he had, inadvertently, spared the country a civil war; for it soon transpired that Prince Max of Baden had handed over his powers to an unworkable coalition, or " directory " as it was called. It consisted of six Socialists, half of whom were inexorably opposed to the other half; three of them, including Chancellor Ebert, were Democrats with bourgeois affiliations, while the other three were " Independents " and Bolshevik sympathisers. On November 9th Communists were holding meetings all over Berlin trying to whip up the masses to fling out their masters and take control of offices and industries. Some of them had surged into the Kaiser's Berlin palace and harangued the crowds from the balcony—the same balcony from which William II had addressed the people at the outbreak of war. The new Chancellor was beside himself, for with his Cabinet split in two he did not see what he could do to restore order. Late that night, while the Kaiser was preparing his dawn departure and von Hindenburg, who had taken over the supreme command from his sovereign, was sleeping from exhaustion, Ebert sat alone in the Chancellery wondering distractedly how he could prevent a total breakdown. Suddenly the telephone rang with a call from Spa. " Gröner speaking," said a crisp military voice. The High Command, said the General, would help Ebert to restore and maintain order, so long as he would provision the army and promise to co-operate in the suppression of Bolshevism. With a sob of relief Ebert accepted the offer.

But if William II had remained in Germany this secret pact could not have taken place, for the Social Democrats had demanded the Emperor's abdication and the army would have been caught between divided loyalties, unable to support a government opposed to its Supreme War Lord. As it was, the High Command raised a force of 400,000 reliable soldiers from the disintegrating mass of the Imperial Army, and during the next six months put down the Communists in two bloody encounters, in January and March. Between these clashes Germany held the first free election in her history. The result revealed that Communist agitation was out of all proportion to its actual strength, for the extreme left polled only 2,300,000 votes. The Social Democrats emerged as the strongest single party with 11,500,000 votes and 163 seats. But the ballot also showed that the majority of people in Germany had not swung left at all, for the parties of the right and centre, although divided among themselves, polled over 16,000,000 votes. Thus the Social Democrats were able to form a coalition with the Democrats and the Catholics, and Ebert became the first President of the Weimar Republic. It had been proved beyond dispute that the widespread desire for William II's abdication had not sprung from disillusionment with the monarchical system, but from President Wilson's warning that unless Germany rid herself of the rulers who had led her into the war she could expect no mercy.

And what could she expect now that the Kaiser had gone? The fallen monarch followed the events taking place in Paris with grim interest. The tiny village of Amerongen had become a scene of feverish activity, and remained so throughout 1919, for the British pledge to bring William to trial focused world attention upon him. The Emperor had arrived in Holland with a staff of servants, including chauffeur, valet, and cook, and a suite of thirty officers and aides. Count Bentinck put up some of them, while others found accommodation in the village inn or in neighbouring houses. Meanwhile dozens of journalists had arrived from all over the world, clamouring to get a glimpse of the famous refugee. Dutch troops, however, guarded all the points of entrance, and no one, not even members of the family, could gain admission to the grounds without presenting a white card signed by Count Bentinck; nor could they leave without surrendering a blue card. The house itself, surrounded by a wide moat with a drawbridge, was a perfect place for seclusion; but the fact that the journalists did not succeed in tracking down their prey immediately gave rise to a rumour that the Kaiser had gone mad, and that his bedroom had been transformed into a padded cell guarded night and day by male nurses!

The Kaiser had several official visitors, for he had left Germany without making a formal abdication—or indeed any abdication at all—and the Berlin jurists argued that it was imperative to secure a signed document, otherwise it would be impossible for the German Government to make peace. The Kaiser acquiesced, and on

November 28th renounced the throne, both as Emperor and King of Prussia. It was a very chilly abdication. It released the officials of the German Empire, all officers and non-commissioned men, from their oath of fealty to the Sovereign, and bade them " help those in possession of actual power in Germany to protect the German people against the threatening dangers of anarchy, famine, and foreign domination." That was all. It contained no warm message to the German people, no praise for the valour of soldiers and civilians during the four years of war. The truth was that William II was still burning with indignation at the way his subjects had cast him aside in order to get an easy peace. He blamed Prince Max of Baden bitterly, and told Count Bentinck repeatedly that his cousin had " tricked him " behind his back.

On the same day that the Emperor signed his abdication the Empress arrived from Germany to join her husband. She had remained with her daughter, the Duchess of Brunswick, at the New Palace throughout the weeks of revolution. Although the guards had put red cockades on their uniforms, they had protected the royal ladies and prevented anyone from molesting them. The Empress was a broken woman. She still suffered from a bad heart, and now her anguish for Germany's plight, and her fear for her husband's safety, had reduced her strength still further. She believed that the forces of evil had triumphed and spent much of her time weeping lest the cruel English arrive to take away her Wilhelm.

The Kaiser, on the other hand, soon regained his composure, and waited with courage for the outcome of the Paris peace talks. He flung himself into dealing with the enormous correspondence which had opened up—much of it unflattering. He read the London *Times* every morning (always four days late) and sent for all the English books which had any first-hand bearing on the events leading up to the war, or the war itself. Although the members of his entourage bade him farewell one by one and returned to Germany, he did not seem to mind. He was left with only four gentlemen. His youngest aide, the vigorous, ebullient, Captain Ilsemann, was the one on whom he depended most, and Ilsemann had no intention of leaving. Indeed, the gay Captain finally married Count Godard Bentinck's daughter, Elizabeth, and remained with the ex-sovereign for the rest of his days.

Ilsemann encouraged William II to take up wood-cutting again as a form of exercise, and soon it had become a regular routine. At eleven there was always a break for coffee which was served in the playhouse built for the Bentinck children. The Emperor liked to spread army maps on the table and go over the battles and victories with his aides. The most brilliant strategical conception of the war, he said, was Winston Churchill's Gallipoli. ("You don't know how nearly you were through," Captain Ilsemann once commented to Count Bentinck's English niece.) The figure in the dark blue serge suit with the long white beard and the black homburg hat, that wended its way back to the house for luncheon, did not seem to have any resemblance to the former ruler of Germany; it was only when the military greatcoat was flung over his shoulders that a flash of the past came back. Yet in truth William II was not very different. He was still impulsive and unpredictable; he still grasped at fantastic straws; still fitted events into patterns which pleased him; still blamed everyone but himself for the world catastrophe. He eagerly devoured any piece of information or any book which opened up a new channel of escape for him. He claimed that the Socialists had worked for years to undermine German morale, and that mothers had been paid a weekly sum to write distressing letters to their sons at the front in an attempt to break their morale. He was fascinated and perturbed by the scurrilous anti-semitic book *The Protocols of Zion* which his brother, Prince Henry, gave to him to read, and which attributed to the Jews the outbreak of the world war, and the subsequent spread of Bolshevism.

Every night he sat up with his host and his aides talking until the small hours of the morning. At first he avoided political questions and entertained Count Bentinck by vivacious reminiscences. But as the weeks passed he lost his reserve and poured out his heart, claiming that no man had been so badly deceived or so ill-used as himself. The question that baffled him most was how the German people had been able to discard him so easily. Although he still accused Prince Max of treachery, his most bitter hatred now centred on von Hindenburg. He told his host that if the Field Marshal had defended the Emperor's flight to Holland, his former subjects would not have accused him of running away, but would have understood that he had sacrificed himself in their interests. He felt that Hindenburg, more than any other person, had destroyed the people's faith in him; but for the Field Marshal he believed that he might have been recalled to Germany within a few weeks.

But not only Prince Max and von Hindenburg received the backlash of his tongue. Prince Bülow was condemned for his duplicity, Bethmann-Hollweg for his stupidity, Ludendorff for his insolence, and George V and Nicholas II for their failure to defend the monarchical principle. Gradually, William II found explanations for every happening which left his ego intact. Why had a man so well intentioned been so cruelly treated? The answer lay with the Deity. God had placed him upon the throne and God, for some mysterious reason, had removed him. Perhaps to test his faith; perhaps to prepare him for further responsibilities, perhaps, who could say, even greater glories. "I bear my personal fate with resignation," he wrote in his memoirs, "for the Lord knows what He does and what He wishes. He knows why He subjects me to this test. I shall bear everything with patience and await whatever God still holds in store for me."[1] Every morning at 8.45 he attended the family prayers conducted by Count Bentinck; and with imperial habitude commanded all the members of his entourage to do likewise.

The Kaiser would not have been human if he had not derived a certain grim satisfaction from the Versailles Peace Treaty: his subjects had cast him aside for a favourable peace, and now they had reaped a fitting reward for their disloyalty. The German people were utterly stunned by the terms. They had expected to lose Alsace-Lorraine to the French; they knew that their fleet would be scuppered; and they were not surprised to find that the British had appropriated their colonies. But what they did not expect was to be treated as a pariah nation. They had established a democracy for the first time in their history and their government was composed of men who had nothing to do with the events leading to the war; yet they were not even to be allowed to take part in the League of Nations. Furthermore, some of their richest areas were to be torn from them and given away or loaned to Poland, Belgium, and France; and on top of all this they were to pay fantastic and impossible reparations. "Now that we see the terms as a whole," wrote young Harold Nicolson, one of the members of the British

[1] *My Memoirs:* William II.

Foreign Office team, to his father, "we realise that they are much too stiff. They are not stern merely but actually punitive, and they abound with what Smuts calls 'pin-pricks' as well as dagger-thrusts. . . . Yet the real crime is the reparations and indemnity chapter, which is immoral and senseless. There is not a single person among the younger people here who is not unhappy and disappointed at the terms. The only people who approve are the old fire-eaters."[1]

After the first shock the German people were enraged. All parties and all shades of opinion united in monster demonstrations. President Ebert ordered every place of amusement closed for a week, while his government sent passionate letters of protest to Paris. But it was to no avail. A few alterations were made, but the treaty stood as designed. Finally, under bitter protest, Germany agreed to sign if the clauses so dear to the heart of Mr. Lloyd George were deleted; these were the demand that Germany admit sole responsibility for the war, and surrender her Kaiser and most of her leading citizens to trial before Allied tribunals. But the Allies remained firm.[2] Ebert rang up the High Command and begged the generals to offer some hope if hostilities were re-opened. Germany would be trampled underfoot, that he knew, but it would be better to fight to the last ditch than to submit to such unbearable humiliation and such monstrous injustice. The High Command, however, replied sadly that no resistance was possible. So at Versailles, on June 28th, 1919, Germany signed. But the signature was tantamount to a new declaration of war, for in the breast of every German burned a resolve to arm again, secretly if necessary, until the day came when Germany could avenge herself. William II's Second Punic War had ceased to be a fancy. "The war to end wars," the Kaiser is said to have remarked, "has resulted in a peace to end peace."

The Kaiser now waited grimly to see how the clauses dealing with his trial, and the trial of Germany's most prominent men, would be implemented. The first salvo was fired on November 1, 1919, when the Allied Powers addressed a note to Berlin (sent by

[1] *Peacemaking*: Harold Nicolson.

[2] If Germany's war guilt had not been admitted, Mr. Lloyd George told a London audience on March 3, 1921, the Versailles Treaty would have been untenable.

special messenger because the German Ambassador in Paris refused to transmit it) demanding the surrender of 830 German citizens accused of having committed " acts of violation of the laws and customs of war " or " morally responsible " for crimes committed by their subordinates. The lists included nearly every leading figure in German life: all the princes, ex-Chancellor von Bethmann-Hollweg, Field Marshals von Hindenburg and von Falkenhayn, and so on down the line. Von Hindenburg was not impressed. " If they want to shoot an old man like myself who has only done his duty and nothing more let them come and take me." However, he exerted himself on behalf of his Emperor. He wrote General Foch a letter begging him " as the supreme head of an army which through centuries has upheld the tradition of true soldier's honour and knightly sentiments as to its highest ideal " not to press for the surrender of the Kaiser. " I put myself entirely at the Allied Powers' disposal in place of my royal master," he concluded.[1] The Crown Prince also stepped forward and offered himself for trial as a scape-goat for the rest.

No notice was taken, however, either of Hindenburg's offer or that of the Prince, and on the 10th of January 1920 the Dutch Government received a demand from the Allies for the extradition of the Kaiser. The Dutch Government, however, refused to oblige. William II had been accorded exile by the Netherlands, said the Dutch Foreign Minister; and since Holland was not a signatory to the Versailles Treaty she was not bound by its articles, and would not give him up.

The French and the Americans had never liked the idea of the war criminal clauses; nor had the British Foreign Office. The diplomats told Mr. Lloyd George that he was making a laughing stock of the country, and it was high time that Britain seized the excuse afforded by the Dutch to drop the whole matter. " Mr. Lloyd George was genuinely indignant," wrote Mr. Churchill, " but by this time among responsible people in England he was alone. The victorious Allies therefore submitted to the Dutch refusal. . . ."[2]

In the early spring of 1920 the Kaiser bought Doorn House, a small schloss standing in a park of 60 acres, four miles from Amerongen

[1] *Hindenburg: The Wooden Titan:* Sir John Wheeler-Bennett.

[2] *World Crisis:* Winston S. Churchill.

in the province of Utrecht. He was able to equip it with his own possessions as the German Government allowed him to remove furniture, pictures, and silver from the palaces at Potsdam and Berlin. As the residence was not big enough for guests the Kaiser built lodge houses near the main gate with suites for visitors, and offices for the Master of the Household; he also enlarged the Orangerie, a building near the main house.

The Empress was deeply relieved that her husband no longer was in danger, but she was homesick for Germany and the companionship of her children. Furthermore, she was distressed by the new rift which had sprung up between the Kaiser and the Crown Prince. Her hopeless, feckless, dissolute first-born son represented almost everything of which she disapproved, yet she adored him. The Kaiser was angry because the Prince had followed him into exile. He argued that while he, the Emperor, had left Germany because the High Command had implored him to do so, the Prince had done the opposite. Despite the generals' exhortation for him to remain, he had fled to Holland two days after his father. Queen Wilhelmina had assigned him a parsonage on the desolate island of Wieringen on the Zuyder Zee. There he lived, accompanied by one aide, for the next four years.

In May 1920 the Queen allowed the Crown Prince to visit his parents at Doorn. His youngest brother, Prince Joachim, was also present, but it was not a happy meeting. Joachim also had left Germany at the time of the revolution, and had bought a villa in Switzerland. He spent most of his time carousing with women and gambling across the border in Italy. The Kaiser blamed the Crown Prince for the boy's demoralisation. The family reunion had a tragic climax, for a few weeks after the gathering at Doorn Joachim shot himself.

The shock undermined the Empress, who declined steadily and died in April 1921. Her body was sent back to Potsdam for burial. All her children were present except for the Crown Prince who was not allowed to return to Germany; thousands of people lined the route in the park of the New Palace along which the funeral procession passed.

The Kaiser was deeply afflicted. He had grown closer to his wife during the awful years of the war than at any time in his marriage, and now in his exile he was desolate. "It was heart-rending," said a member of his suite, "to see the man who once was the most powerful ruler in Christendom slowly ascend, a grey and lonely figure, the steep stairs to his room. His little court was unable to make him forget his unutterable grief for the loss of his helpmate." Just as his mother had done in the case of a family bereavement, he ordered the Empress's room to be locked, and kept exactly as she had left it, with the toilet articles on the tables, and the intimate photographs and books in their places. Every morning for the rest of his life he visited the room, and bowed his head in silent prayer.

However the loneliness that hung over Doorn was soon to be dispelled. A year after the Empress's death the ex-Kaiser received a letter from a small boy who declared that when he grew up he intended to fight for the fallen monarch. The signature was familiar. The Kaiser recalled the boy's father, Prince Schoenaich-Carolath, who had been killed in the war; and his mother, born the Princess Hermine of Reuss. William was so touched by the letter that he invited the child and his mother to visit him at Doorn. The mother came by herself and within a week she was engaged to the Kaiser; they were married six months later on November 5th, 1922. It was not a love match, but a *mariage de convenance*. The Princess Hermine was twenty-eight years younger than William and very different from the first Empress. She was argumentative, lively, tactless, and aggressive. No one in the Kaiser's household liked her; they said she was hard and ambitious and trouble-making; that she had prompted her child to write the Kaiser in order to trap him; that she had proposed to the Emperor herself, and married him because she believed that the Hohenzollerns would one day be restored to the throne. On the other hand, George Viereck, the American-born German propagandist, who acted as the Kaiser's literary agent and often visited Doorn (and who later became an ardent Nazi supporter), declared that the Kaiser confided to him that the Princess Hermine "saved my reason if not my life." He told Viereck that he discussed everything with her, did not write a line without her approval, and had great faith in her ability to see through people, referring proudly to her "X-ray eyes." And when Daisy, Princess of Pless, sent him a letter of congratulation he replied with touching simplicity: "I have found peace and happiness again after such terrible years of loss and trials, through the affection of this winning lady who has consented to be my wife and to bring sunshine into this house of darkness, sorrow and mourning."[1] The household, despite their resentment of the new mistress of Doorn, admitted that whatever her shortcomings she brought the Kaiser happiness.

For fifteen years William II lived in the dream that one day God might recall him to the throne of his forbears. His faith in the Almighty not only afforded him deep solace but gave him hope which, although always illusory, enabled him to bear his exile with courage and dignity. Now that he was no longer subjected to the torment and strain of political responsibility, his character mellowed and he became more calm and considerate. " A great gentleman," the Dutch said; while his household—perhaps for the first time in his life—became genuinely attached to him. He followed a clockwork routine: 9 a.m. Prayers; 9.15 Newspapers; 10.30 Exercise (wood-cutting); 12.0 Correspondence; 1.0 Luncheon; 2 to 4 Sleep; 4 to 8 Work and Reading; 8.0 Dinner. When he was alone with his household he liked to read aloud after dinner, and despite the imperfect knowledge of his attendants often chose English books. He was fond of P. G. Wodehouse but he sometimes was irritated by the fact that his listeners only laughed when he laughed. Occasionally, he told a friend, he laughed when there was no joke at all; then when the merriment of his entourage had died away he fixed them with his steely blue eyes and asked them to explain the joke.

The Kaiser, however, was not often alone. The guest houses at Doorn nearly always were full, sometimes with his children and relations, sometimes wi h eminent men from Germany who kept him abreast of current affairs. He still was very much the Emperor; and although he read widely he gained little understanding of political affairs or human psychology. He was incapable of learning from facts, for he simply altered them to fit the patterns his imagination conjured up, or to satisfy his emotional desires. He continued to view the world in the same fanciful and distorted light as when he had been on the throne.

As he believed that God had subjected him to cruel adversity to test his faith and resolve, he worked remorselessly to clear his name

[1] *Better Left Unsaid:* Daisy, Princess of Pless.

of war-guilt. He made no verbal pronouncements, for he had promised the Queen of Holland to remain aloof from political issues, but he authorised the publication of many articles (not under his own name but through agents) attacking " the infamous Treaty of Versailles." And in 1922 he published an apologia in the form of an autobiographical work entitled *My Memoirs*. The theme was familiar. " Not Germany, but the alliance of her foes, prepared the war according to a definite plan, and intentionally caused it." The book is not interesting historically because of its glaring omissions and half-truths, but it is a striking revelation of the author's character. William II wrote throughout as though he merely had played the role of a constitutional monarch, fastening the blame for Germany's mistakes on his advisers, with not so much as a mention of the fact that these counsellors came and went at his bidding. " The menace of the war was not realised," he wrote with Olympian detachment, " because the Foreign Office . . . completely eliminated from its calculations war as a possible instrument of entente statesmanship." The only person for whom he had a good word to say was Admiral Tirpitz who, probably more than any other single person, was responsible for Germany's downfall by his antagonism of Britain.

The memoirs did little to enhance William II's reputation. " No more disarming revelation of inherent triviality, lack of understanding and sense of proportion, and, incidentally, of literary talent, can be imagined," wrote Mr. Winston Churchill gloomily. " It is shocking to reflect that upon the word or nod of a being so limited there stood attentive and obedient for thirty years the forces which, whenever released, could devastate the world."[1]

However, the scholars came to the Kaiser's rescue. Throughout the twenties all the great powers—Germany, Austria, Russia, France, and Britain—allowed their diplomatic exchanges leading to the conflict to be assembled and published, and a score of historians produced analytical studies of the period. Gradually it became clear that whatever the failings of the Kaiser he had not, as was commonly supposed, planned or plotted or even desired a big war —only a little war! No longer was he an evil or cruel despot, but just a blunderer; a " careless tourist " who, in the words of Churchill, " flung down his cigarette in the ante-room of the

[1] *Contemporary Portraits:* Winston S. Churchill.

magazine which Europe had become," then went yachting and returned, "to find the building impenetrable with smoke." "His undeniable cleverness and versatility," wrote Churchill, "his personal grace and vivacity, only aggravated his dangers by concealing his inadequacy . . . but underneath all this posing and its trappings was a very ordinary, a vain, but on the whole well-meaning man, hoping to pass himself off as Frederick the Great. . . ."[1] Mr. Lloyd George, however, declared that there were other blunderers as well. He overlooked the fact that he once had led a campaign to hang the Kaiser and declared that all the Foreign Secretaries of the period were guilty of gross incompetence. "War could and should have been avoided," he wrote in memoirs published in the thirties. "I am convinced after a careful perusal of all the documents available on all sides that the Kaiser never had the remotest idea that he was plunging—or being plunged—into a European war. . . . He was not anticipating a costly war but a cheap diplomatic triumph."[2]

The Kaiser not only worked to destroy the "war-guilt clause" of the Versailles Treaty but to re-establish himself with the German people. His anger at von Hindenburg had turned to a deep hatred and he now privately accused the Field Marshal deliberately of having betrayed his imperial master in order to transfer the affections of the German people to himself. The old soldier's gesture of offering himself for trial in place of the Kaiser was dismissed by William II as a theatrical gesture to win popularity—an act reeking of the basest hypocrisy. It could not be denied that Hindenburg had replaced the Emperor as the father-figure of Germany; that wherever he went he was honoured for the great battles he had won, and for his services in leading the German armies home in the bitter hour of defeat. When the Peace Treaty was signed he retired and went to live in Hanover with his wife, but he still remained the greatest man in Germany. His massive frame seemed to breathe an air of confidence and strength but it was misleading; at heart he had no courage. His failure to speak up for the Kaiser sprang from moral cowardice, not disloyalty. He was a fervent monarchist and on the fateful November 9th had proffered William II advice which

[1] *Contemporary Portraits:* Winston S. Churchill.
[2] *War Memoirs:* David Lloyd George.

any soldier might have given. He could not allow his Emperor to be captured by the Communists and "dragged to Berlin;" therefore he had begged him to leave. The Field Marshal, however, was shocked by the reaction of the German people at the news of the Kaiser's flight; he was abashed by the fury and contempt of the monarchists and suddenly saw the action in a different light. In the storm of universal condemnation he feared that he might be accused of treason for the part he had played. It was not a creditable performance, and William II was not alone in condemning the reticence of the Field Marshal. "But what should one think," wrote the Crown Prince's Chief of Staff, Count von der Schulenburg, to Count Westrarp, "of the individual gentlemen who preferred to desert their King and Master, rather than admit the truth which freed the Kaiser from guilt but incriminated them heavily?"[1]

The Kaiser was determined to force von Hindenburg into the open, and soon after moving to Doorn, in the spring of 1921, wrote to the Field Marshal that his exclusion from Germany was the cause of "burning anguish in my soul," and added: "As you know, I forced myself to the difficult and terrible decision to leave the country only upon the urgent declaration of yourself . . . that only by my doing so would it be possible to obtain more favourable armistice terms for our people and spare them a bloody civil war." This last assertion was not strictly accurate, as the Kaiser's departure had not affected the armistice terms; he had left in order to save himself from falling into the hands of the Communists.

Hindenburg did not refer to William II's pointed observation for many months; but finally, perhaps under pressure from von der Schulenburg, was prevailed upon to shoulder the responsibility. In a letter written in July 1922, beginning "Most Serene Highness, Great and Mighty Kaiser! Most Gracious Kaiser, King and Lord!" Hindenburg wrote: "I take the responsibility for Your Majesty's resolve to go into exile, a step taken on that unhappy ninth of November as a result of the united demand of all your advisers. I have already given as the reason the menace of the danger that Your Majesty sooner or later might have been arrested by mutinous troops and might be surrendered to the enemy at home or abroad. The Fatherland had at all costs to be spared such insult and disgrace."[2]

[1] *The Life of Crown Prince William:* Klaus Jonas.

[2] *Hindenburg: The Wooden Titan:* Sir John Wheeler-Bennett.

The Kaiser did not reply for two months, then wrote acidly that he had been compelled to wait a long time before the persons involved could be persuaded to come forward and declare publicly "that I was forced to depart from Spa on the urgent advice of my political advisers and against my own conviction. I thank you for having now taken this step, which is necessary not only in the interests of historical truth, but equally for my personal reputation and the honour of my House. . . . Convinced that you were loyally discharging a difficult task, you gave to your Kaiser and King counsel which you thought it your duty to give. . . . Whether that view was correct cannot be finally decided until all the facts of those unhappy days are known."[1]

William II was disappointed to find that Hindenburg's statement aroused little interest. 1918 seemed a long way back; furthermore most people felt that whatever advice the Kaiser had received the final responsibility for his flight must remain his and his alone.

However, the correspondence is important for other reasons; for the Emperor's unconcealed disapproval of von Hindenburg, and his dream of regaining his throne, produced a curious situation in 1930/31 which facilitated Herr Hitler's climb to power. The seventy-seven-year-old Field Marshal was recalled from retirement in 1925, much against his will, and elected President of the German Republic. Germany had been through seven years of upheaval, but Hindenburg's re-emergence coincided with a turn of the tide. For the next four years things improved steadily until in 1929 the New York stock-market collapsed and dealt the economy a savage blow. Once again there was unemployment and widespread suffering; and at last the dangerous, hate-laden voice of Corporal Hitler began to gain followers. He not only struck a resonant chord by blaming the Versailles Treaty for all Germany's woes, but excited his audiences by declaring that the German Army had been undefeated, and that the Fatherland would not have been vanquished if it had not been stabbed in the back by the "Jews and Socialists" who had organised the revolution. He referred to Ebert's Government—the men who had signed the armistice—as "the November Criminals." In 1928 Hitler's National Socialist Party won only 12 seats in the Reichstag; but in 1930 the number had swollen to 132.

[1] *Hindenburg: The Wooden Titan:* Sir John Wheeler-Bennett.

The note that Hitler sounded did not displease the Kaiser. He had always loathed the Socialists for forcing him off the throne and he was glad that someone was reminding the people of the iniquitous war-guilt clause. However, in 1930 William II was faced by a dilemma. The new Chancellor, the Catholic leader Doctor Heinrich Brüning, was strongly in favour of restoring the monarchy as a means of preventing Hitler from capturing the support of the right wing. Did the Kaiser's best chance lie with Brüning and Hindenburg, or with the rising star, Hitler?

It is not surprising that the Kaiser made the wrong choice, for he still lived in a world distorted by false premises and illusory hopes. It would have been possible for Brüning to restore the monarchy, but not to bring back William II. The Socialists and Trade Unions would not tolerate either the ex-Kaiser or the Crown Prince, but they were perfectly willing to support a Regency in the name of one of the Kaiser's grandsons. Hindenburg, however, still smarted from the rebuke that William II had administered in his letter of 1922; still was sensitive to whispered taunts that he had not served his Emperor loyally. When Brüning raised the question of the monarchy Hindenburg flatly refused to consider a restoration unless his "Lord and Master," William II, was recalled to the throne. "A re-introduction of the monarchy in the struggle against the Nazis might well have been possible," wrote Brüning in 1957, "but it broke up when Hindenburg declared to me he would champion a restoration of the monarchy only if William II were to become Kaiser. That was naturally out of the question and because of that everything was doomed to failure."[1] Thus the last chance of bringing back the Hohenzollerns was lost; also the last possibility of stopping Hitler.

Only William II could have broken the impasse. If he had written to the Field Marshal and asked him to declare a Regency in favour of his grandson von Hindenburg almost certainly would have responded. But William II did not see the situation in this light. He believed that he could retrieve the throne for himself under Hitler. In 1931–32 the leading Nazis were loud in their praise of the Hohenzollerns. The Crown Prince, who had returned to Germany in 1923, had known Goering during the war, and in the early thirties made the acquaintance of Goebbels, Roehm, and

[1] *The Life of Crown Prince William:* Klaus Jonas.

Hitler. " My goal," the Führer assured him in a private conversation, "is the restoration of the Empire under a Hohenzollern." With William II, however, the Nazis were more explicit. Goering visited the Kaiser at Doorn in 1932 and assured both the Emperor and his wife that Hitler's most ardent desire was to reinstate the exiled monarch.

Consequently, the Empress Hermine became one of Hitler's most fervent supporters and encouraged her husband in his wild aspirations. William allowed two of his sons, Prince August William and Prince Oskar, to join the National Socialist Party, thereby making an exception to the principle of non-participation in politics by members of his House. He also raised no objection when the Crown Prince came out openly in support of Hitler; and when his grandson, Prince Louis Ferdinand, wrote to him asking his opinion of the new movement he made his attitude clear. " In Hitler he sees the leader of a strong Nationalist movement which is the embodiment of the national energy. He does not yet know what will come of it, or claim that the movement pleases him in all its details, but he is firmly convinced that only national forces will lead Germany forward again."[1]

In the Reichstag elections of July 1932 the Nazis won 240 seats and became the largest single political party. The following year von Hindenburg, who was now practically senile, decided that he had no option but to invite Hitler to become Chancellor. The Führer soon showed his hand as far as the Hohenzollerns were concerned. In the autumn of 1933 Goering, the new Prussian Minister-President, informed the Kaiser that he could not continue to draw revenue from his German estates. Instead the new Government would grant the Kaiser and his sons a generous annual allowance; but if they criticised the Nationalist Socialists the payments would stop immediately. An even more ominous indication of Hitler's views was demonstrated in January 1934 when the Nazis broke up celebrations in Berlin in honour of the ex-Kaiser's 75th birthday.

Despite these occurrences the Empress Hermine continued to believe in Hitler's good intentions for another year. On June 27th, 1934, she wrote to Mr. Poultenay Bigelow, of Boston, Massachusetts, a boyhood friend of the Kaiser, and told him that young

[1] *The Life of Crown Prince William:* Klaus Jonas.

Randolph Churchill had visited Doorn. Churchill hoped to interview the Kaiser on Hitler, but the Emperor switched the conversation to the Chinese-Japanese war, reverting to the well-worn theme of the "Yellow Peril." His twenty-three-year-old visitor, however, did not allow His Majesty's reticence to prevent him from stating his own views on Germany's leader; and the Empress Hermine told Bigelow that "young Churchill knew nothing of the new Germany which she admired so much and she was shocked when he referred to Hitler as 'a danger and an enemy.'"[1]

However, the Empress Hermine could no longer mistake Hitler's attitude when, in January 1935, the Kaiser requested the Crown Prince to call on the Chancellor and discuss with him the possibility of William II's return to Germany. The son did as he was bidden but Hitler stated categorically that there could be no question of His Majesty's return.

The Kaiser's dream was shattered; yet, strangely enough, the last six years of his life were the most tranquil of his long existence. For the first time he was free of the tempting and tormenting vision of personal glory; for the first time he could look at events with a measure of detachment. Although he still referred to himself as "the most mis-used man on earth" the phrase had an empty ring as his emotions no longer were involved. Of course he now loathed the Nazis. He not only resented Hitler's broken promises and his references to "the Hohenzollern parasites," but he was shocked to find that members of his own entourage—gentlemen who were hand-picked in Berlin and sent to Doorn on tours of duty—were spying on him.[2] Did he remember, one wonders, his mother's bitter complaints about the spies that Prince Bismark infiltrated into her household?

There is no doubt that as the political scene darkened the Kaiser's thoughts turned with ever increasing frequency towards his mother's country. He seemed to delight in all things English: in speaking the language, in reading English books, and in receiving English

[1] *The Life of Crown Prince William:* Klaus Jonas.

[2] Hitler still regarded the monarchists as dangerous and feared that a plot against his regime might be hatched at Doorn House. A conspiracy did begin in 1938—not at Doorn but in Berlin—organised by high army officers and members of the aristocracy. It ended in the abortive attempt on Hitler's life in July 1944.

visitors. In 1937 he took an almost pathetic interest in the details of George VI's coronation ceremony. Like other old men he dwelt nostalgically on the scenes of his childhood. He talked constantly of his beloved grandpapa and grandmama, but it was a bit confusing because grandpapa was William I of Germany, and grandmama was Queen Victoria of England. When he gave dinner-parties he frequently showed his guests one of the first documentaries ever made—the film of Queen Victoria's Diamond Jubilee.

It would be wrong to suggest that the Kaiser's dislike of Hitler was only due to pique. William II was deeply, almost obsessively, religious, and as the dictator's pathological hatreds and racial prejudices became increasingly pronounced he undoubtedly experienced a genuine revulsion. Although like all Germans he regarded the Versailles Treaty as an abomination, he was appalled by the thought of another European war. He had always had a very personal, almost childish, conception of God and he now turned to his Bible more frequently than ever in order to discover an explanation for the new punishment that seemed to be awaiting mankind.

In 1938, when Mr. Chamberlain prevented war by flying to Munich, the Kaiser was so relieved that he wrote impulsively to the widowed Queen Mary—the same Princess May who so many years ago, after a dinner at Cowes, had written in her diary, "fancy me, little me, sitting next to William!!!" It was the Kaiser's first communication to any member of the British royal family since the war. "May I," he wrote, "with a grateful heart relieved from a sickening anxiety by the intercession of Heaven unite my warmest sincerest thanks to the Lord with yours and those of the German and British People that He saved us from a most fearful catastrophe by helping the responsible statesmen to preserve Peace! I have not the slightest doubt that Mr. N. Chamberlain was inspired by Heaven and guided by God who took pity on His children on Earth by crowning his mission with such relieving success. God bless him. I kiss your hand in respectful devotion as ever."[1] The letter was signed "Your affte. cousin—William." Queen Mary promptly replied thanking him for his letter and saying that she had sent it to her son George VI asking him to show it to the Prime Minister and then to place it among the royal archives.

[1] *Queen Mary:* James Pope-Hennessy.

The Kaiser's figure suddenly seemed to be thrown into bright relief by the monstrous and darkening shadow of Hitler. He seemed to be acquiring a strange new prestige. For the first time since 1914 he received favourable references in the English press. Many people both inside and outside Germany began to look back wistfully to the days when he sat upon the throne; and some even referred to him as an elder statesman—a man of dignity and restraint. "Time," wrote Winston Churchill in 1937, "has brought him a surprising and paradoxical revenge on his conquerors. He has reached a phase when the greater part of Europe, particularly his most powerful enemies, Great Britain and France, would regard the Hohenzollern restoration they formerly abhorred beyond expression as a comparatively hopeful event and as a sign that dangers were abating. . . ."[1]

In 1939, a fortnight before the second world war broke out, the Kaiser received two distinguished British writers who were in close touch with the Foreign Office—Mr. Robert Bruce Lockhart and Mr. John Wheeler-Bennett. The eighty-year-old Kaiser dressed for the occasion in grey-blue English tweed with a white waistcoat and lavender topped boots. In his tie he wore a huge cameo of Queen Victoria. He talked incessantly and with great animation. As Sir John Wheeler-Bennett was contemplating a life of him, his conversation centred mainly on the past. William II still considered himself cruelly misjudged. He spoke scathingly of official historians, accusing them of gross misrepresentation; and he asserted, as he had done so often before, that he alone had prevented a Franco-Russian-German war against England at the time of the Boer War. "For that," he said, "I got 1918." He told his guests that the 1914 war would never have happened if he had not been deceived by England's attitude. Then he added, rather disconcertingly, that he had only wanted to fight the Russians! "Yet if he felt bitterness," wrote Sir Robert Bruce Lockhart, "the Kaiser made a brave effort to conceal it. Probably he was too interested in his own conversation, for he talked not only with his tongue, but with all the physical force left in him. His eyes danced and sparkled; his good arm was freely moved to point a warning finger or to make a broad sweep to far distant menaces like Russia and Japan. And when he made a sly hit at the English, a foxy smile lit up his whole face. He talked

[1] *Great Contemporaries:* Winston S. Churchill.

much, too, of the imperialist greed which had been the downfall of all great nations and told us that in his years of trial he had evolved a new theory. No nation should occupy more land than Providence intended for it. Providence in its own good time would punish those who sinned against this law.

" I asked him if his reference to punishment was meant to apply to the British Empire or to the Third Reich of Hitler. He paused for a moment and then replied firmly : ' To all empires and, therefore, to both.' In his talk he did no more than touch on the crisis of the moment. He did not like or trust the Poles and said so, but, mindful of his pact with Providence, added that he had no wish to see them incorporated in Germany. He was careful, too, not to say much about the Nazis, although he made it clear that he was opposed to them. Indeed, at one moment he burst into anger. ' I am a prisoner in my own house,' he said : ' They [the Nazis] treat me far worse than the Socialists ever treated me.' "[1]

The Empress Hermine was even more outspoken against the Nazis than the Kaiser. " They are evil," she said, " and great harm will come from them." She warned the visitors not to trust any members of the Kaiser's household apart from his aide, Freiherr von Sell. Only one reference was made to the approaching war and that was when the guests made their farewell. " Come back and see me again next summer if you can," said the Kaiser. And then he added : " but you won't be able to because the machine is running away with *him* as it ran away with *me*." This remark was not as wise as it sounded ; for whatever the Kaiser meant by " the machine " neither World War I nor World War II was started by excessive military pressure on the ruler. Indeed, Hitler had to lash his army forward ; the reluctance of the generals to set fire to Europe caused him to refer contemptuously to " mastiffs who had forgotten how to bite."

In May 1940, when Hitler's attack on the West was launched, German troops fought their way through Holland. Queen Wilhelmina and her Government flew to London to organise the continued resistance of the Dutch Empire. Winston Churchill had just become Prime Minister and as he read of the ferocious attack on the Low Countries he feared for the Kaiser's safety. He instructed the Foreign Office to offer the Kaiser refuge in England.

[1] *Comes the Reckoning :* Sir Robert Bruce Lockhart.

If William accepted the offer an R.A.F. plane would fly to Holland within the next few hours and pick up the Kaiser and his wife. The message was transmitted through the British Embassy in The Hague to the Burgomaster of Utrecht, Baron von Nagell. The Baron immediately drove to Doorn House with the communication. The Kaiser was still in bed but he was ushered into the bedroom. William II was surprised by the offer and childishly pleased. His first inclination was to accept it. The Empress Hermine was overjoyed and immediately began to pack her bags. Baron von Nagell said that no doubt the Kaiser would like time to consider the offer, and that he would return in an hour for His Majesty's answer.

Upon reflection William II knew that he could not go. He was a German; and whatever he thought of Herr Hitler he must support his country, right or wrong. Indeed, sixteen Hohenzollern princes including three of his grandsons were serving with the Wehrmacht; furthermore, he was still haunted by the decision he had made at Spa on the fateful 9th November 1918. When the Dutch Burgomaster reappeared, William asked him to convey to the British Government his sincerest thanks; but that as he had been accused of running away once before, whatever happened now he would stay where he was. And finally, that as he had received much kindness from the Dutch people he did not wish to desert them in their misfortune.

As the mighty German Army poured through Holland and swept past Doorn many hundreds of German officers tried to catch a glimpse of their former Supreme War Lord. Hitler issued strict orders that there was to be no fraternisation between the Wehrmacht and the exiled sovereign, but the attraction proved so great that the Gestapo finally posted a military detachment at the gate-house with a special S.S. officer in charge. The Kaiser amused himself by walking down to the lodge and engaging the storm-trooper in conversation. Apparently the young man was so flattered and impressed that soon he was clicking his heels and bowing before the former sovereign in the true style of a Prussian guards officer. Despite Hitler's orders the Kaiser talked with many German army officers, who were smuggled into Doorn through secret back entrances.

On May 26th, 1940, the Kaiser's grandson, Prince William of Prussia, the eldest son of the Crown Prince, died from wounds in the fighting near Valenciennes. His body was sent back to Potsdam and he was buried on May 29th in the Antike Tempel. Fifty thousand people thronged to his funeral service and the occasion became the most formidable monarchist demonstration since the collapse of the Hohenzollern dynasty. Hitler was enraged, and a week later General von Dommes, the Kaiser's Court Chamberlain, returned to Doorn from Berlin with news of impending disaster. The Führer had sent out instructions that all members of the House of Hohenzollern were immediately to be dismissed from the army. Rumours were circulating that he intended taking severe reprisals against them and their families. General von Dommes implored the Kaiser to placate Hitler by a conciliatory gesture. It was sad that William II consented, for the gesture constituted the last official act of his life. The German armies entered Paris on June 14th; and the following day the Kaiser sent to Hitler a brief telegram of congratulations, the text of which was published in Germany and caused much dismay to monarchists who were conspiring against Hitler.

The Kaiser lived for one more year. During these twelve months England stood alone against the might of Germany. Once again, despite the staggering victories of the Wehrmacht, the war was not won. Was history repeating itself? The Kaiser believed that it was, but he died on June 5th, 1941, a few weeks before the German attack brought Russia into the war and six months before the entry of America.

The Kaiser's wife and his daughter, the Duchess of Brunswick, were with him during his last hours. He was buried at Doorn, and his death caused scarcely a ripple of interest in either Germany or Britain, for people were too preoccupied with the present struggle to cast their minds back a quarter of a century. The tragedy of William II was the tragedy of birth. He possessed neither the intellect nor the character to shoulder the burden thrust upon him. " It was not his fault," wrote Winston Churchill, " it was his fate."

Alas, it was the fate of all of us, for the Kaiser unwittingly set in motion a chain of events which for the past fifty years have acted and reacted on one another with explosive force, driving the world relentlessly towards a point of no return.

THE END

Acknowledgements

I would like to thank the following publishers for allowing me to quote from books published by them: Appleton-Century for *The Edwardian Era* by Andre Maurois; The Cambridge University Press for the *Holstein Papers* edited by N. Rich and M. H. Fisher; the Carnegie Endowment for International Peace for the *German Documents Collected by Karl Kautsky* edited by Max Montgelas and Walther Schucking; Cassell & Co., Ltd., for *Queen Victoria's Relations* by Meriel Buchanan, *Better Left Unsaid* by Daisy, Princess of Pless, *My Memoirs* by William II; Constable & Co., Ltd., for *An English Wife in Berlin*, by Princess Blücher, *Memoirs* by Max, Prince of Baden; Ernest Benn, Ltd., for *History of the English People* by Elie Halevy, *Germany* by G. P. Gooch; Faber & Faber, Ltd., for *The Empress Frederick Writes to Sophie* edited by Arthur Gould Lee; Her Majesty's Stationery Office for *British Documents on the Origin of the War* edited by Gooch and Temperley; Hutchinson & Co., Ltd., for *My Memoirs* by Admiral von Tirpitz, *Embassies of Other Days* by Walpurga Paget; Alfred A. Knopf, Inc., for *Queen Mary* by John Pope Hennessy and *Prince Eulenburg, The Kaiser's Friend* by Johannes Haller, translated by Ethel Colburn Mayne; Ivor Nicholson & Watson, Ltd., for *Letters of Czar Nicholas and Empress Marie* edited by Edward Bing; John Murray for *The Queen Thanks Sir Howard* by Mary McClintock, *The Letters of Queen Victoria*, *Daisy, Princess of Pless*, *Scenes & Memories*, by Walpurga Paget; Macdonald & Co., Ltd., for *The Kaiser and His Court* by Admiral von Müller edited by Walter Gorlitz; Macmillan & Co., Ltd., for *Henry Ponsonby, His Life from His Letters* by Arthur Ponsonby, *Letters of the Empress Frederick* edited by Sir Frederick Ponsonby; The Macmillan Company, New York, for *The Origins of the Second World War* by Sidney Fay; Methuen & Co., Ltd., for *Memories of the Fatherland* and *Memoirs of the Kaiser's Court* by Anne Topham; *My Early Life* by William II, *German Diplomatic Documents* edited by E. T. S. Dugdale;

Acknowledgements

G. P. Putnam's Sons for *Great Contemporaries* by Winston S. Churchill and *Kaiser and Chancellor* by Karl Novak; Putnams & Co., Ltd., for *Comes the Reckoning* by Sir Robert Bruce-Lockart, *Memoirs* by Prince von Bülow; Routledge & Kegan Paul, Ltd., for *The Life of Crown Prince William* by Klaus Jonas; Charles Scribner's Sons for *The World Crisis* by Winston S. Churchill; A. P. Watt & Son for *Twenty-five Years* by Viscount Grey; and for *Die Grosse Politik der Europaischen Kabinette* edited by Friedrich Thimme.

I would also like to thank Sir Harold Nicolson and Constable & Co. for permission to quote from *King George V*, *Lord Carnock* and *Peacemaking*; Sir John Wheeler Bennett and Macmillan & Co. for *Hindenburg: The Wooden Titan*; A. P. Watt & Son and Lord Esher for *The Letters and Journals of Reginald, Viscount Esher*.

19 Chester Square VIRGINIA COWLES
London
August, 1963

INDEX

Index

Index